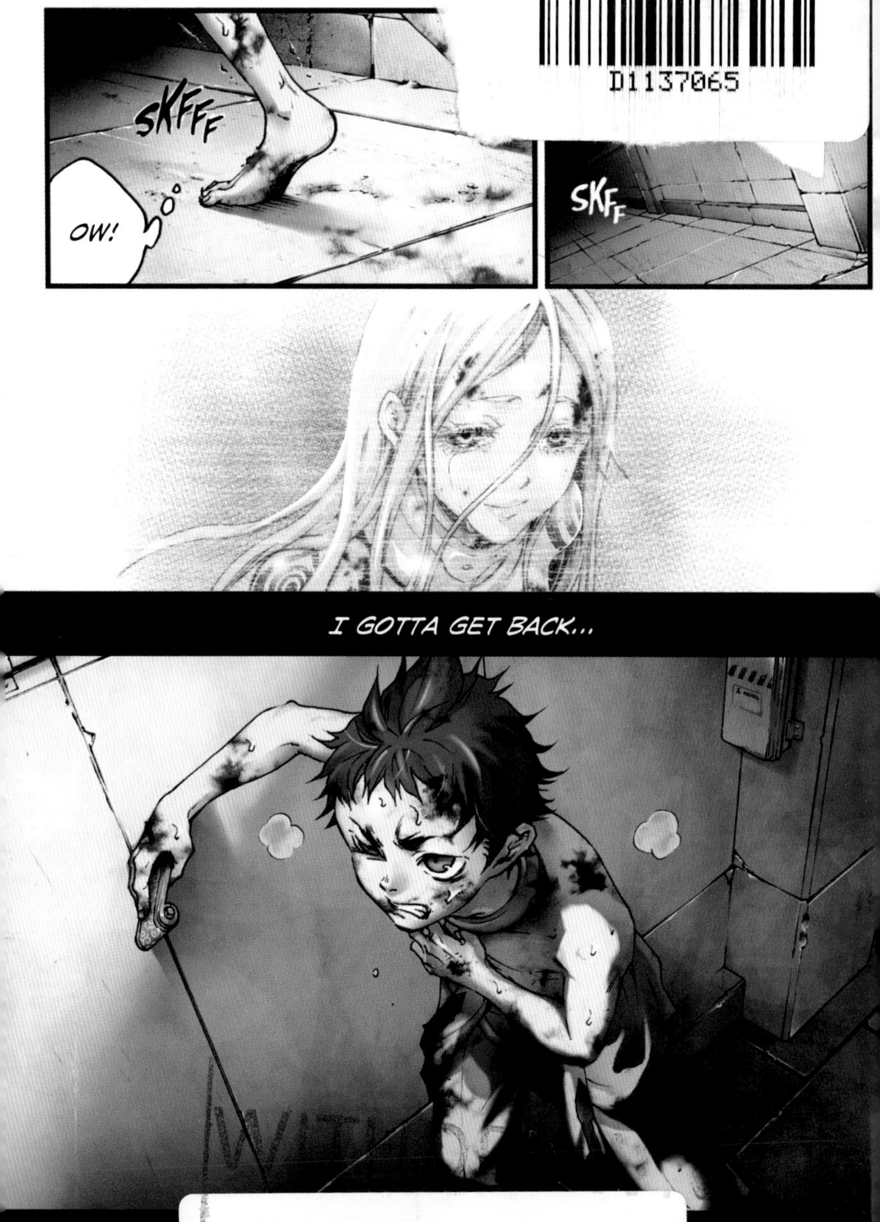
SKFF
SKFFFF
OW!
I GOTTA GET BACK...

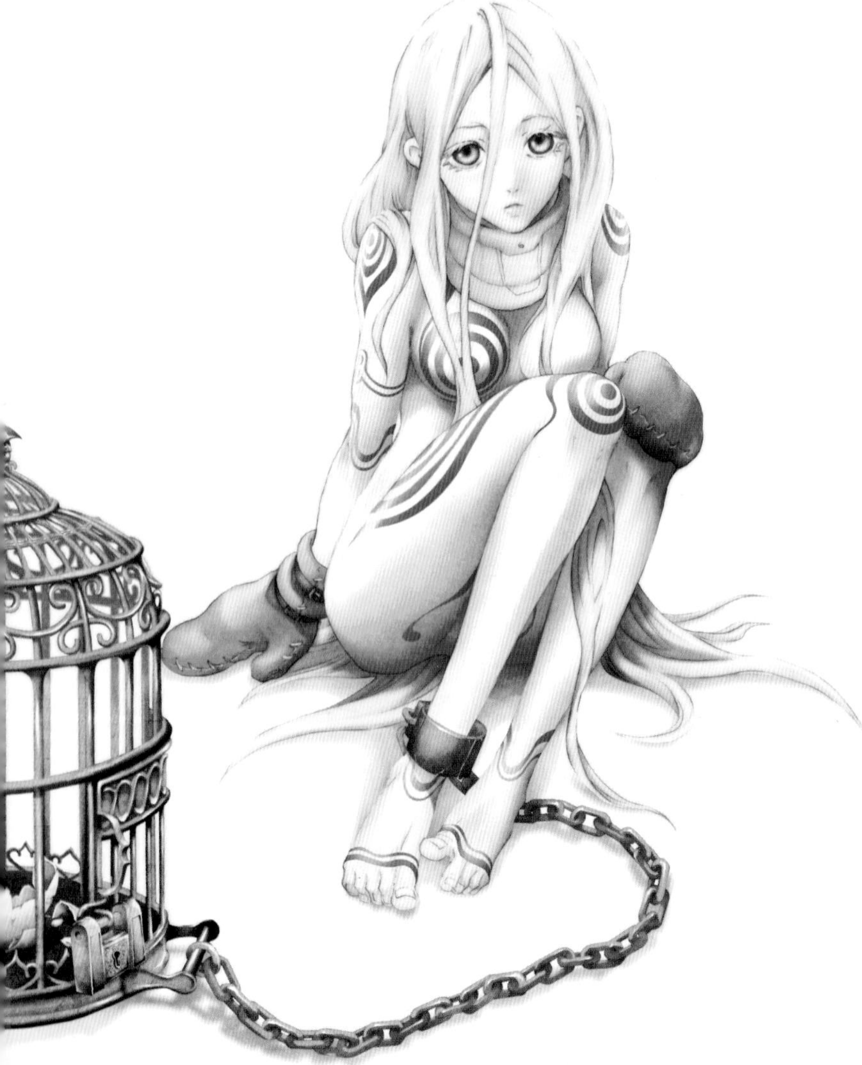

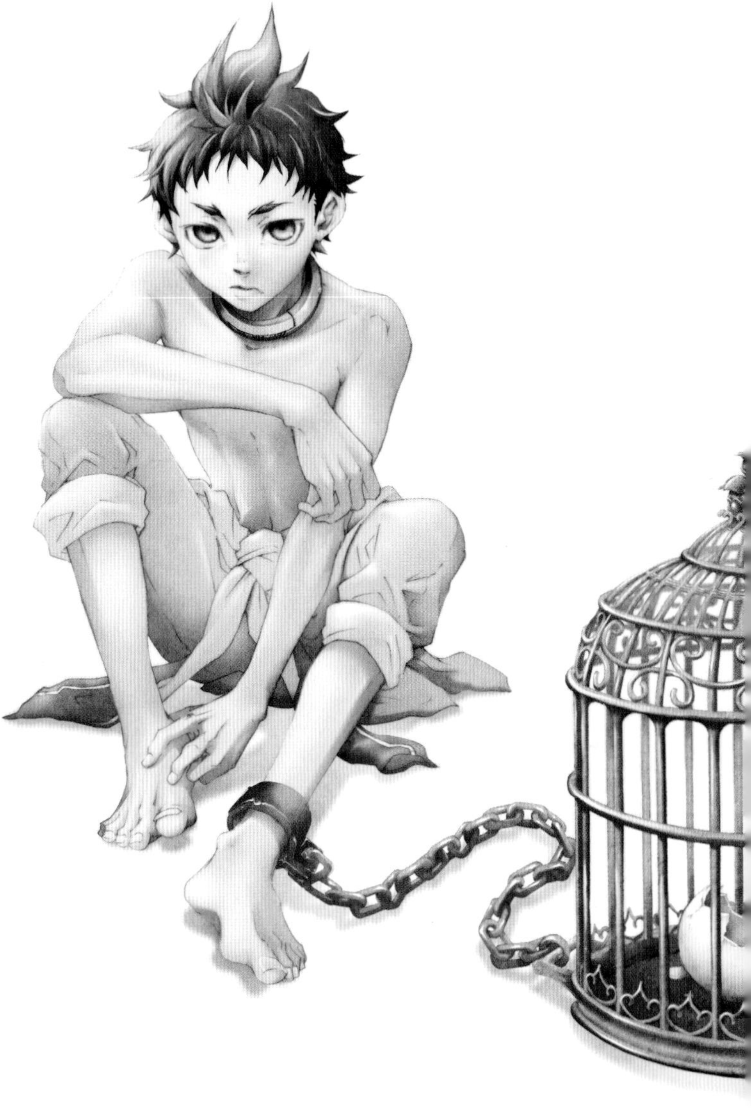

DEADMAN WONDERLAND

STORY & ART BY JINSEI KATAOKA, KAZUMA KONDOU

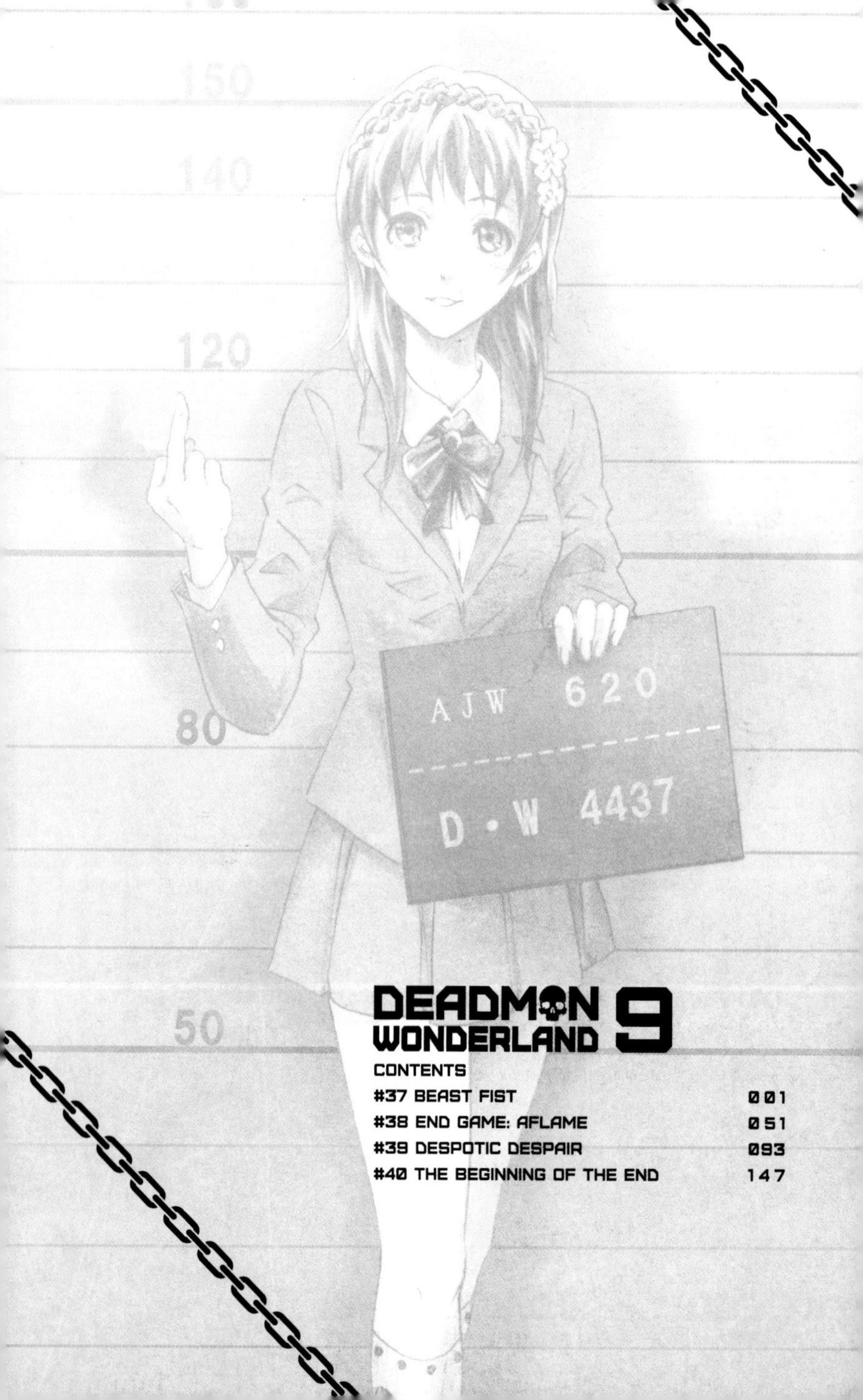
150
140
120
AJW 620
D・W 4437
80
50

DEADMAN WONDERLAND 9

CONTENTS

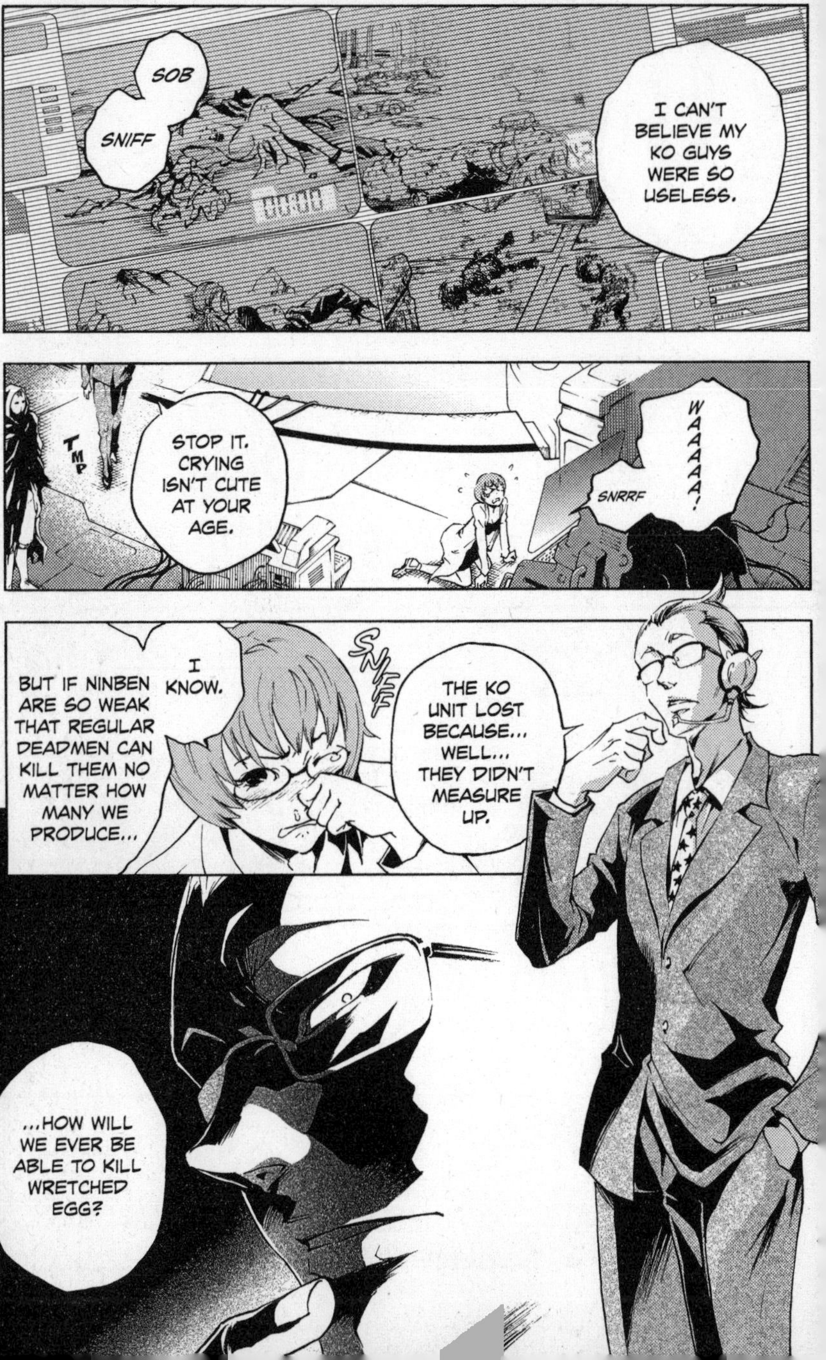
I CAN'T BELIEVE MY KO GUYS WERE SO USELESS.
SOB
SNIFF
WAAAAAA!
SNRRF
STOP IT. CRYING ISN'T CUTE AT YOUR AGE.
TMP
THE KO UNIT LOST BECAUSE... WELL... THEY DIDN'T MEASURE UP.
SNIFF
I KNOW.
BUT IF NINBEN ARE SO WEAK THAT REGULAR DEADMEN CAN KILL THEM NO MATTER HOW MANY WE PRODUCE...
...HOW WILL WE EVER BE ABLE TO KILL WRETCHED EGG?

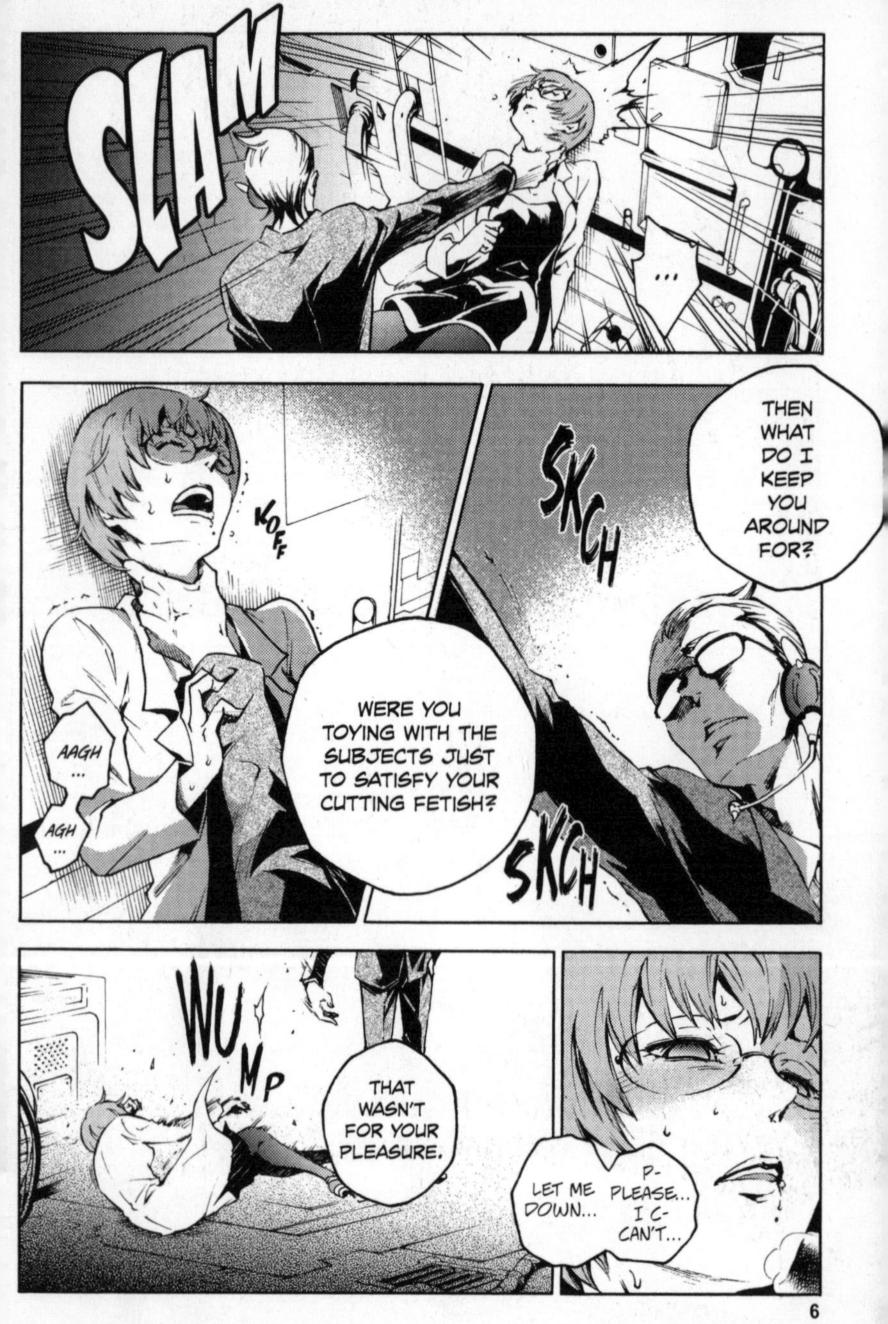
SLAM
...
THEN WHAT DO I KEEP YOU AROUND FOR?
SKCH
WERE YOU TOYING WITH THE SUBJECTS JUST TO SATISFY YOUR CUTTING FETISH?
SKCH
KOFF
AAGH ...
AGH ...
P- PLEASE... I C- CAN'T...
LET ME DOWN...
WUMP
THAT WASN'T FOR YOUR PLEASURE.

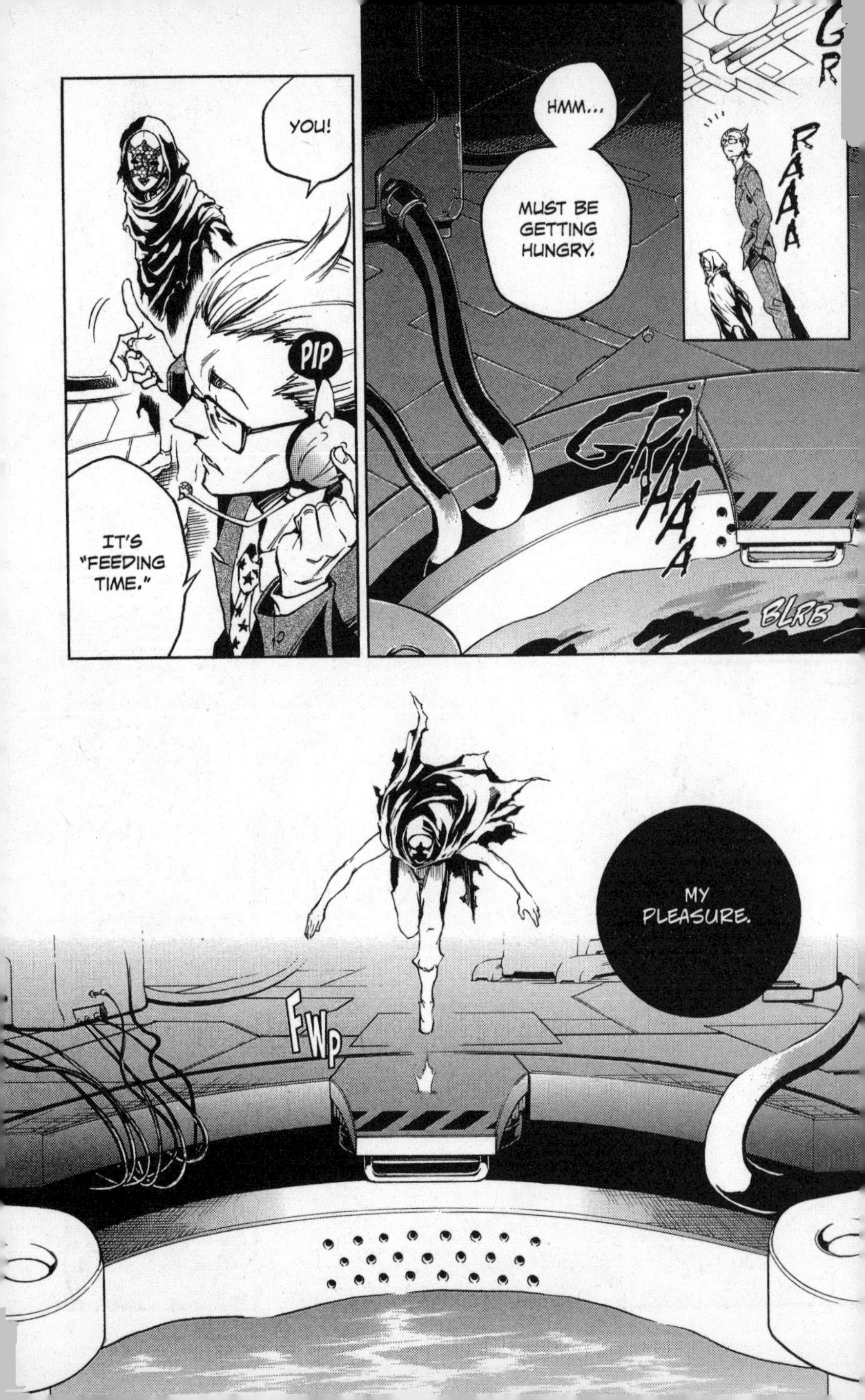
GR
RAAA
HMM...
MUST BE GETTING HUNGRY.
GRAAAA
BLRB
YOU!
PIP
IT'S "FEEDING TIME."
MY PLEASURE.
FWP

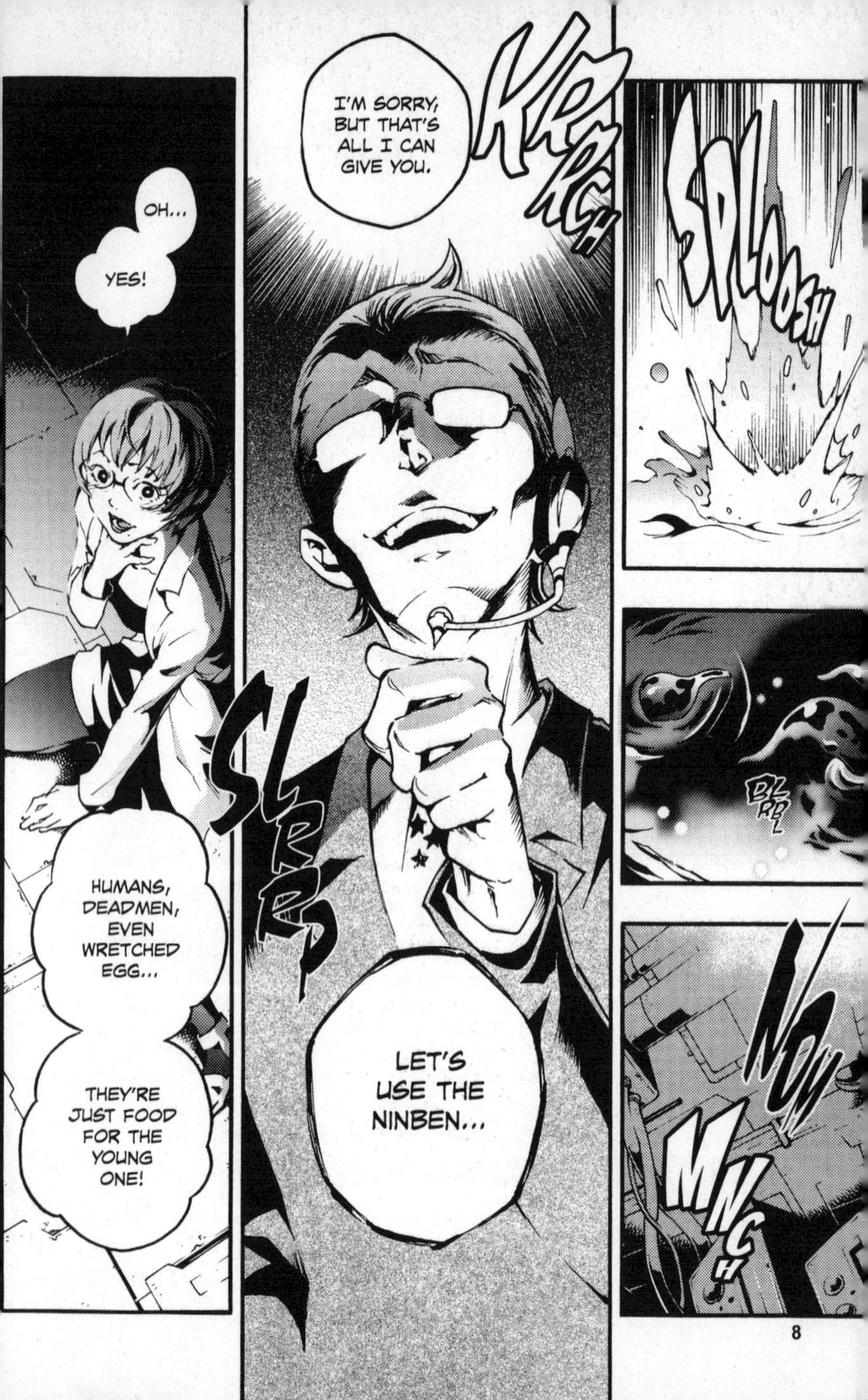
SPLOOSH
BLRBL
NOM
MNCH
I'M SORRY, BUT THAT'S ALL I CAN GIVE YOU.
SLRRP
LET'S USE THE NINBEN...
OH...
YES!
HUMANS, DEADMEN, EVEN WRETCHED EGG...
THEY'RE JUST FOOD FOR THE YOUNG ONE!

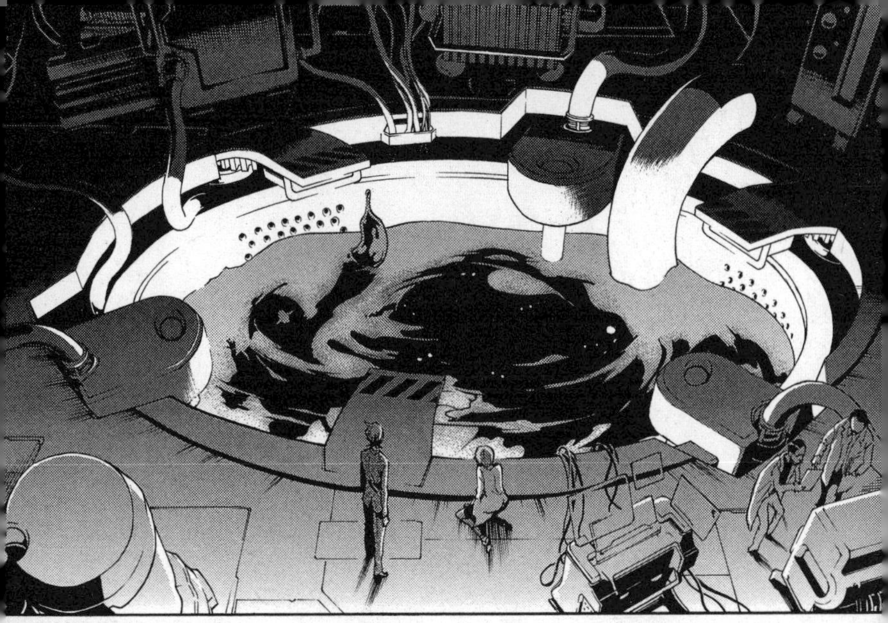

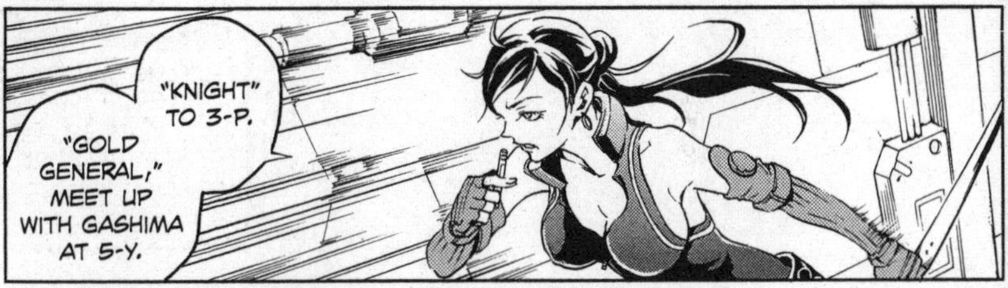
"KNIGHT" TO 3-P.
"GOLD GENERAL," MEET UP WITH GASHIMA AT 5-Y.

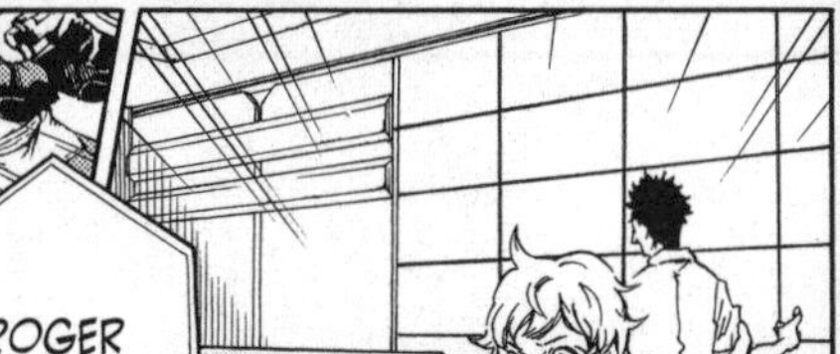
TAP TAP

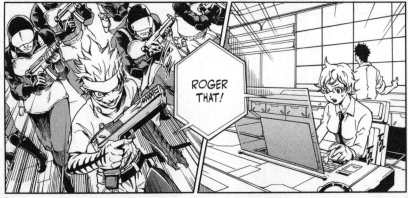

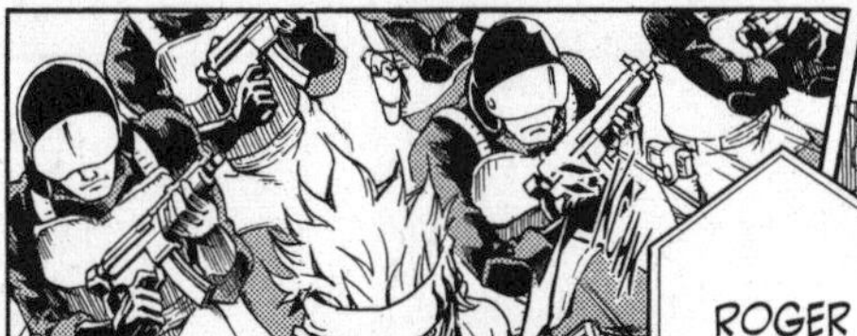
ROGER THAT!

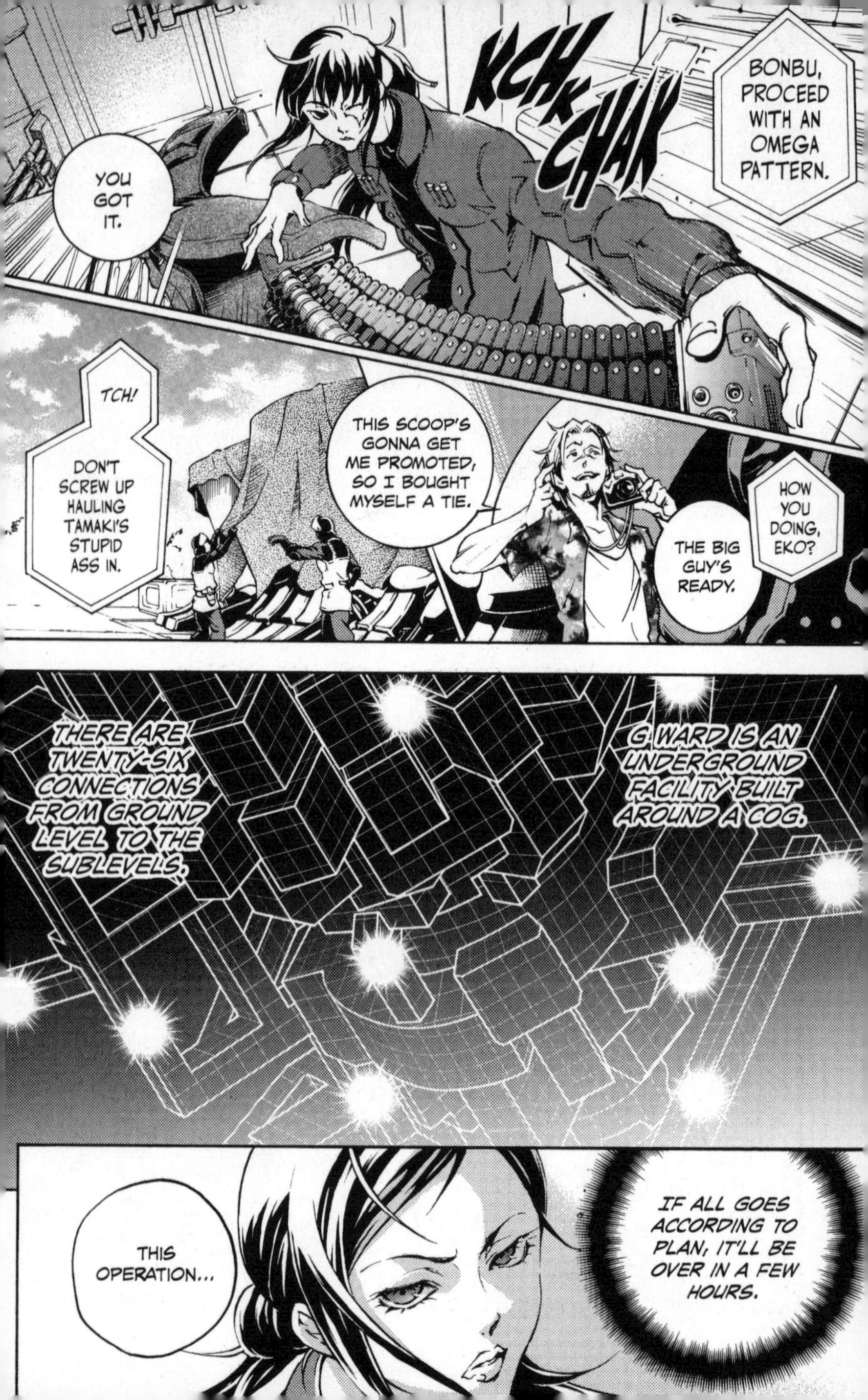
BONBU, PROCEED WITH AN OMEGA PATTERN.
KCHK CHAK
YOU GOT IT.
HOW YOU DOING, EKO?
THE BIG GUY'S READY.
THIS SCOOP'S GONNA GET ME PROMOTED, SO I BOUGHT MYSELF A TIE.
TCH!
DON'T SCREW UP HAULING TAMAKI'S STUPID ASS IN.
G WARD IS AN UNDERGROUND FACILITY BUILT AROUND A COG.
THERE ARE TWENTY-SIX CONNECTIONS FROM GROUND LEVEL TO THE SUBLEVELS.
IF ALL GOES ACCORDING TO PLAN, IT'LL BE OVER IN A FEW HOURS.
THIS OPERATION...

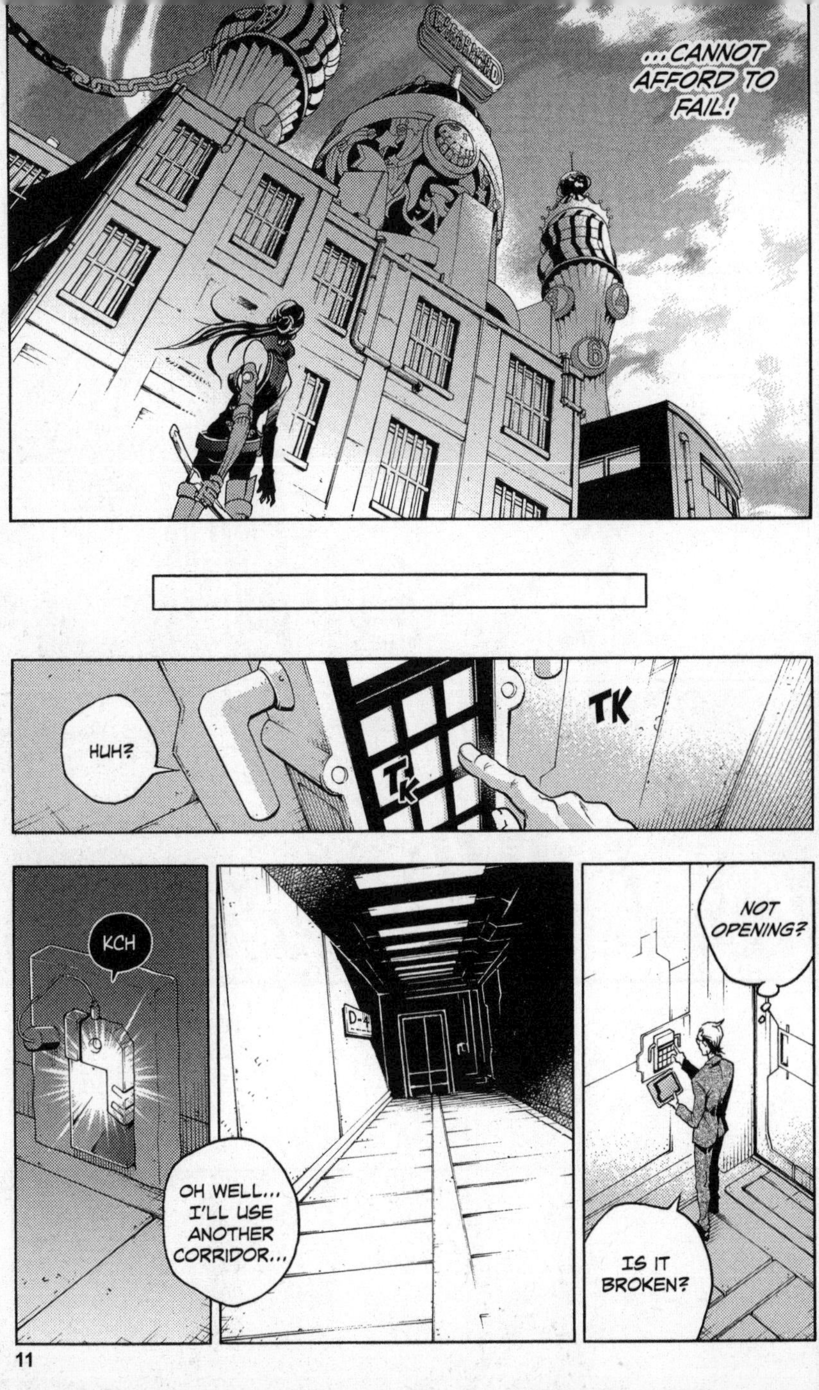
...CANNOT AFFORD TO FAIL!
TK
TK
HUH?
NOT OPENING?
IS IT BROKEN?
D-4
OH WELL... I'LL USE ANOTHER CORRIDOR...
KCH

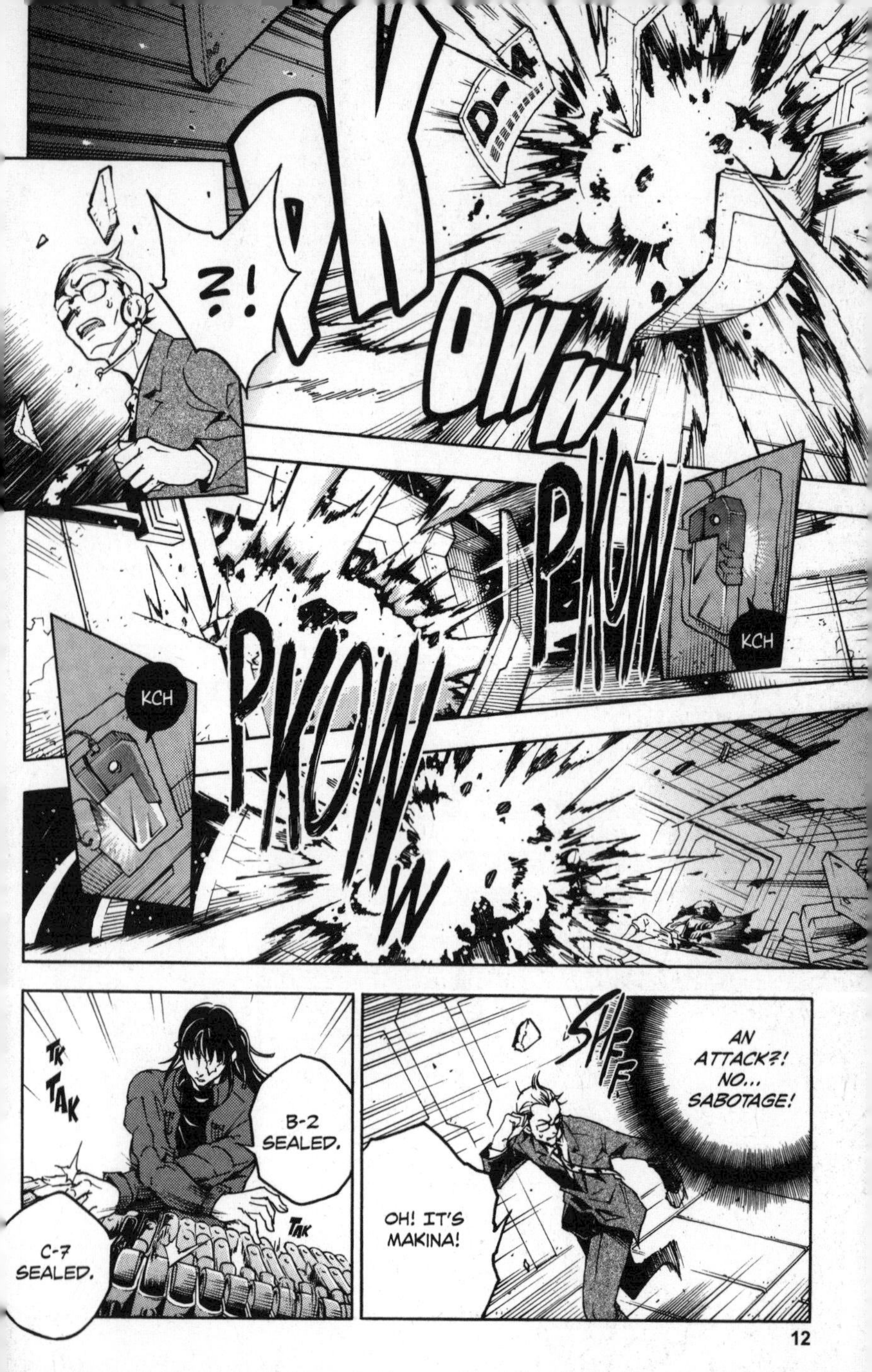
?!
PKOW
KCH
PKOW
KCH
SHFF
AN ATTACK?! NO... SABOTAGE!
OH! IT'S MAKINA!
TK TAK
B-2 SEALED.
TAK
C-7 SEALED.

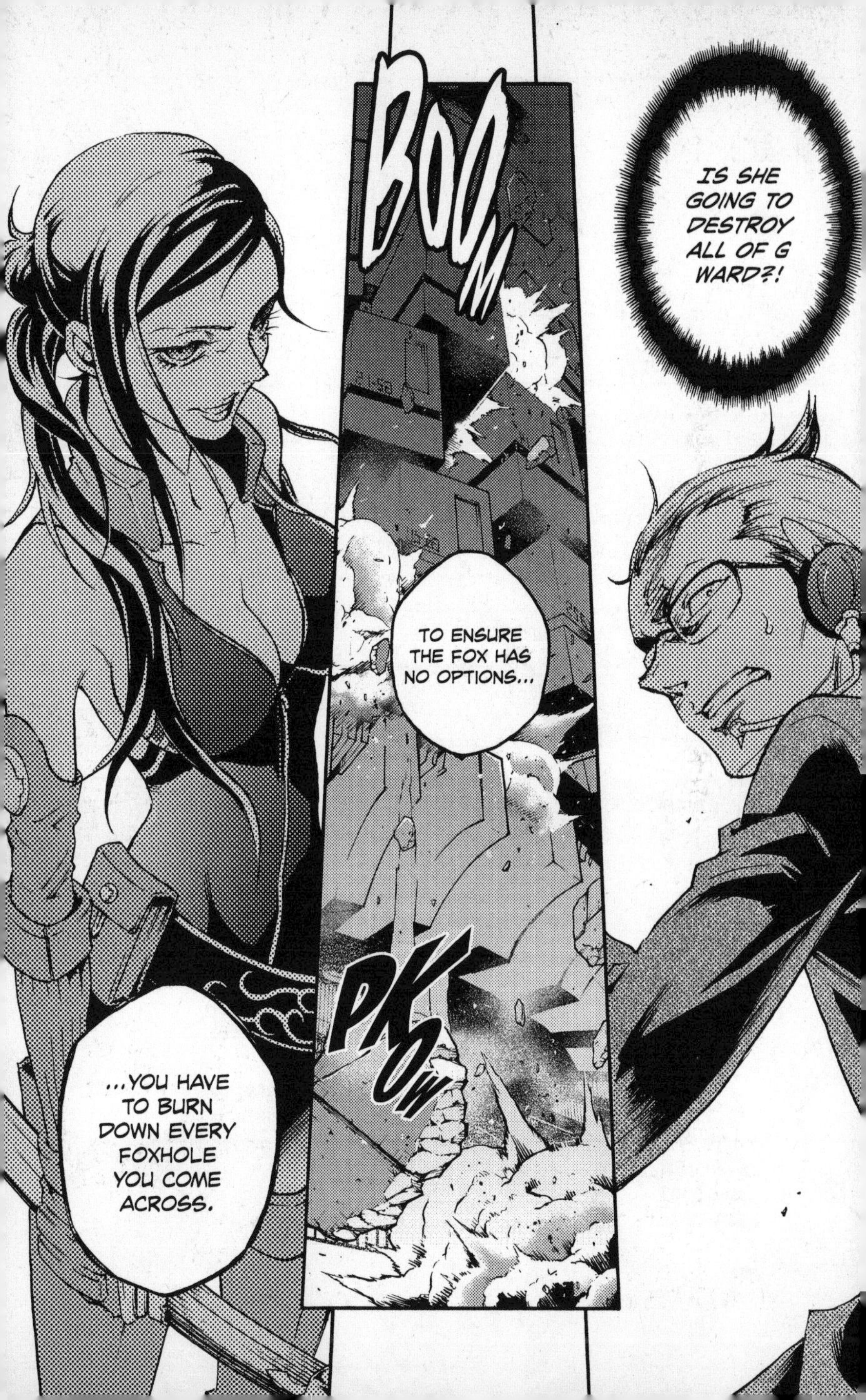
IS SHE GOING TO DESTROY ALL OF G WARD?!
BOOM
TO ENSURE THE FOX HAS NO OPTIONS...
PKOW
...YOU HAVE TO BURN DOWN EVERY FOXHOLE YOU COME ACROSS.

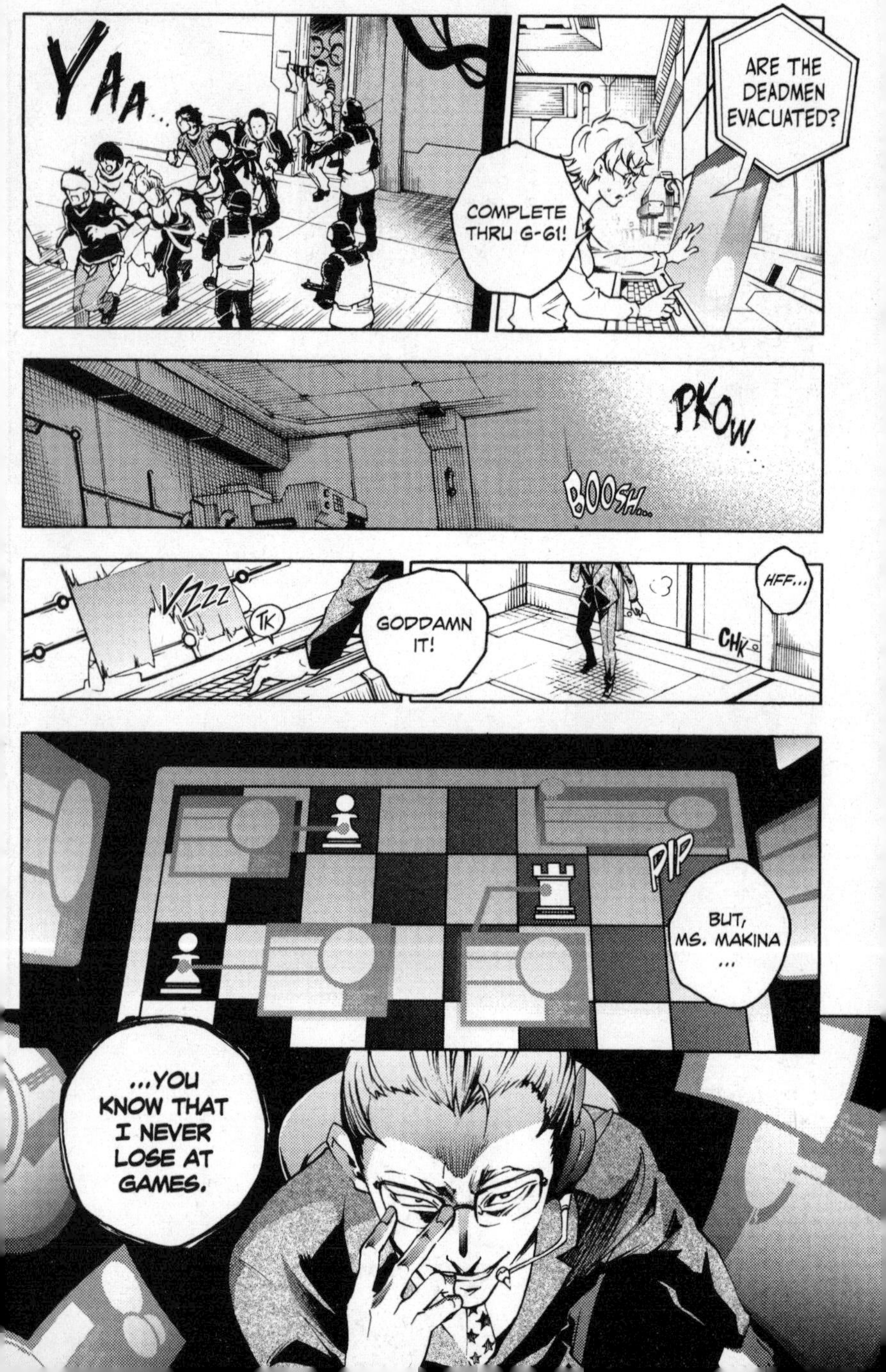
ARE THE DEADMEN EVACUATED?
COMPLETE THRU G-61!
YAA...
PKOW...
BOOSH...
HFF...
CHK
GODDAMN IT!
TK
VZZZ
PIP
BUT, MS. MAKINA ...
...YOU KNOW THAT I NEVER LOSE AT GAMES.

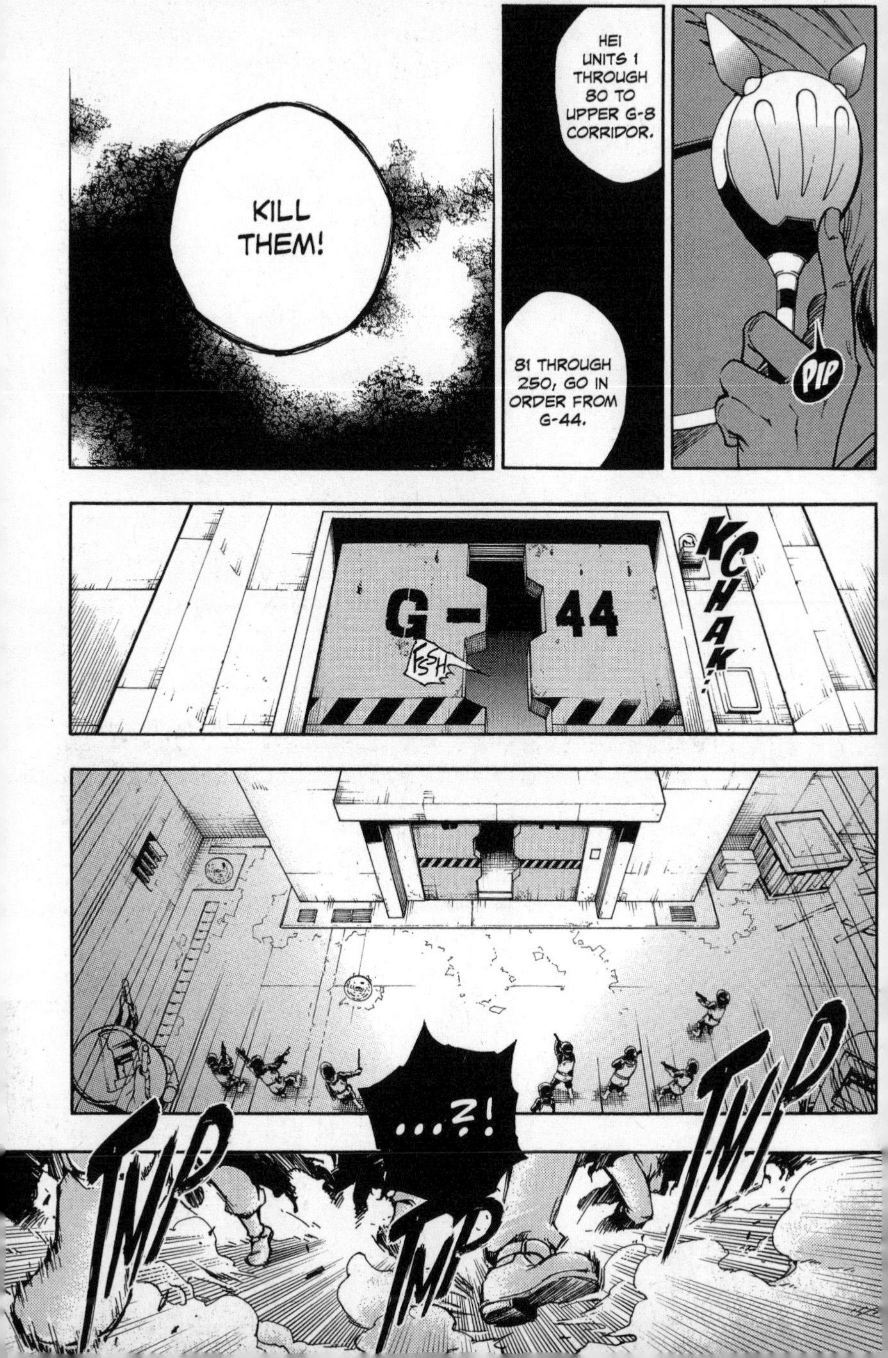
PIP
HEI UNITS 1 THROUGH 80 TO UPPER G-8 CORRIDOR.
81 THROUGH 250, GO IN ORDER FROM G-44.
KILL THEM!
KCHAK!
G-44
FSSH
TMP
TMP
TMP
...?!

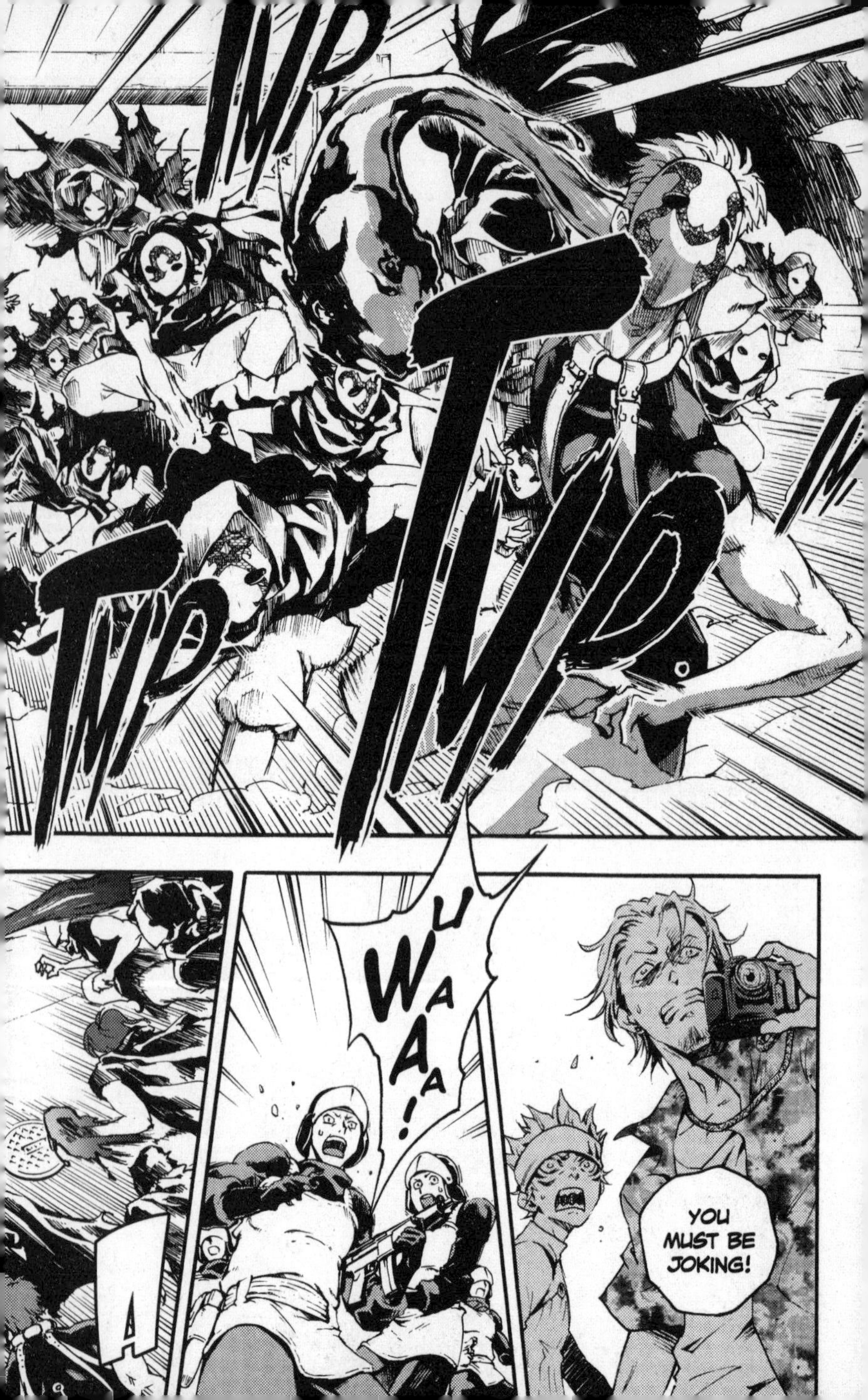
TMP
TMP
UWAAAA!
YOU MUST BE JOKING!
A

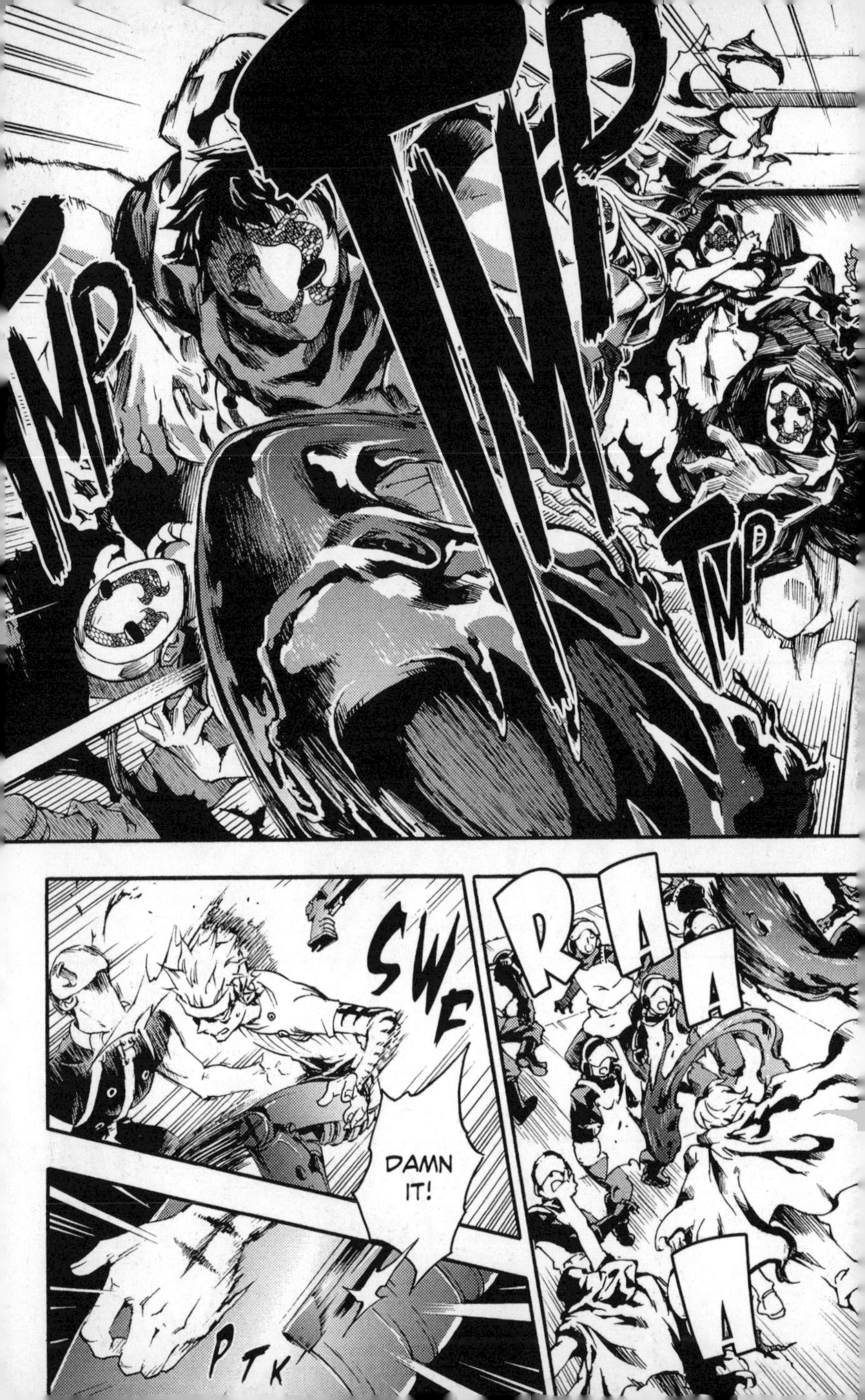

TMP
TMP
RAAA
SWF
DAMN IT!
PTK

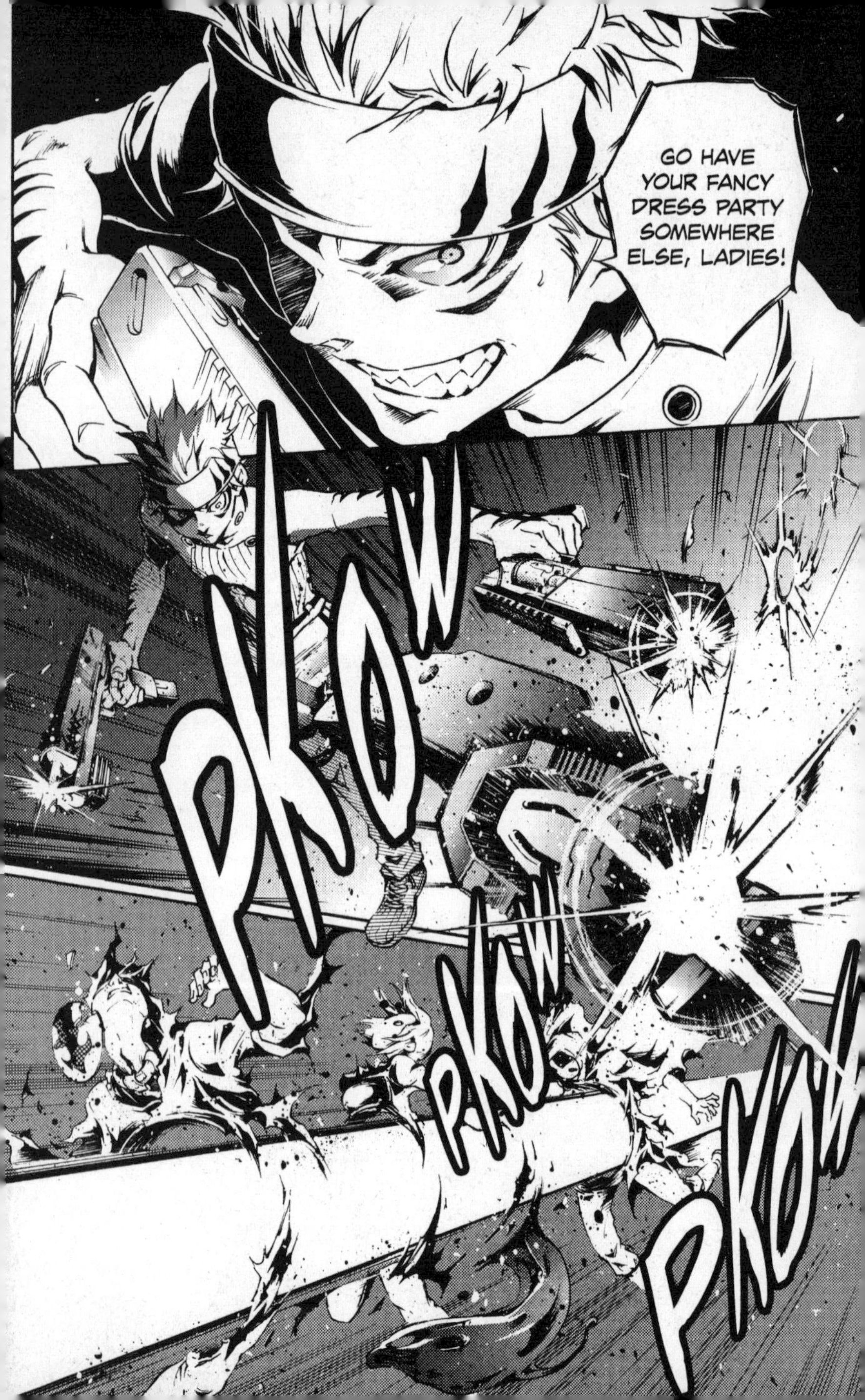
GO HAVE YOUR FANCY DRESS PARTY SOMEWHERE ELSE, LADIES!
PKOW
PKOW
PKOW

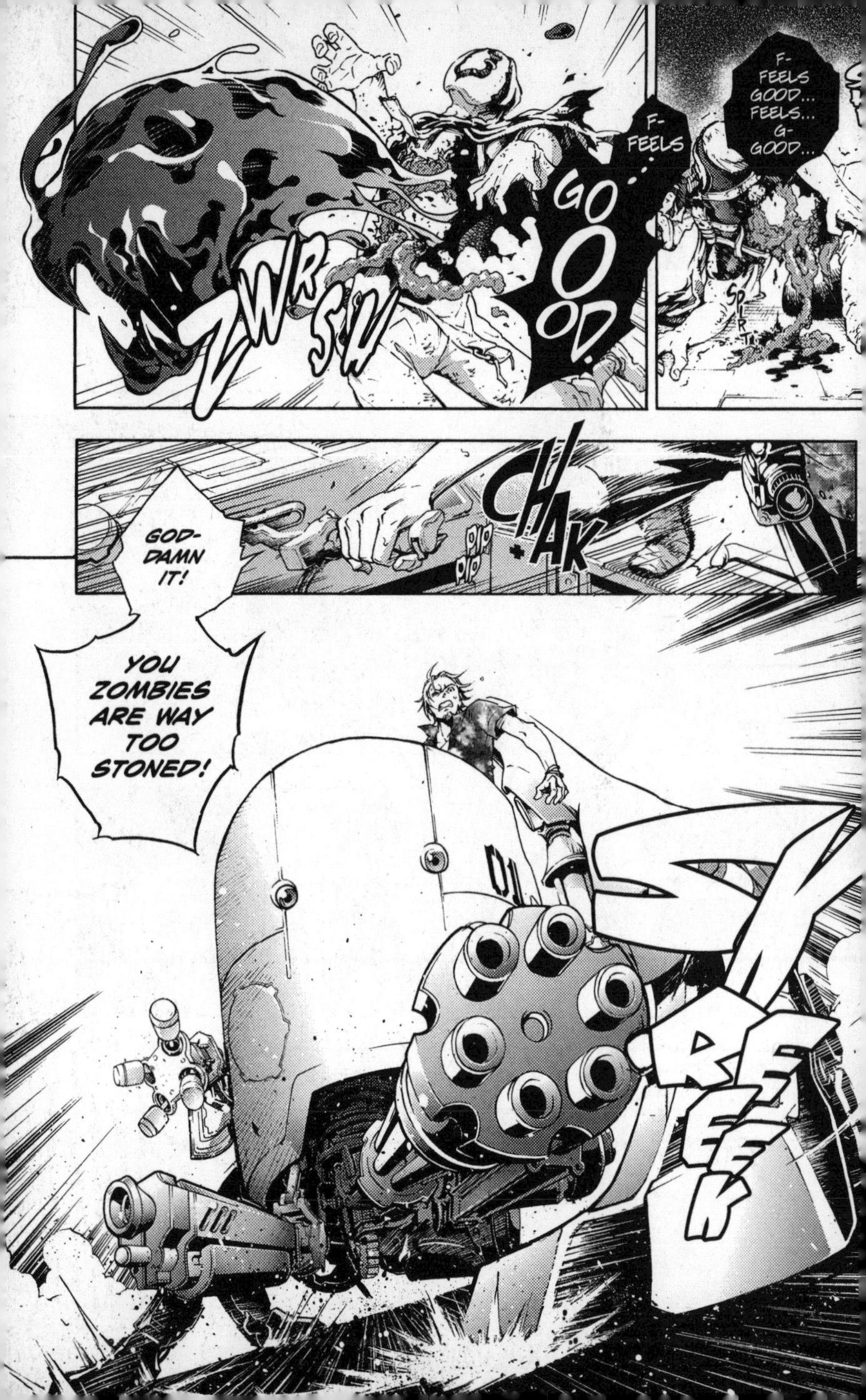
F-
FEELS GOOD... FEELS... G-GOOD...
SPLRT
F-
FEELS
GOOOOD.
ZWRSH
CHAK
PIP PIP
GOD-DAMN IT!
YOU ZOMBIES ARE WAY TOO STONED!
SKREEEEK

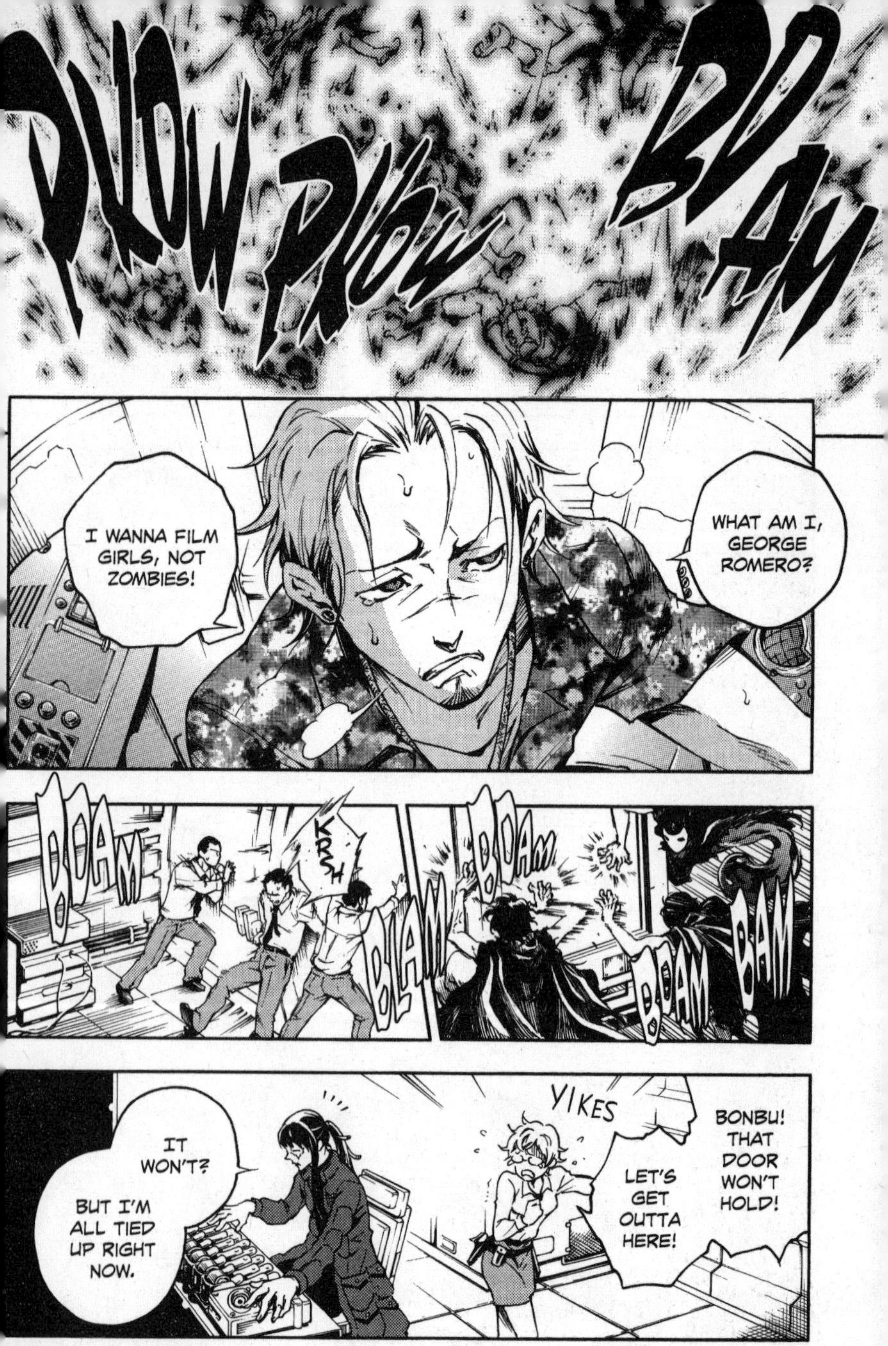
BZAM
PKOW
PKOW
WHAT AM I, GEORGE ROMERO?
I WANNA FILM GIRLS, NOT ZOMBIES!
BAM
BLAM
BLAM
BLAM
KRSH
BLAM
BONBU! THAT DOOR WON'T HOLD!
YIKES
LET'S GET OUTTA HERE!
IT WON'T?
BUT I'M ALL TIED UP RIGHT NOW.

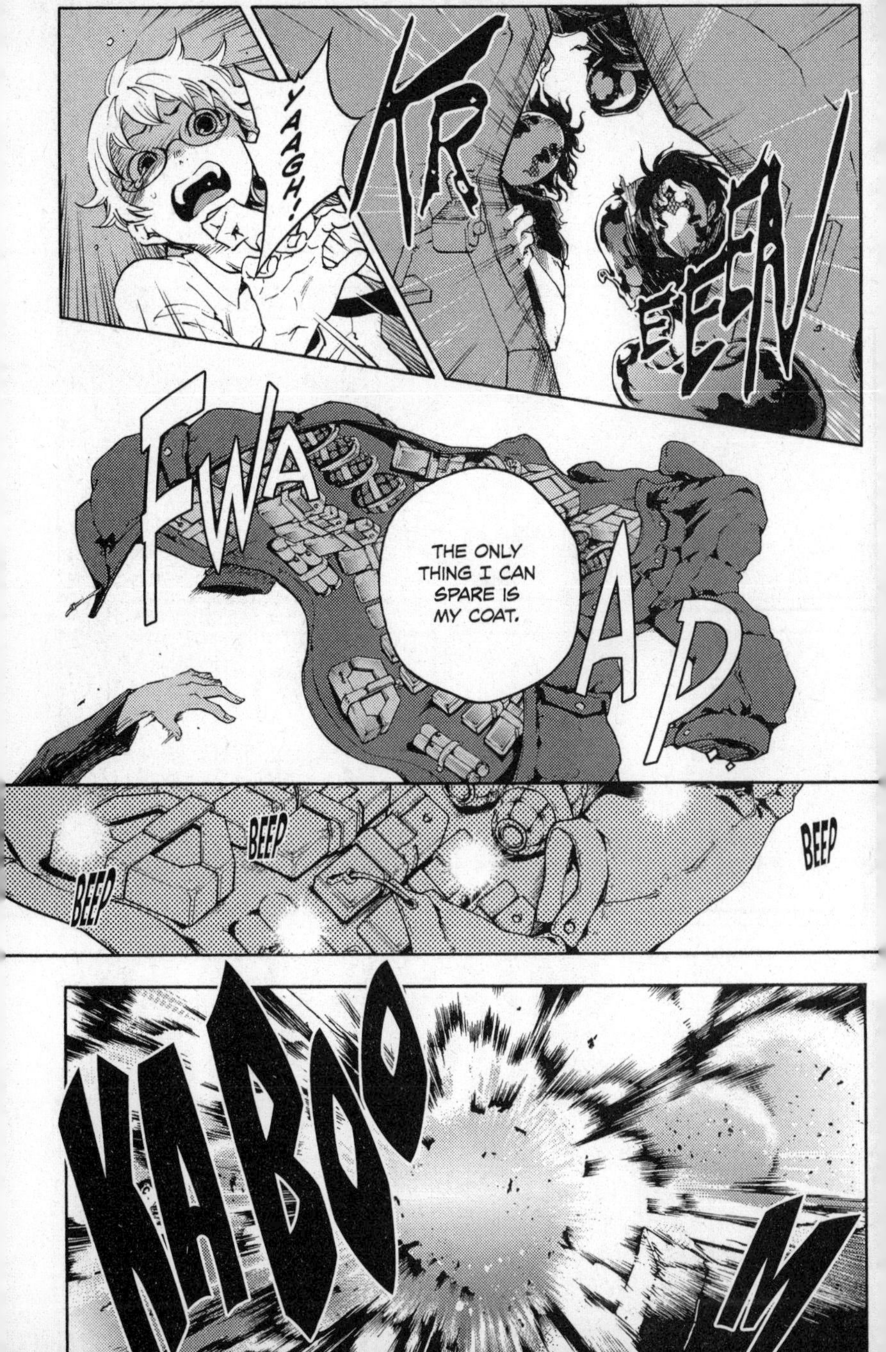
KREEEN
YAAAGH!
FWAAP
THE ONLY THING I CAN SPARE IS MY COAT.
BEEP
BEEP
BEEP
KABOOM

TIME LOST... 132 SECONDS.

WOW ...

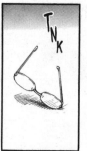

TNK

LET'S GET ON WITH THE OPERATION.

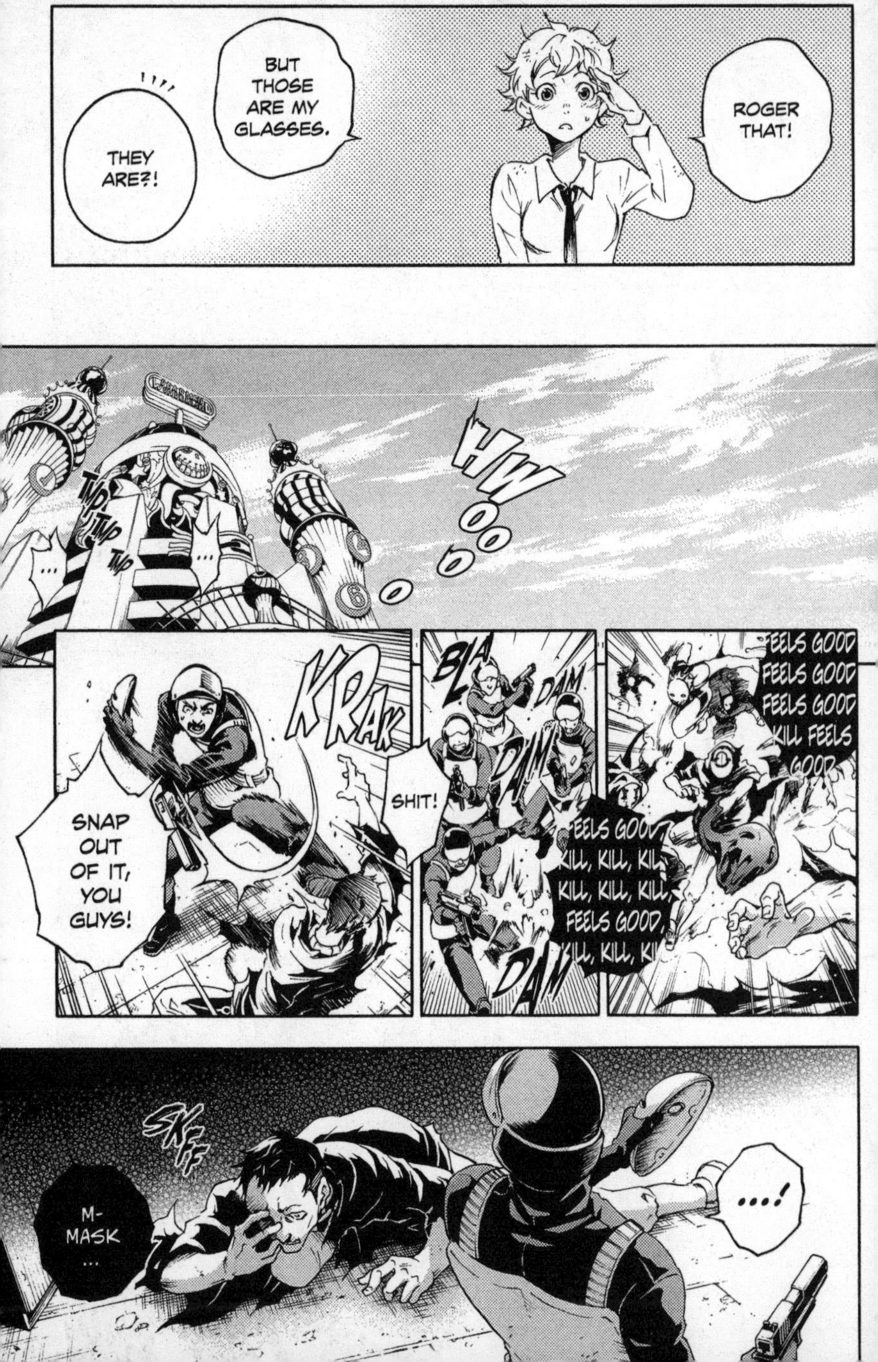
ROGER THAT!
BUT THOSE ARE MY GLASSES.
THEY ARE?!
HWOOOOO
...
TMP TMP TMP
...
FEELS GOOD FEELS GOOD FEELS GOOD KILL FEELS GOOD
BLAM
DAM
DAM
FEELS GOOD KILL, KILL, KIL KILL, KILL, KILL, FEELS GOOD, KILL, KILL, KI
DAM
KRAK
SHIT!
SNAP OUT OF IT, YOU GUYS!
...!
SKFF
M-MASK ...

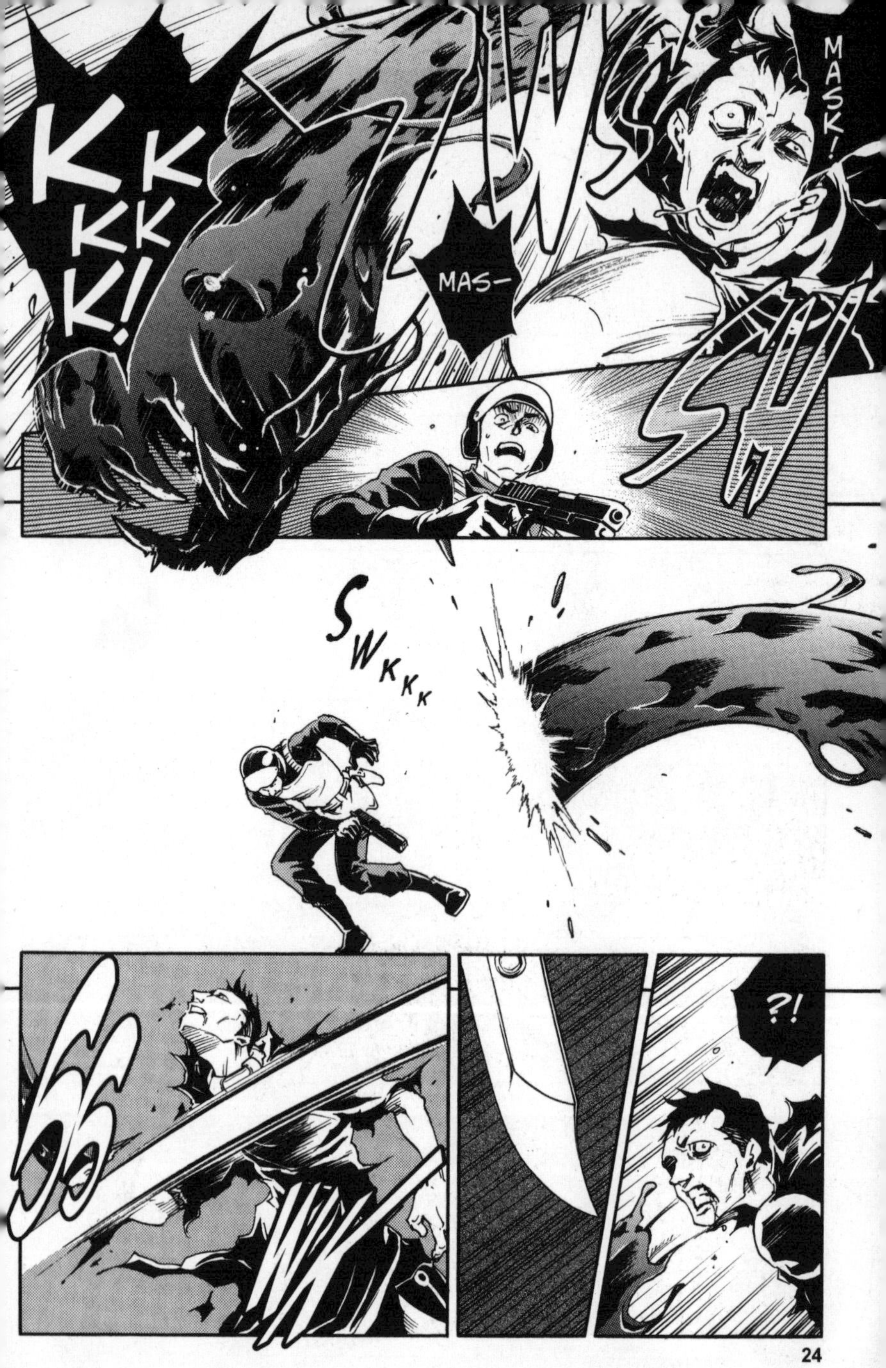
MASK!
MAS—
KKKKK!
SWKKK
?!

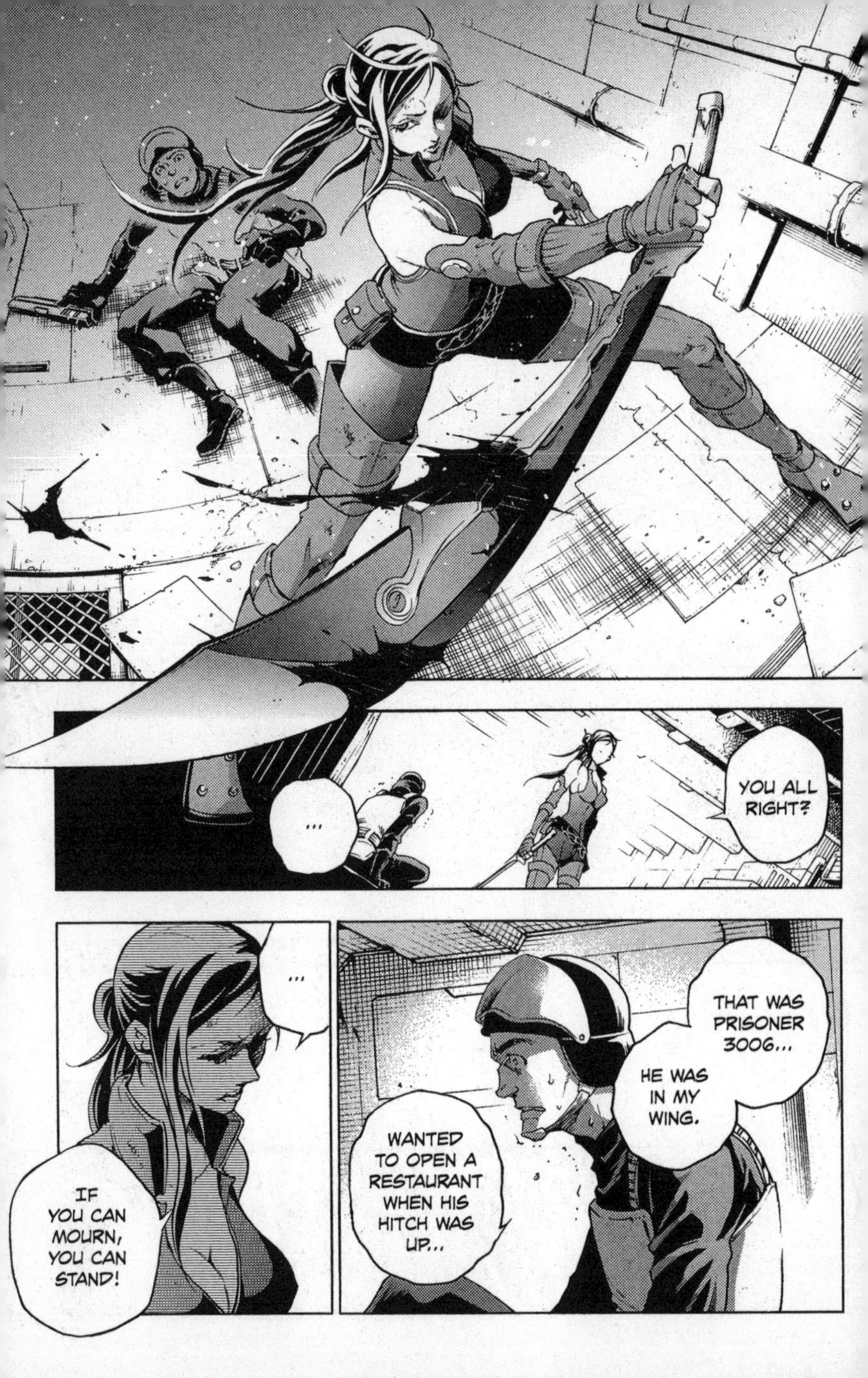
YOU ALL RIGHT?
...
THAT WAS PRISONER 3006...
HE WAS IN MY WING.
WANTED TO OPEN A RESTAURANT WHEN HIS HITCH WAS UP...
...
IF YOU CAN MOURN, YOU CAN STAND!

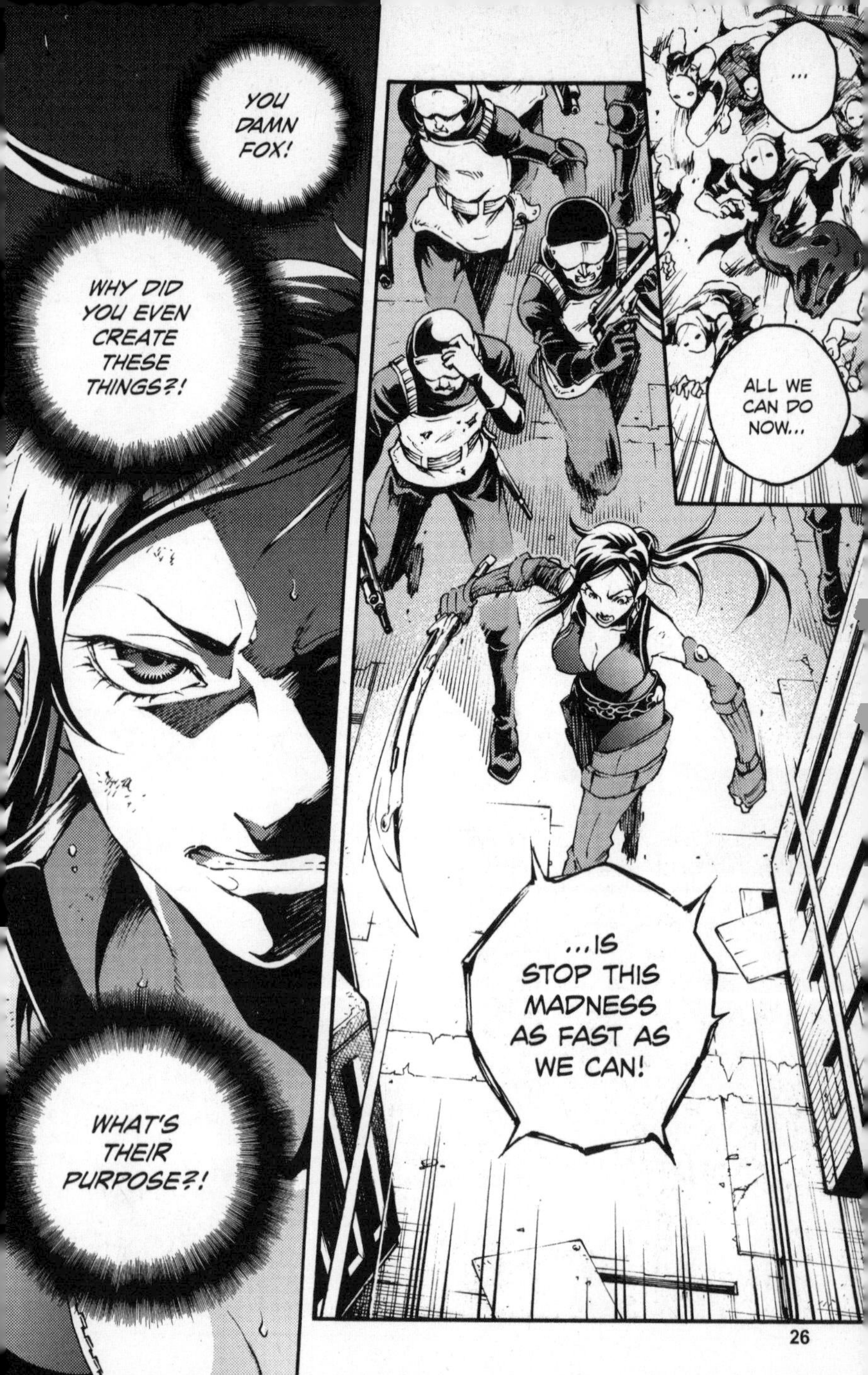
...
ALL WE CAN DO NOW...
...IS STOP THIS MADNESS AS FAST AS WE CAN!
YOU DAMN FOX!
WHY DID YOU EVEN CREATE THESE THINGS?!
WHAT'S THEIR PURPOSE?!

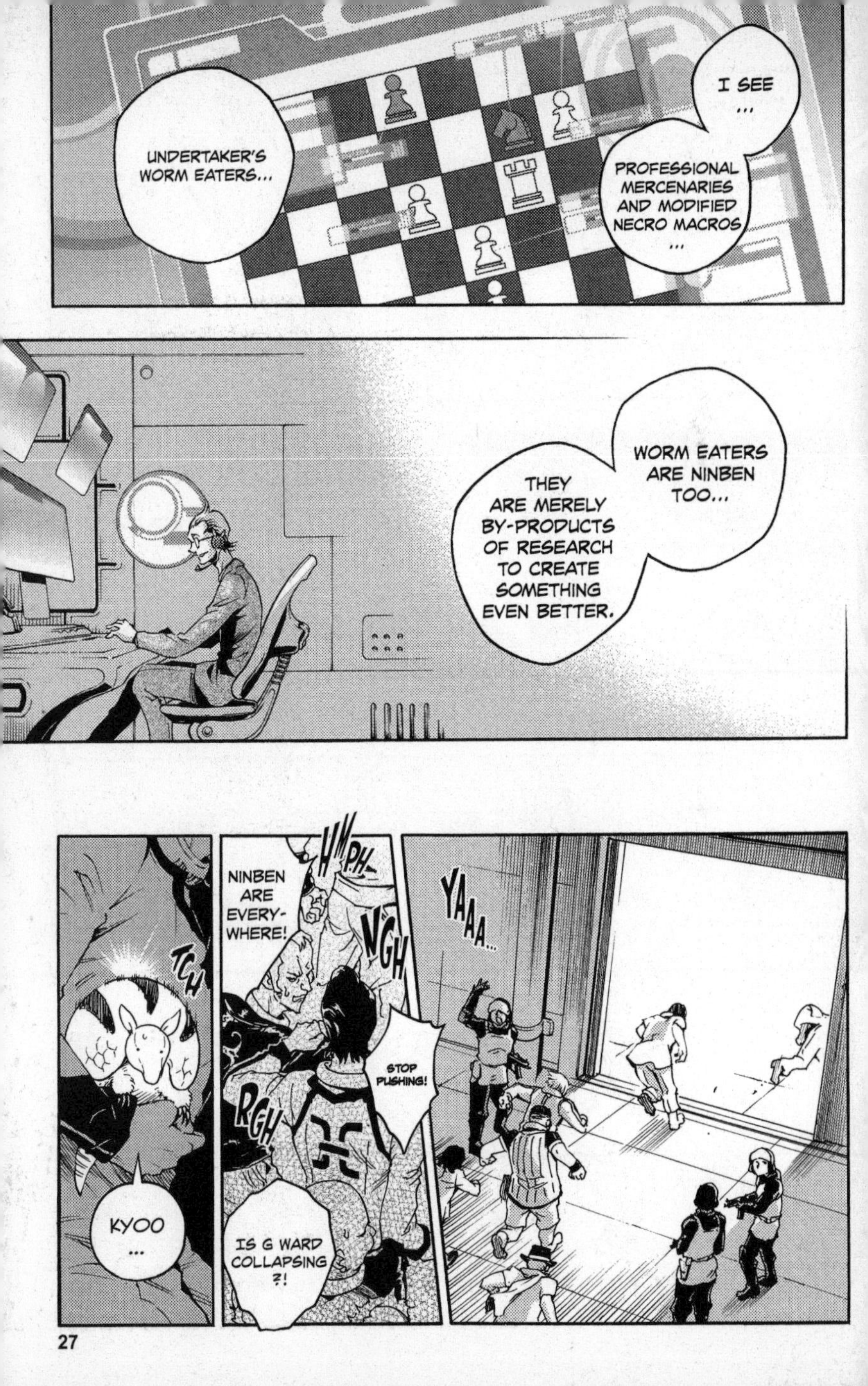
I SEE ...
PROFESSIONAL MERCENARIES AND MODIFIED NECRO MACROS ...
UNDERTAKER'S WORM EATERS...
WORM EATERS ARE NINBEN TOO...
THEY ARE MERELY BY-PRODUCTS OF RESEARCH TO CREATE SOMETHING EVEN BETTER.
YAAAA...
HMPH
NINBEN ARE EVERY-WHERE!
NGH
STOP PUSHING!
RGH
IS G WARD COLLAPSING ?!
TCH
KYOO ...

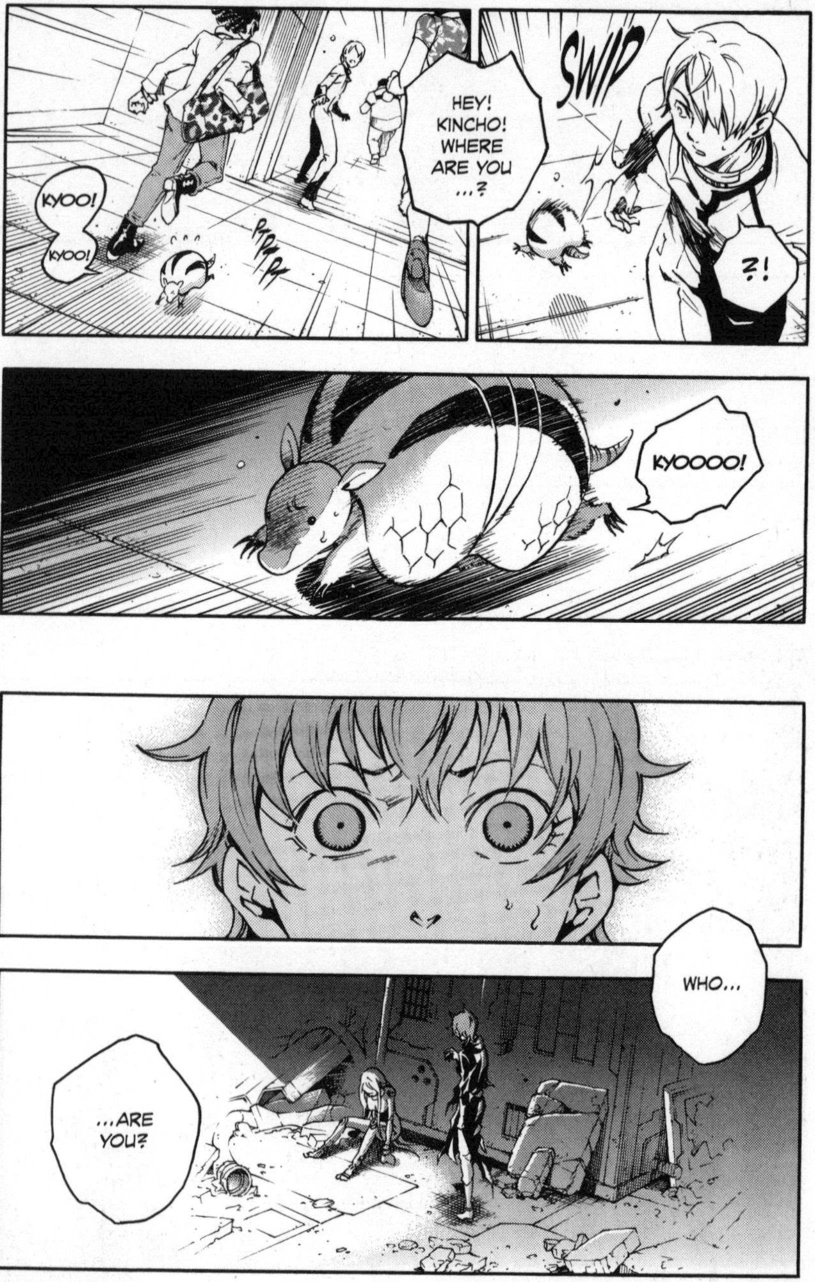
SWIP
?!
HEY! KINCHO! WHERE ARE YOU ...?
KYOO!
KYOO!
KYOOOO!
WHO...
...ARE YOU?

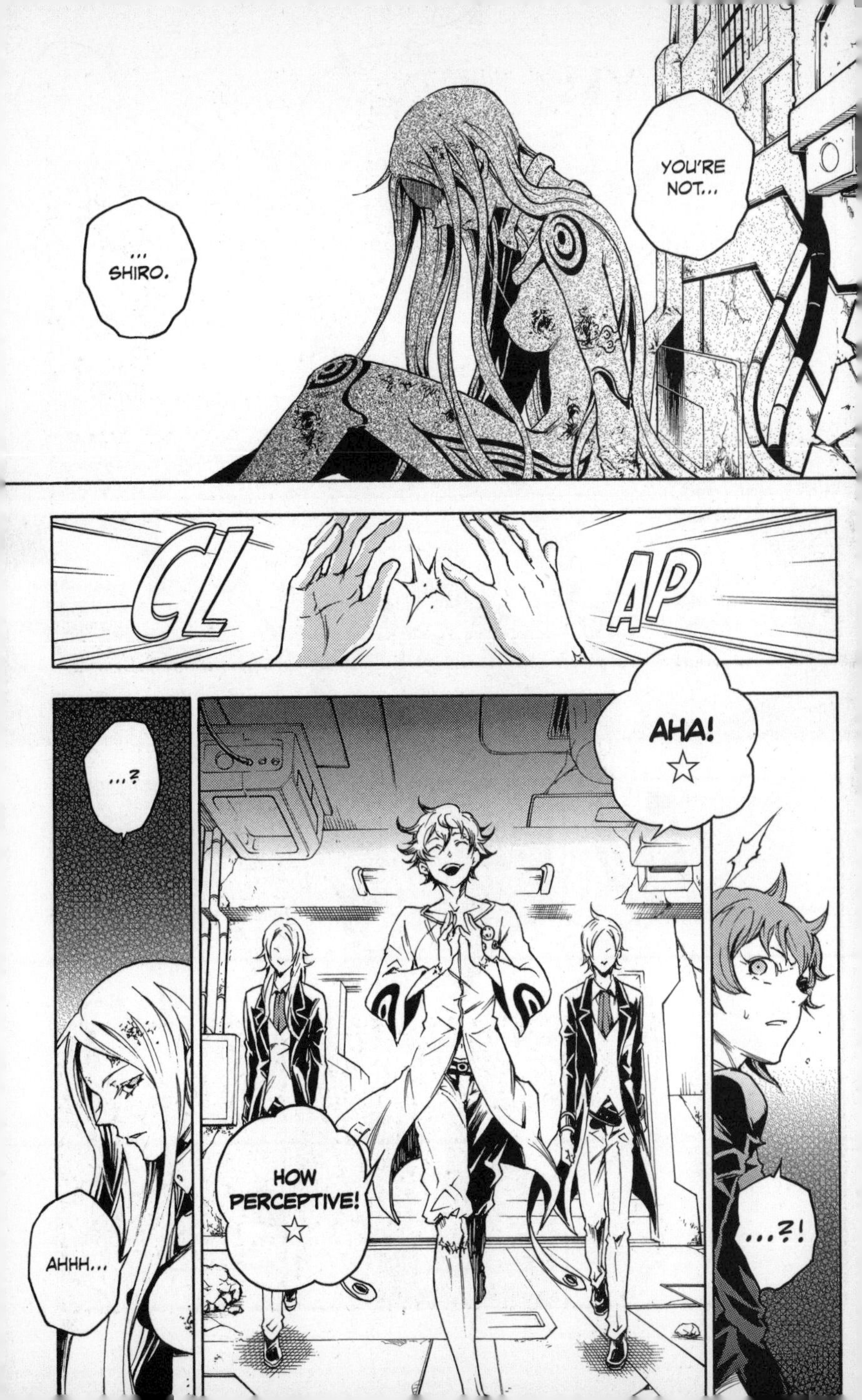
YOU'RE NOT...
... SHIRO.
CLAP
...?!
AHA! ☆
HOW PERCEPTIVE! ☆
...?
AHHH...

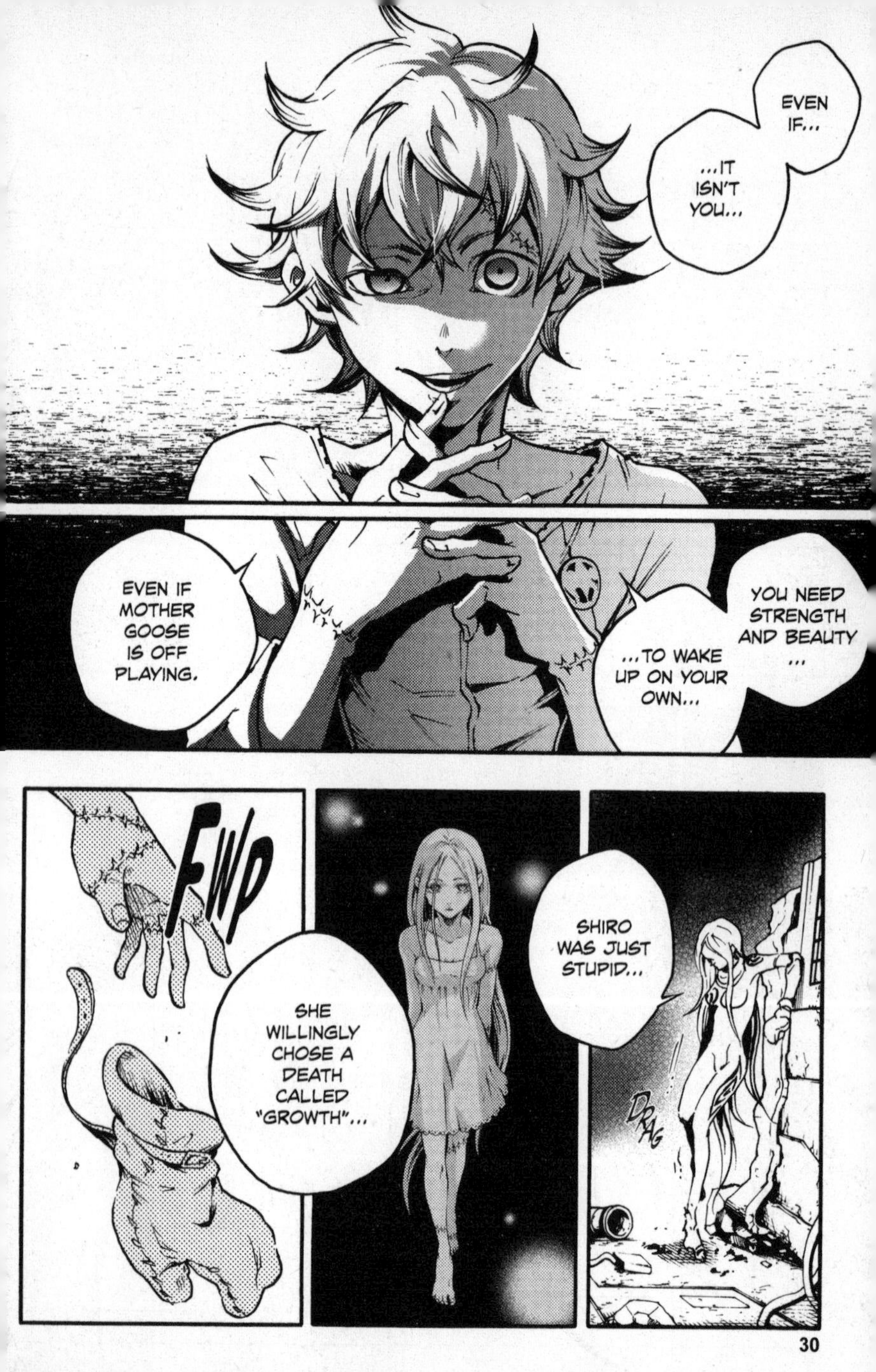
EVEN IF...
...IT ISN'T YOU...
YOU NEED STRENGTH AND BEAUTY ...
...TO WAKE UP ON YOUR OWN...
EVEN IF MOTHER GOOSE IS OFF PLAYING.
SHIRO WAS JUST STUPID...
DRAG
SHE WILLINGLY CHOSE A DEATH CALLED "GROWTH"...
FWP

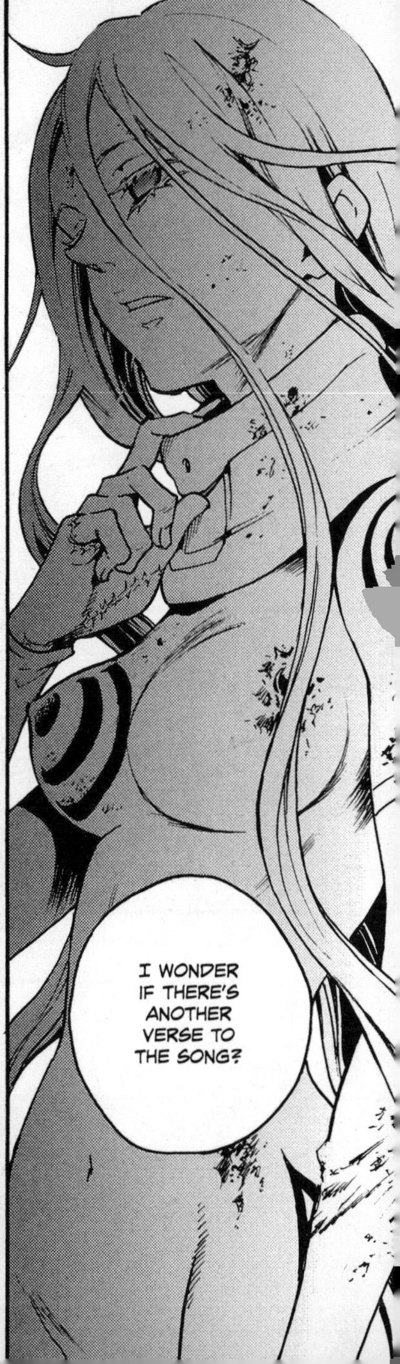
I WONDER IF THERE'S ANOTHER VERSE TO THE SONG?

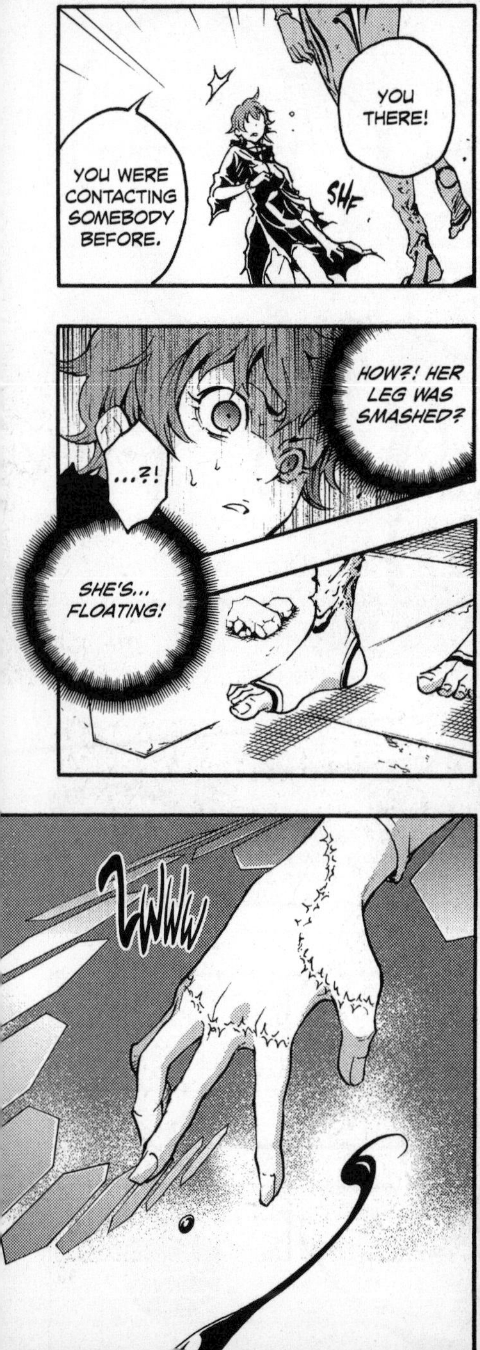
YOU THERE!
SHF
YOU WERE CONTACTING SOMEBODY BEFORE.
HOW?! HER LEG WAS SMASHED?
...?!
SHE'S... FLOATING!
ZWWW

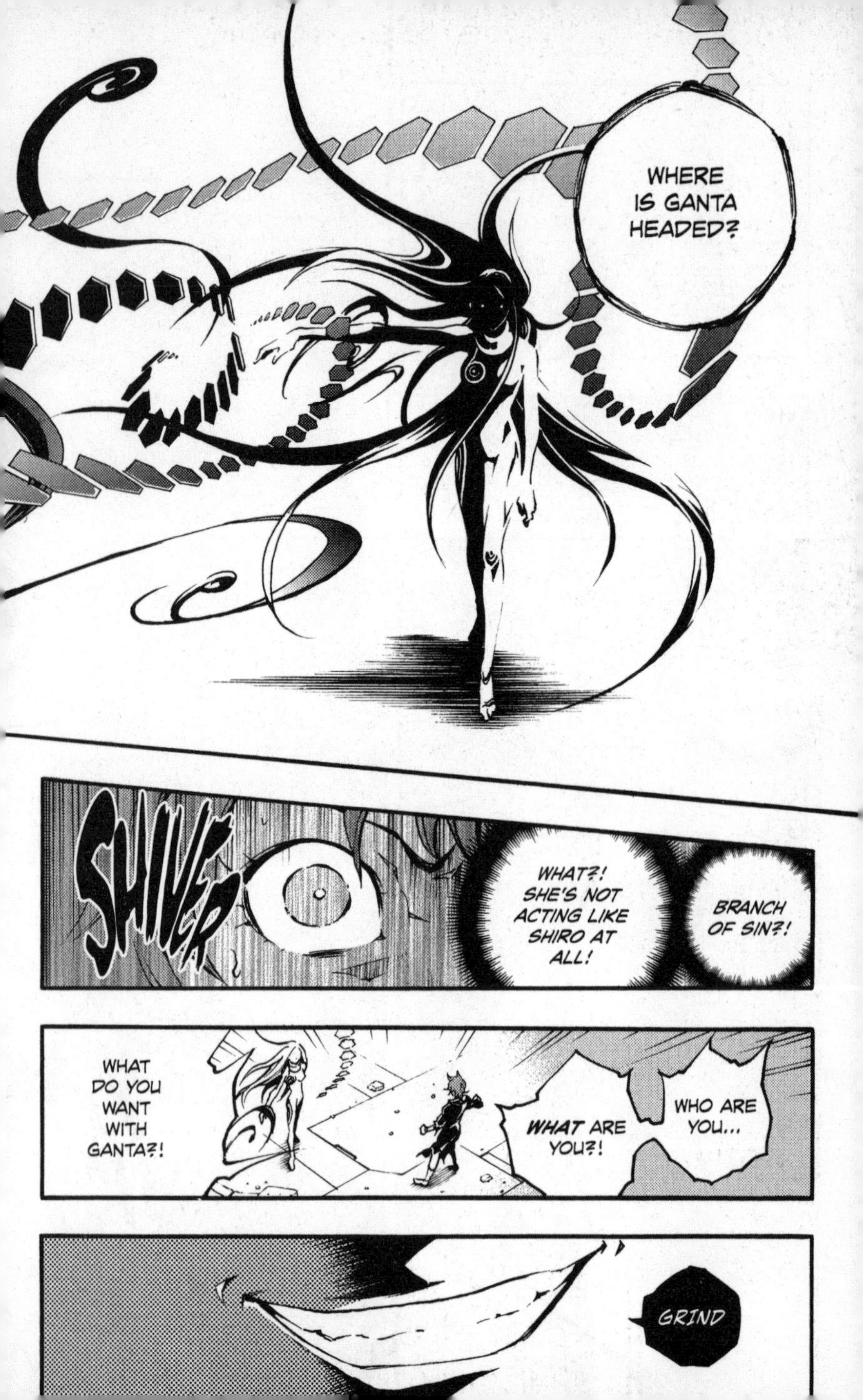
WHERE IS GANTA HEADED?
BRANCH OF SIN?!
WHAT?! SHE'S NOT ACTING LIKE SHIRO AT ALL!
SHIVER
WHO ARE YOU...
WHAT ARE YOU?!
WHAT DO YOU WANT WITH GANTA?!
GRIND

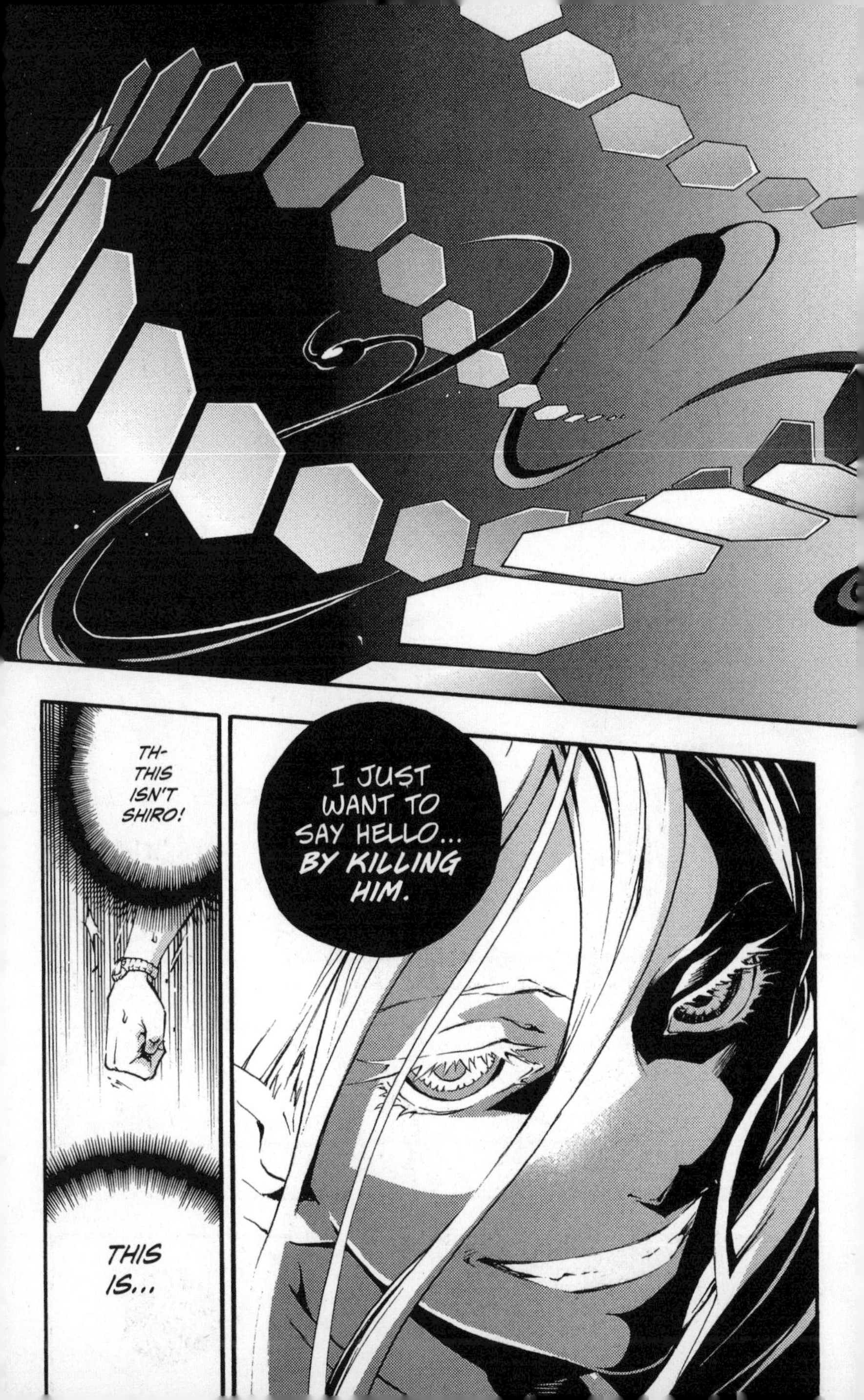
I JUST WANT TO SAY HELLO... BY KILLING HIM.
TH-THIS ISN'T SHIRO!
THIS IS...

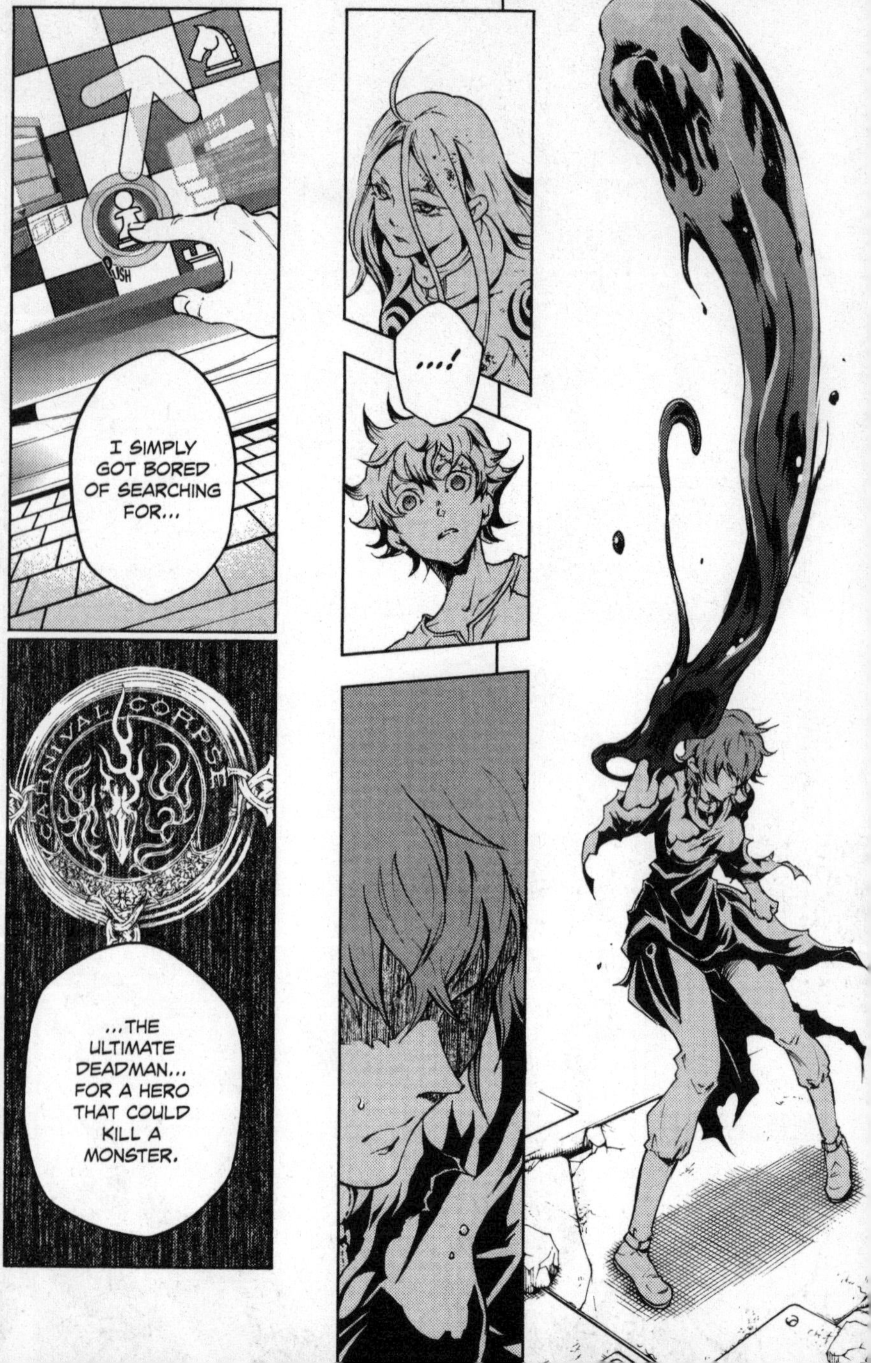
...!
PUSH
I SIMPLY GOT BORED OF SEARCHING FOR...
CARNIVAL CORPSE
...THE ULTIMATE DEADMAN... FOR A HERO THAT COULD KILL A MONSTER.

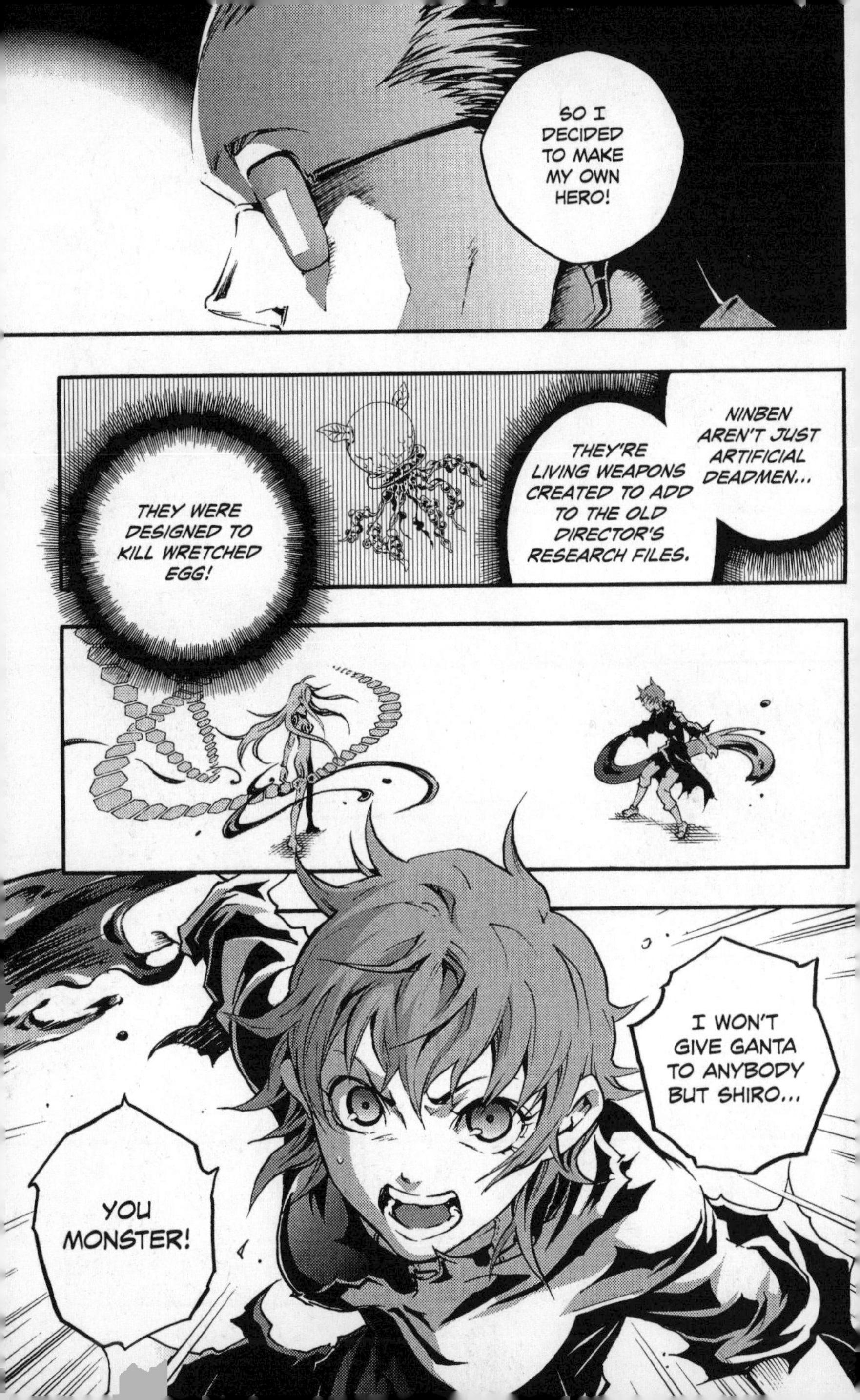
SO I DECIDED TO MAKE MY OWN HERO!
NINBEN AREN'T JUST ARTIFICIAL DEADMEN...
THEY'RE LIVING WEAPONS CREATED TO ADD TO THE OLD DIRECTOR'S RESEARCH FILES.
THEY WERE DESIGNED TO KILL WRETCHED EGG!
I WON'T GIVE GANTA TO ANYBODY BUT SHIRO...
YOU MONSTER!

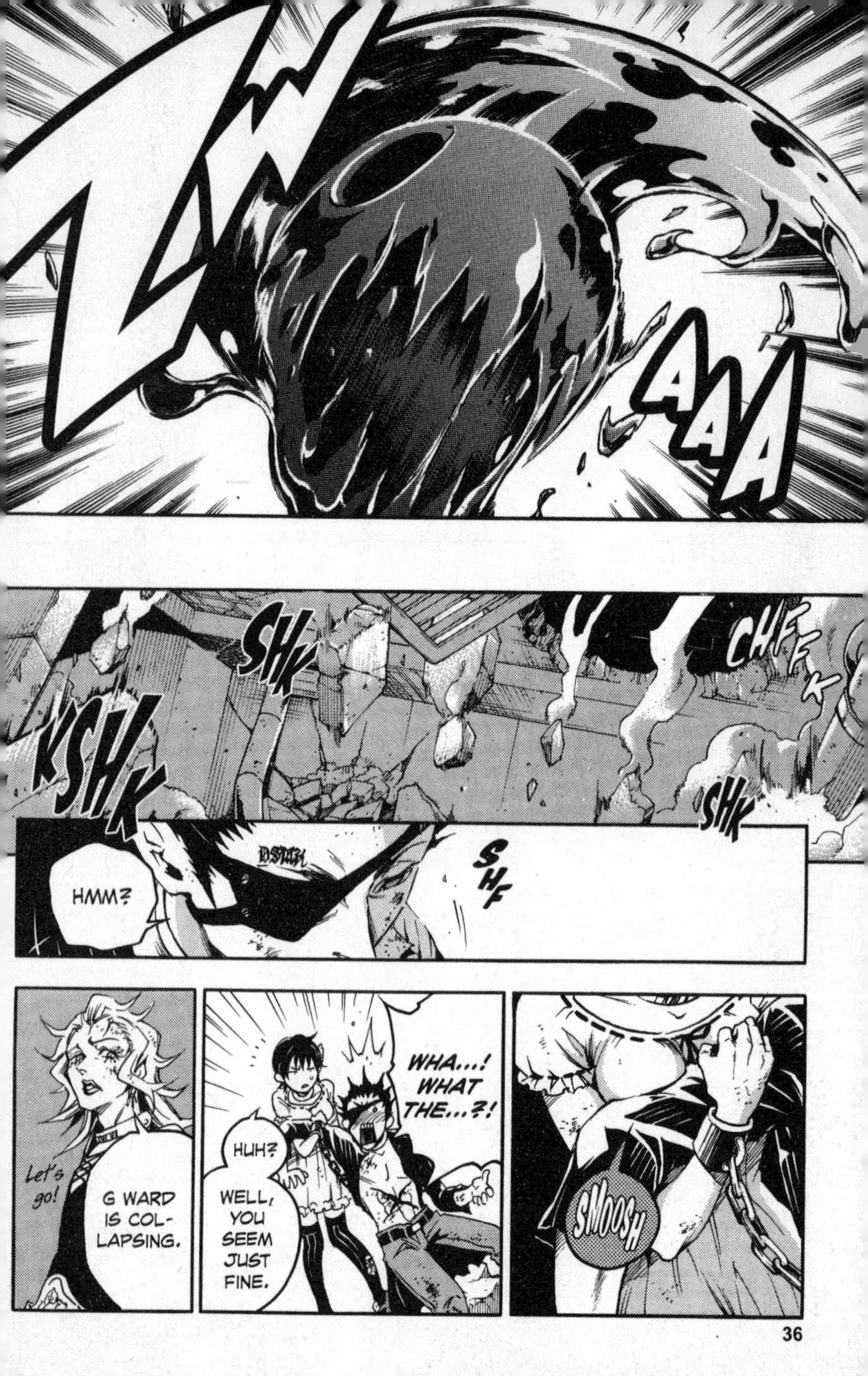
ZAAAA
CHFFK
SHK
KSHK
SHK
SHF
HMM?
SMOOSH
WHA...! WHAT THE...?!
HUH?
WELL, YOU SEEM JUST FINE.
G WARD IS COL-LAPSING.
Let's go!

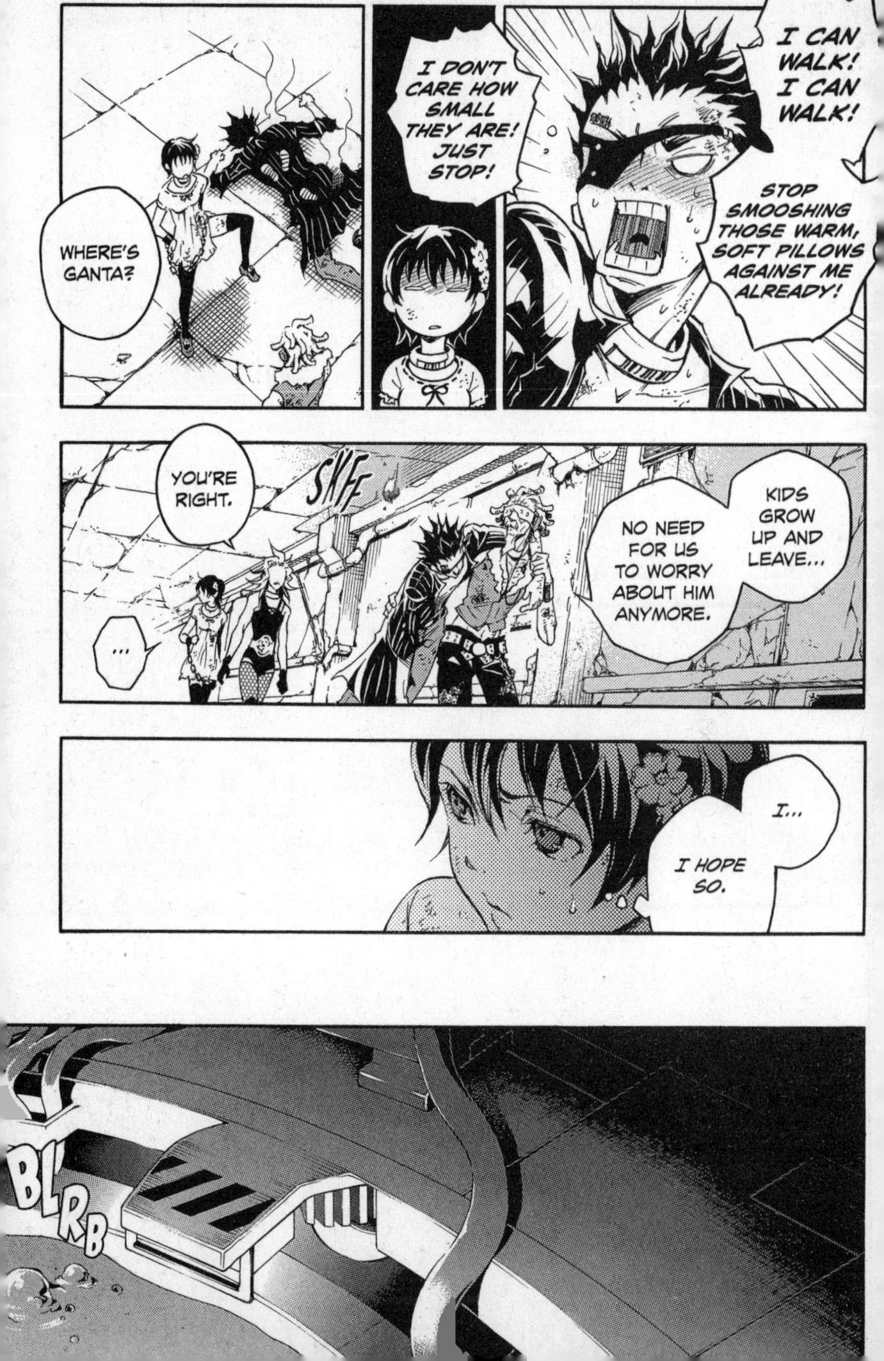
I CAN WALK! I CAN WALK!
STOP SMOOSHING THOSE WARM, SOFT PILLOWS AGAINST ME ALREADY!
I DON'T CARE HOW SMALL THEY ARE! JUST STOP!
WHERE'S GANTA?
KIDS GROW UP AND LEAVE...
NO NEED FOR US TO WORRY ABOUT HIM ANYMORE.
SHFF
YOU'RE RIGHT.
...
I...
I HOPE SO.
BLRB

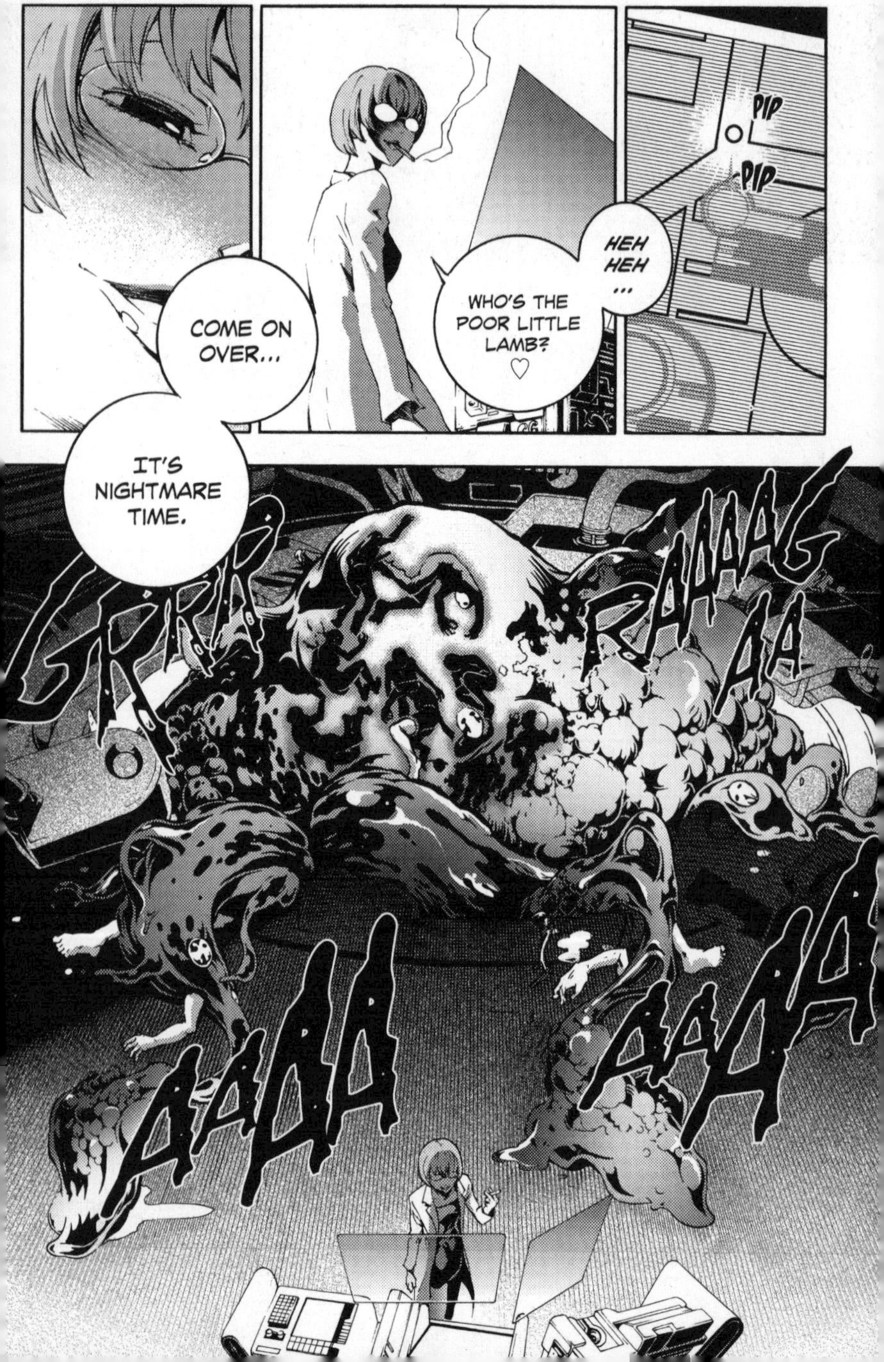
PIP
PIP
HEH HEH ...
WHO'S THE POOR LITTLE LAMB? ♡
COME ON OVER...
IT'S NIGHTMARE TIME.
RAAAG
AAA
GRRR
AAAA
AAAA

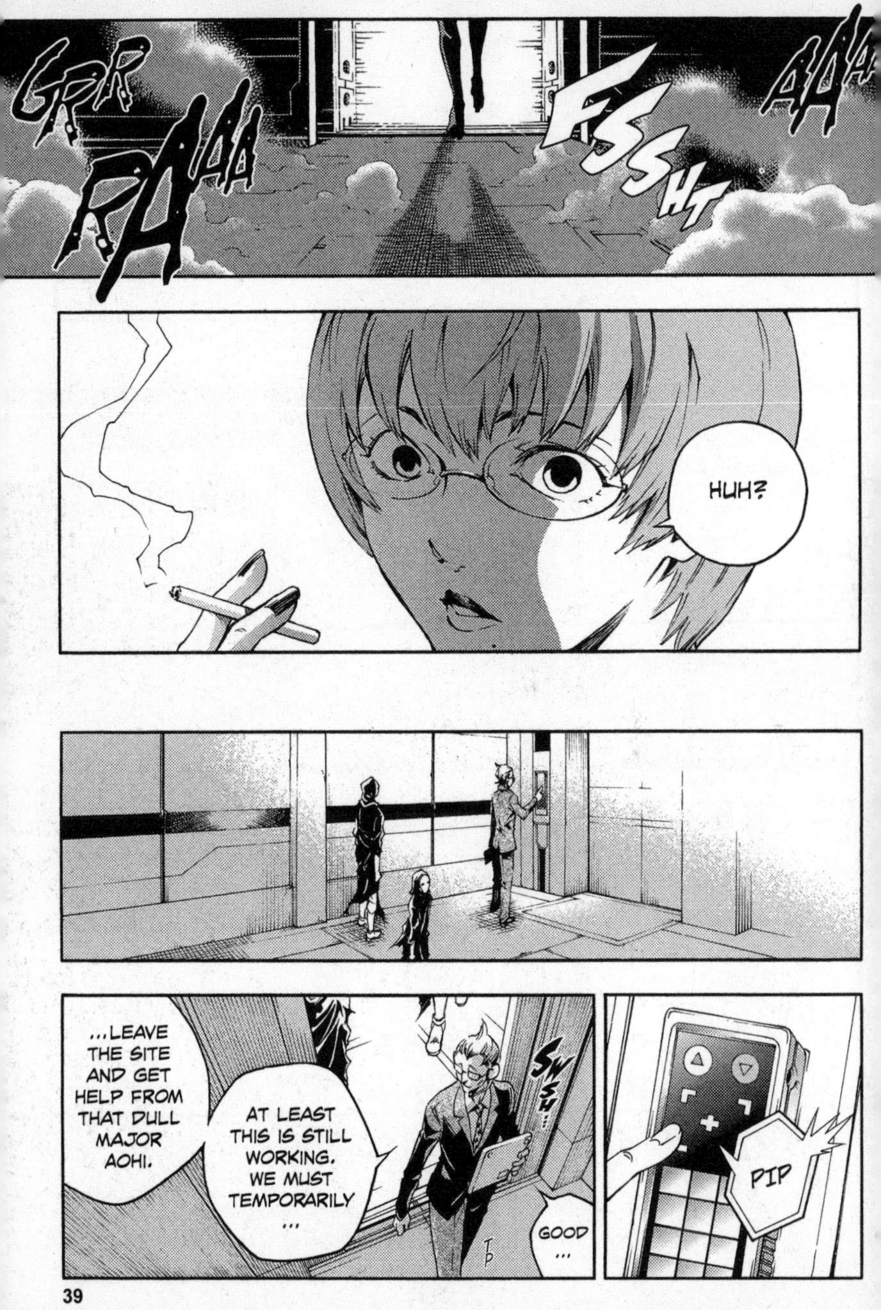
AAA
FSSHT
GRR RAAAA
HUH?
PIP
GOOD ...
SWSH...
TP
AT LEAST THIS IS STILL WORKING. WE MUST TEMPORARILY ...
...LEAVE THE SITE AND GET HELP FROM THAT DULL MAJOR AOHI.

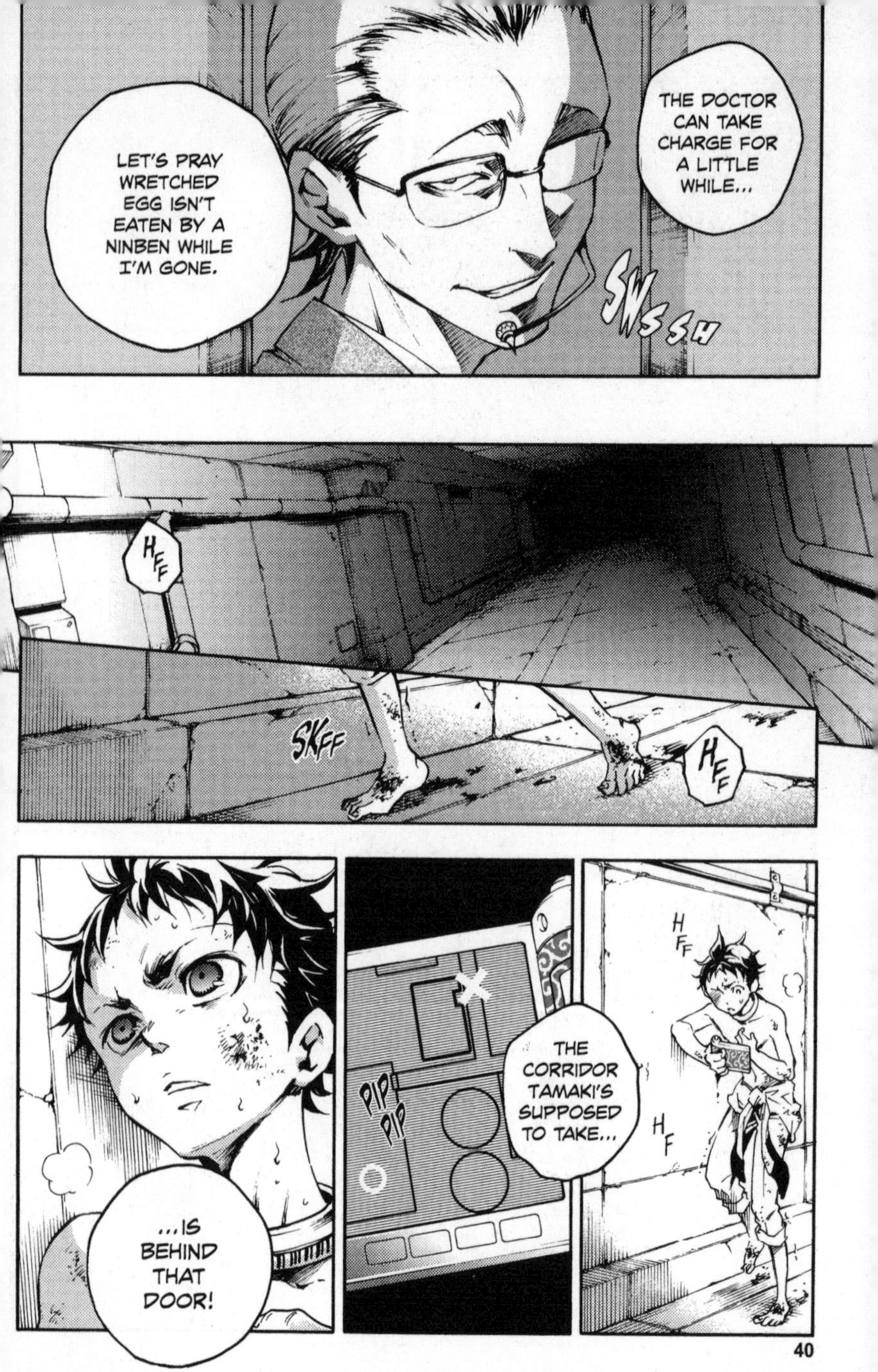
THE DOCTOR CAN TAKE CHARGE FOR A LITTLE WHILE...
LET'S PRAY WRETCHED EGG ISN'T EATEN BY A NINBEN WHILE I'M GONE.
SWSSH
HFF
HFF
SKFF
HFF
HF
THE CORRIDOR TAMAKI'S SUPPOSED TO TAKE...
PIP PIP
...IS BEHIND THAT DOOR!

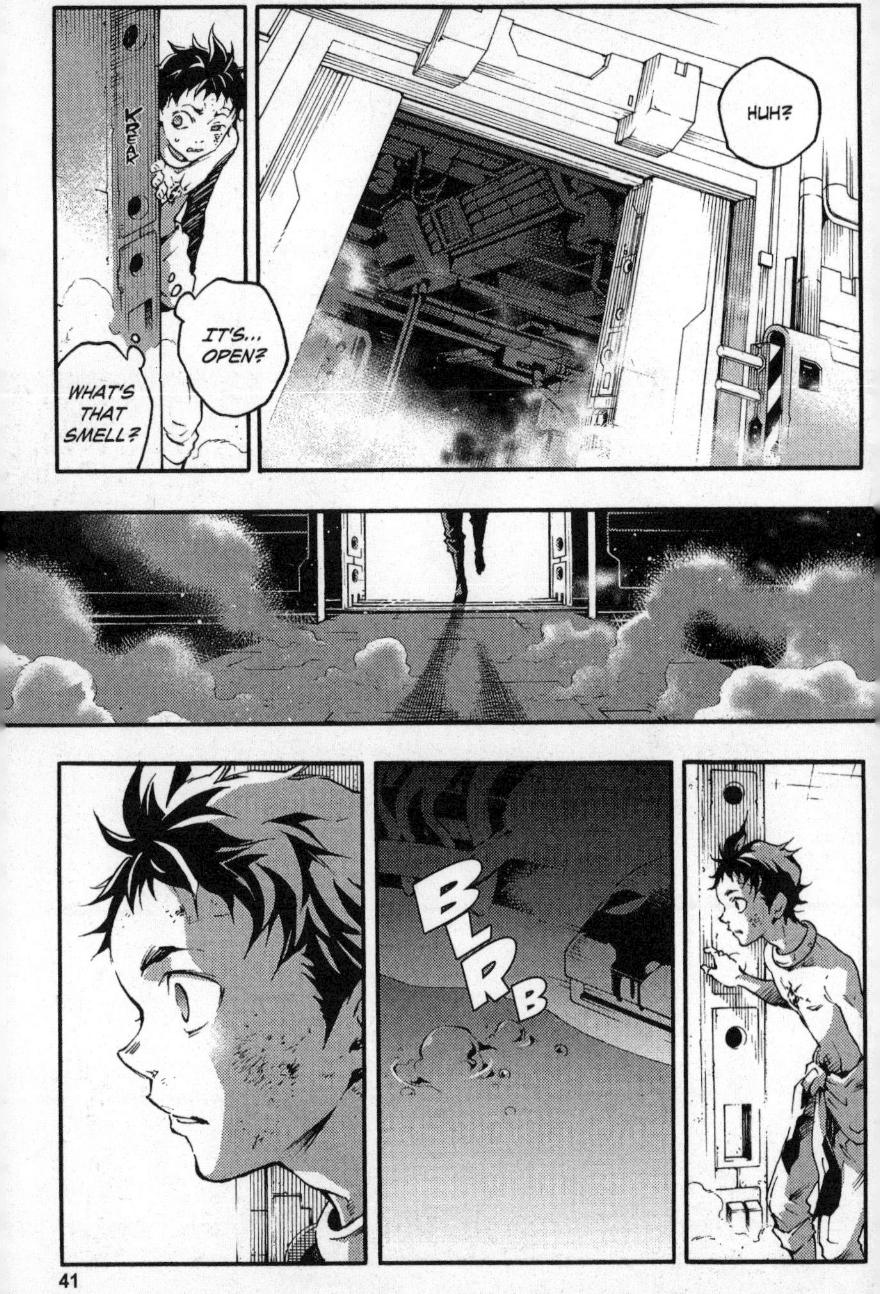
HUH?
KREAK
IT'S... OPEN?
WHAT'S THAT SMELL?
BLRB

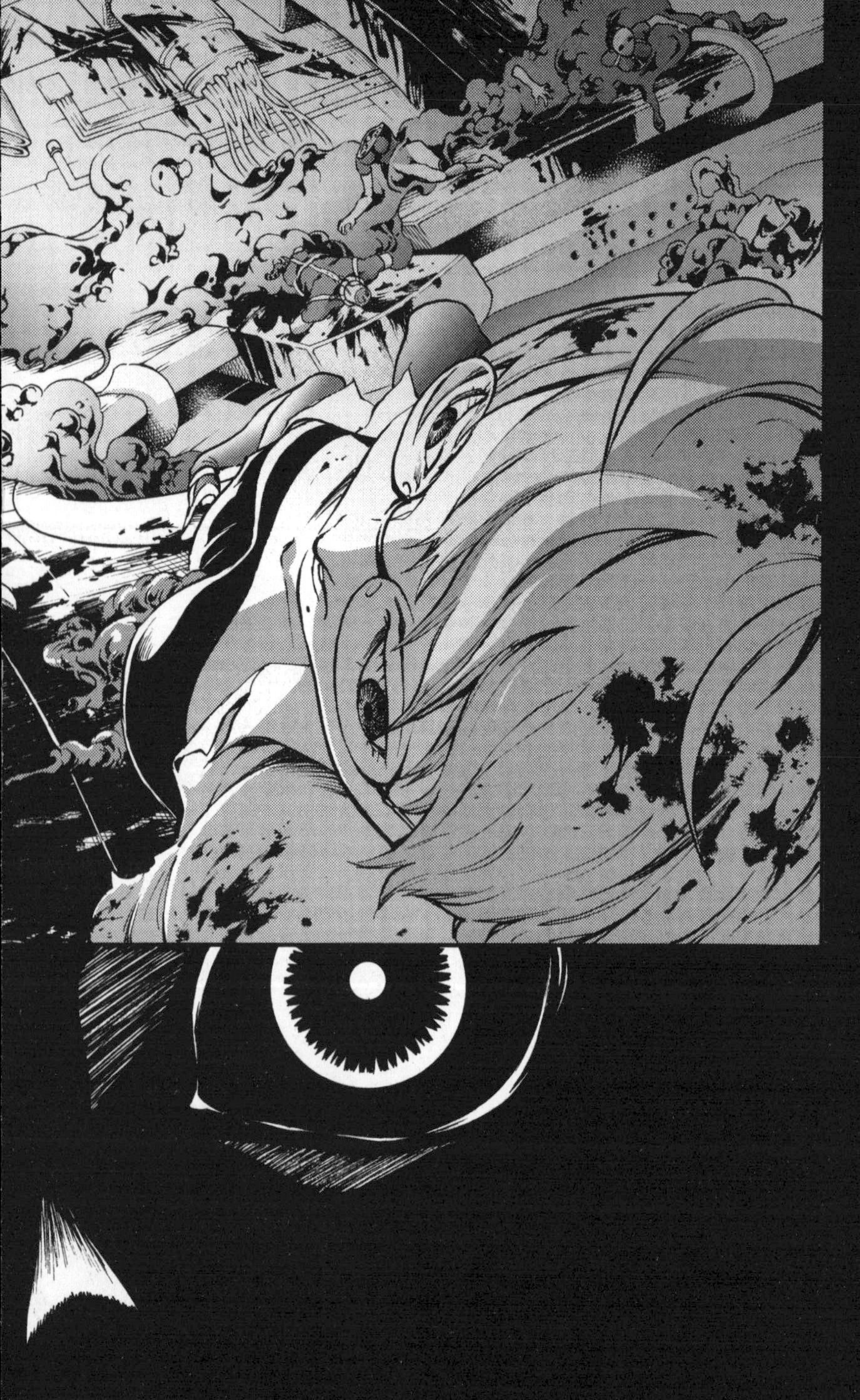

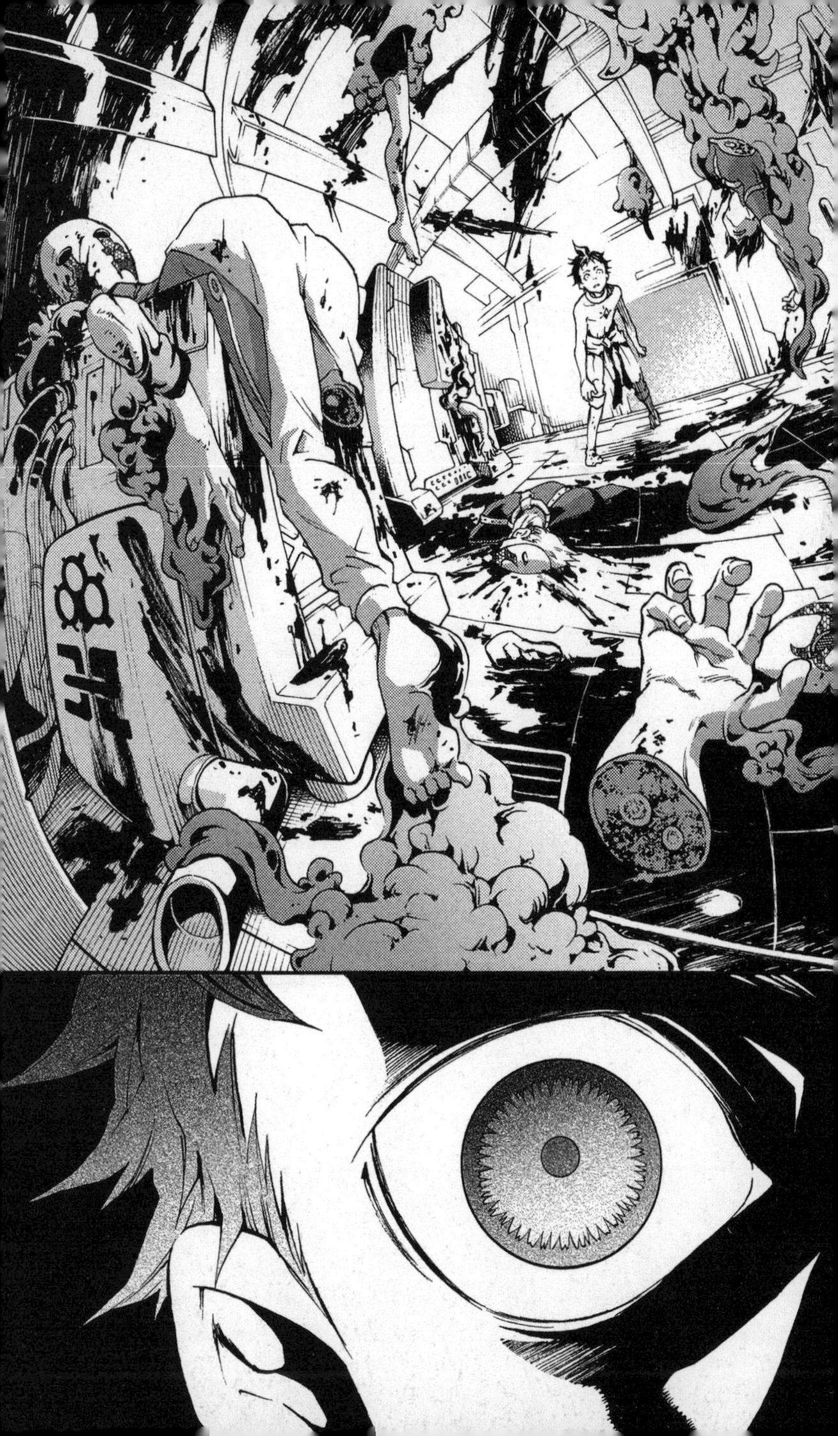

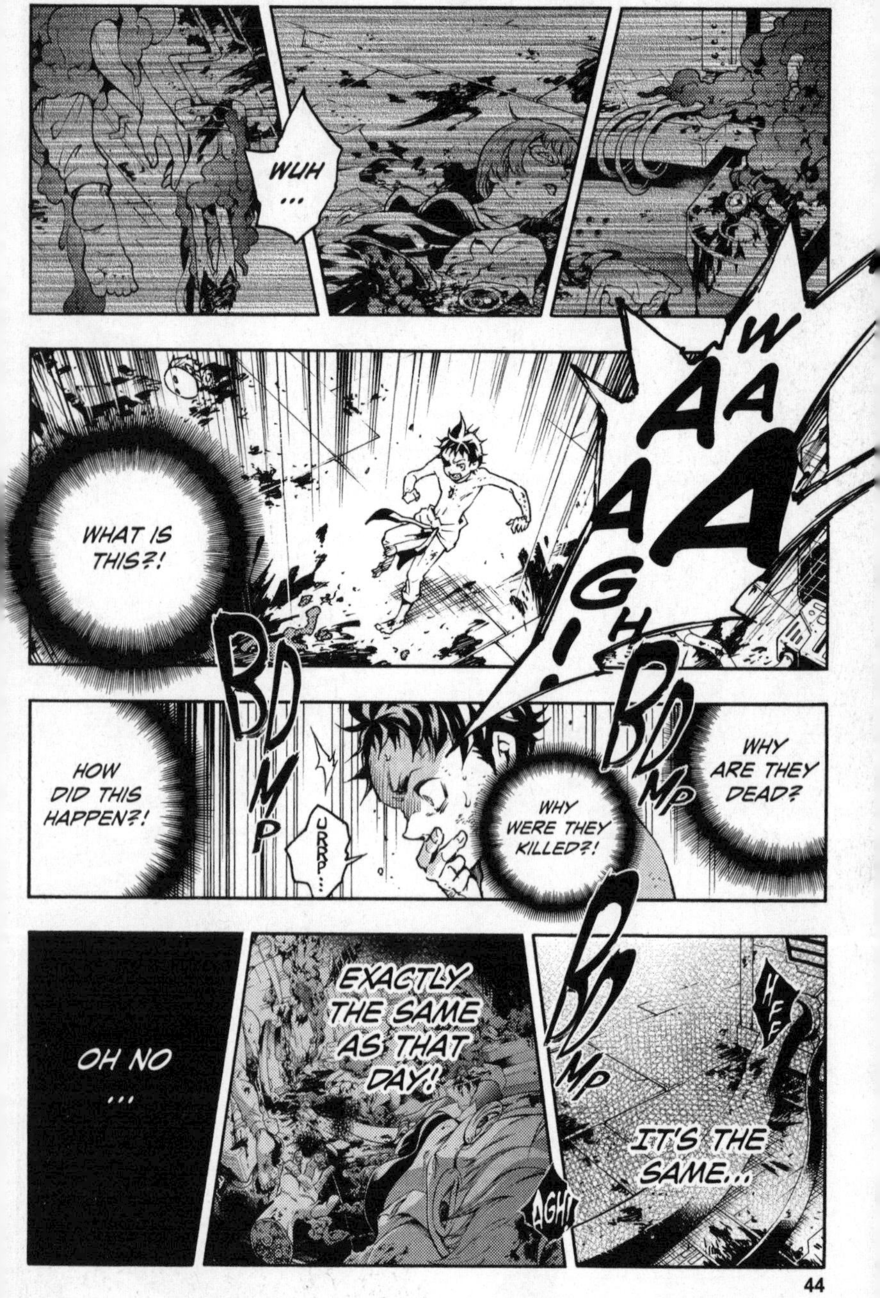
WUH ...
WAAAAAGH!!
WHAT IS THIS?!
BDMP
WHY ARE THEY DEAD?
BDMP
WHY WERE THEY KILLED?!
URRP...
BDMP
HOW DID THIS HAPPEN?!
HFF
BDMP
IT'S THE SAME...
AGH!
EXACTLY THE SAME AS THAT DAY!
OH NO ...

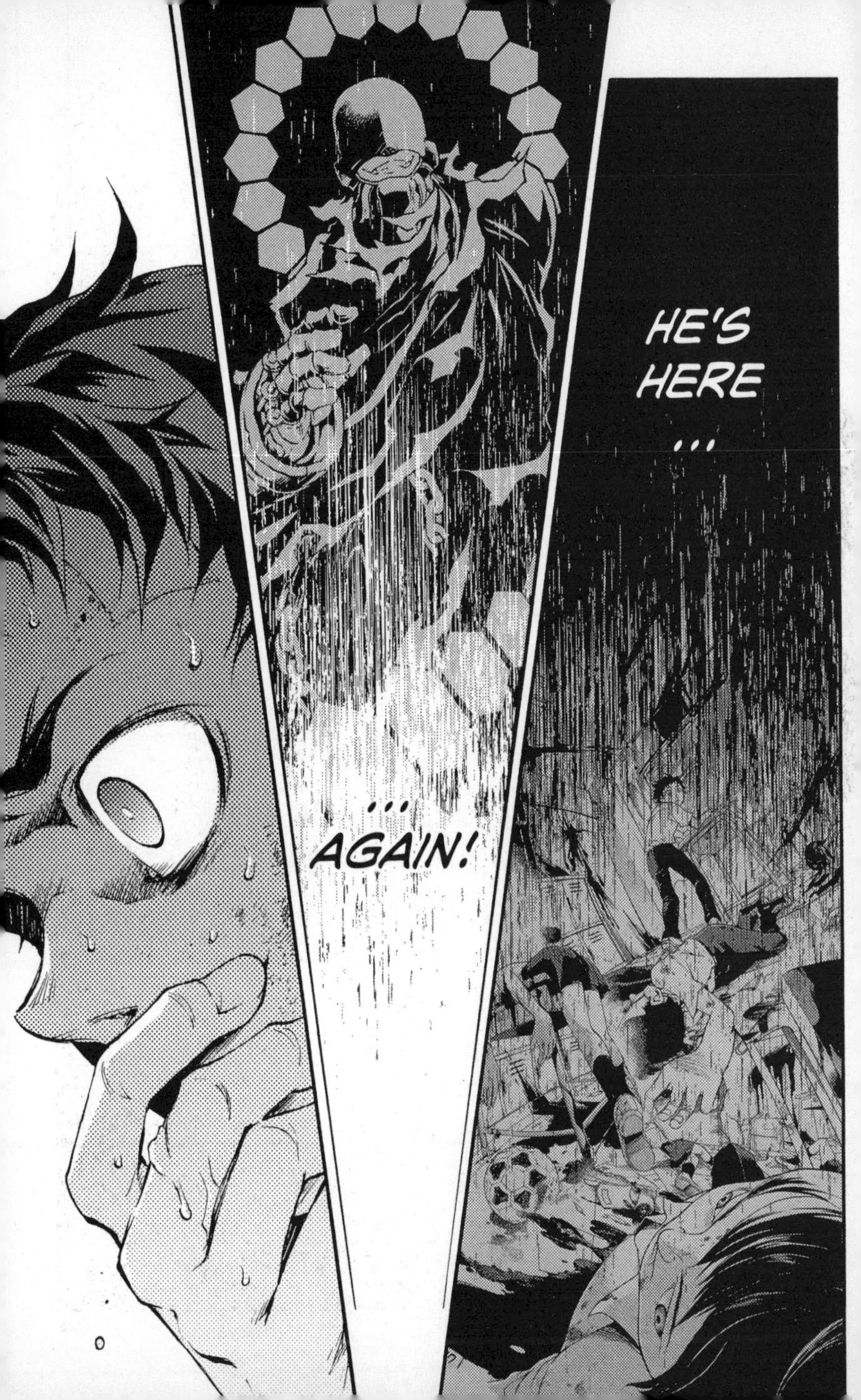
HE'S HERE ...
... AGAIN!

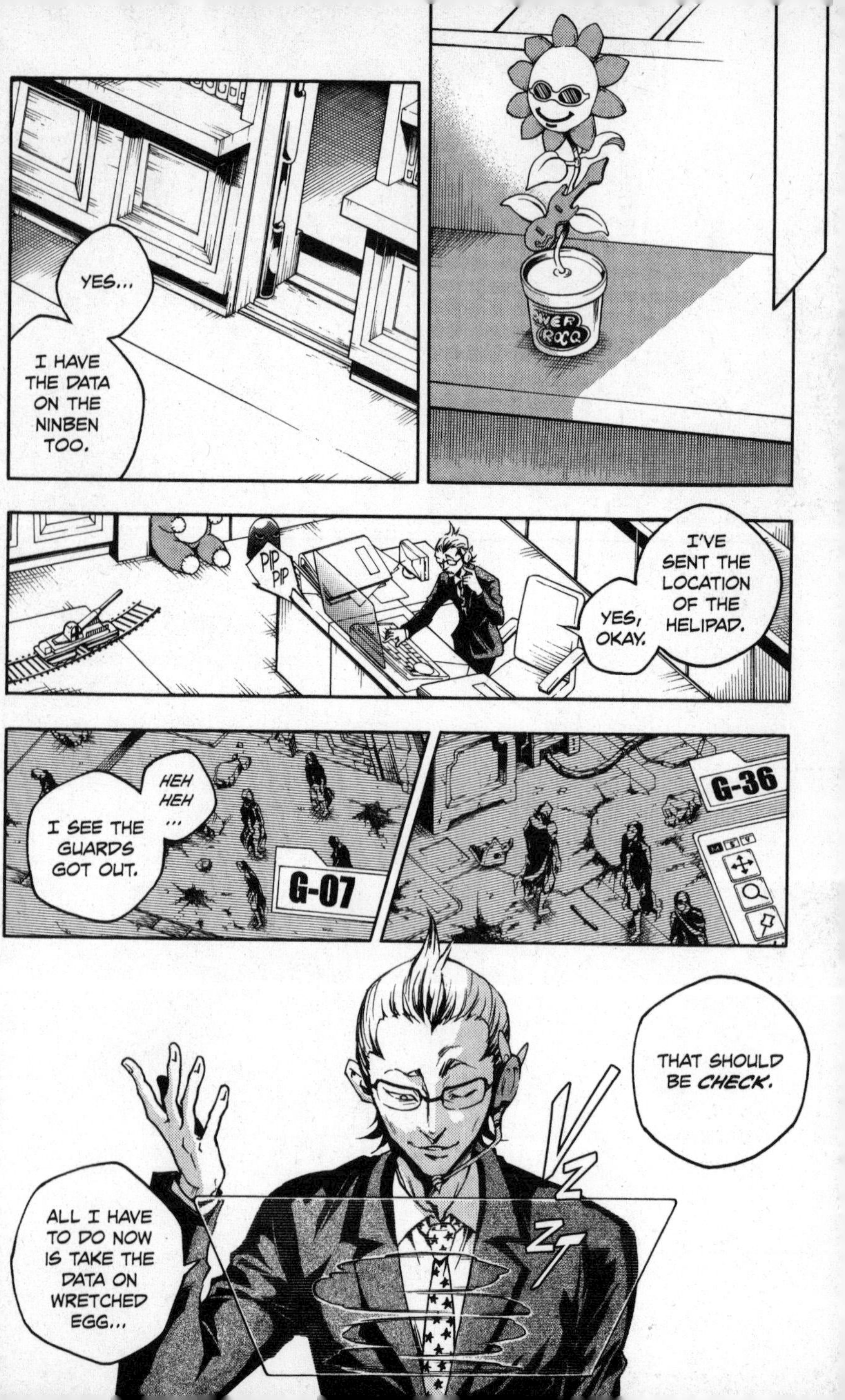

YES...
I HAVE THE DATA ON THE NINBEN TOO.
I'VE SENT THE LOCATION OF THE HELIPAD.
YES, OKAY.
PIP PIP
G-36
HEH HEH ...
I SEE THE GUARDS GOT OUT.
G-07
THAT SHOULD BE *CHECK*.
ALL I HAVE TO DO NOW IS TAKE THE DATA ON WRETCHED EGG...
ZZT

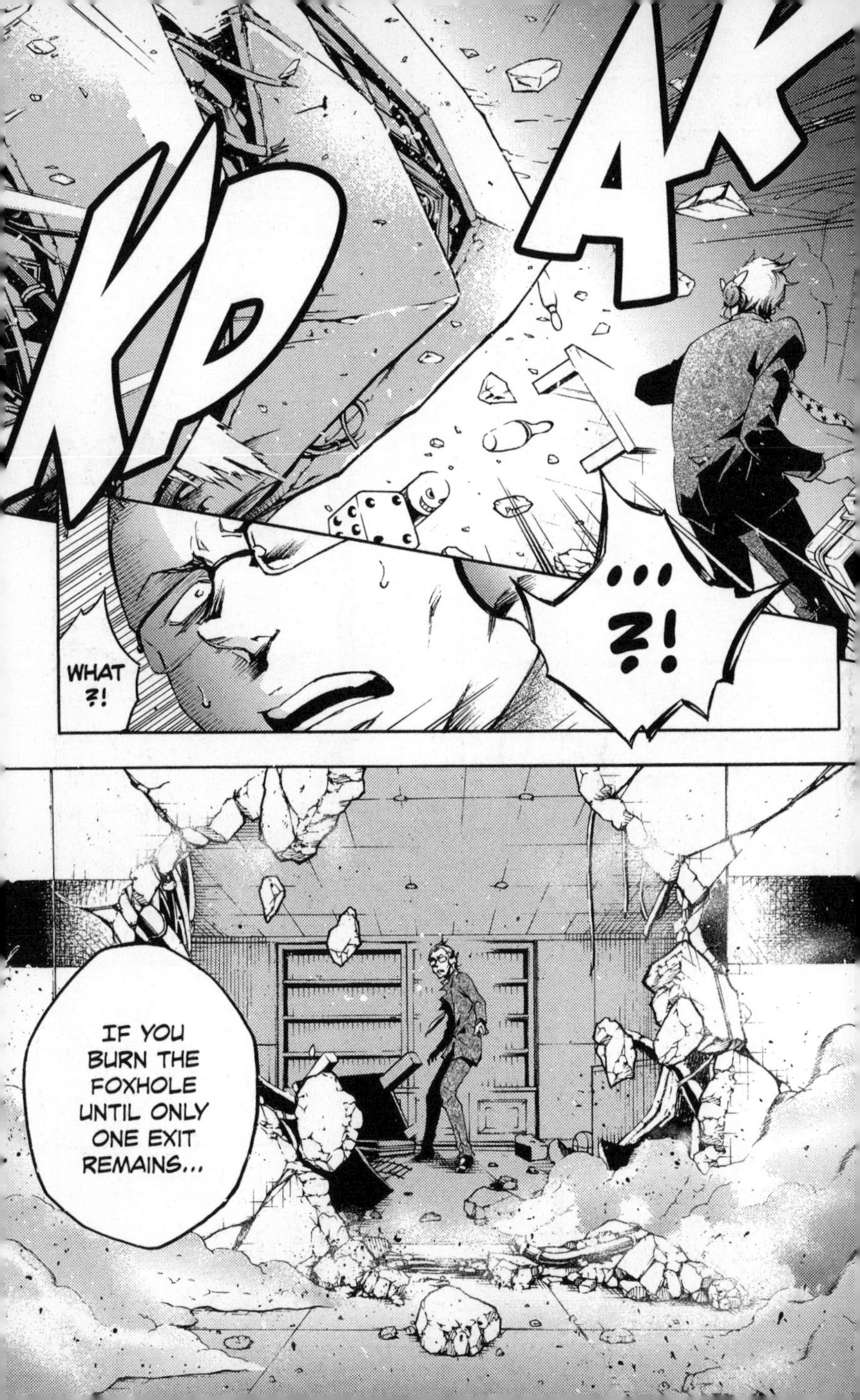
KRAK
...?!
WHAT?!
IF YOU BURN THE FOXHOLE UNTIL ONLY ONE EXIT REMAINS...

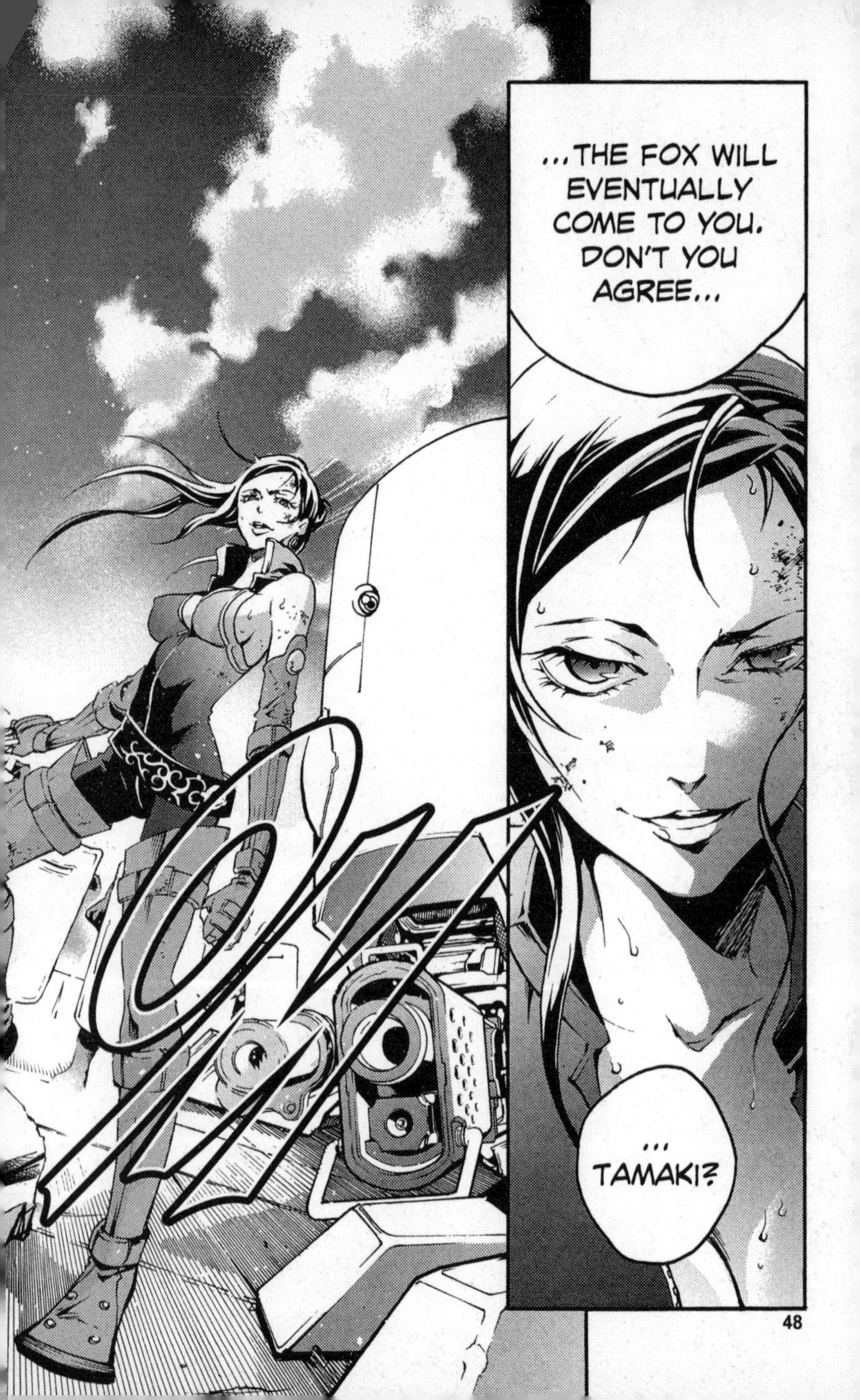
...THE FOX WILL EVENTUALLY COME TO YOU. DON'T YOU AGREE...
... TAMAKI?

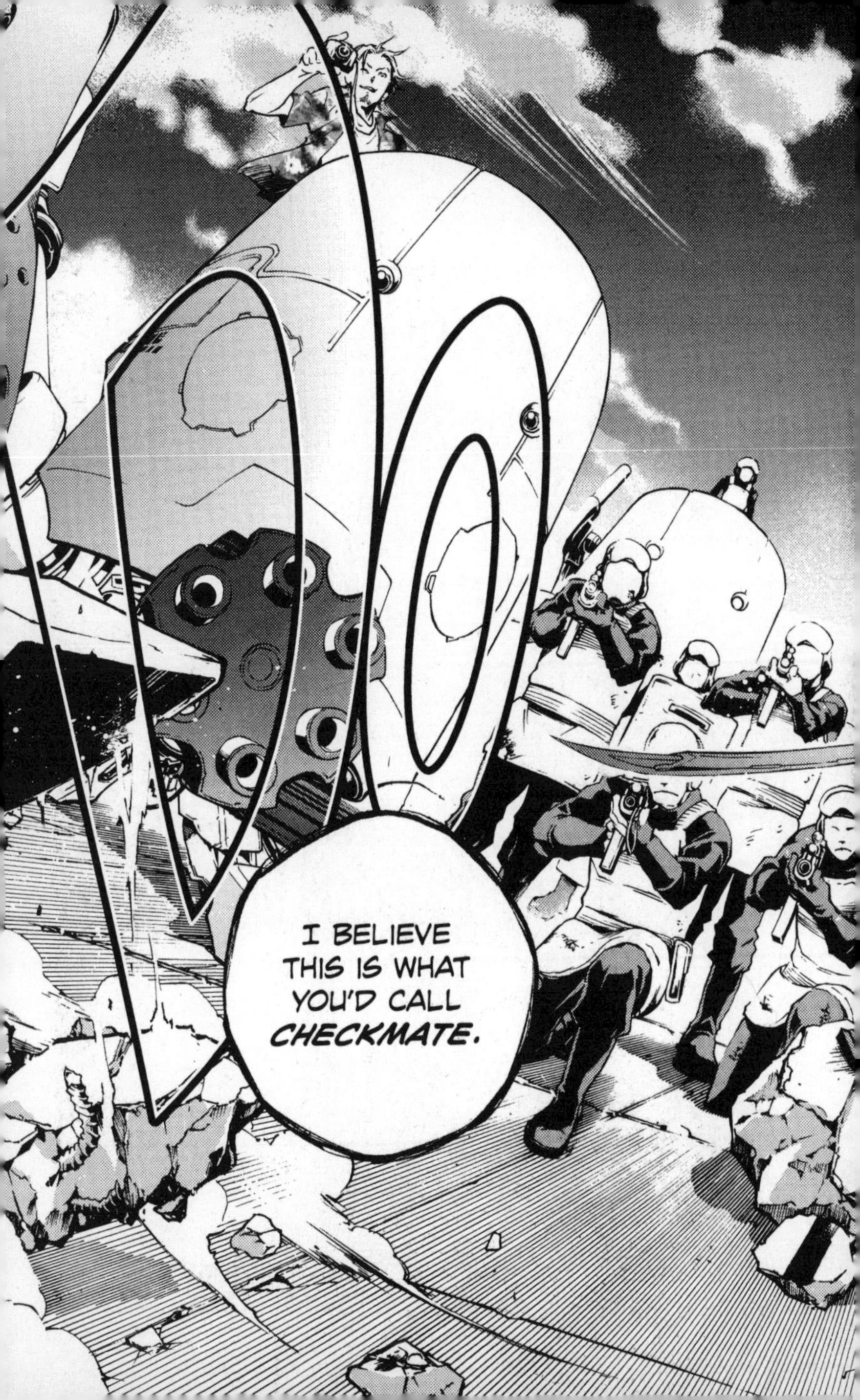
I BELIEVE THIS IS WHAT YOU'D CALL *CHECKMATE*.

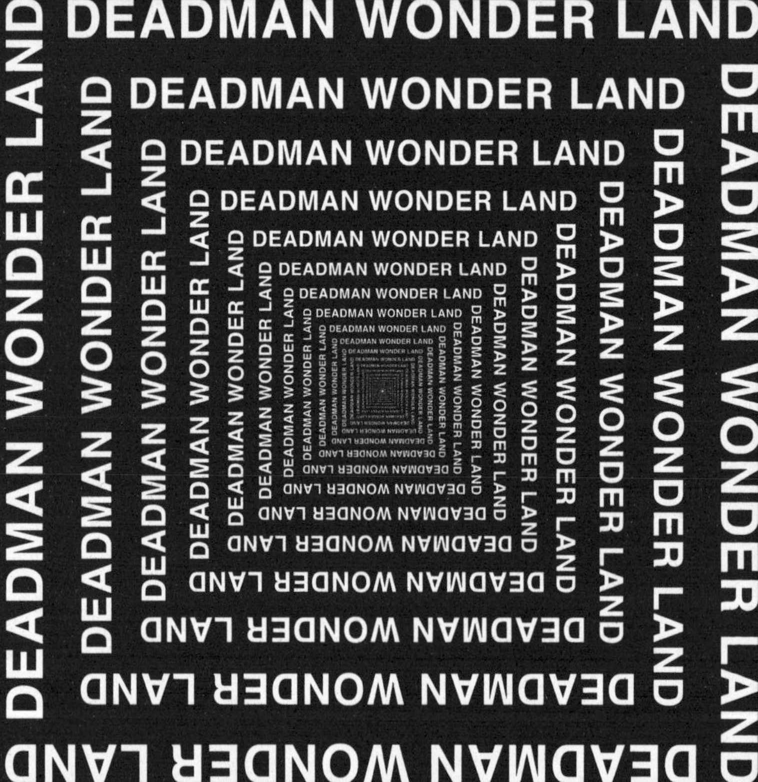
DEADMAN WONDER LAND

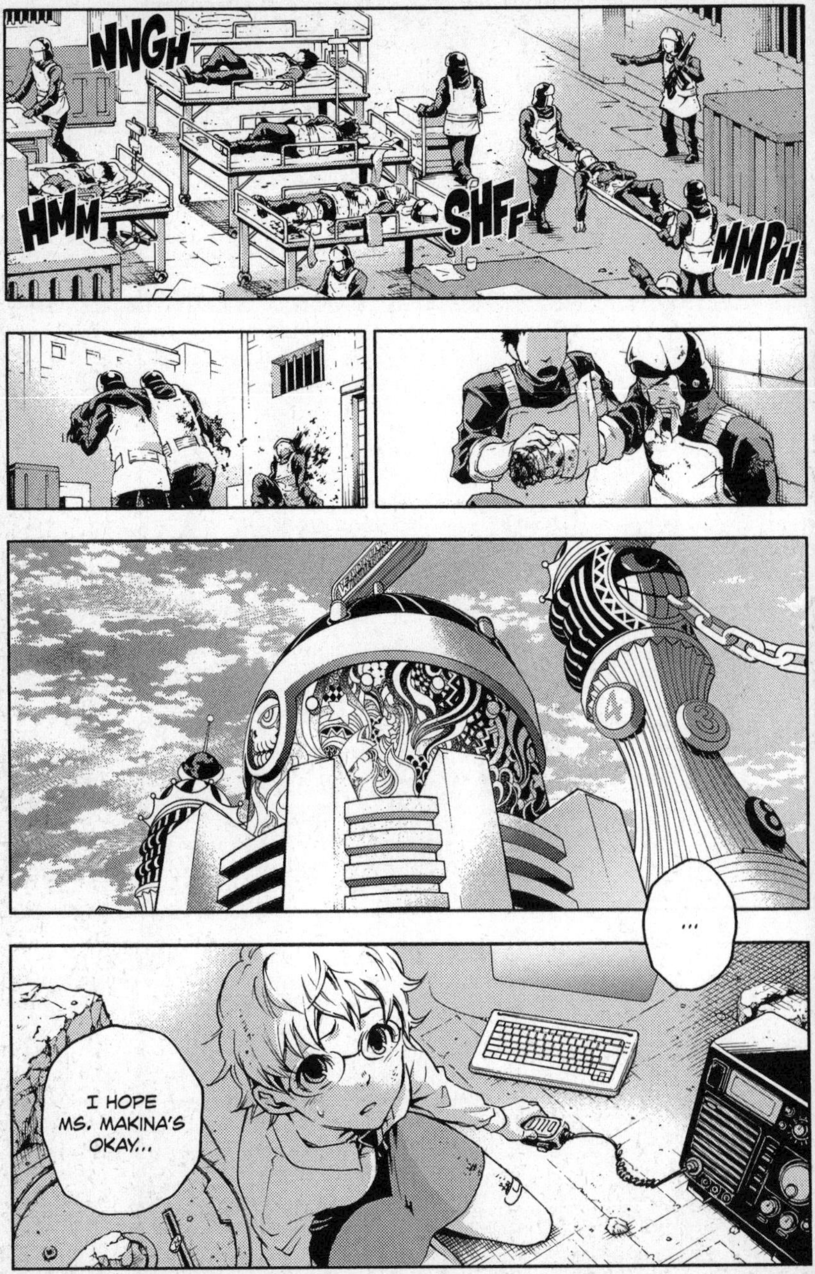
NNGH
SHFF
MMPH
HMM
...
I HOPE MS. MAKINA'S OKAY...

148,000 dead or missing.
Japan was essentially without a government. Restoration took several years with help from the UN and Allied Nations.
—2014 – Seismic Intensity 11.4 – The Great Tokyo Earthquake—
The cause of this unusual "super-shallow" earthquake, where the epicenter is less than 0.5km underground, was still unknown.

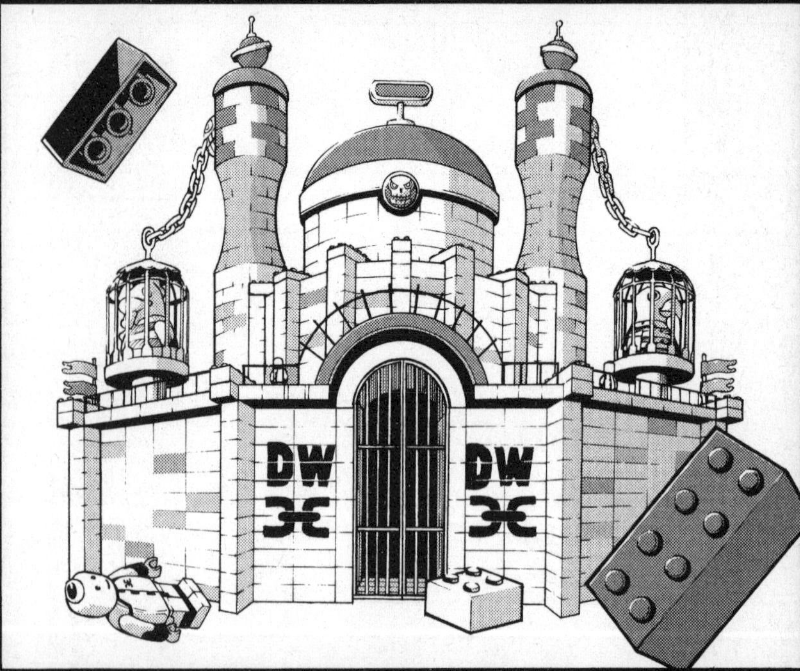
DW
DW

"That's why I started the game."

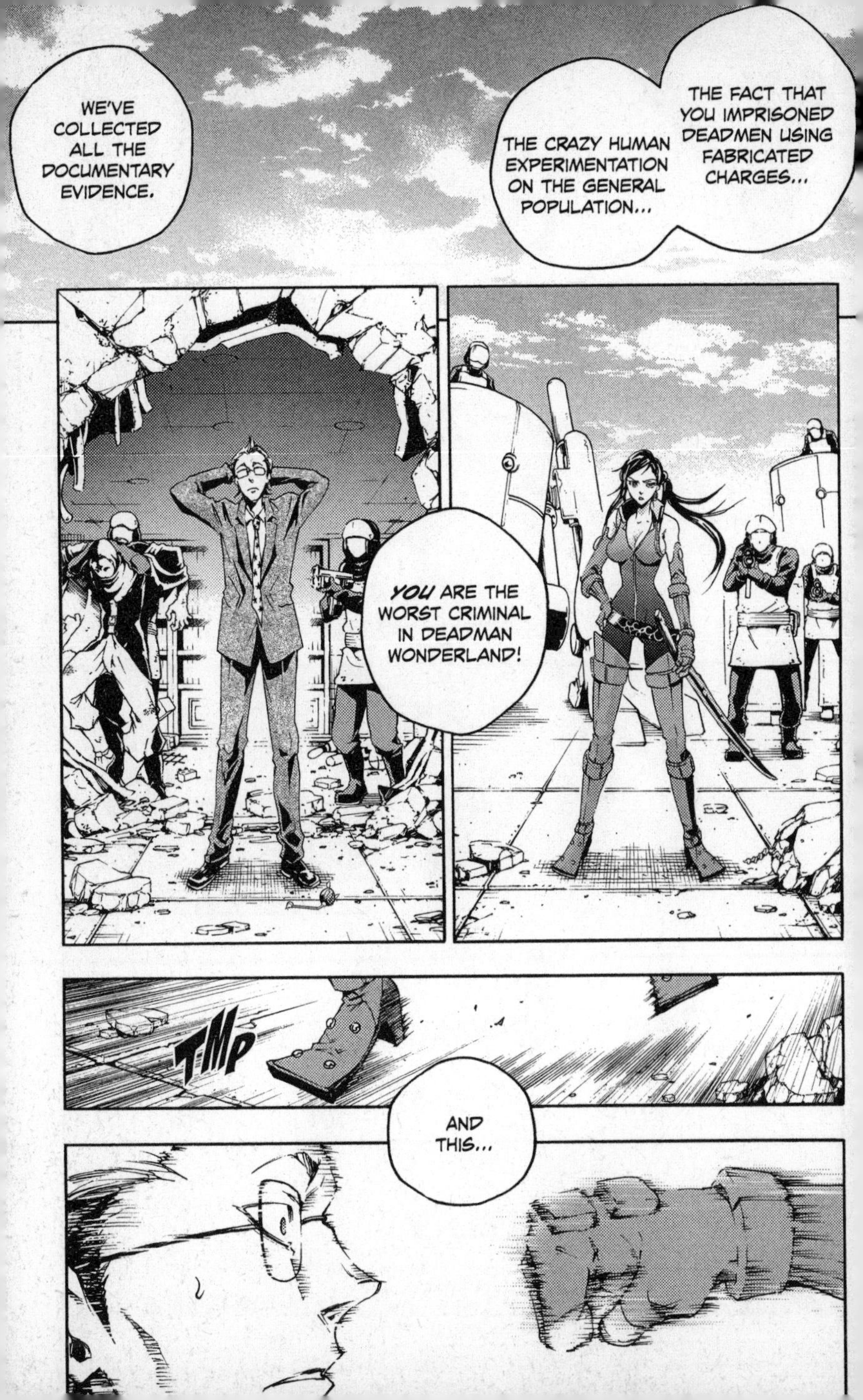
THE FACT THAT YOU IMPRISONED DEADMEN USING FABRICATED CHARGES...
THE CRAZY HUMAN EXPERIMENTATION ON THE GENERAL POPULATION...
WE'VE COLLECTED ALL THE DOCUMENTARY EVIDENCE.
YOU ARE THE WORST CRIMINAL IN DEADMAN WONDERLAND!
TMP
AND THIS...

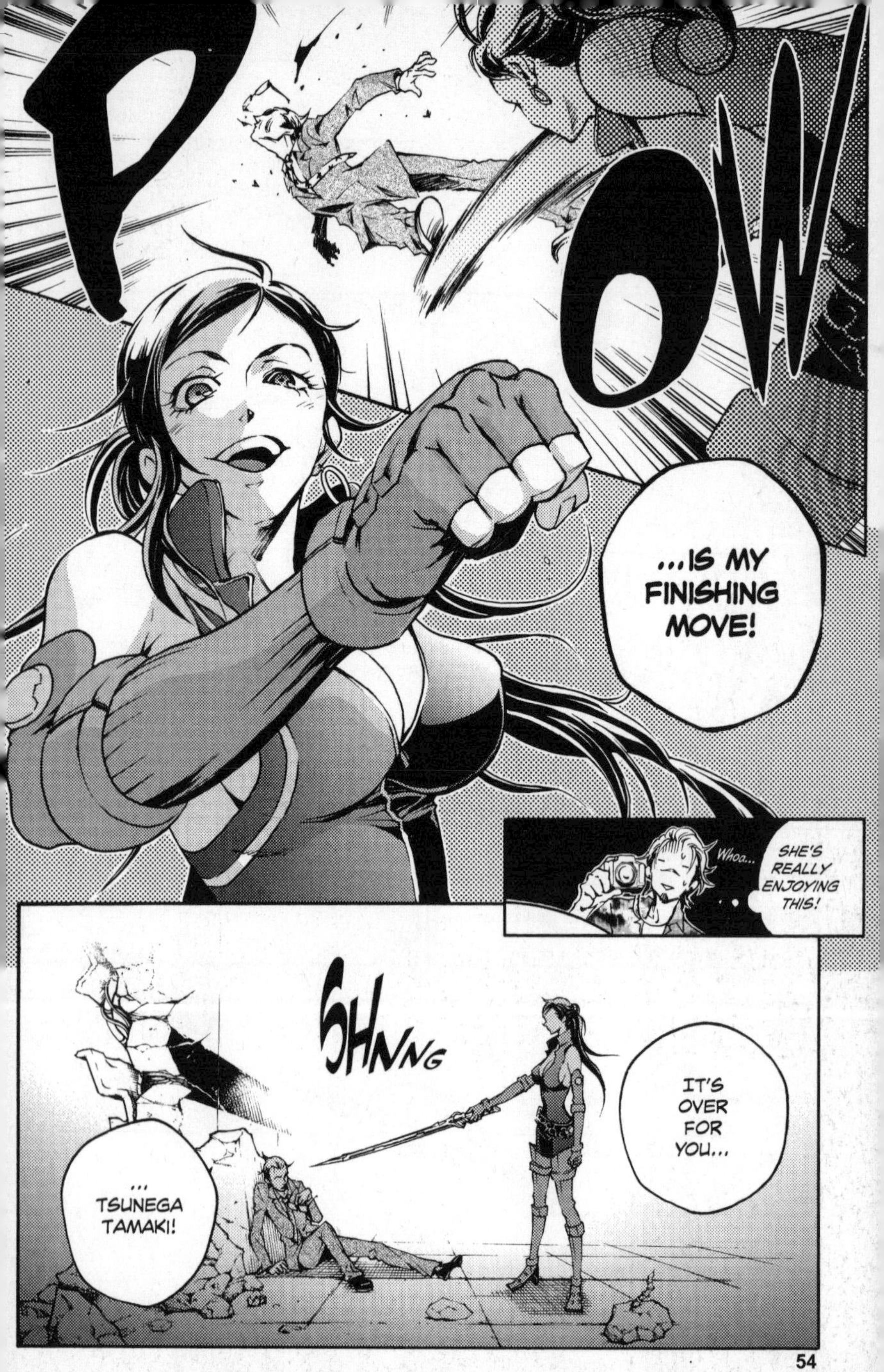
POW
...IS MY FINISHING MOVE!
Whoa...
SHE'S REALLY ENJOYING THIS!
SHNNG
IT'S OVER FOR YOU...
... TSUNEGA TAMAKI!

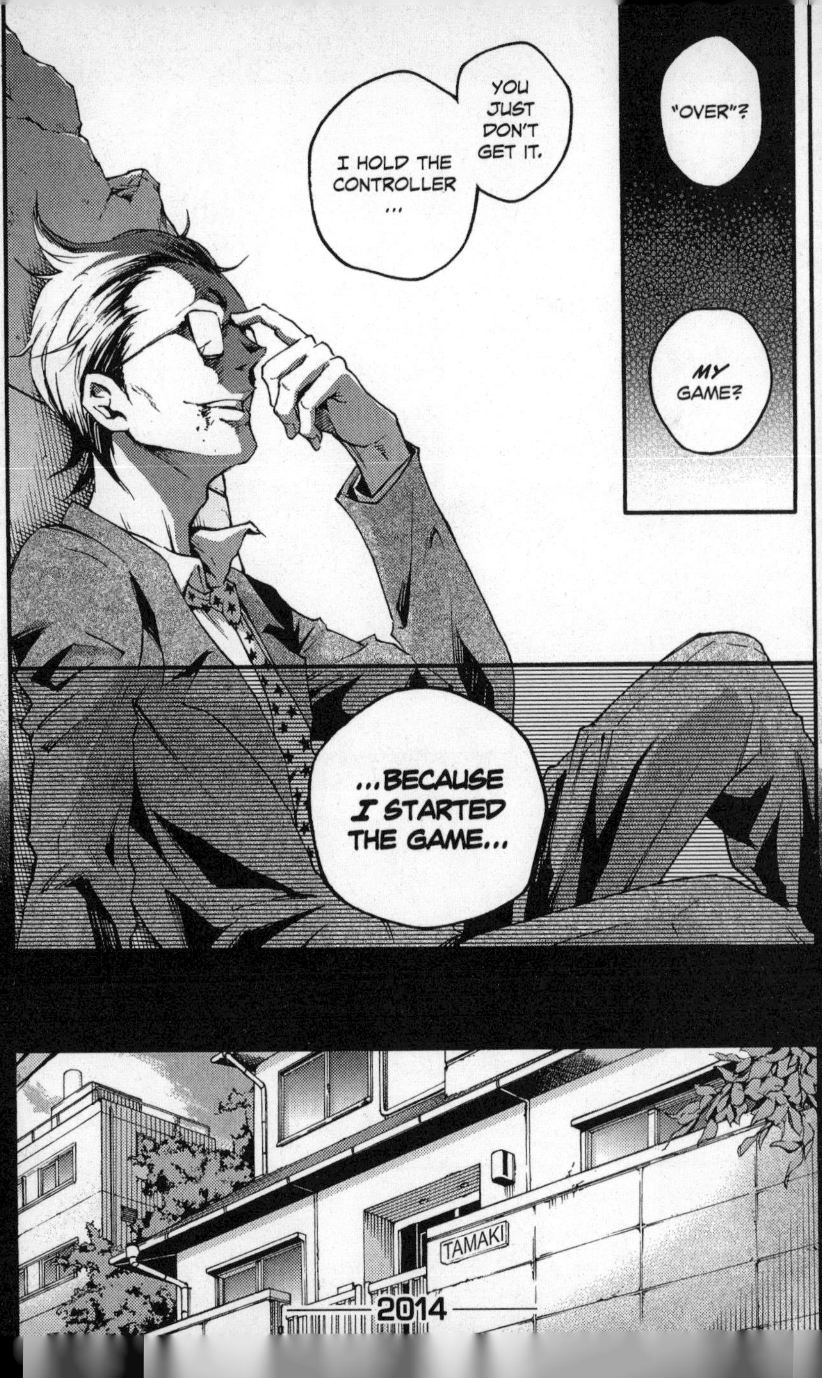
"OVER"?
MY GAME?
YOU JUST DON'T GET IT.
I HOLD THE CONTROLLER...
...BECAUSE I STARTED THE GAME...
TAMAKI
2014

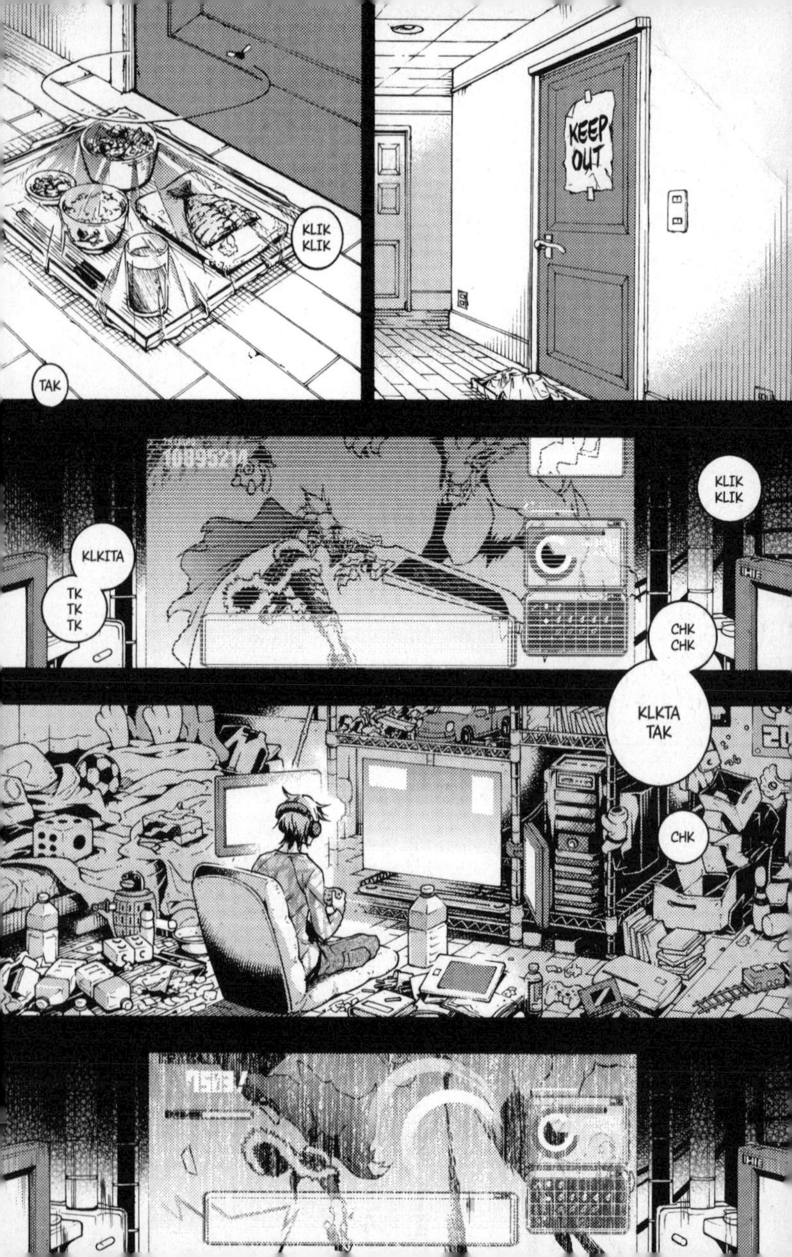
KEEP OUT
KLIK KLIK
TAK
KLIK KLIK
CHK CHK
KLKITA
TK TK TK
KLKTA TAK
CHK

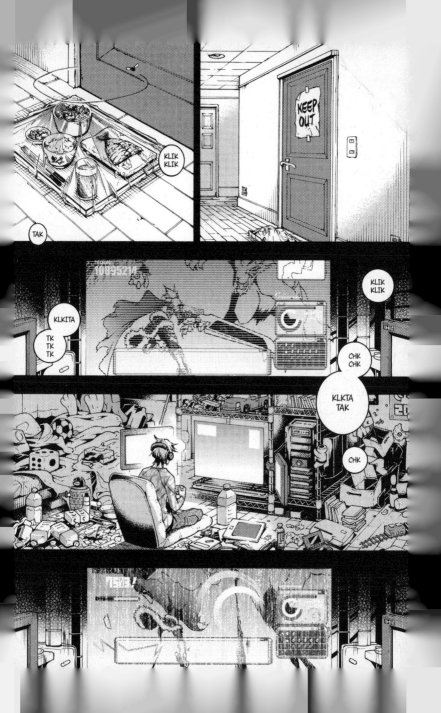

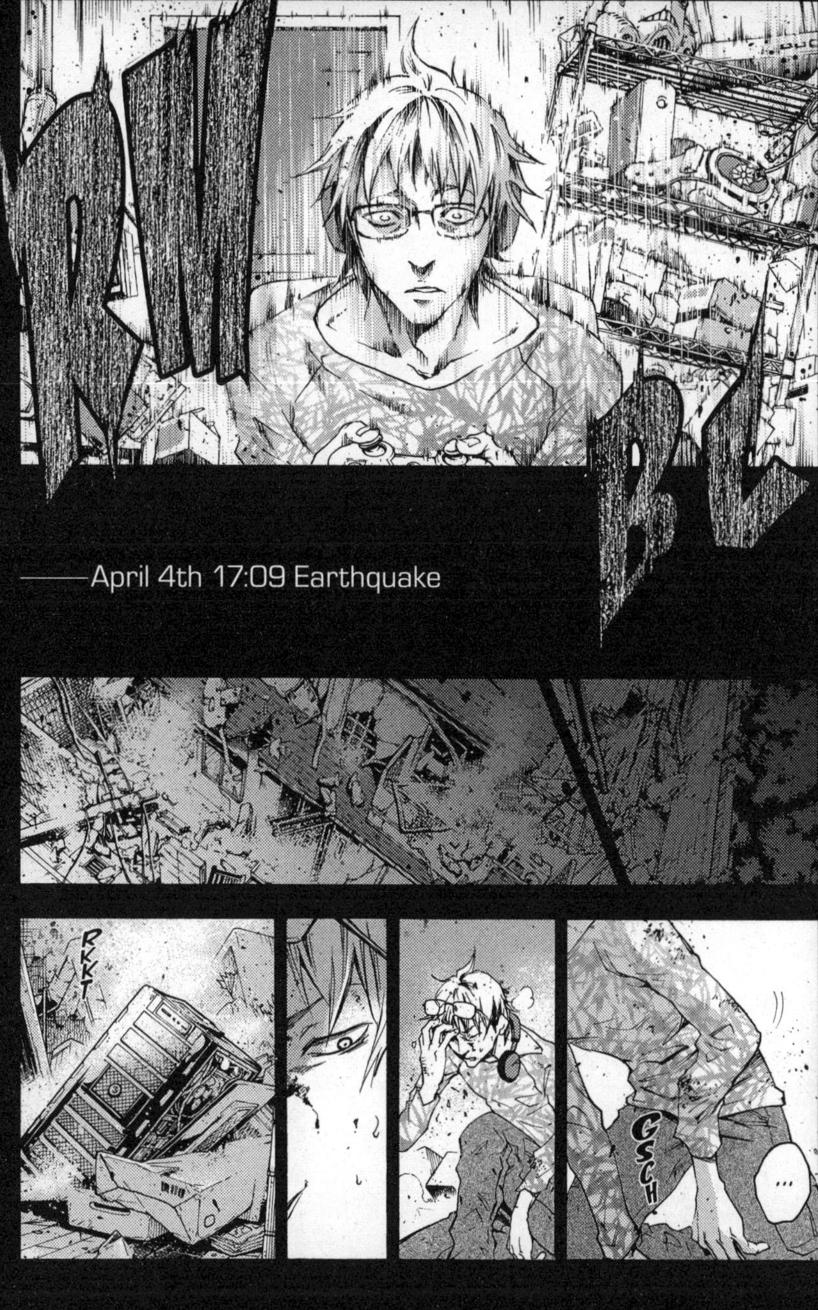
——April 4th 17:09 Earthquake
GSCH
...
RKKT

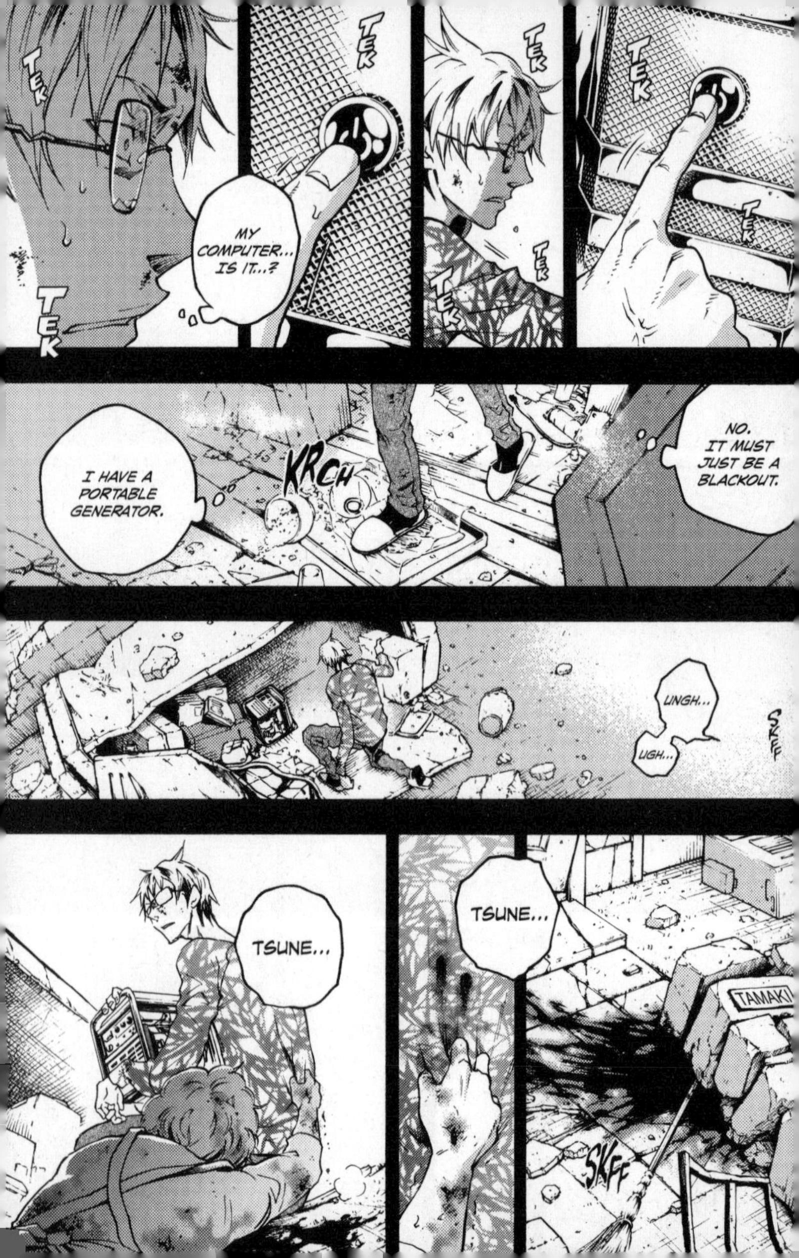
TEK
TEK
TEK
TEK
TEK
TEK
MY COMPUTER... IS IT...?
TEK
TEK
NO. IT MUST JUST BE A BLACKOUT.
KRCH
I HAVE A PORTABLE GENERATOR.
SKFF
UNGH...
UGH...
TAMAKI
TSUNE...
SKFF
TSUNE...

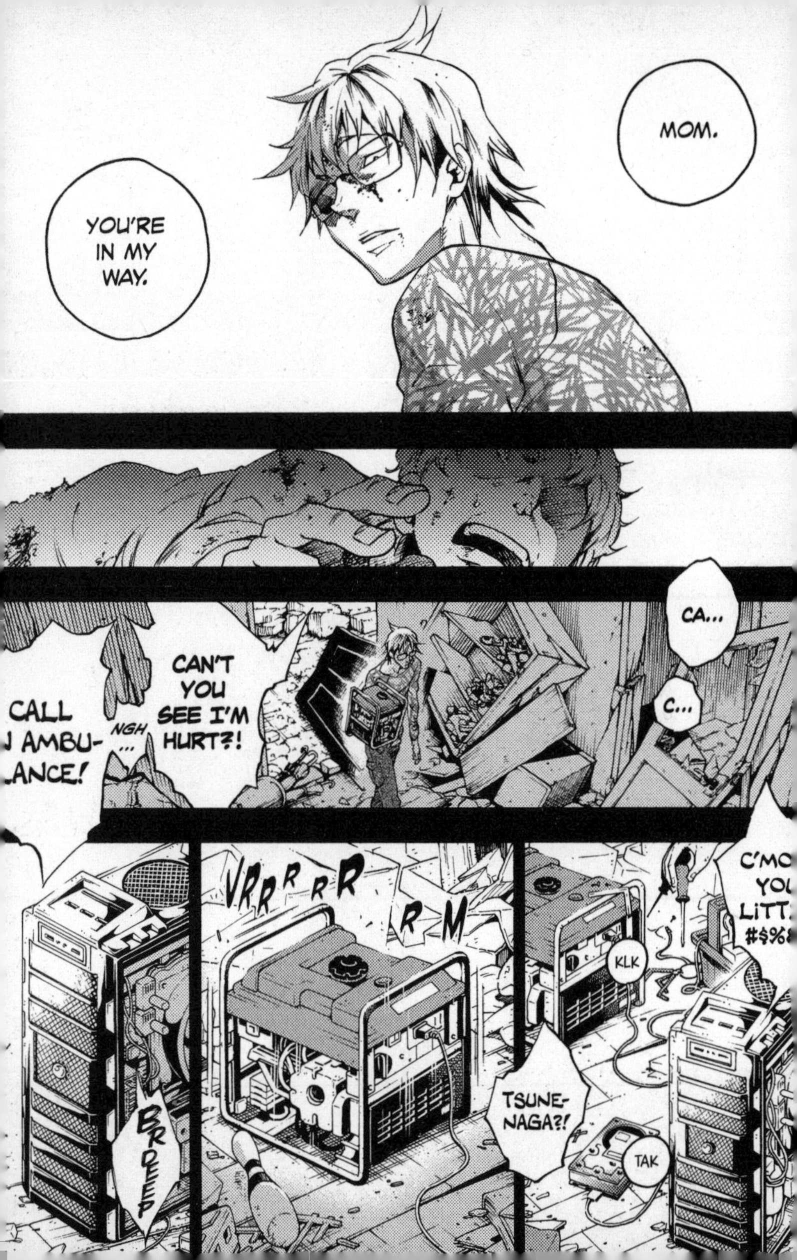
MOM.
YOU'RE IN MY WAY.
CA...
C...
CAN'T YOU SEE I'M HURT?!
NGH...
CALL N AMBU- LANCE!
C'MO YOU LITT #$%
KLK
TSUNE-NAGA?!
TAK
VRRRRRRM
BRDEEP

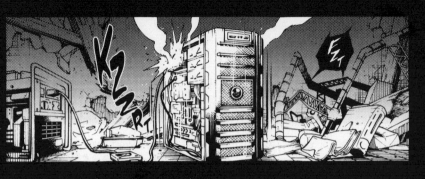

————Same day 18:23

MY WORLD
CRUMBLED.

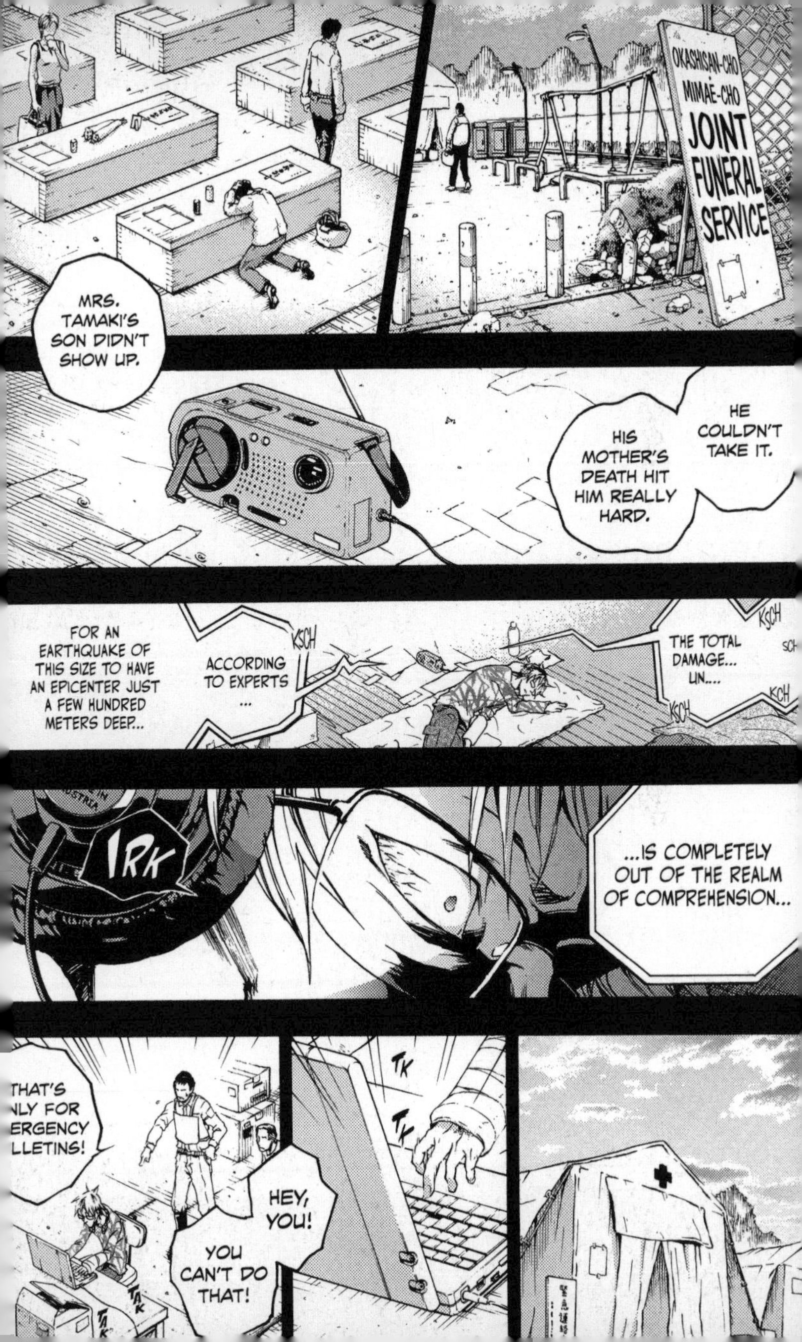
OKASHISAN-CHO MIMAE-CHO JOINT FUNERAL SERVICE
MRS. TAMAKI'S SON DIDN'T SHOW UP.
HE COULDN'T TAKE IT.
HIS MOTHER'S DEATH HIT HIM REALLY HARD.
KSCH
THE TOTAL DAMAGE... UN....
SCH
KSCH
KCH
KSCH
ACCORDING TO EXPERTS ...
FOR AN EARTHQUAKE OF THIS SIZE TO HAVE AN EPICENTER JUST A FEW HUNDRED METERS DEEP...
...IS COMPLETELY OUT OF THE REALM OF COMPREHENSION...
IRK
TK
TK
HEY, YOU!
YOU CAN'T DO THAT!
THAT'S
NLY FOR
ERGENCY
LLETINS!
TAK
TAK

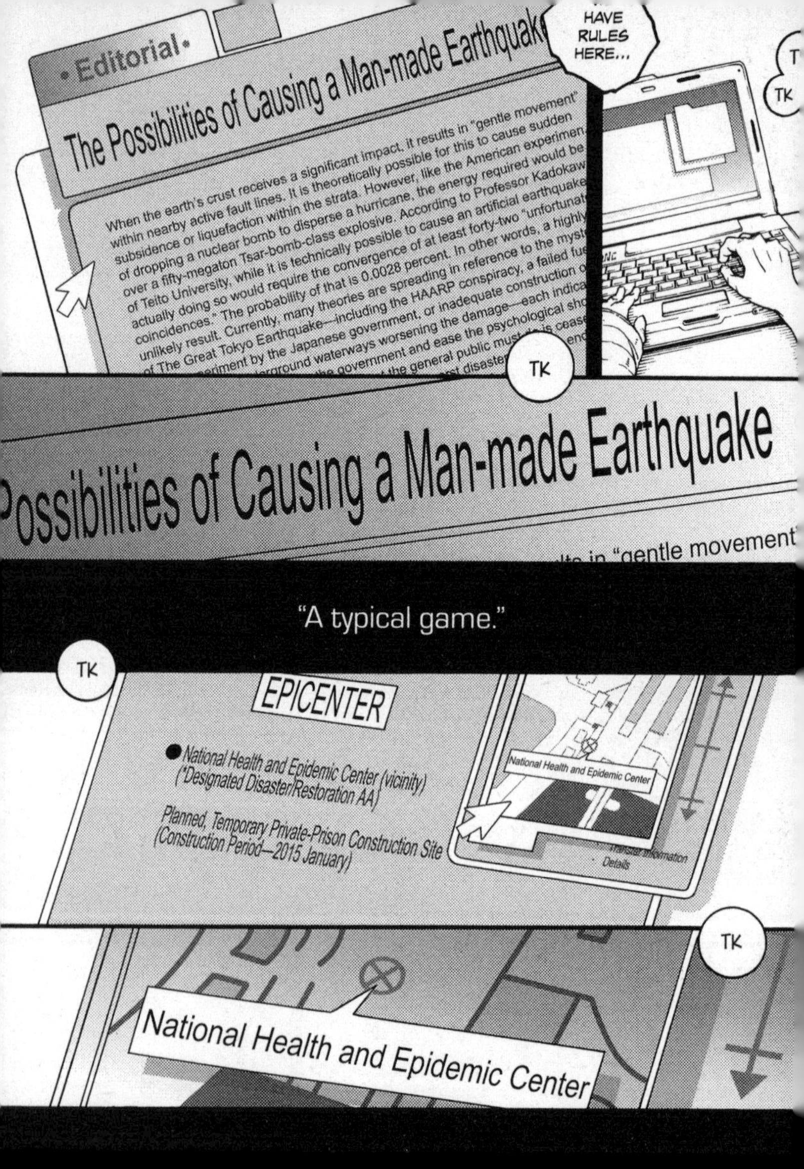
HAVE RULES HERE...
TK
• Editorial •
The Possibilities of Causing a Man-made Earthquake
When the earth's crust receives a significant impact, it results in "gentle movement"
within nearby active fault lines. It is theoretically possible for this to cause sudden
subsidence or liquefaction within the strata. However, like the American experimen
of dropping a nuclear bomb to disperse a hurricane, the energy required would be
over a fifty-megaton Tsar-bomb-class explosive. According to Professor Kadokaw
of Teito University, while it is technically possible to cause an artificial earthquake
actually doing so would require the convergence of at least forty-two "unfortunat
coincidences." The probability of that is 0.0028 percent. In other words, a highly
unlikely result. Currently, many theories are spreading in reference to the myst
of The Great Tokyo Earthquake—including the HAARP conspiracy, a failed fu
TK
Possibilities of Causing a Man-made Earthquake
"A typical game."
TK
EPICENTER
●National Health and Epidemic Center (vicinity)
(*Designated Disaster/Restoration AA)
Planned, Temporary Private-Prison Construction Site
(Construction Period—2015 January)
National Health and Epidemic Center
Details
TK
National Health and Epidemic Center

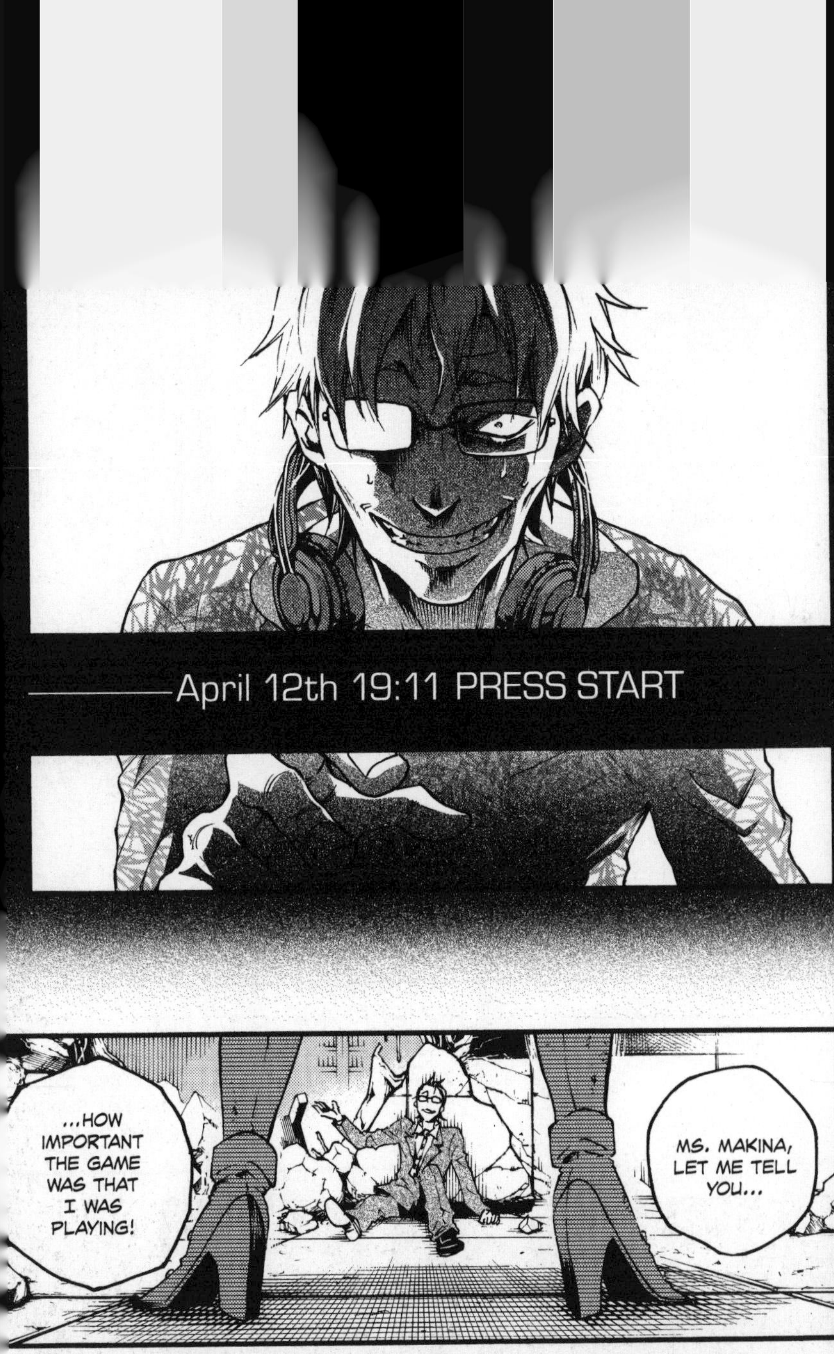
April 12th 19:11 PRESS START
MS. MAKINA, LET ME TELL YOU...
...HOW IMPORTANT THE GAME WAS THAT I WAS PLAYING!

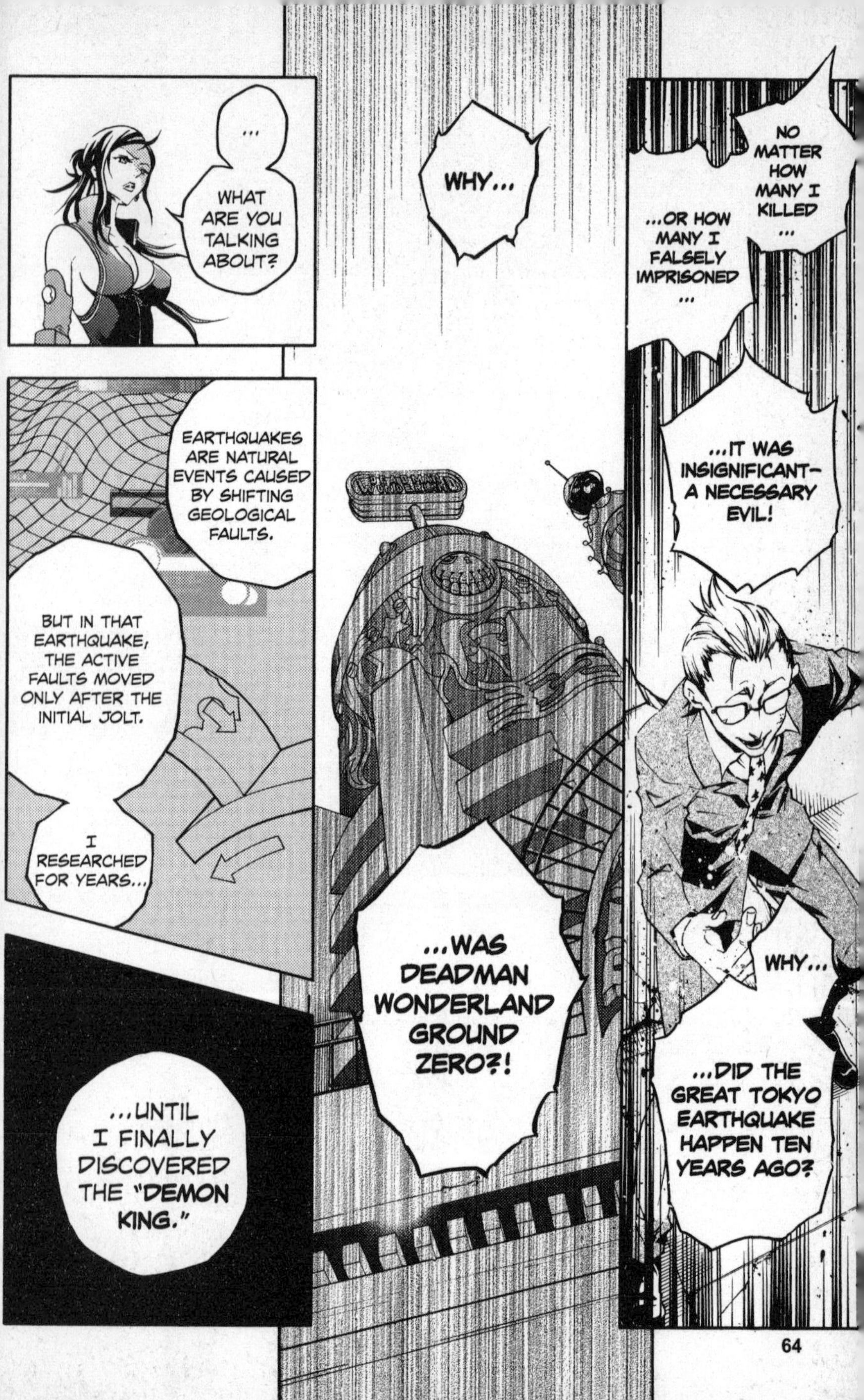
NO MATTER HOW MANY I KILLED ...
...OR HOW MANY I FALSELY IMPRISONED ...
...IT WAS INSIGNIFICANT— A NECESSARY EVIL!
WHY...
...DID THE GREAT TOKYO EARTHQUAKE HAPPEN TEN YEARS AGO?
WHY...
...WAS DEADMAN WONDERLAND GROUND ZERO?!
...
WHAT ARE YOU TALKING ABOUT?
EARTHQUAKES ARE NATURAL EVENTS CAUSED BY SHIFTING GEOLOGICAL FAULTS.
BUT IN THAT EARTHQUAKE, THE ACTIVE FAULTS MOVED ONLY AFTER THE INITIAL JOLT.
I RESEARCHED FOR YEARS...
...UNTIL I FINALLY DISCOVERED THE "DEMON KING."

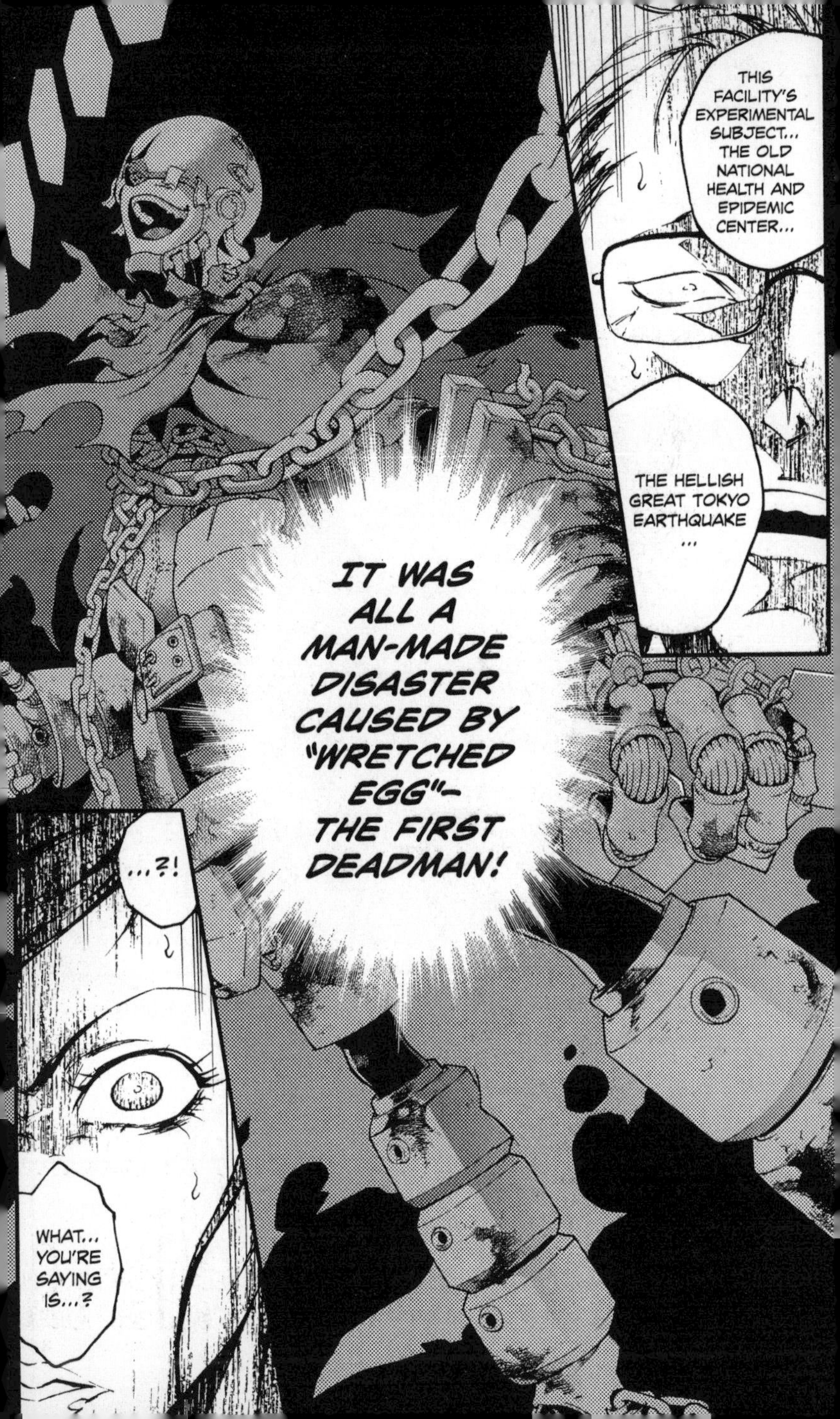
THIS FACILITY'S EXPERIMENTAL SUBJECT... THE OLD NATIONAL HEALTH AND EPIDEMIC CENTER...
THE HELLISH GREAT TOKYO EARTHQUAKE ...
IT WAS ALL A MAN-MADE DISASTER CAUSED BY "WRETCHED EGG"- THE FIRST DEADMAN!
...?!
WHAT... YOU'RE SAYING IS...?

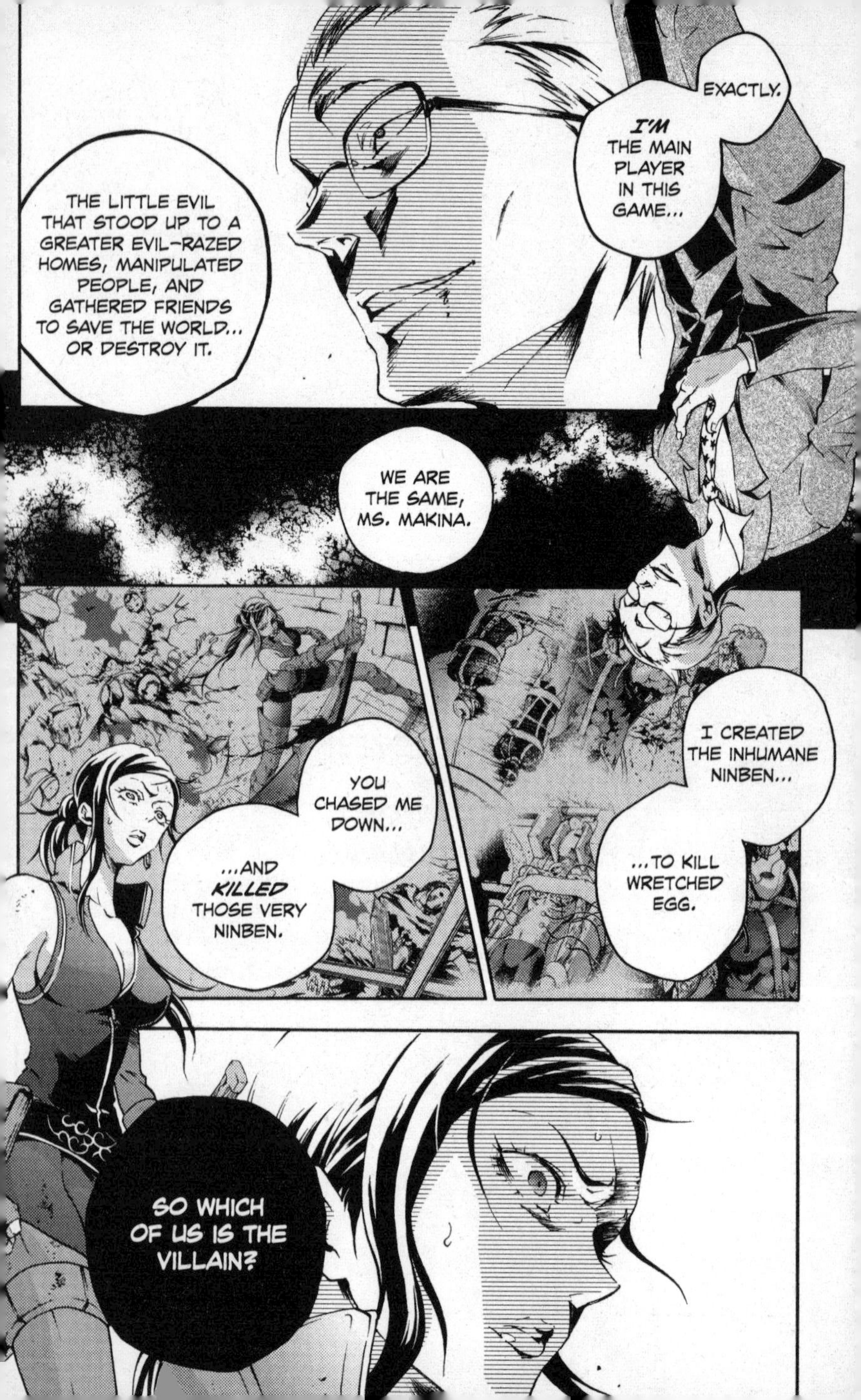
EXACTLY.
I'M THE MAIN PLAYER IN THIS GAME...
THE LITTLE EVIL THAT STOOD UP TO A GREATER EVIL–RAZED HOMES, MANIPULATED PEOPLE, AND GATHERED FRIENDS TO SAVE THE WORLD... OR DESTROY IT.
WE ARE THE SAME, MS. MAKINA.
I CREATED THE INHUMANE NINBEN...
...TO KILL WRETCHED EGG.
YOU CHASED ME DOWN...
...AND *KILLED* THOSE VERY NINBEN.
SO WHICH OF US IS THE VILLAIN?

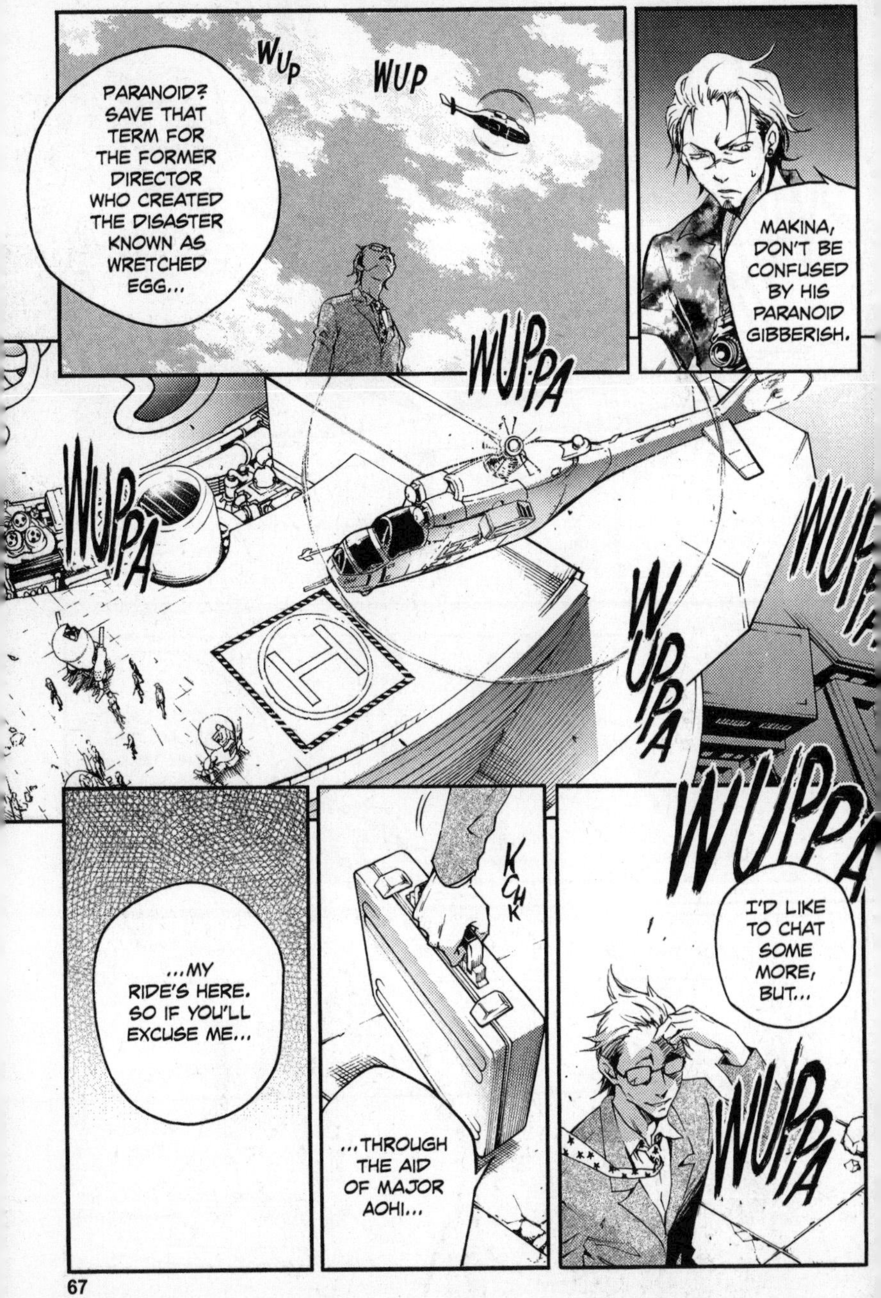
MAKINA, DON'T BE CONFUSED BY HIS PARANOID GIBBERISH.
WUP
WUP
PARANOID? SAVE THAT TERM FOR THE FORMER DIRECTOR WHO CREATED THE DISASTER KNOWN AS WRETCHED EGG...
WUPPA
WUPPA
WUPPA
WUPPA
WUPPA
I'D LIKE TO CHAT SOME MORE, BUT...
WUPPA
KCHK
...THROUGH THE AID OF MAJOR AOHI...
...MY RIDE'S HERE. SO IF YOU'LL EXCUSE ME...

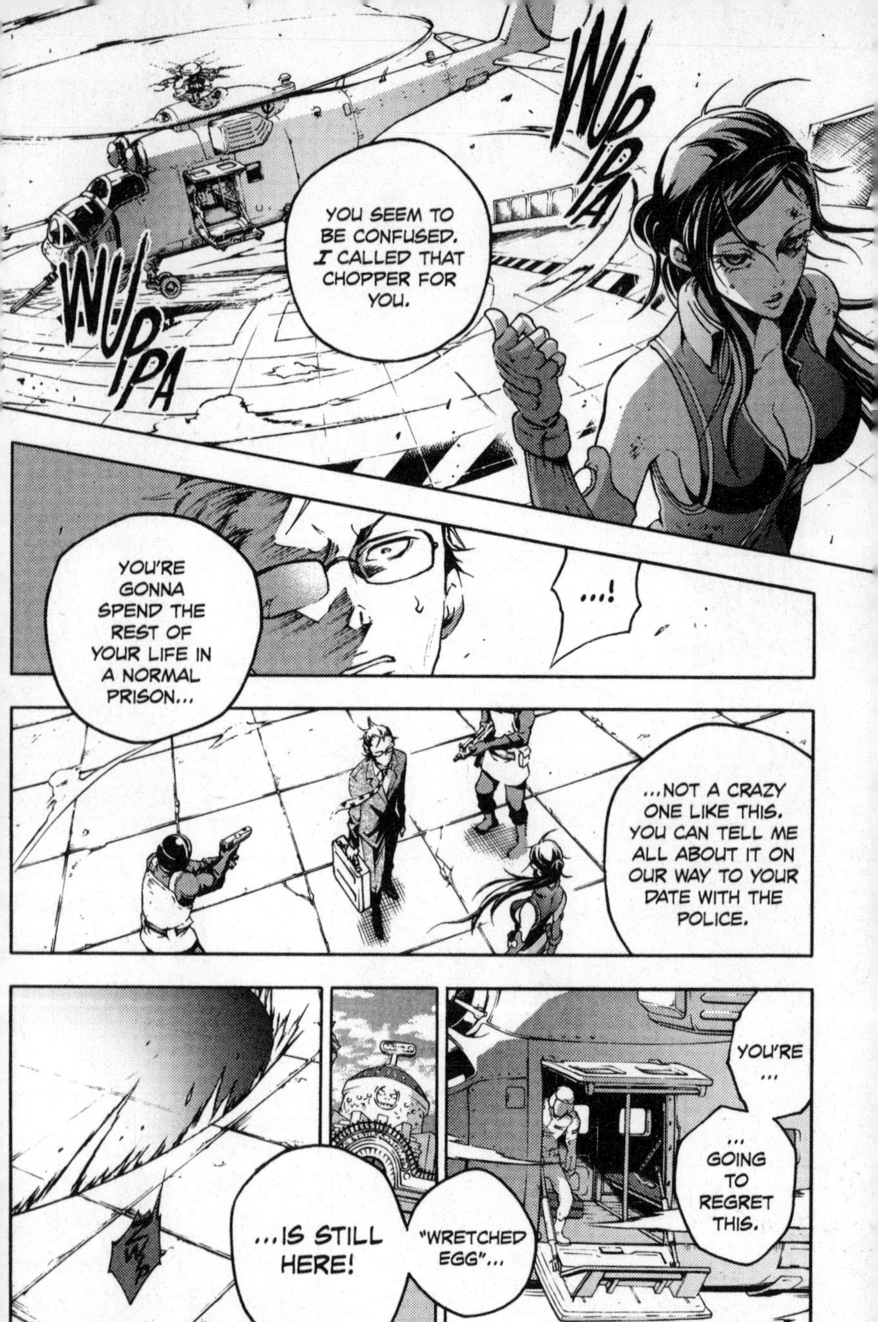
WUPPA
YOU SEEM TO BE CONFUSED. I CALLED THAT CHOPPER FOR YOU.
WUPPA
...!
YOU'RE GONNA SPEND THE REST OF YOUR LIFE IN A NORMAL PRISON...
...NOT A CRAZY ONE LIKE THIS. YOU CAN TELL ME ALL ABOUT IT ON OUR WAY TO YOUR DATE WITH THE POLICE.
YOU'RE ...
... GOING TO REGRET THIS.
"WRETCHED EGG"...
...IS STILL HERE!

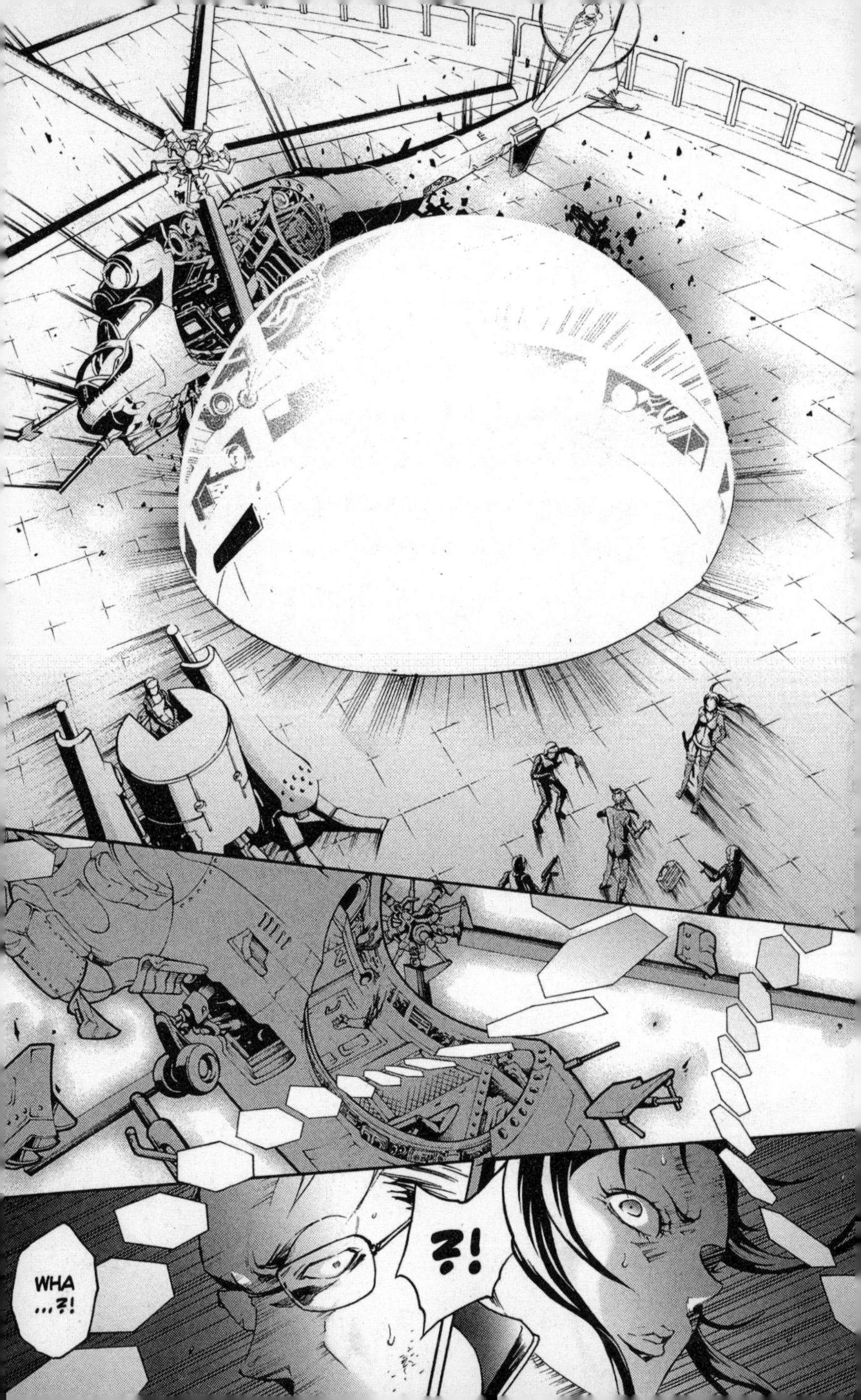
?!
WHA ...?!

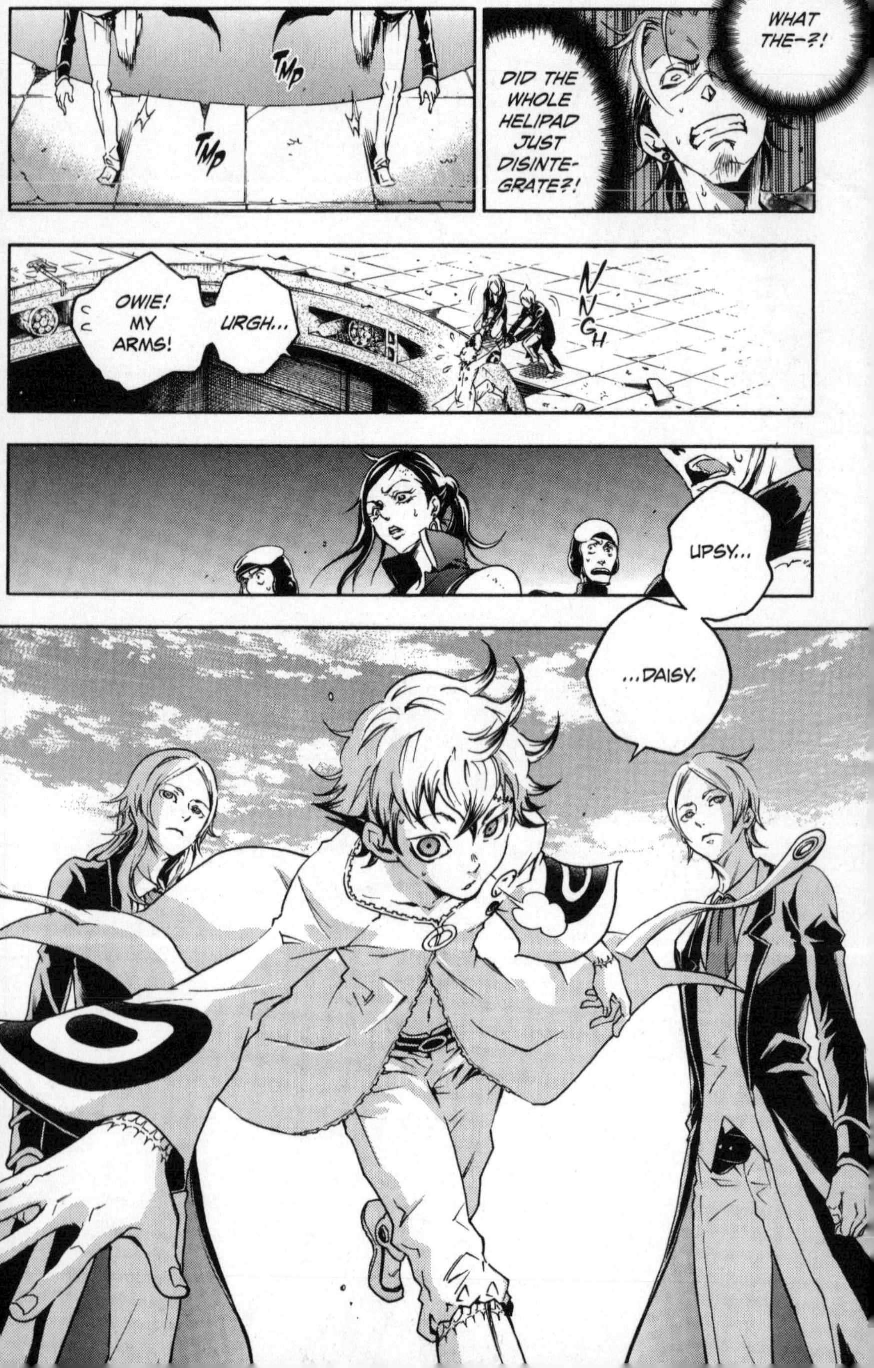
WHAT THE-?!
DID THE WHOLE HELIPAD JUST DISINTEGRATE?!
TMP
TMP
NNGH
URGH...
OWIE! MY ARMS!
UPSY...
...DAISY.

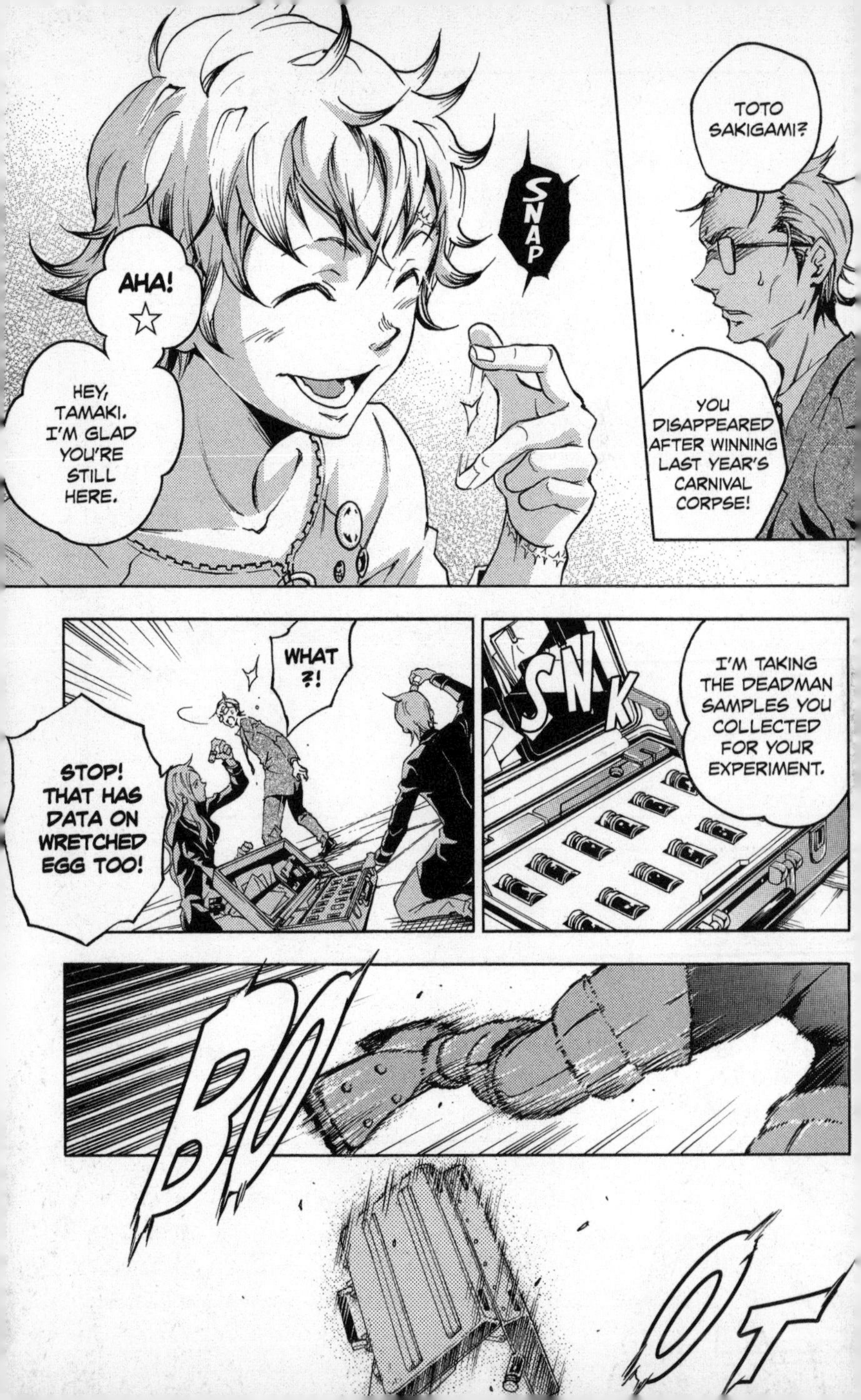
TOTO SAKIGAMI?
YOU DISAPPEARED AFTER WINNING LAST YEAR'S CARNIVAL CORPSE!
SNAP
AHA! ☆
HEY, TAMAKI. I'M GLAD YOU'RE STILL HERE.
SNK
I'M TAKING THE DEADMAN SAMPLES YOU COLLECTED FOR YOUR EXPERIMENT.
WHAT ?!
STOP! THAT HAS DATA ON WRETCHED EGG TOO!
BOOT

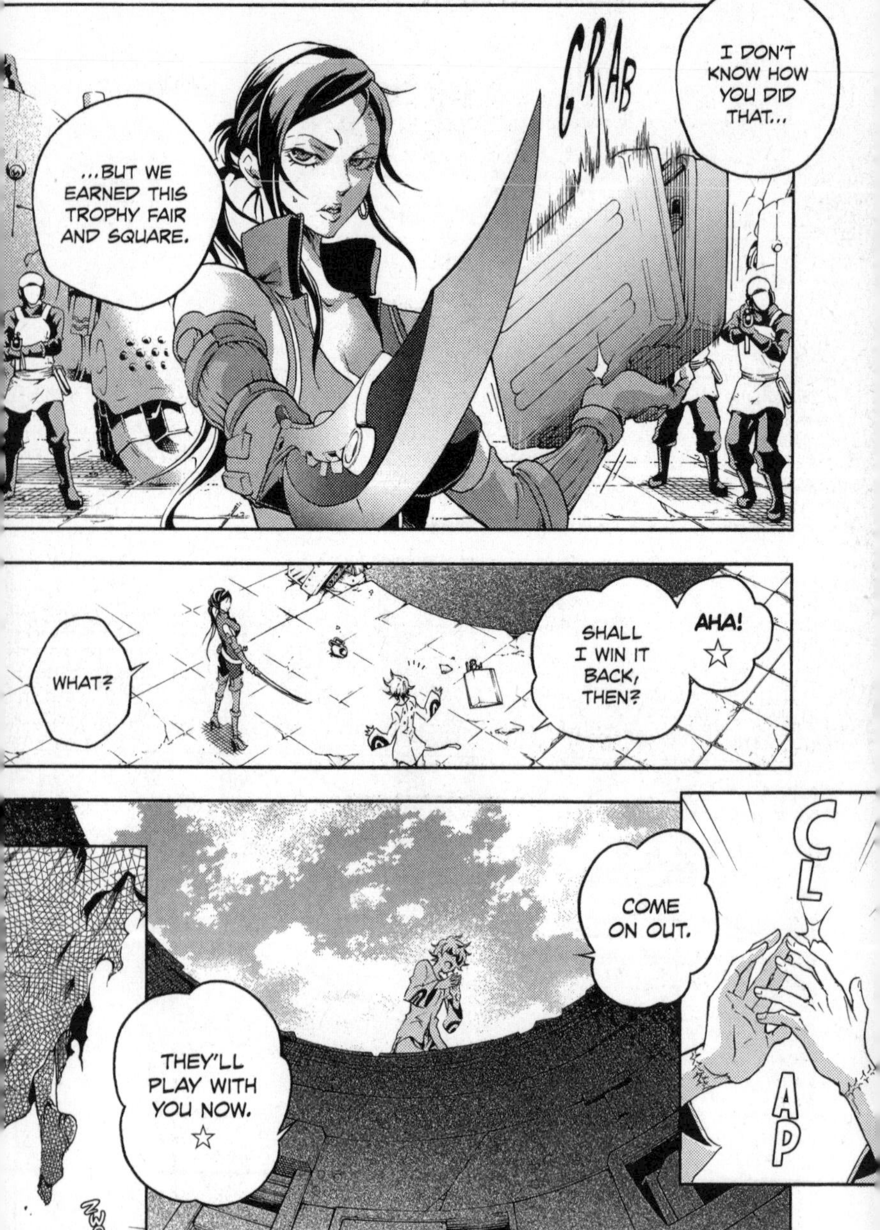
I DON'T KNOW HOW YOU DID THAT...
GRAB
...BUT WE EARNED THIS TROPHY FAIR AND SQUARE.
AHA! ☆
SHALL I WIN IT BACK, THEN?
WHAT?
CLAP
COME ON OUT.
THEY'LL PLAY WITH YOU NOW. ☆

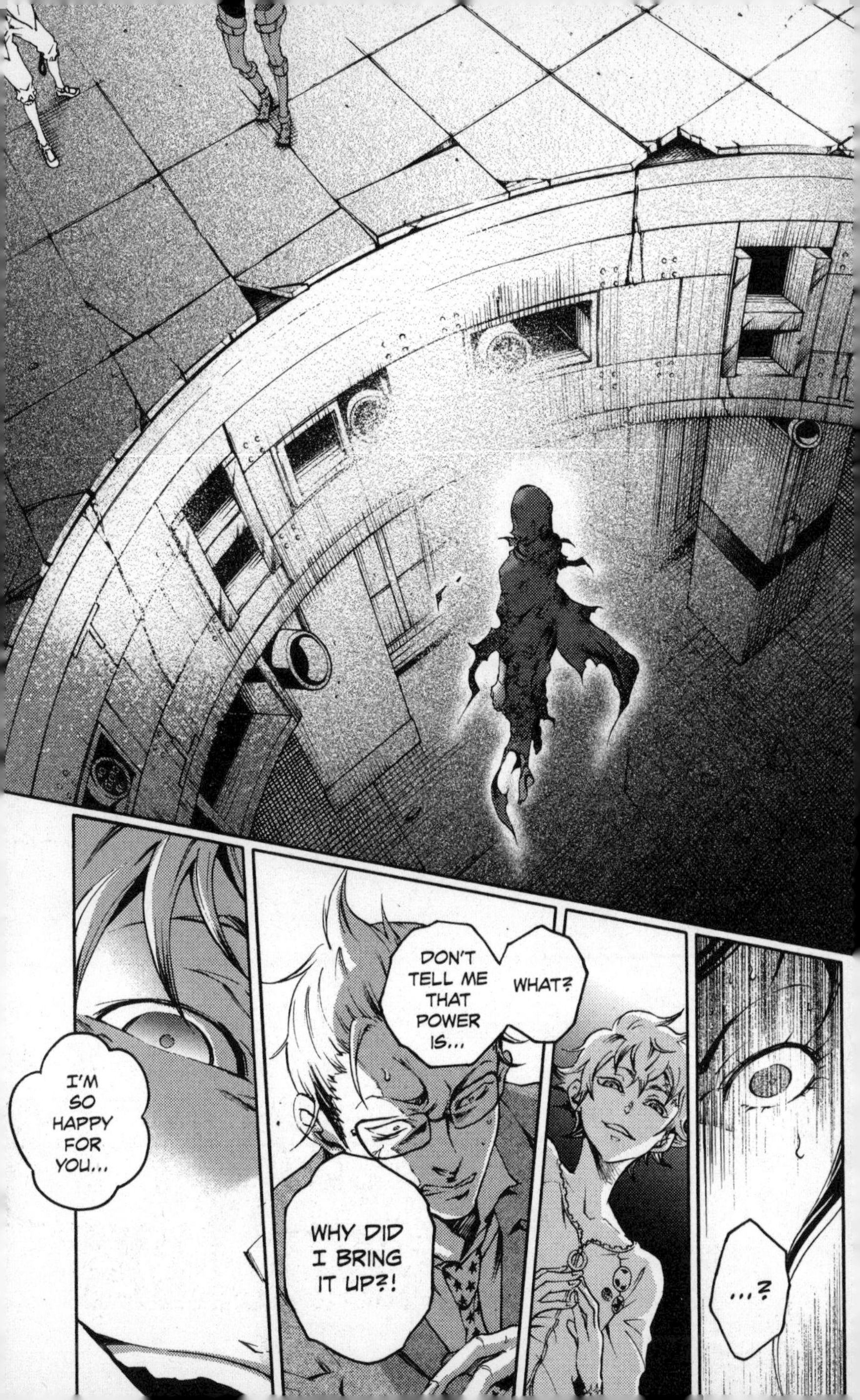

...?
WHAT?
DON'T TELL ME THAT POWER IS...
WHY DID I BRING IT UP?!
I'M SO HAPPY FOR YOU...

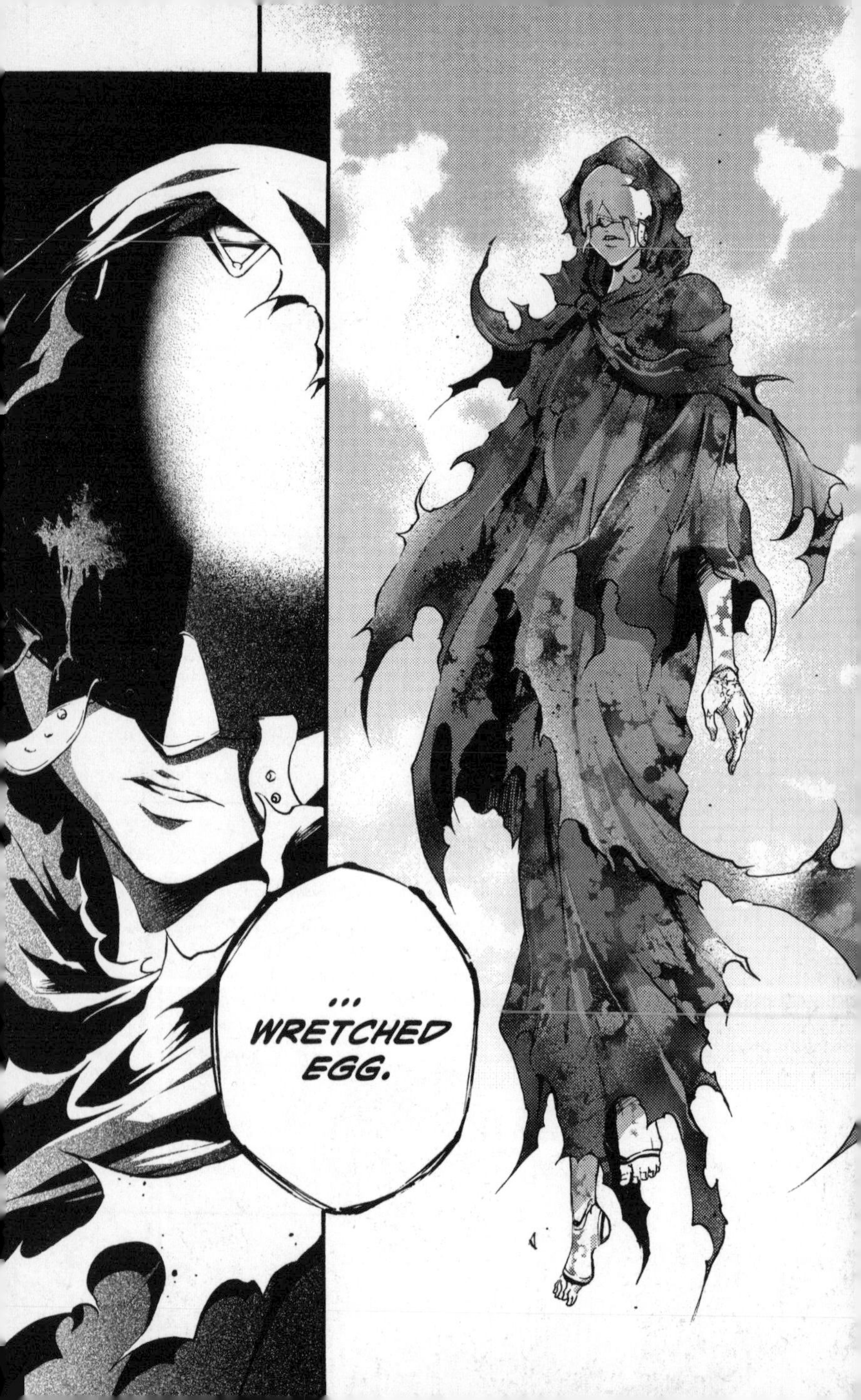
...WRETCHED EGG.

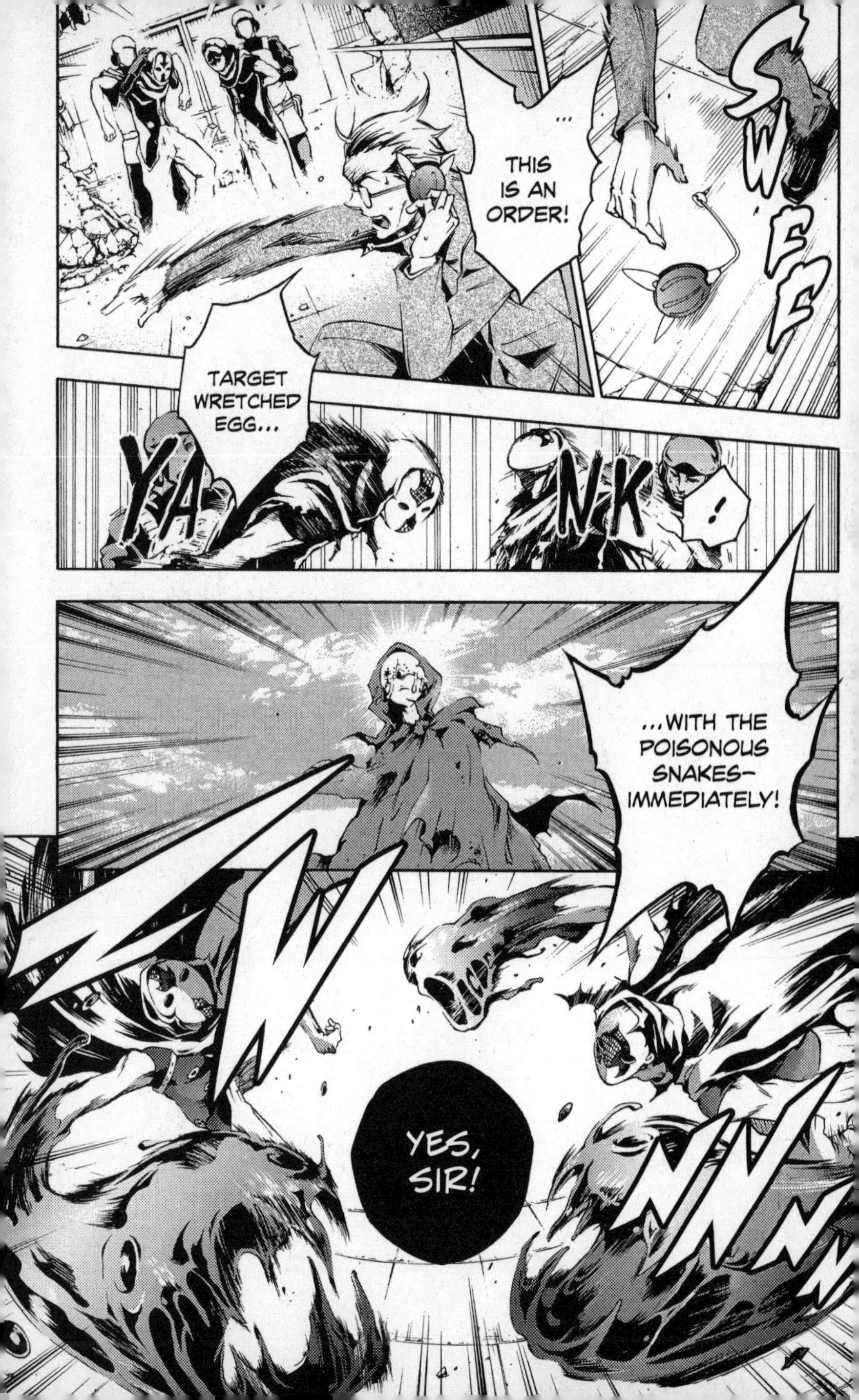
SWEEE
...
THIS IS AN ORDER!
TARGET WRETCHED EGG...
!
YANK
...WITH THE POISONOUS SNAKES— IMMEDIATELY!
YES, SIR!

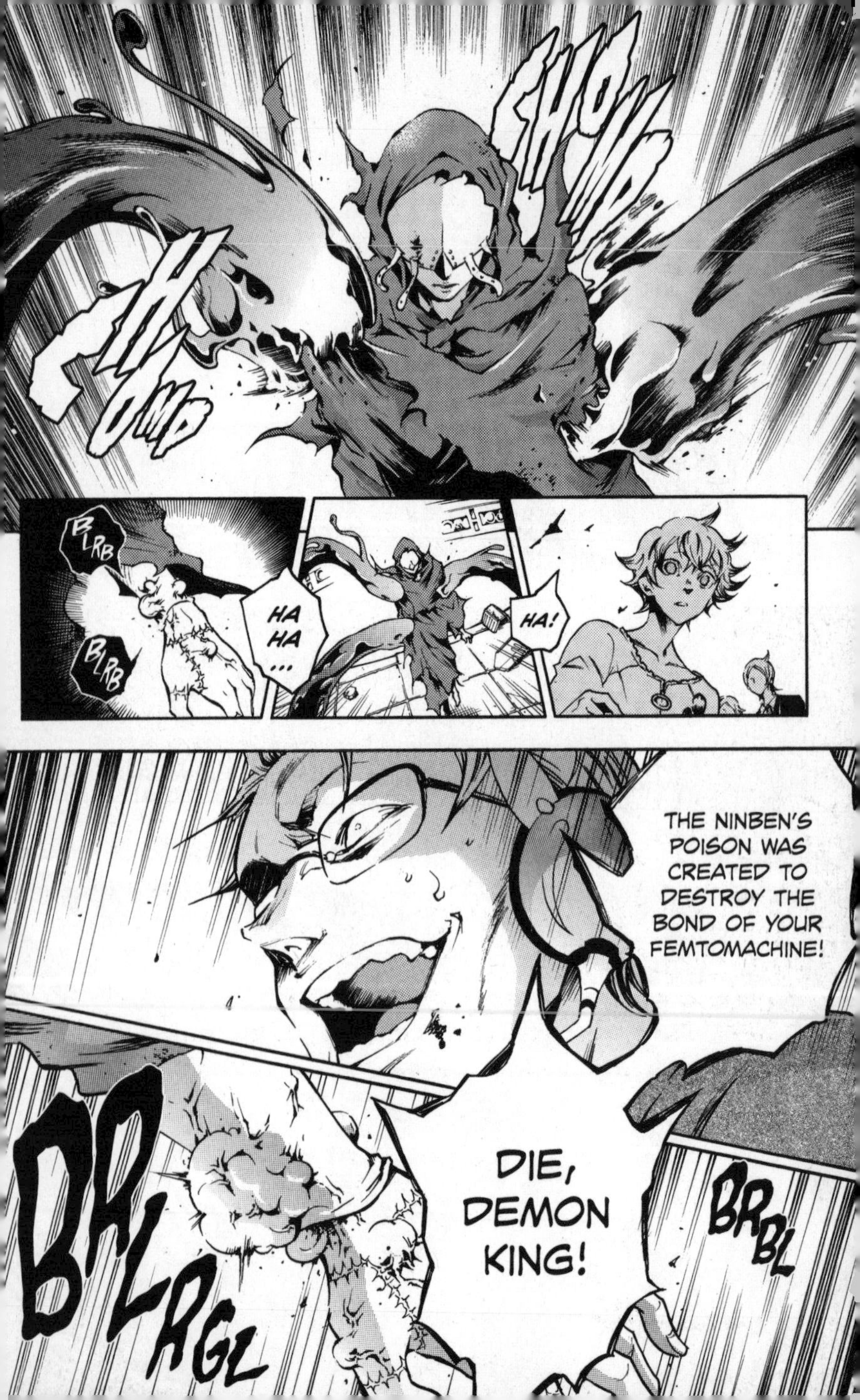
CHOMP
CHOMP
HA!
HA HA ...
BLRB
BLRB
THE NINBEN'S POISON WAS CREATED TO DESTROY THE BOND OF YOUR FEMTOMACHINE!
DIE, DEMON KING!
BRBL
BRLRGL

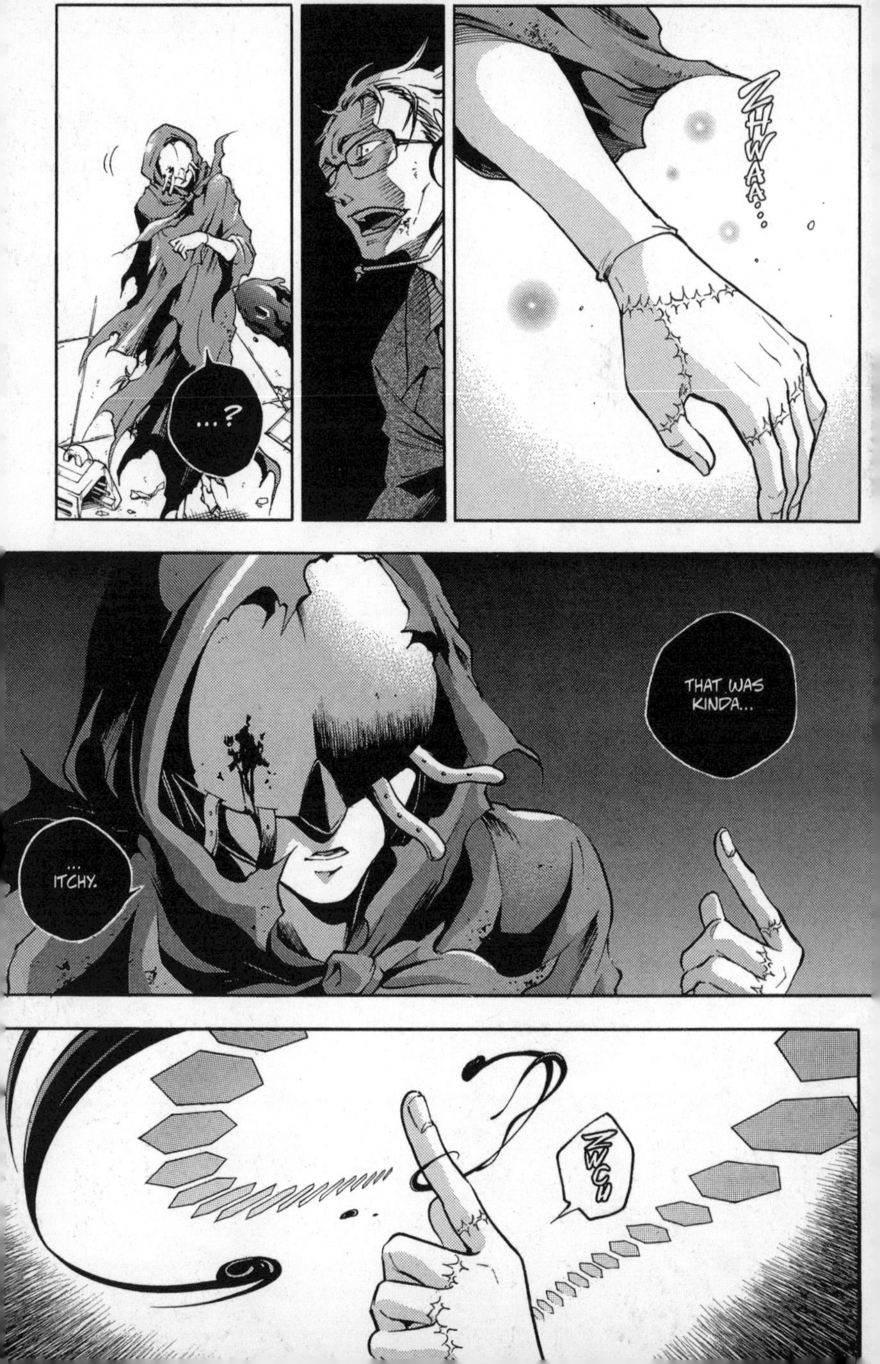
ZHWAA...
...?
THAT WAS KINDA...
...ITCHY.
ZWCH

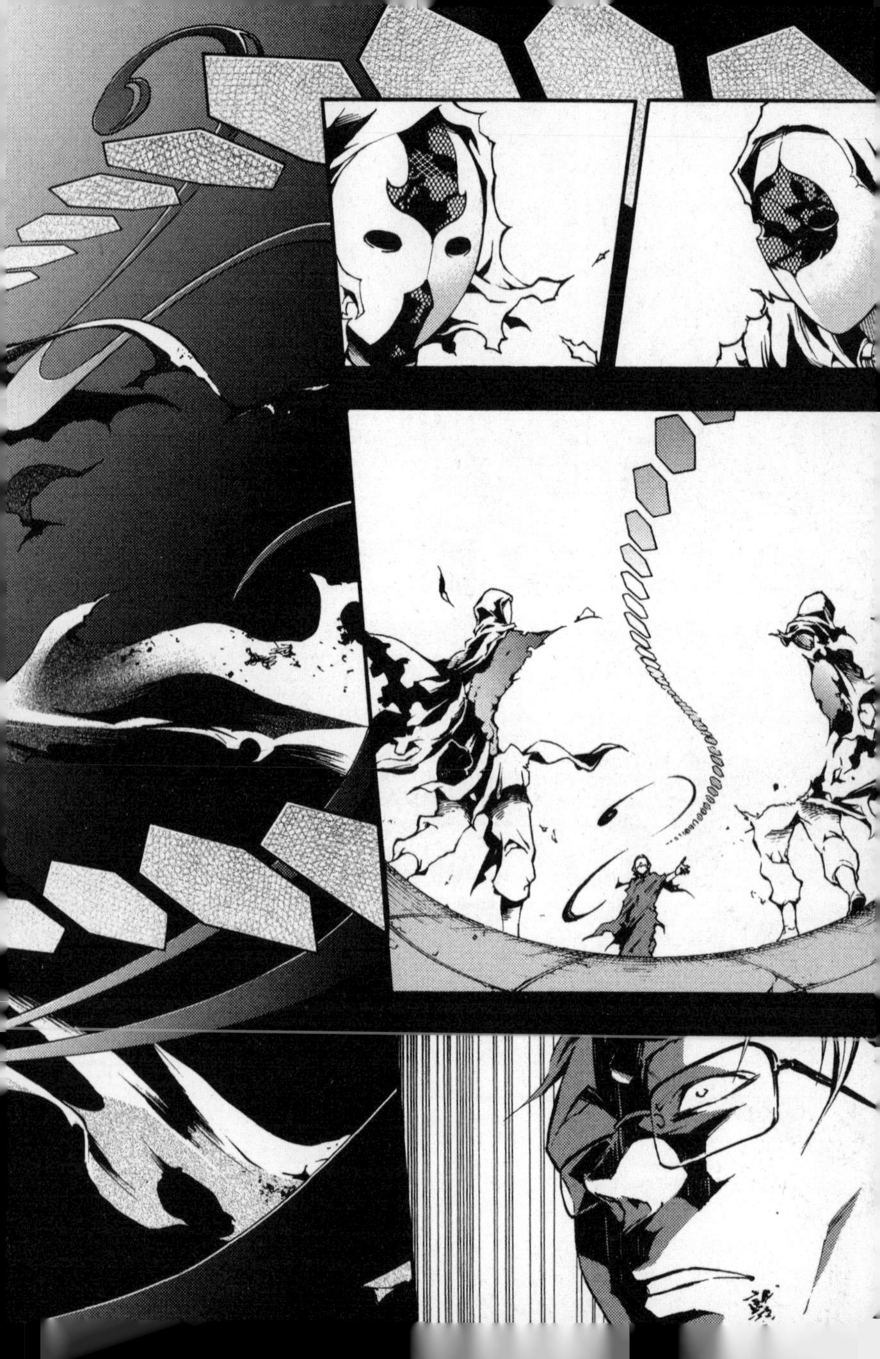

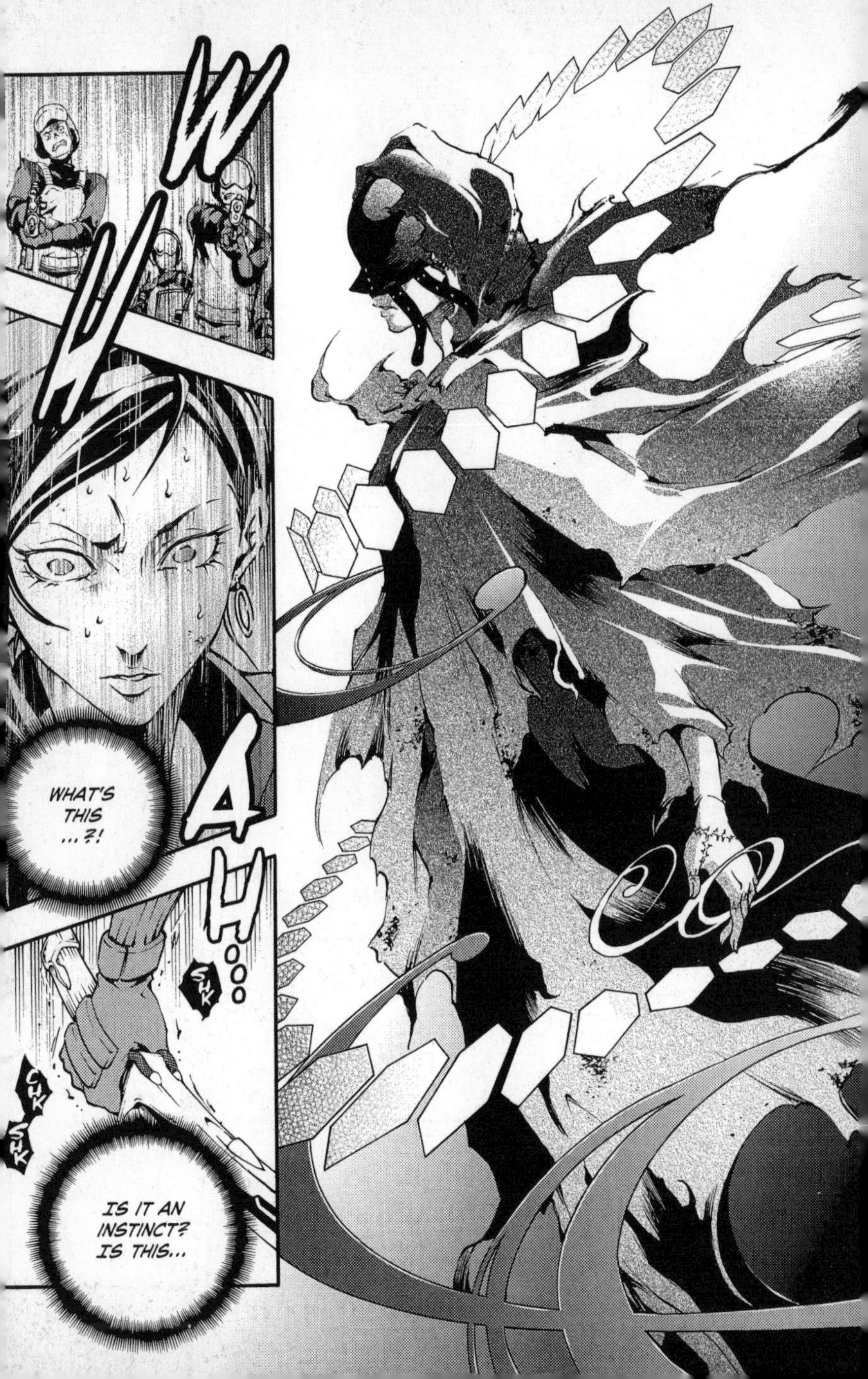
WHA
WHAT'S THIS ...?!
WHOOO
SHK
CHK
SHK
IS IT AN INSTINCT? IS THIS...

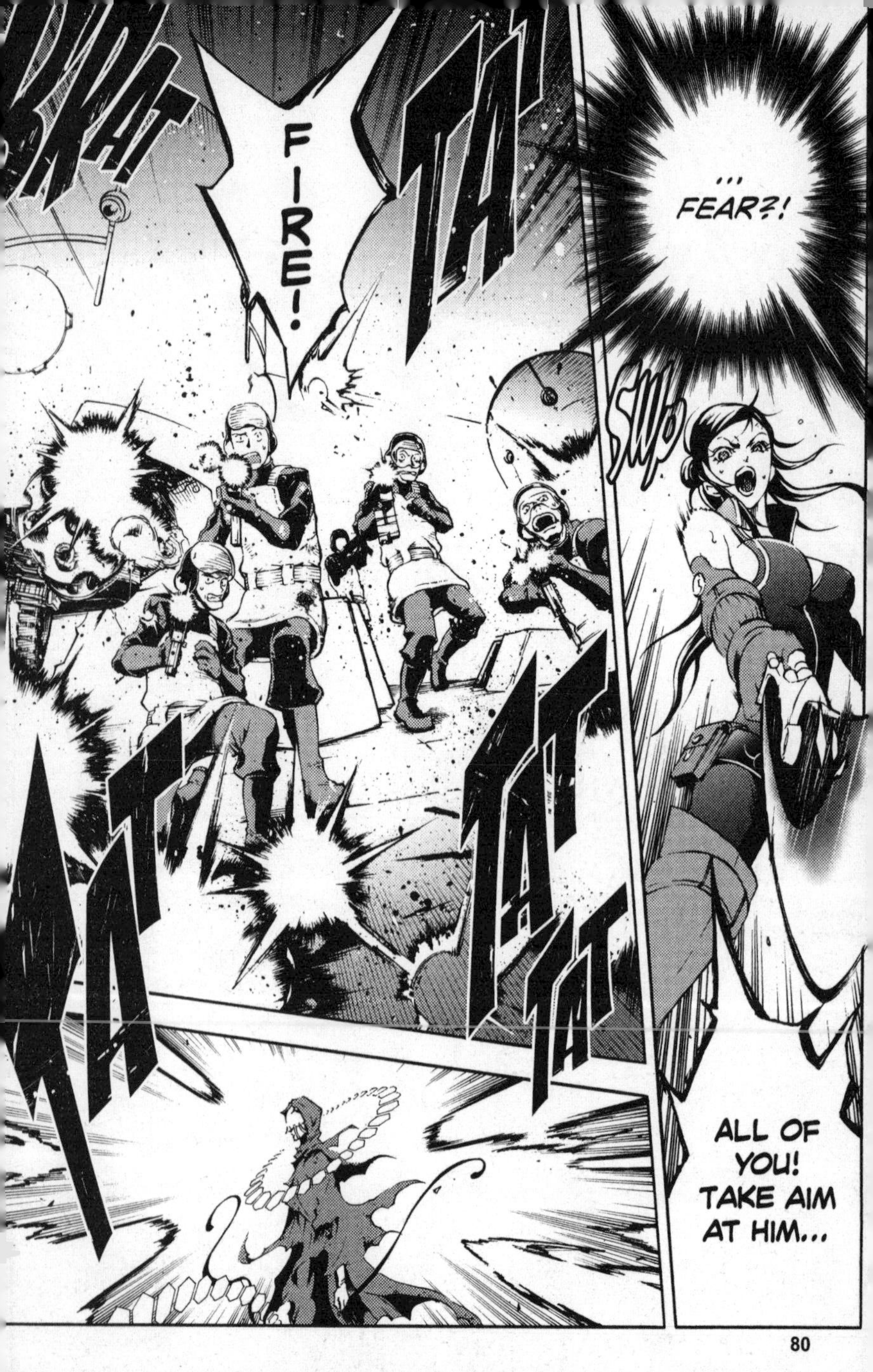
... FEAR?!
ALL OF YOU! TAKE AIM AT HIM...
FIRE!

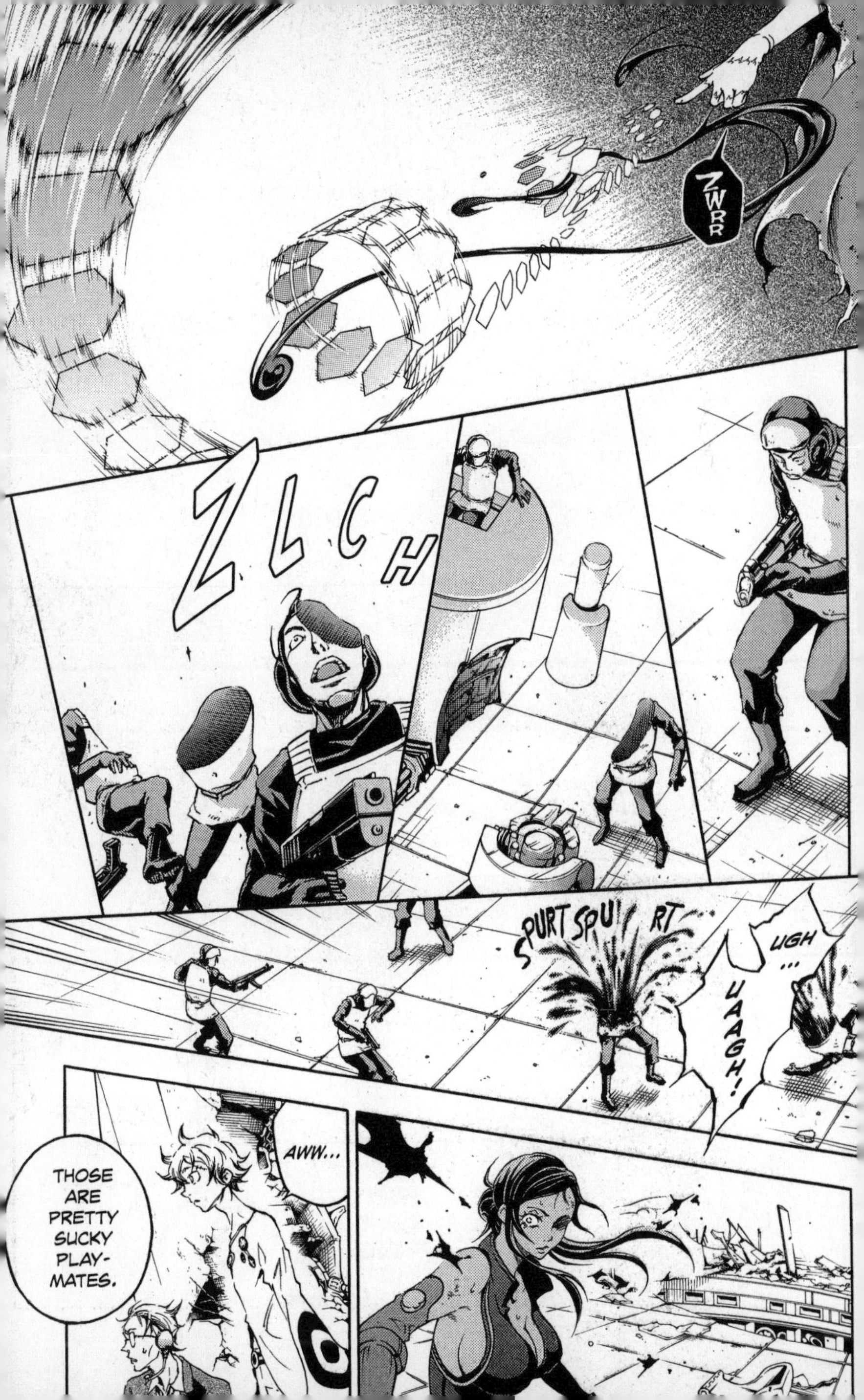
ZWRR
ZLCH
UGH...
UAAGH!
SPURT SPU RT
AWW...
THOSE ARE PRETTY SUCKY PLAY-MATES.

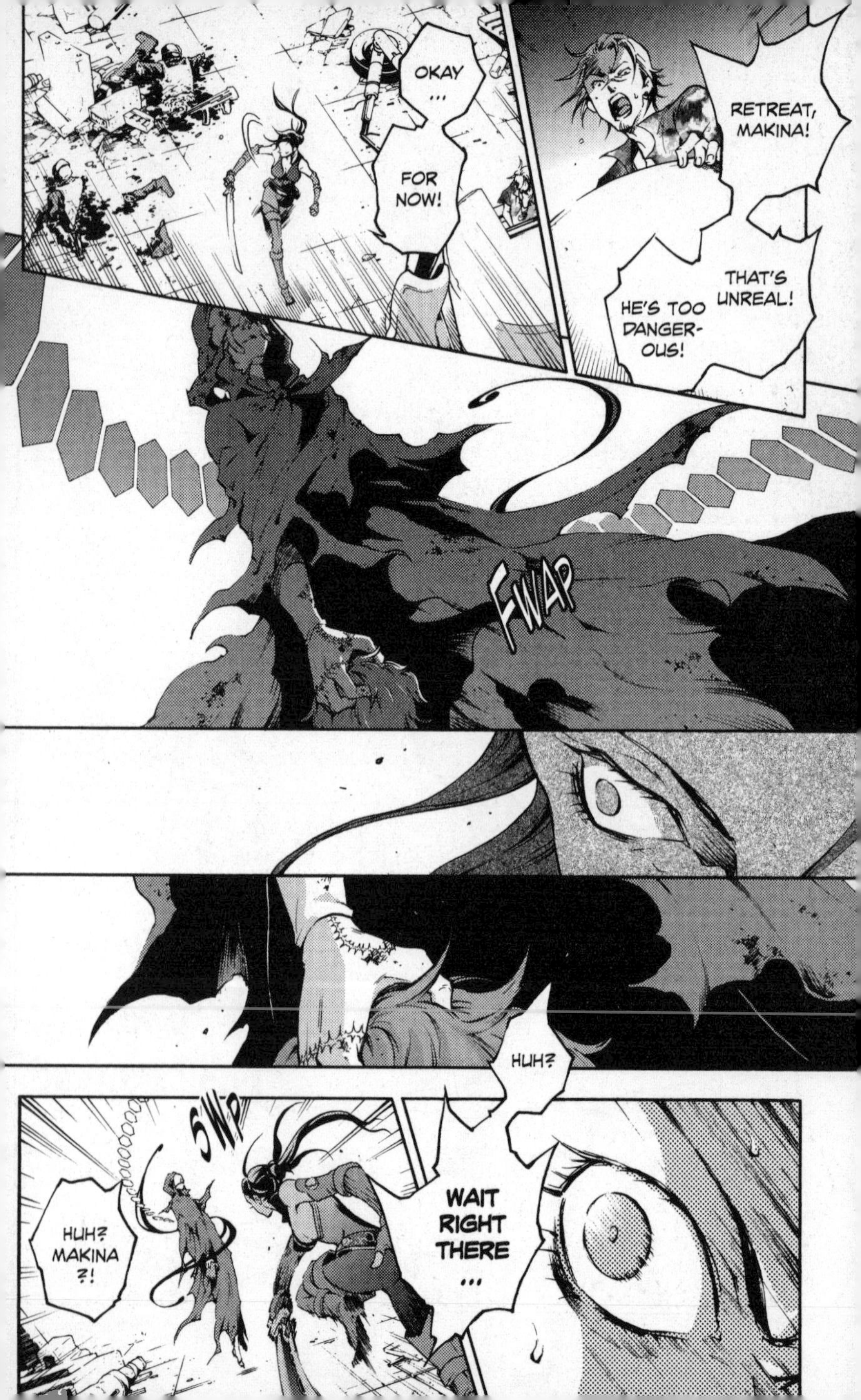
RETREAT, MAKINA!
THAT'S UNREAL!
HE'S TOO DANGER-OUS!
OKAY ...
FOR NOW!
FWAP
HUH?
WAIT RIGHT THERE ...
HUH? MAKINA?!

...YOU BAS-TARD!

HE MAY BE A MONSTER, BUT HE'S GOT INTEL I NEED!

MY WORM EATER BLADE SHOULD CUT HIM FREE!

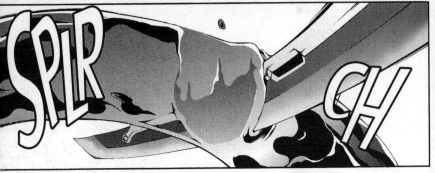

SPLR

CH

WH-WHAT?!

?!

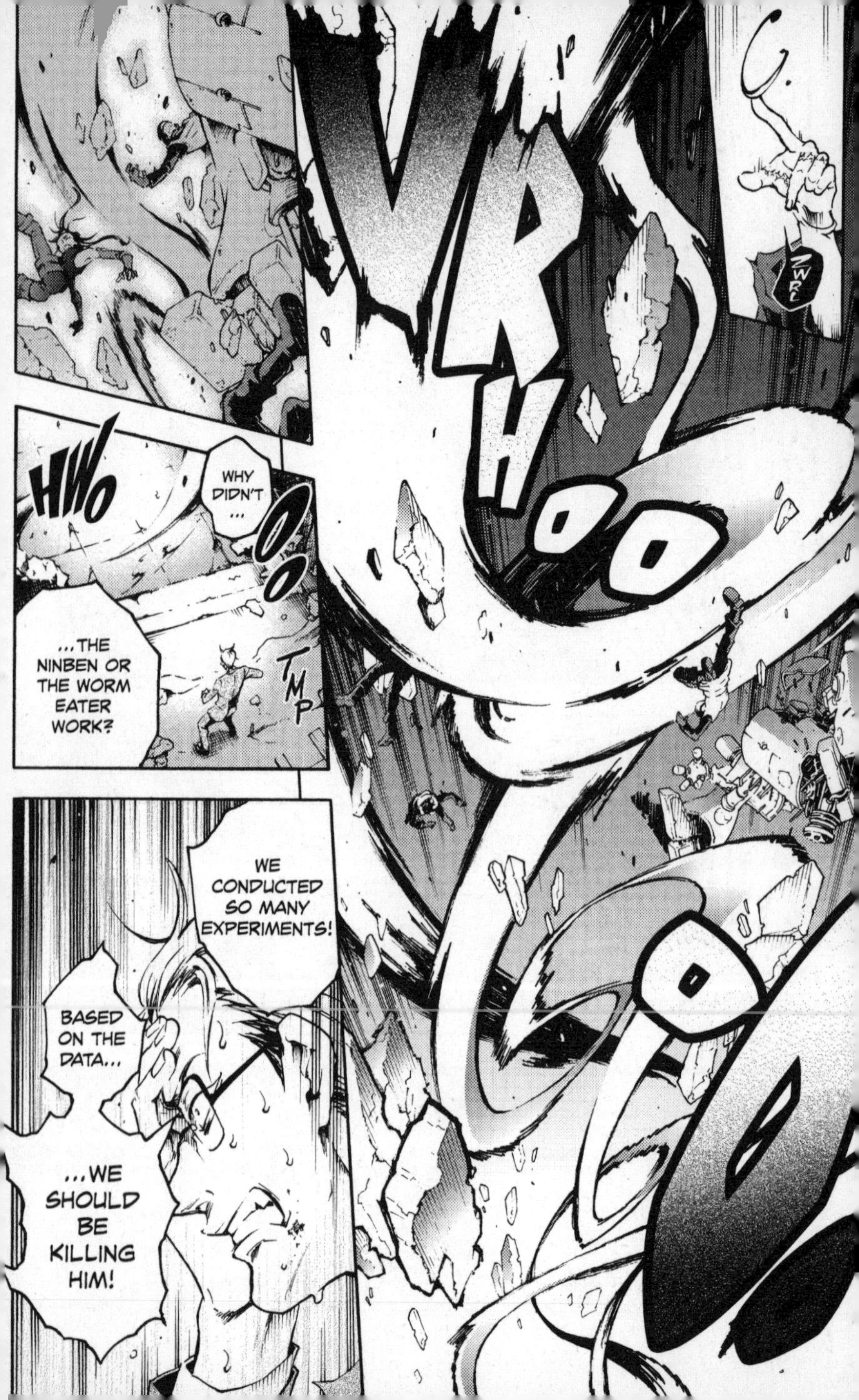
ZWRL
VRHOOO
HWO
WHY DIDN'T ...
OO
...THE NINBEN OR THE WORM EATER WORK?
TMP
WE CONDUCTED SO MANY EXPERIMENTS!
BASED ON THE DATA...
...WE SHOULD BE KILLING HIM!

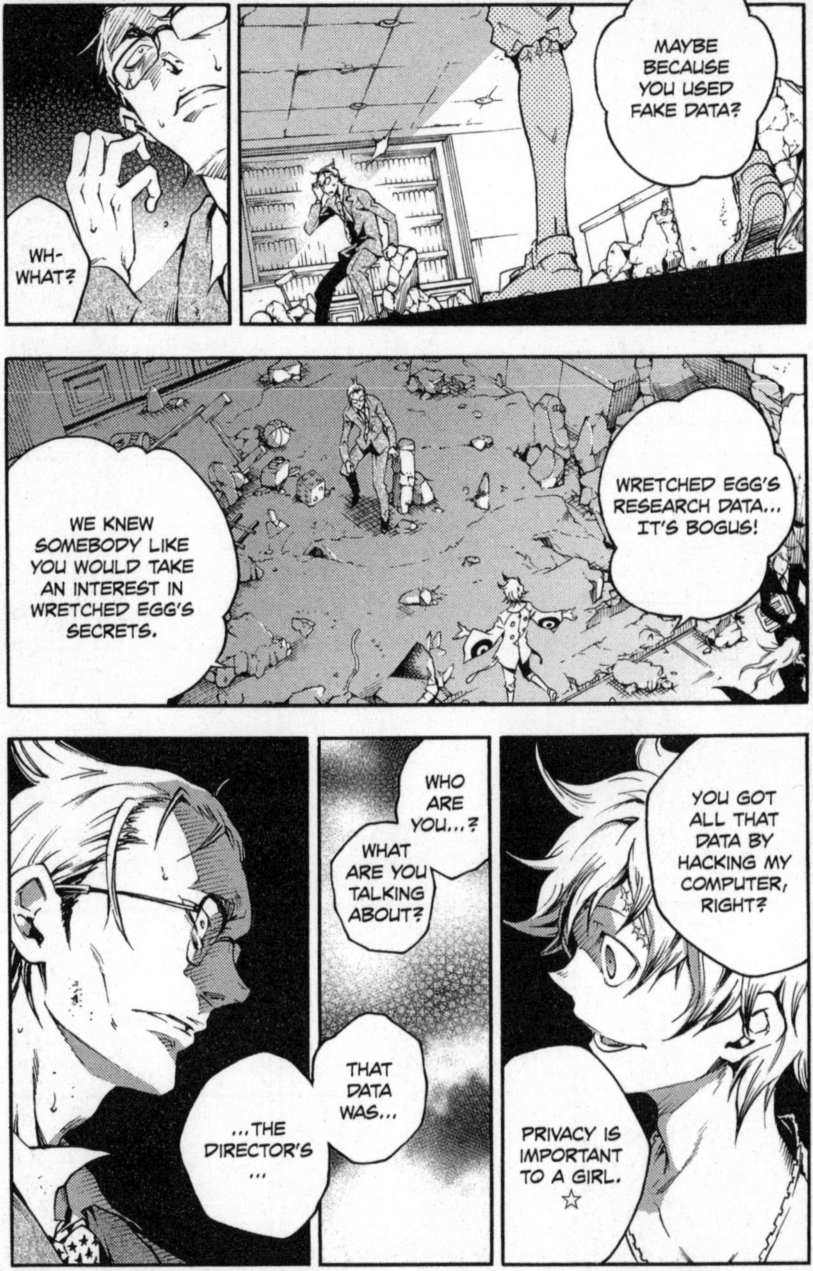
MAYBE BECAUSE YOU USED FAKE DATA?
WH- WHAT?
WRETCHED EGG'S RESEARCH DATA... IT'S BOGUS!
WE KNEW SOMEBODY LIKE YOU WOULD TAKE AN INTEREST IN WRETCHED EGG'S SECRETS.
YOU GOT ALL THAT DATA BY HACKING MY COMPUTER, RIGHT?
PRIVACY IS IMPORTANT TO A GIRL. ☆
WHO ARE YOU...?
WHAT ARE YOU TALKING ABOUT?
THAT DATA WAS...
...THE DIRECTOR'S ...

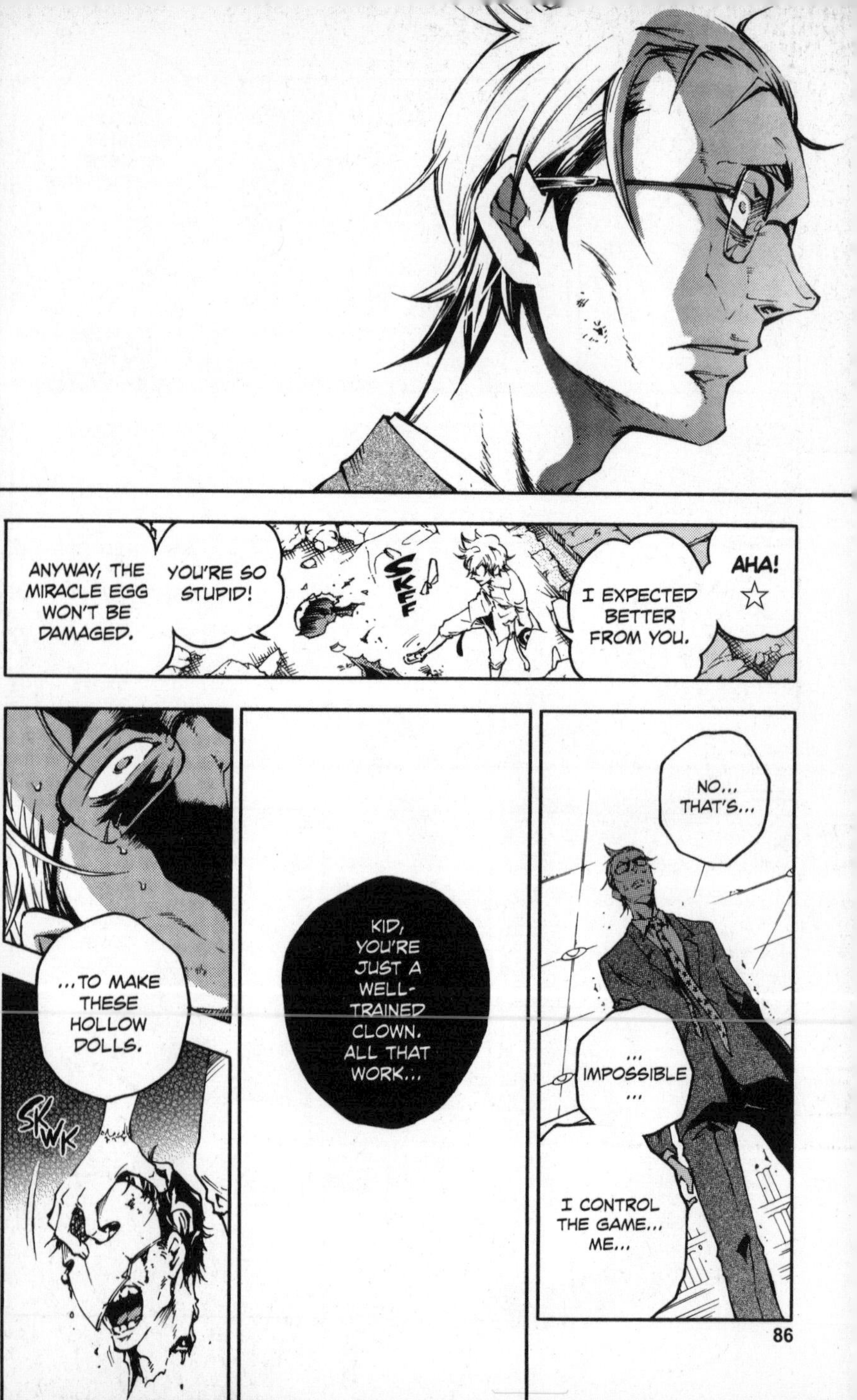
AHA! ☆
I EXPECTED BETTER FROM YOU.
SKEF
YOU'RE SO STUPID!
ANYWAY, THE MIRACLE EGG WON'T BE DAMAGED.
NO... THAT'S...
... IMPOSSIBLE ...
I CONTROL THE GAME... ME...
KID, YOU'RE JUST A WELL-TRAINED CLOWN. ALL THAT WORK...
...TO MAKE THESE HOLLOW DOLLS.
SKWK

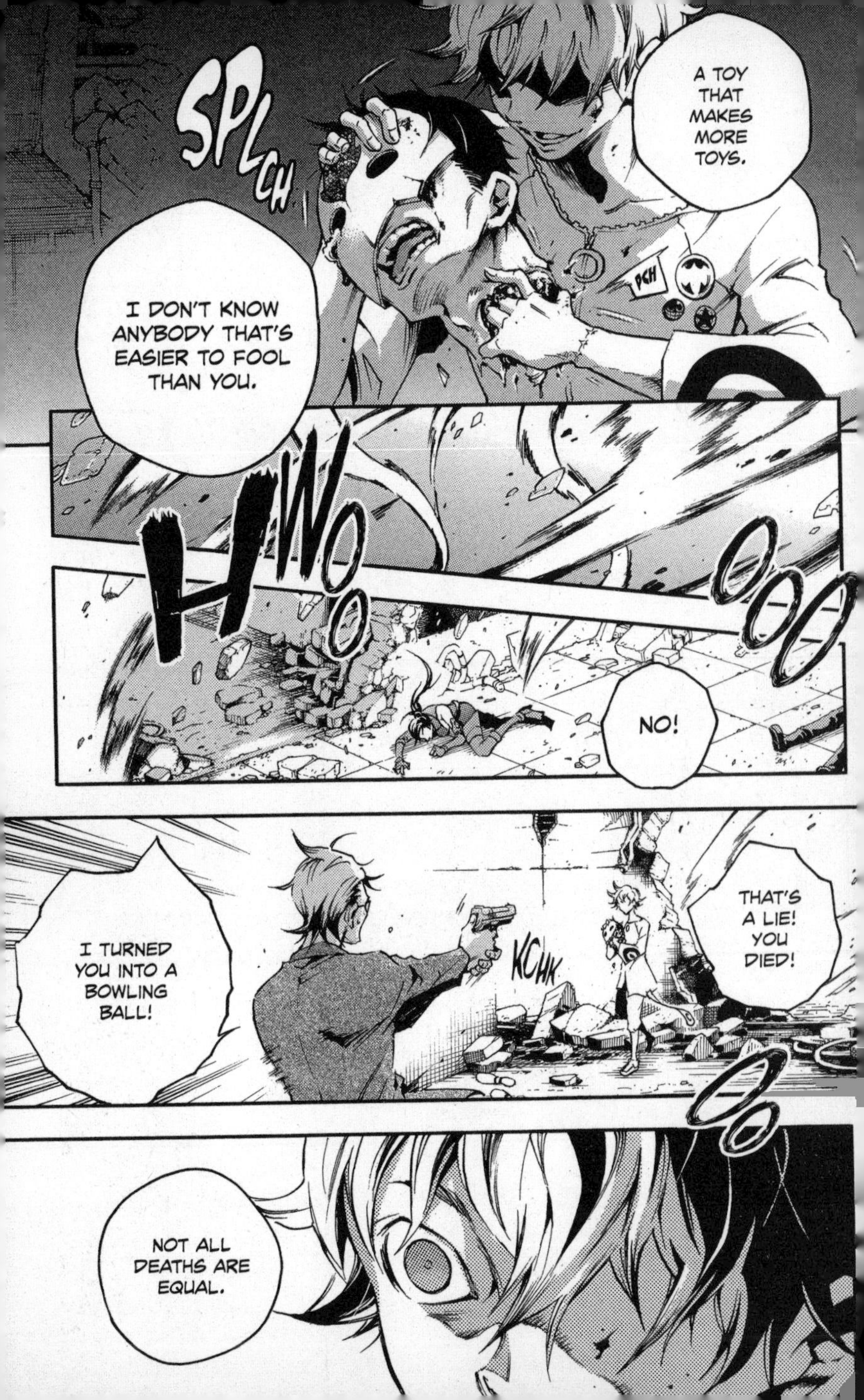
A TOY THAT MAKES MORE TOYS.
SPLCH
PCH
I DON'T KNOW ANYBODY THAT'S EASIER TO FOOL THAN YOU.
HWOOO
NO!
THAT'S A LIE! YOU DIED!
KCHK
I TURNED YOU INTO A BOWLING BALL!
NOT ALL DEATHS ARE EQUAL.

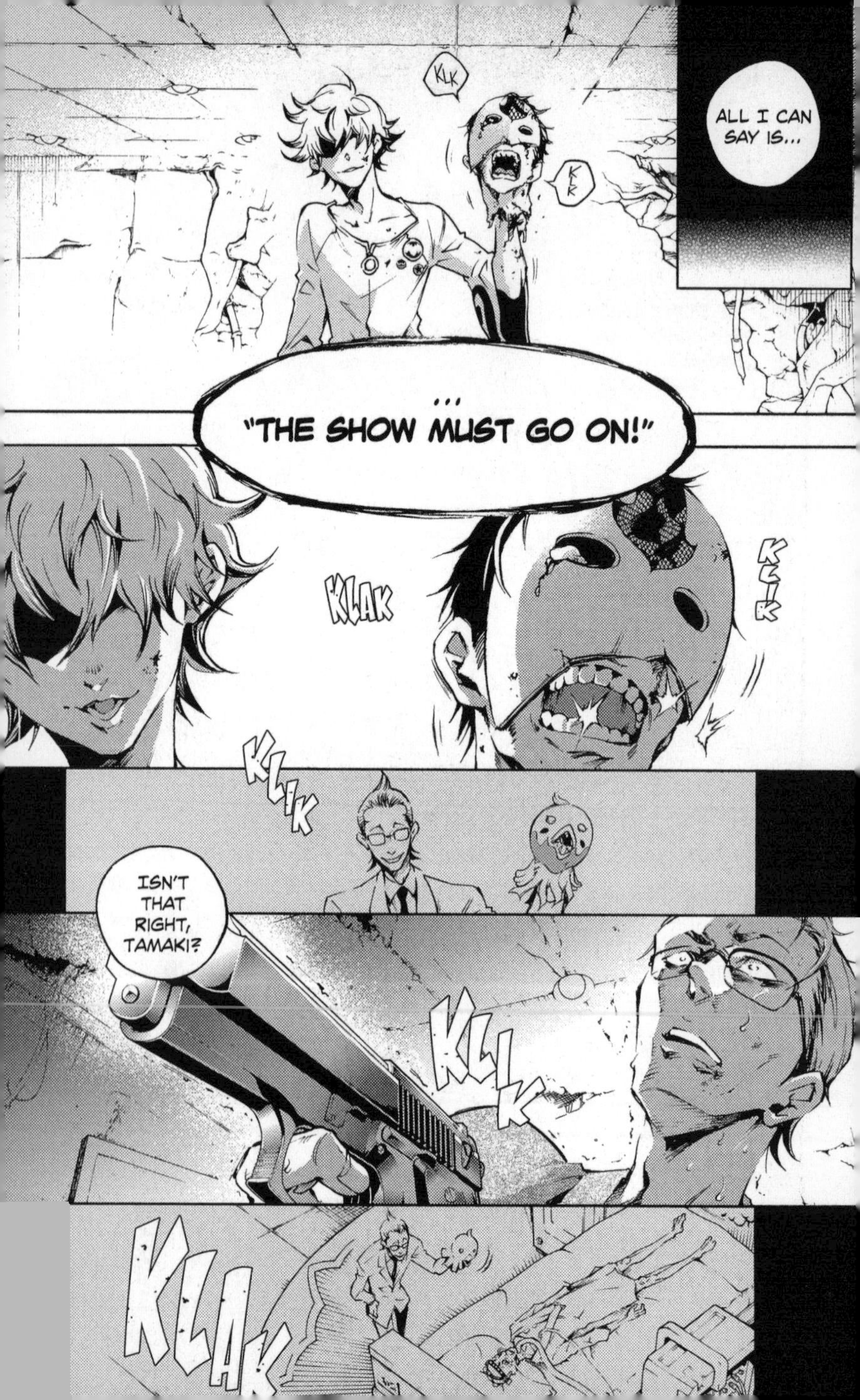
ALL I CAN SAY IS...
KLK
KLK
..."THE SHOW MUST GO ON!"
KLIK
KLAK
KLIK
ISN'T THAT RIGHT, TAMAKI?
KLIK
KLAK

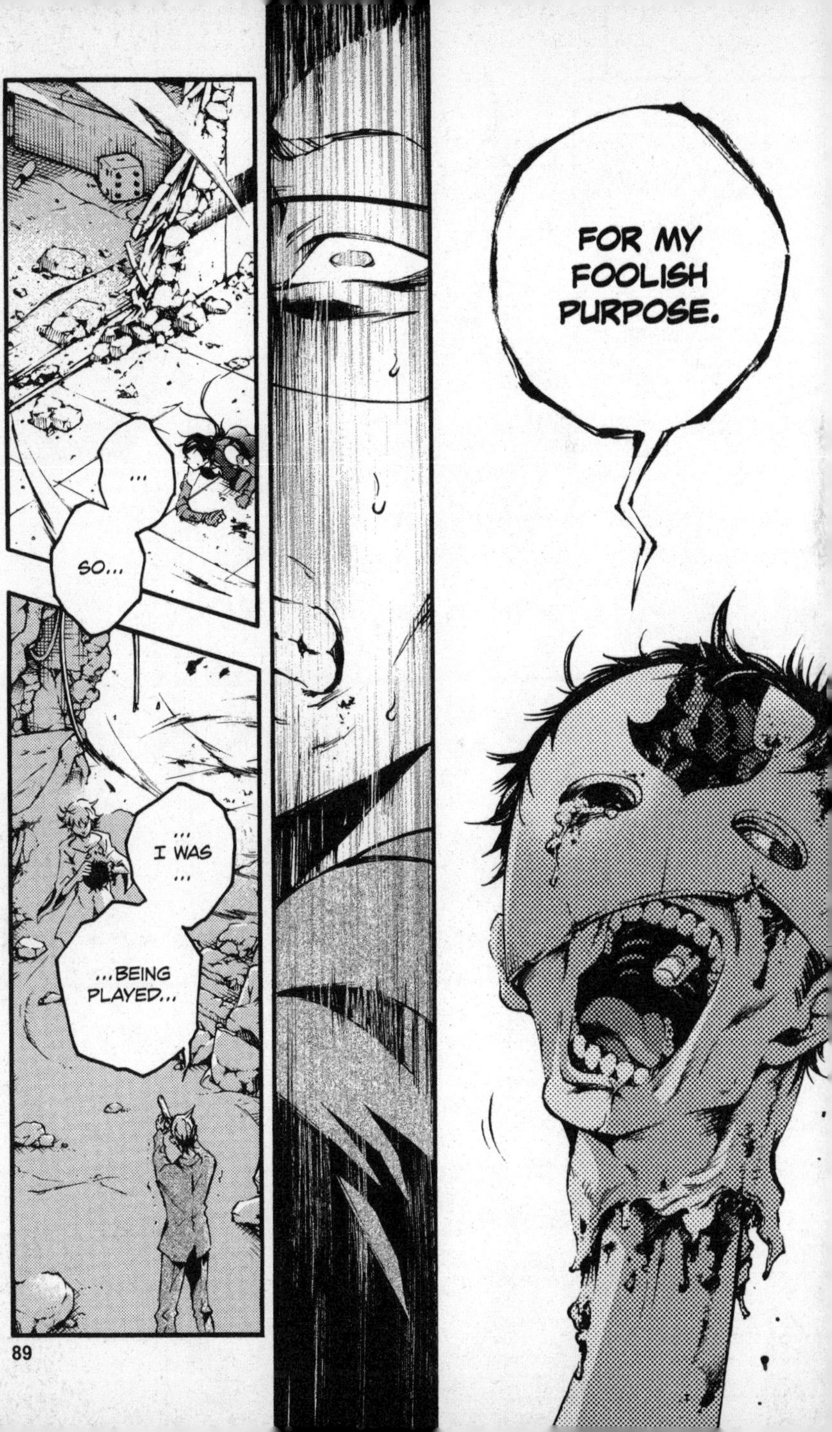
FOR MY FOOLISH PURPOSE.
...
SO...
... I WAS ...
...BEING PLAYED...

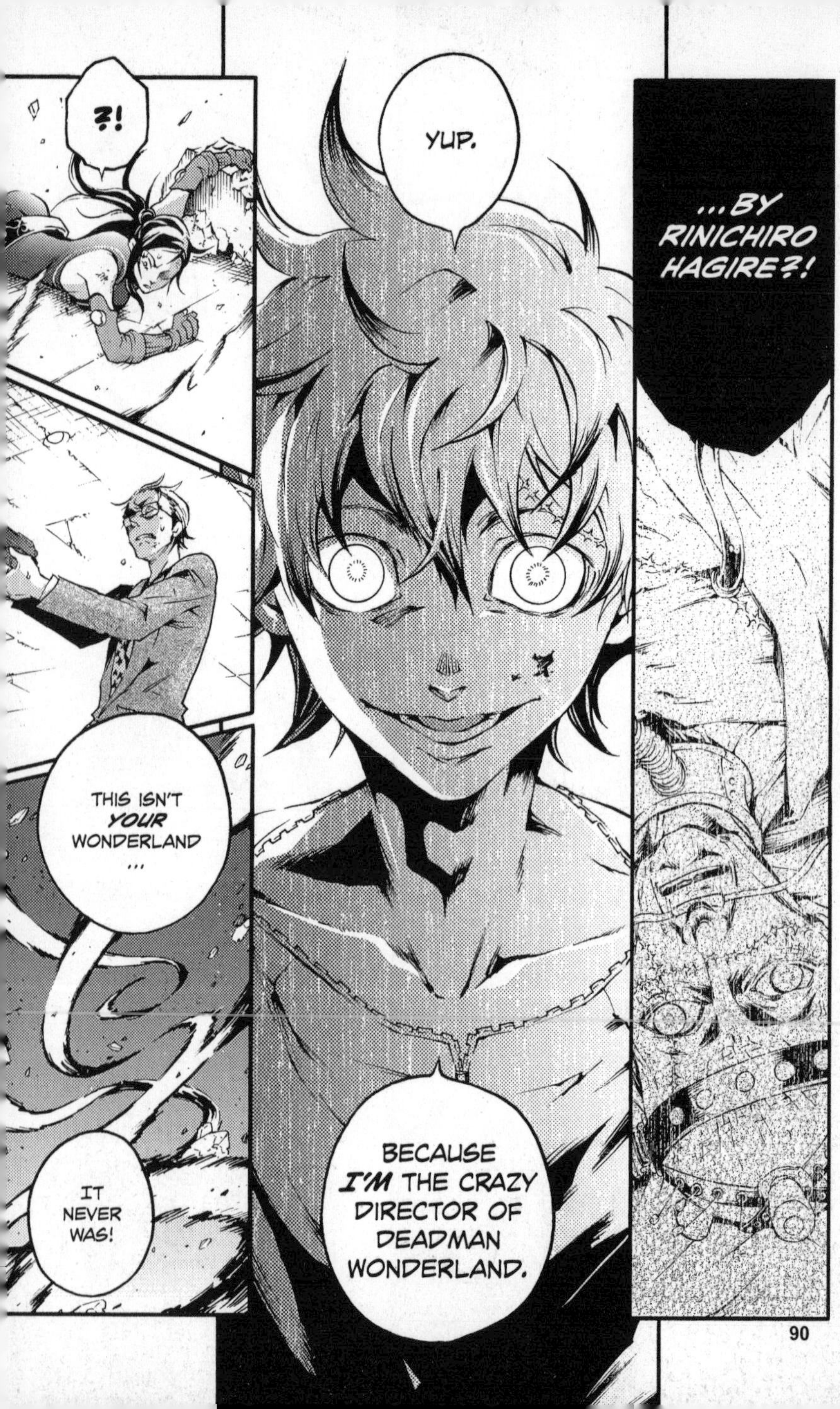
...BY RINICHIRO HAGIRE?!
YUP.
BECAUSE *I'M* THE CRAZY DIRECTOR OF DEADMAN WONDERLAND.
?!
THIS ISN'T *YOUR* WONDERLAND ...
IT NEVER WAS!

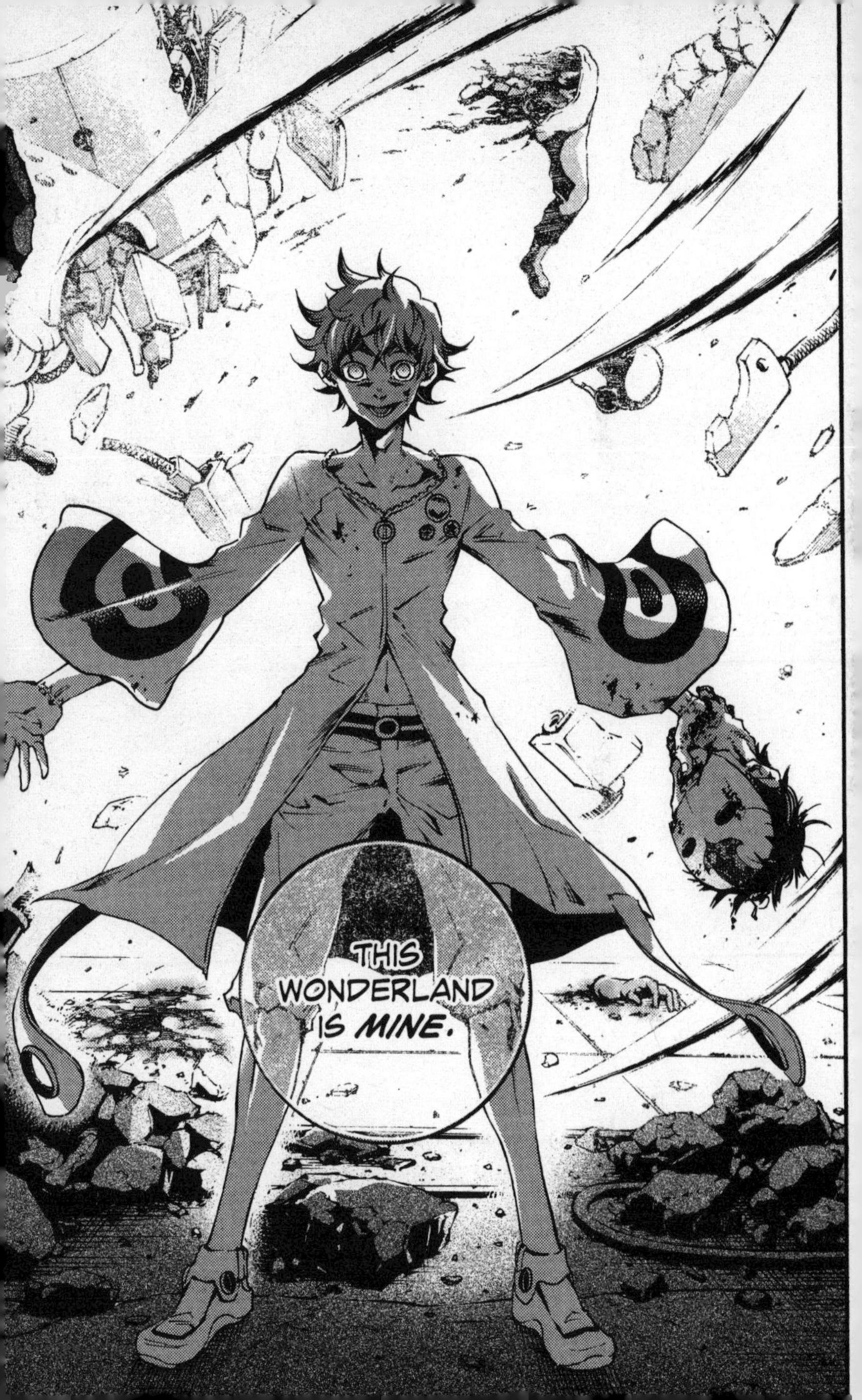
THIS WONDERLAND IS MINE.

DEADMAN
WONDERLAND

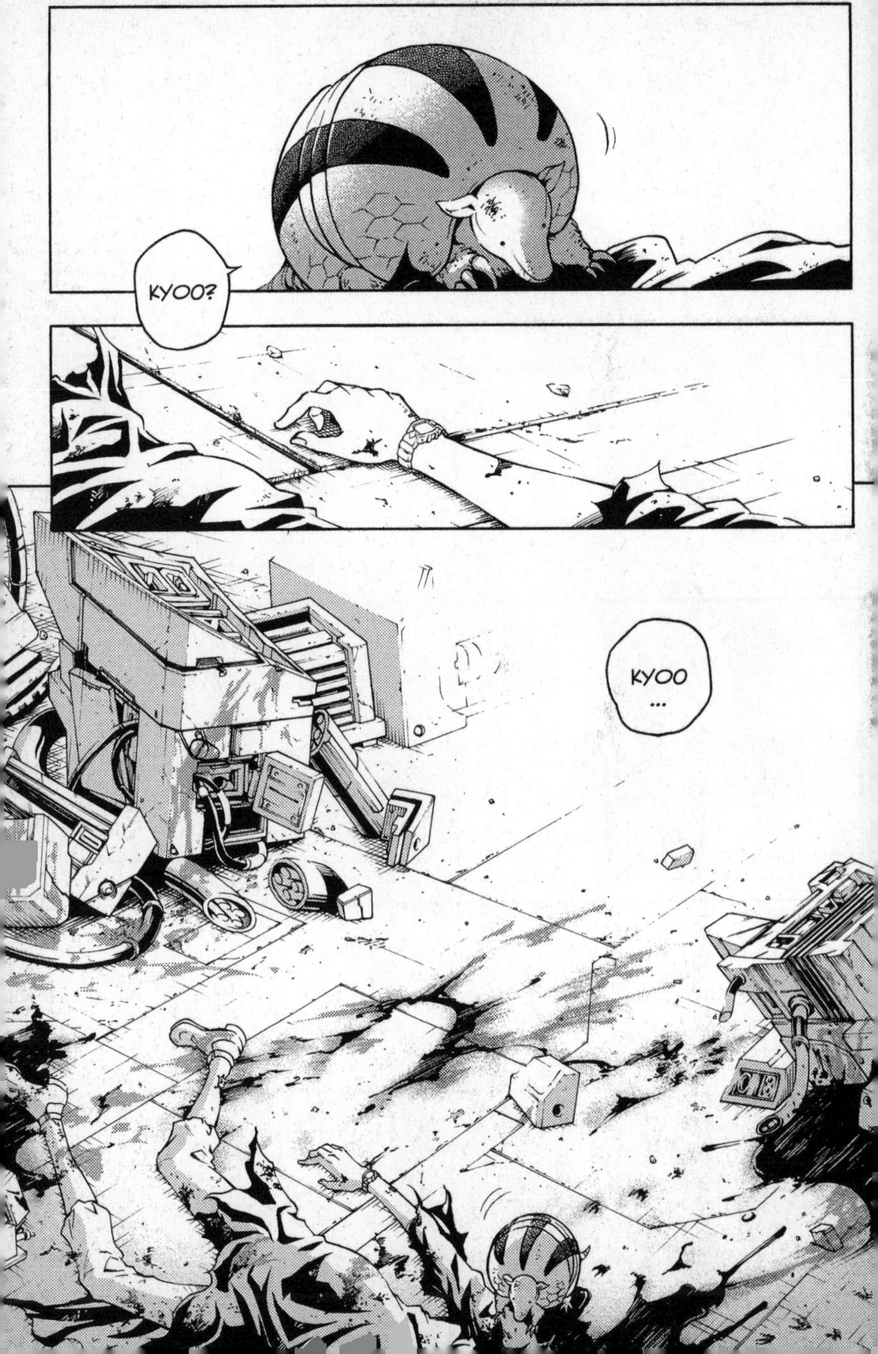
KYOO?
KYOO ...

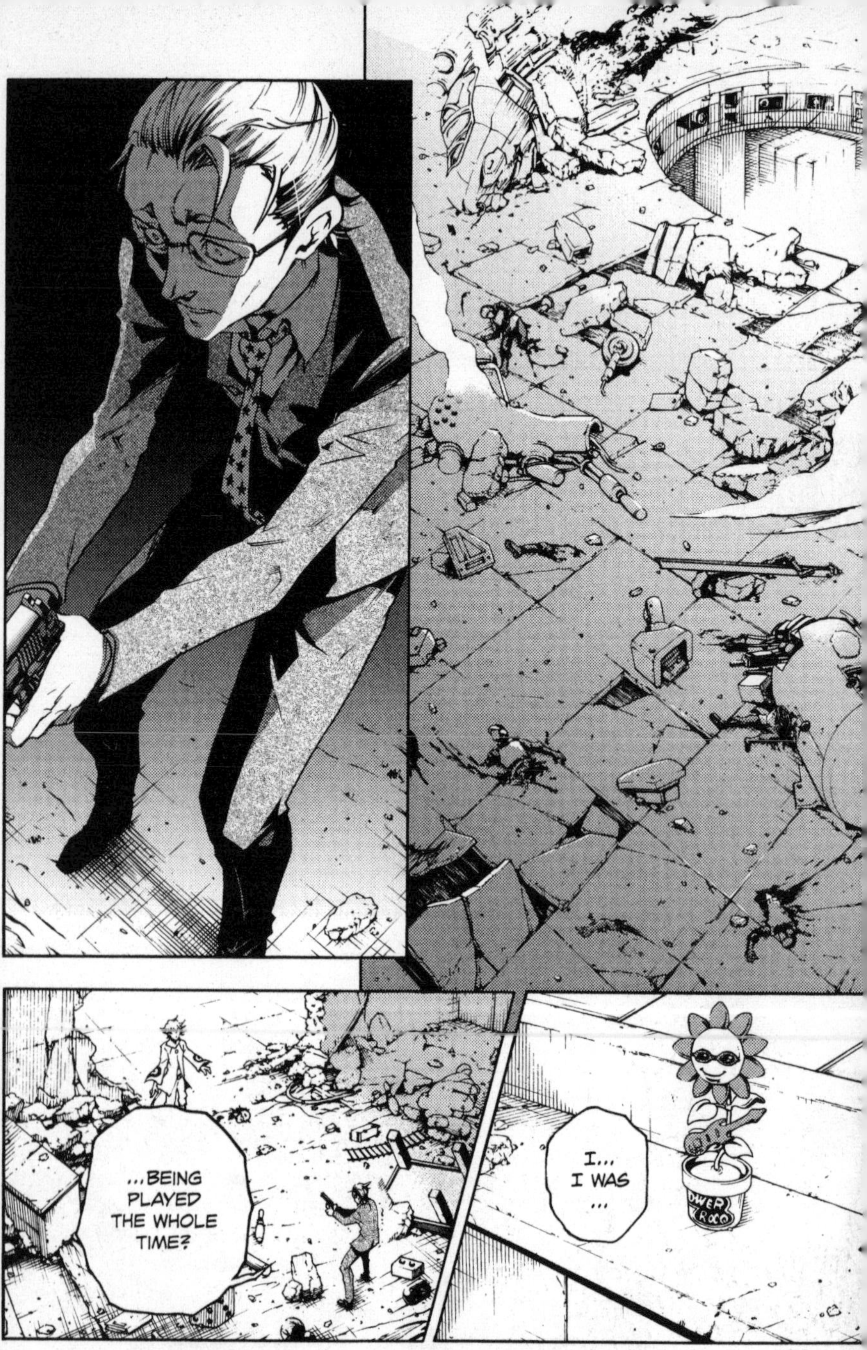
I... I WAS ...
...BEING PLAYED THE WHOLE TIME?

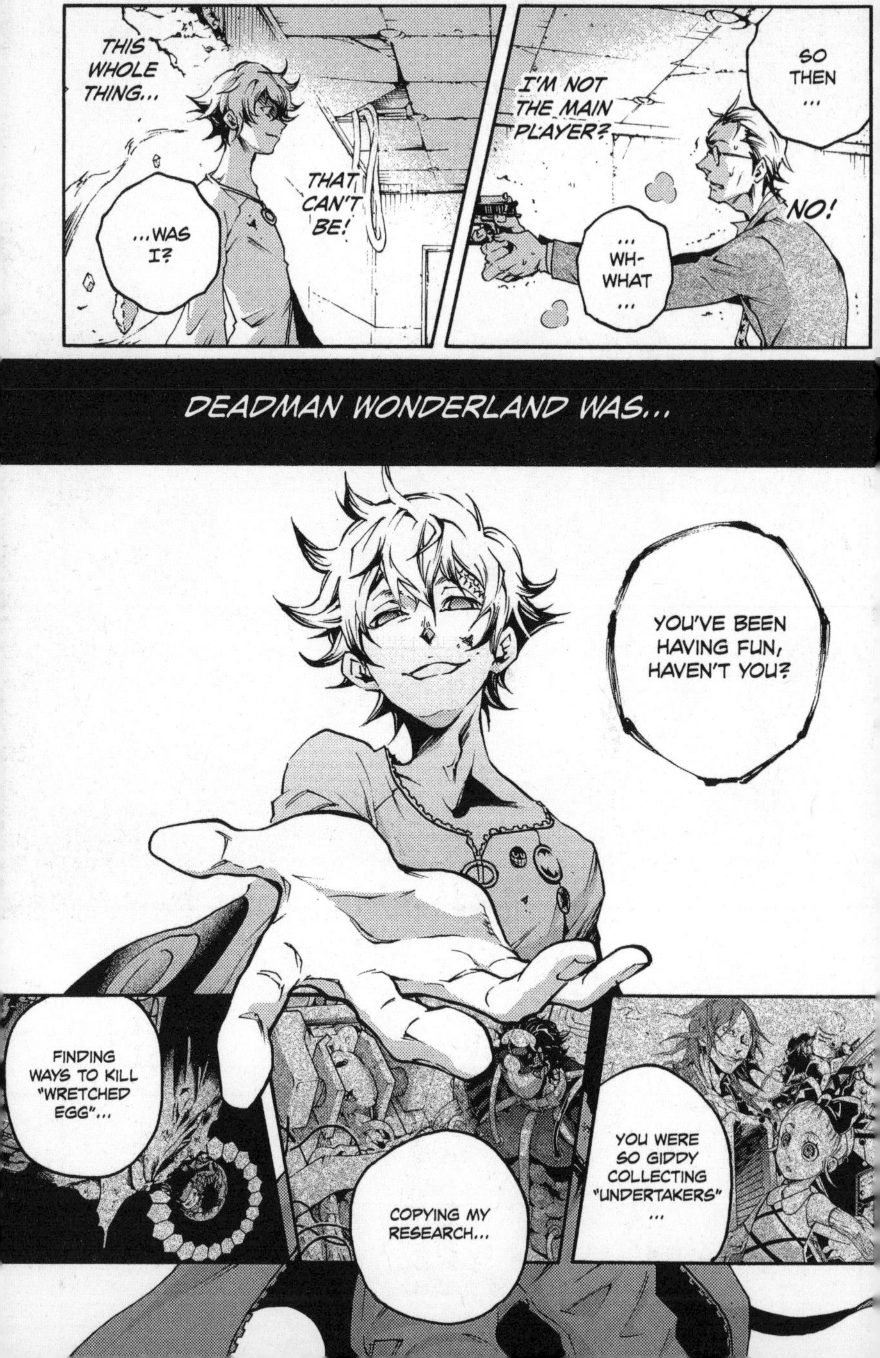
SO THEN ...
I'M NOT THE MAIN PLAYER?
NO!
... WH-WHAT ...
THIS WHOLE THING...
THAT CAN'T BE!
...WAS I?
DEADMAN WONDERLAND WAS...
YOU'VE BEEN HAVING FUN, HAVEN'T YOU?
YOU WERE SO GIDDY COLLECTING "UNDERTAKERS" ...
COPYING MY RESEARCH...
FINDING WAYS TO KILL "WRETCHED EGG"...

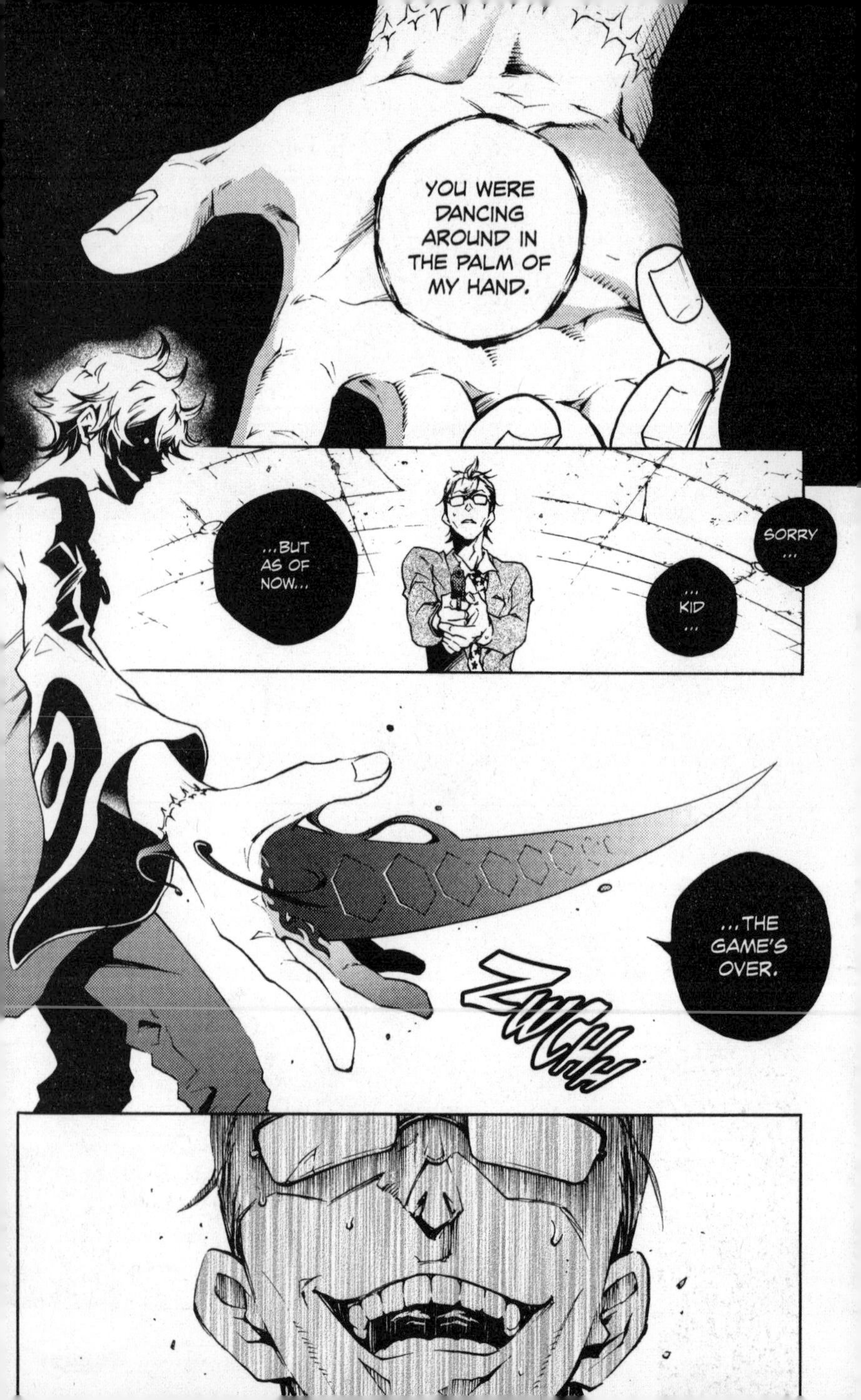
YOU WERE DANCING AROUND IN THE PALM OF MY HAND.
SORRY ...
... KID ...
...BUT AS OF NOW...
...THE GAME'S OVER.
ZUCH!

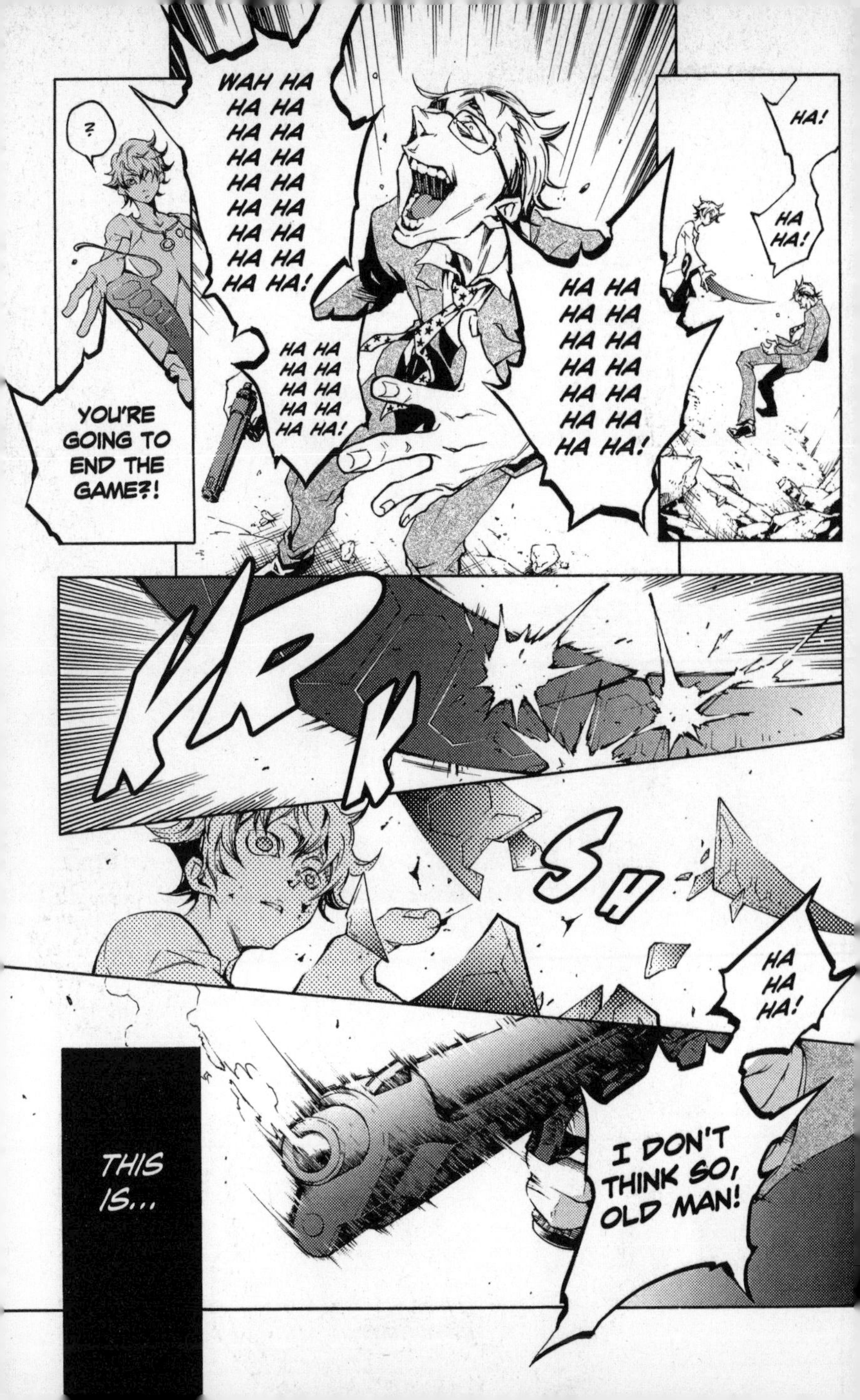
HA!
HA HA!
WAH HA HA HA HA HA HA HA HA HA HA HA HA HA HA HA HA HA!
HA HA HA HA HA HA HA HA HA HA HA HA HA HA!
HA HA HA HA HA HA HA HA HA HA!
?
YOU'RE GOING TO END THE GAME?!
KRK
SH
HA HA HA!
I DON'T THINK SO, OLD MAN!
THIS IS...

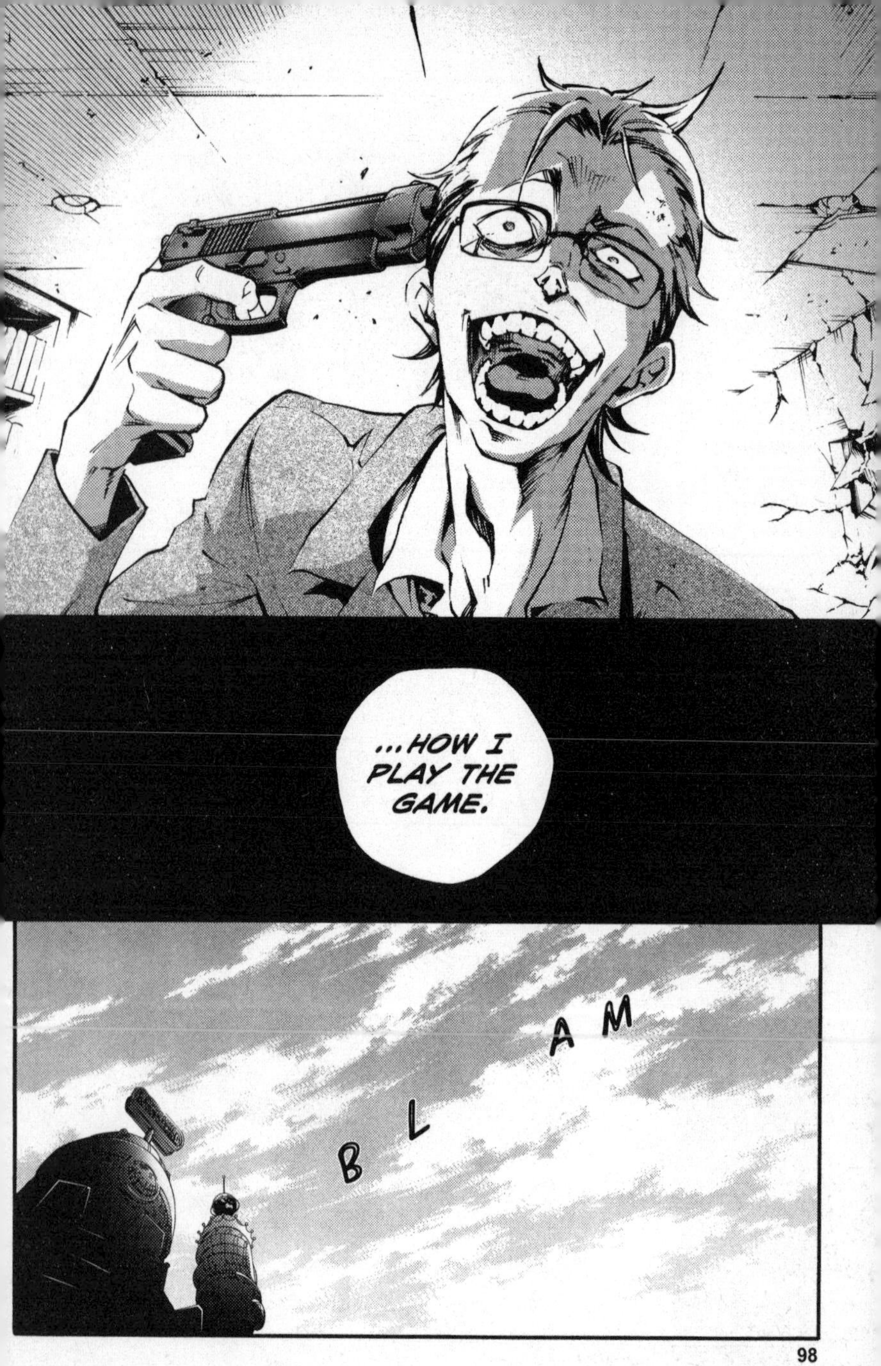
...HOW I PLAY THE GAME.
BLAM

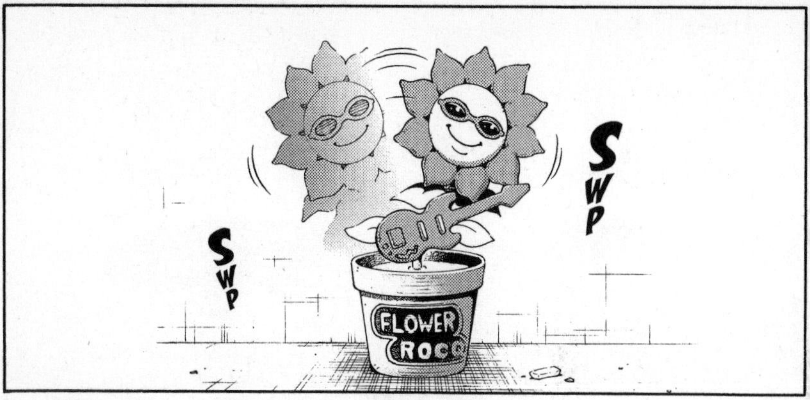
SWP
SWP
FLOWER
ROC

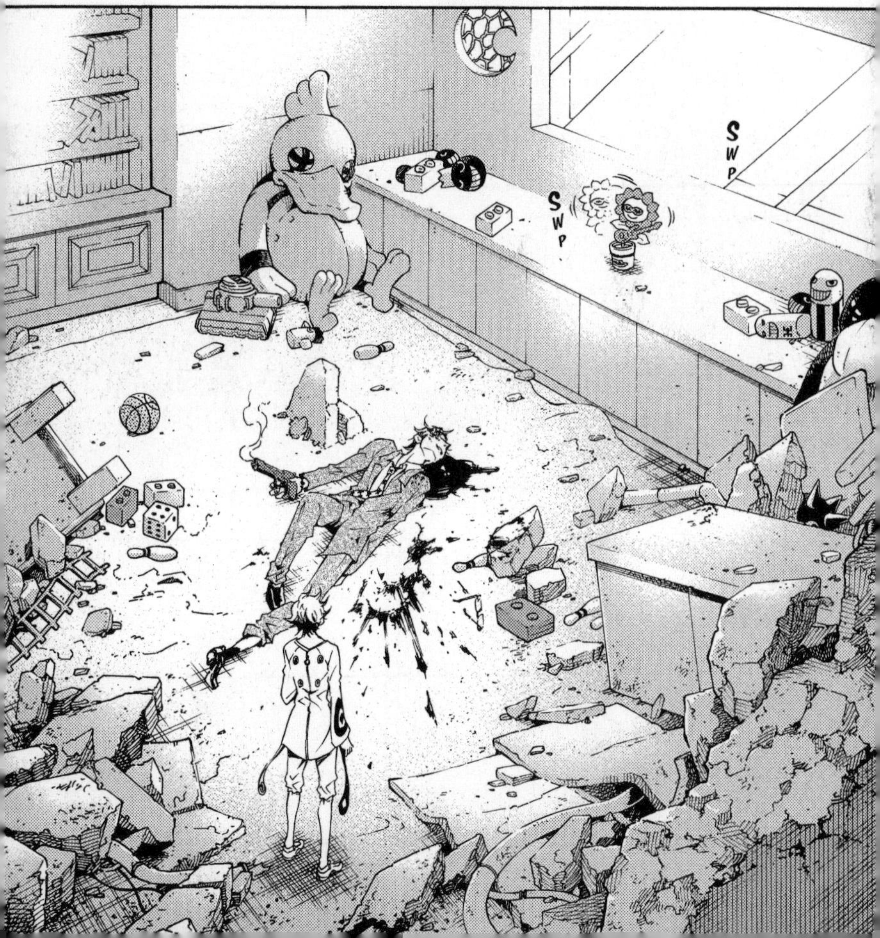
SWP
SWP

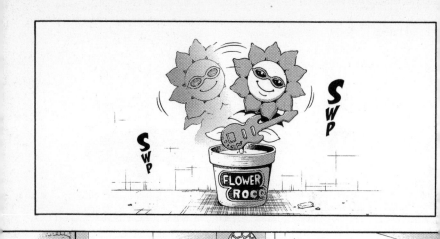

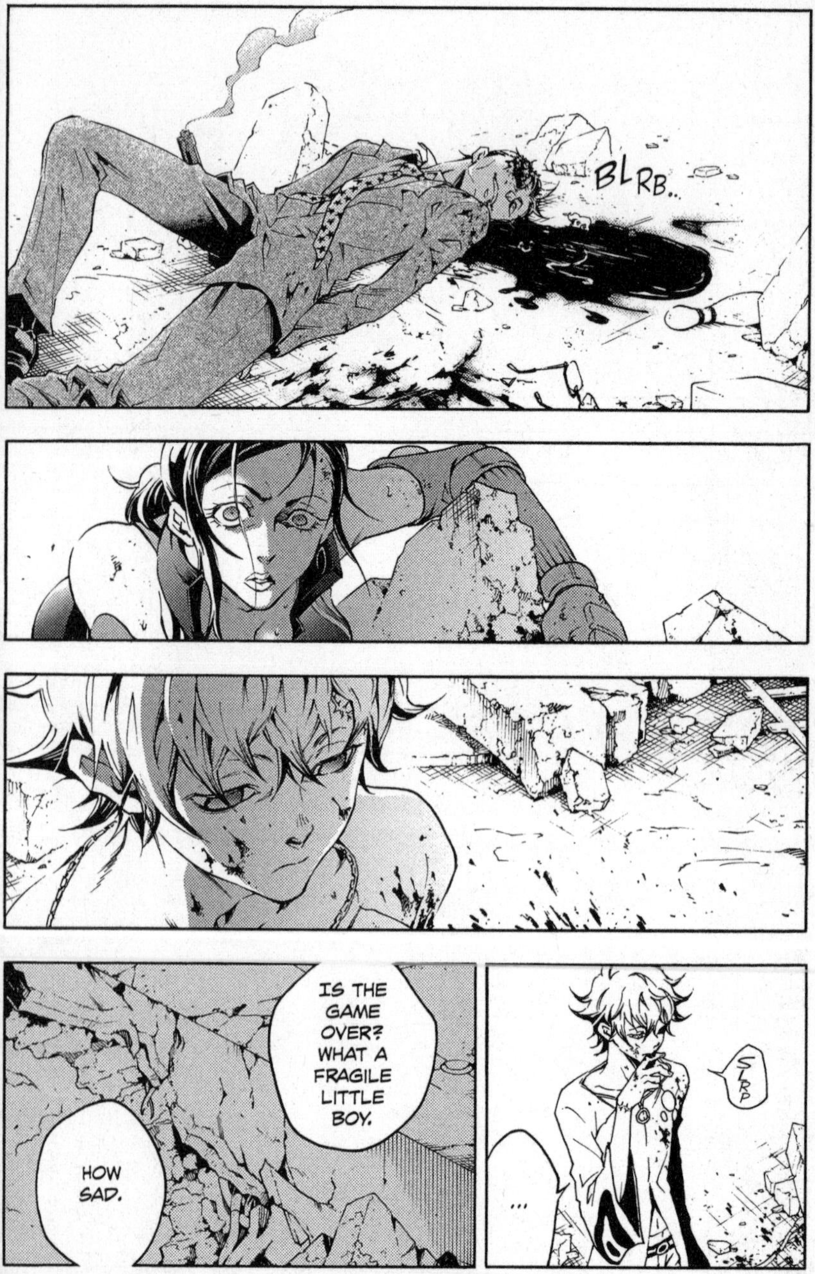
BLRB...
SLRP
...
IS THE GAME OVER? WHAT A FRAGILE LITTLE BOY.
HOW SAD.

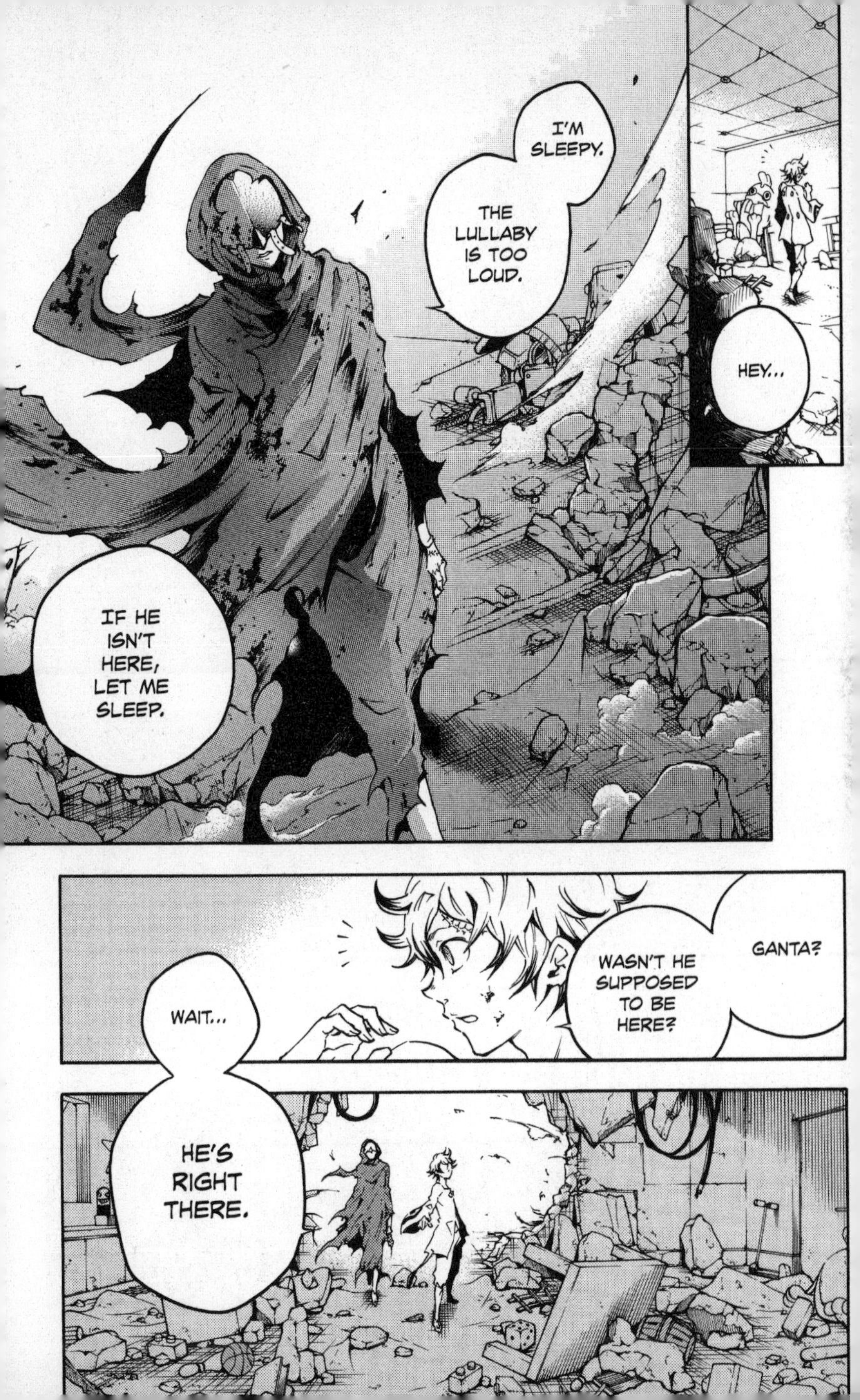
HEY...
I'M SLEEPY.
THE LULLABY IS TOO LOUD.
IF HE ISN'T HERE, LET ME SLEEP.
GANTA?
WASN'T HE SUPPOSED TO BE HERE?
WAIT...
HE'S RIGHT THERE.

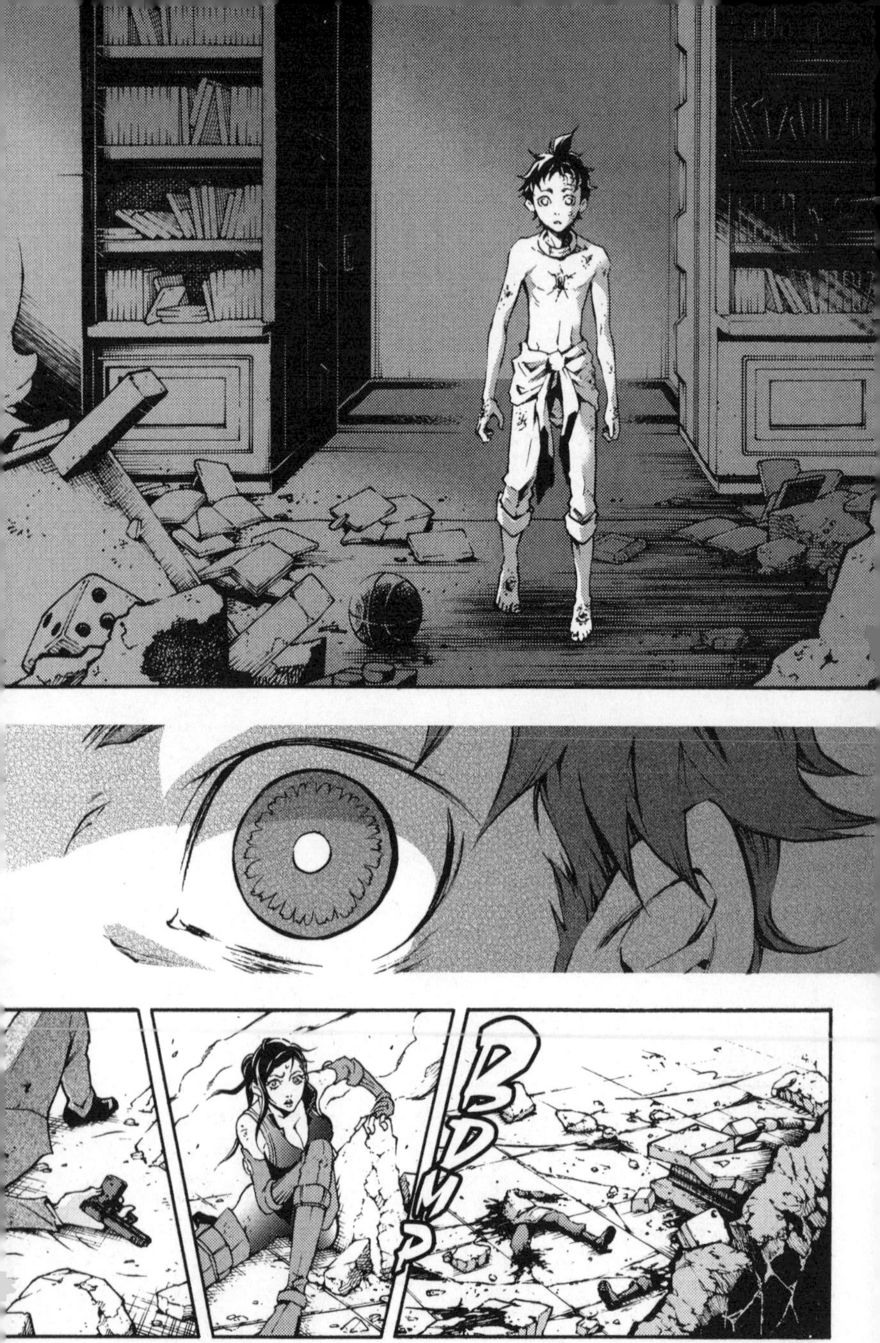
BDMP

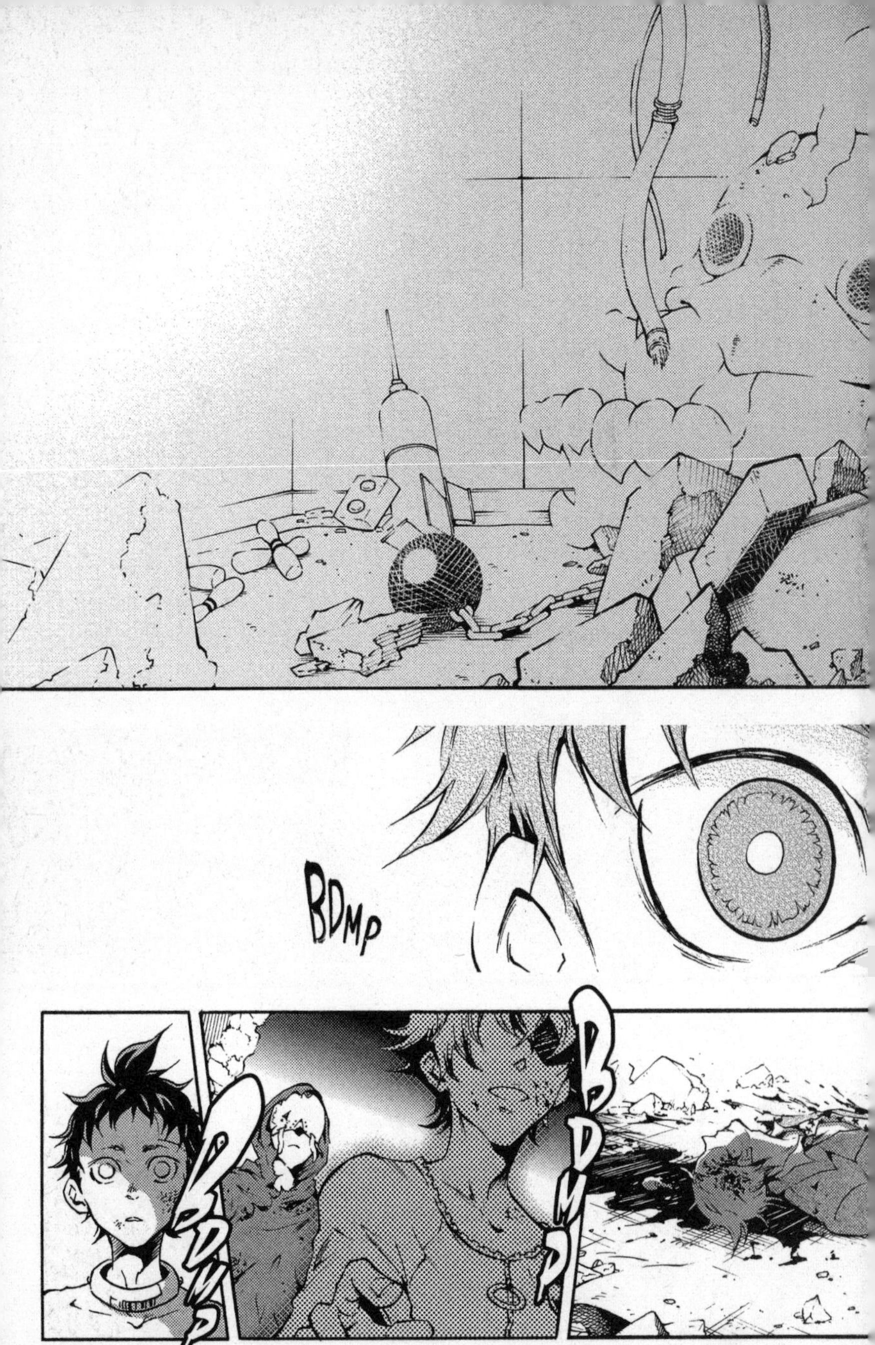
BDMP
BDMP
BDMP

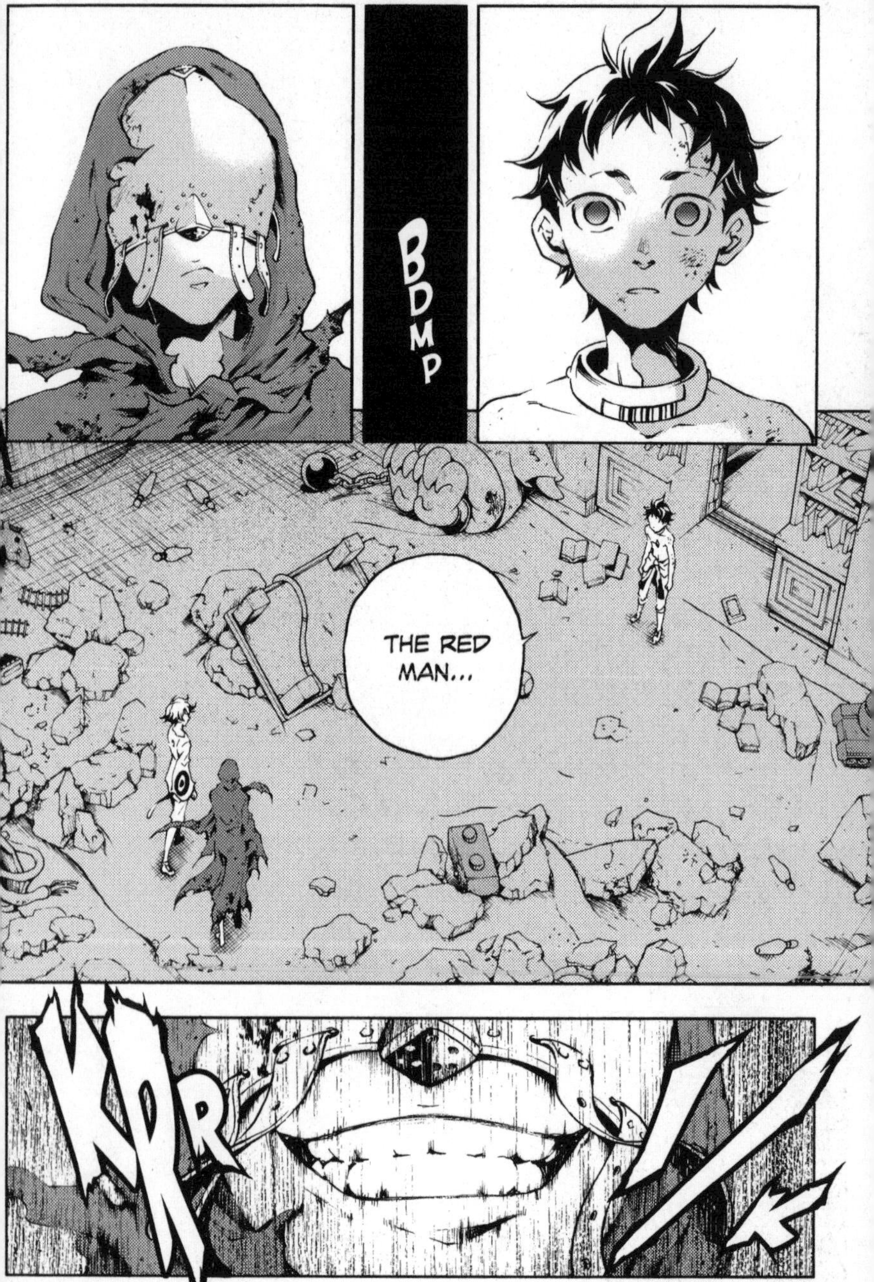
BDMP
THE RED MAN...

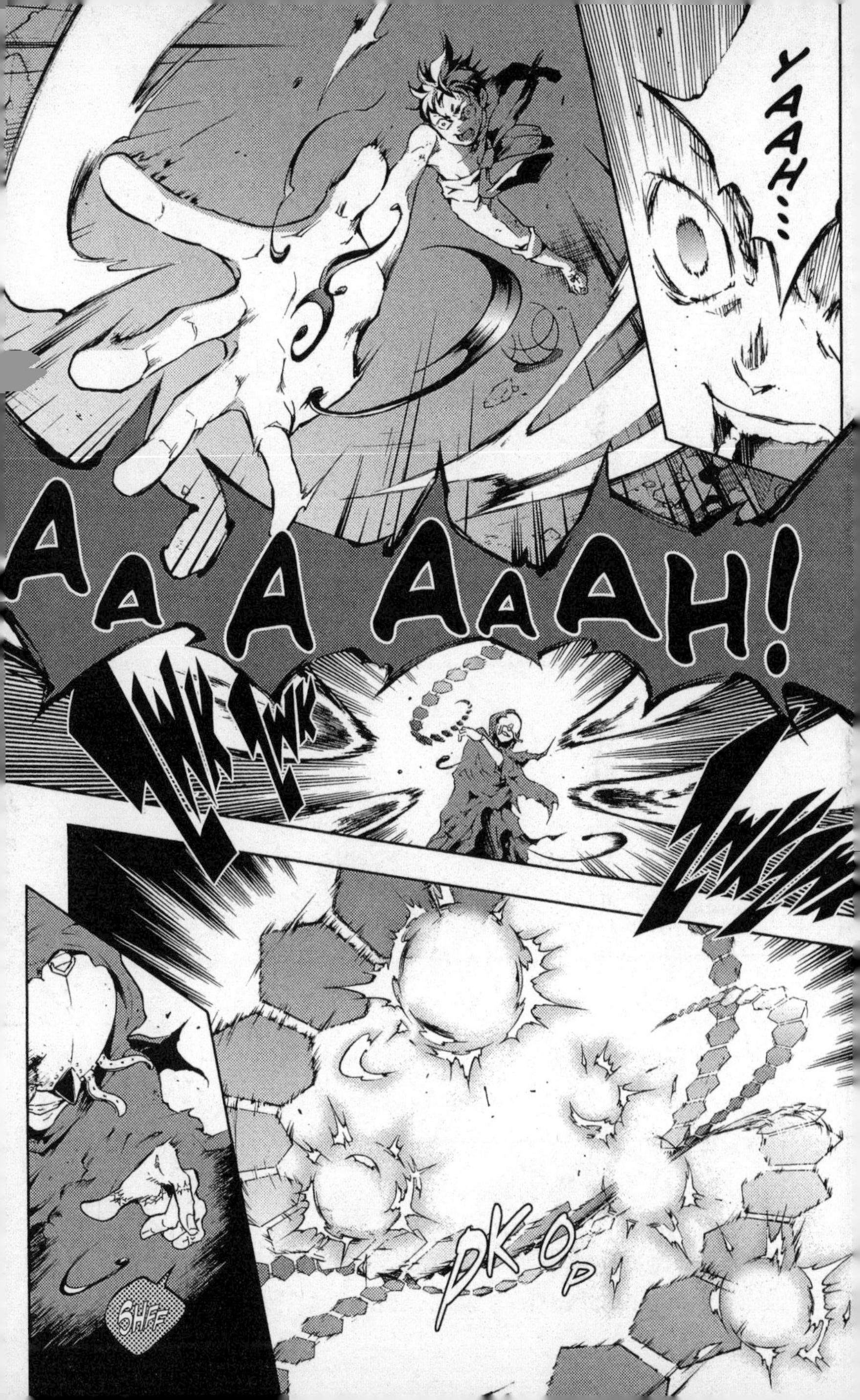
YAAAH...
AAAAAAH!
WHK WHK
PKOP
SHFF

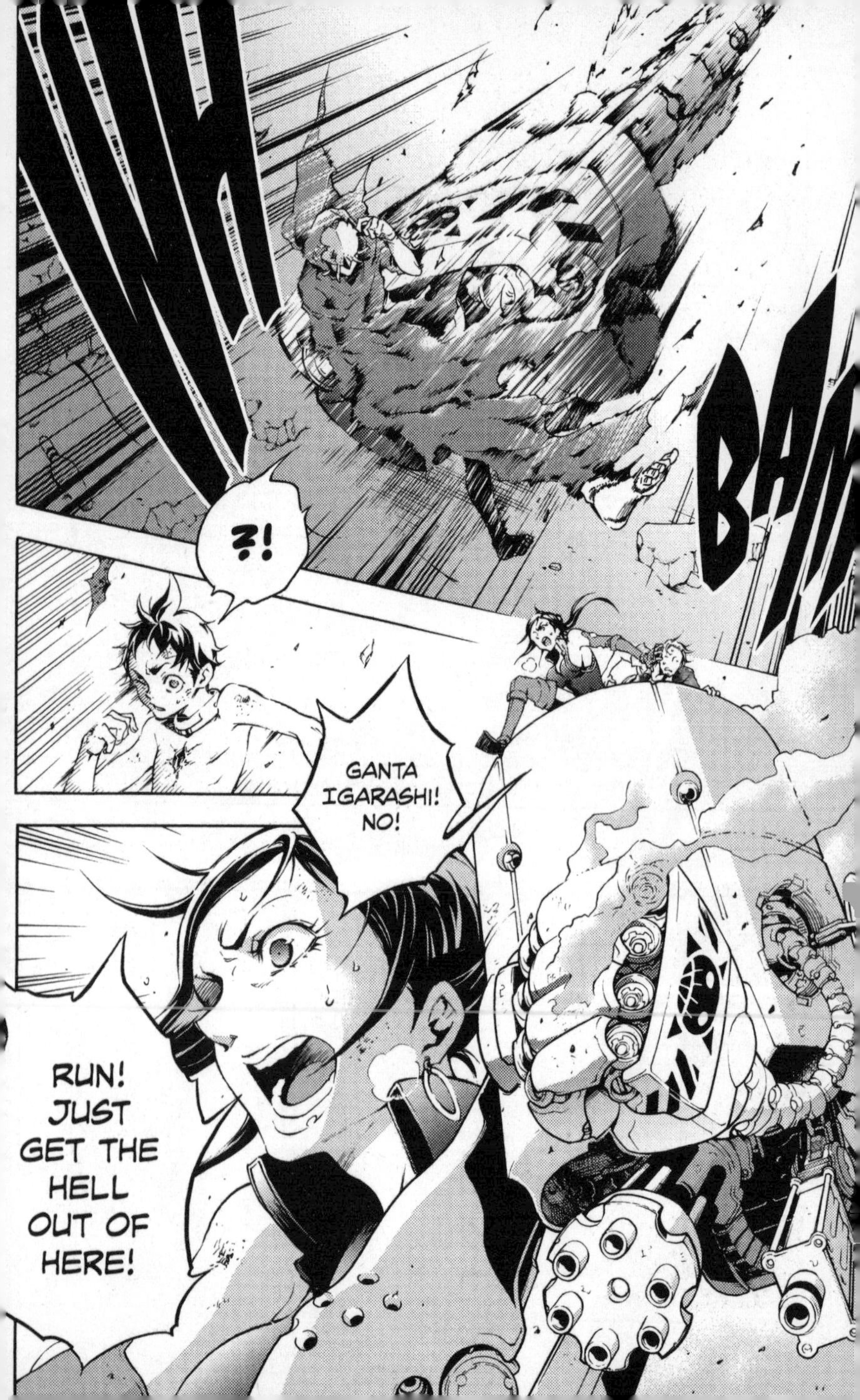
?!
GANTA IGARASHI! NO!
RUN! JUST GET THE HELL OUT OF HERE!

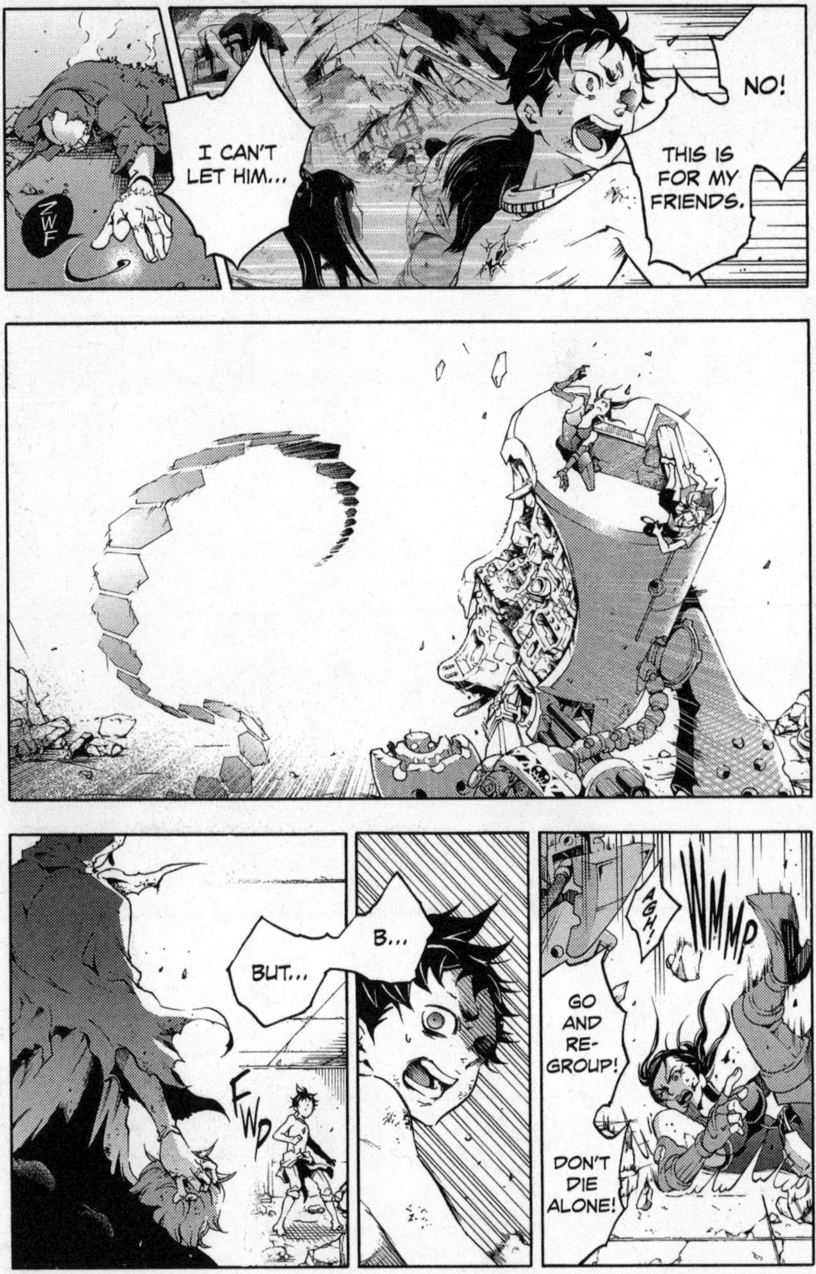
NO!
THIS IS FOR MY FRIENDS.
I CAN'T LET HIM...
ZWF
AGH!
WMMP
GO AND RE-GROUP!
DON'T DIE ALONE!
B...
BUT...
FWP

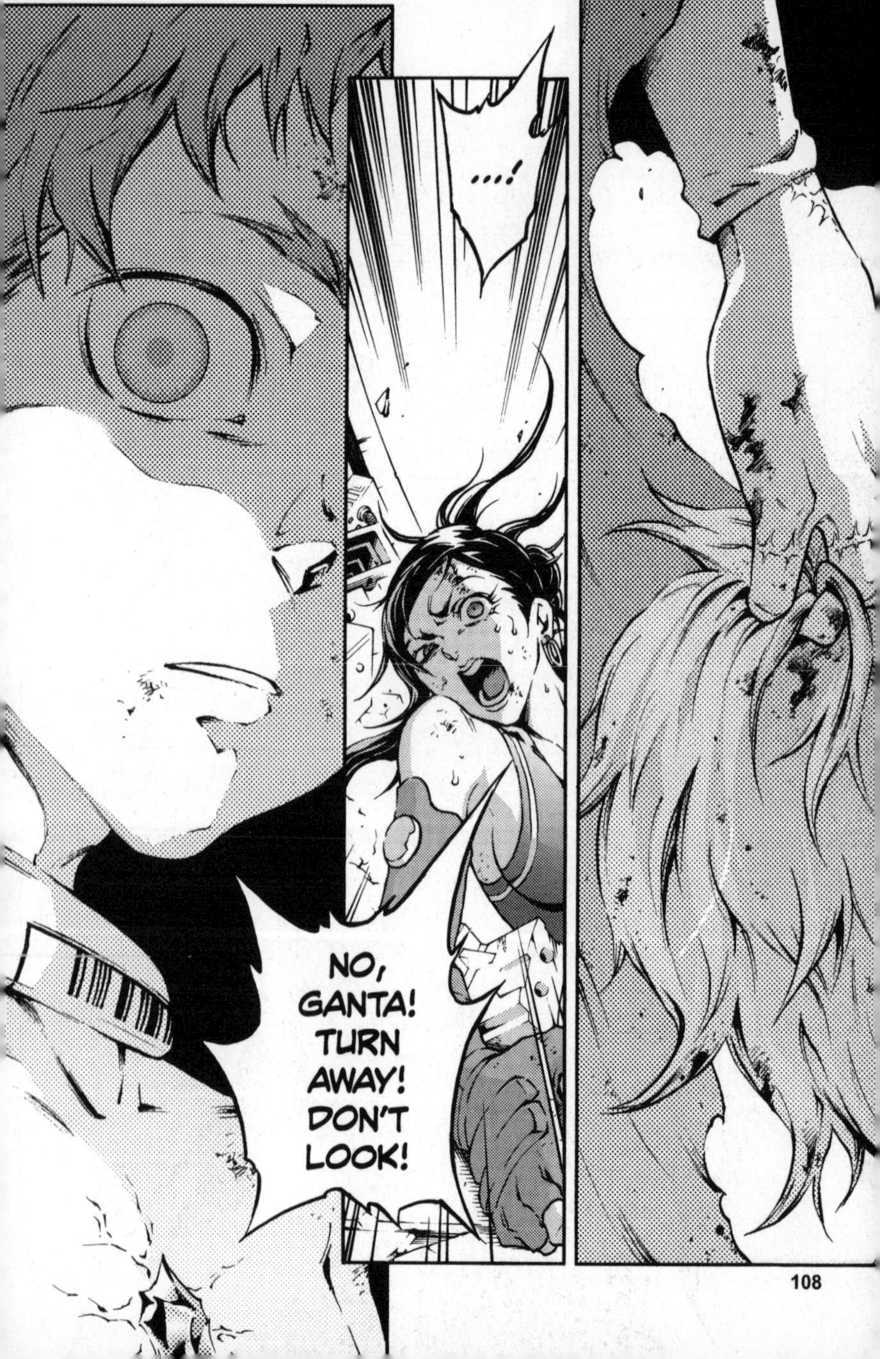
...!
NO, GANTA! TURN AWAY! DON'T LOOK!

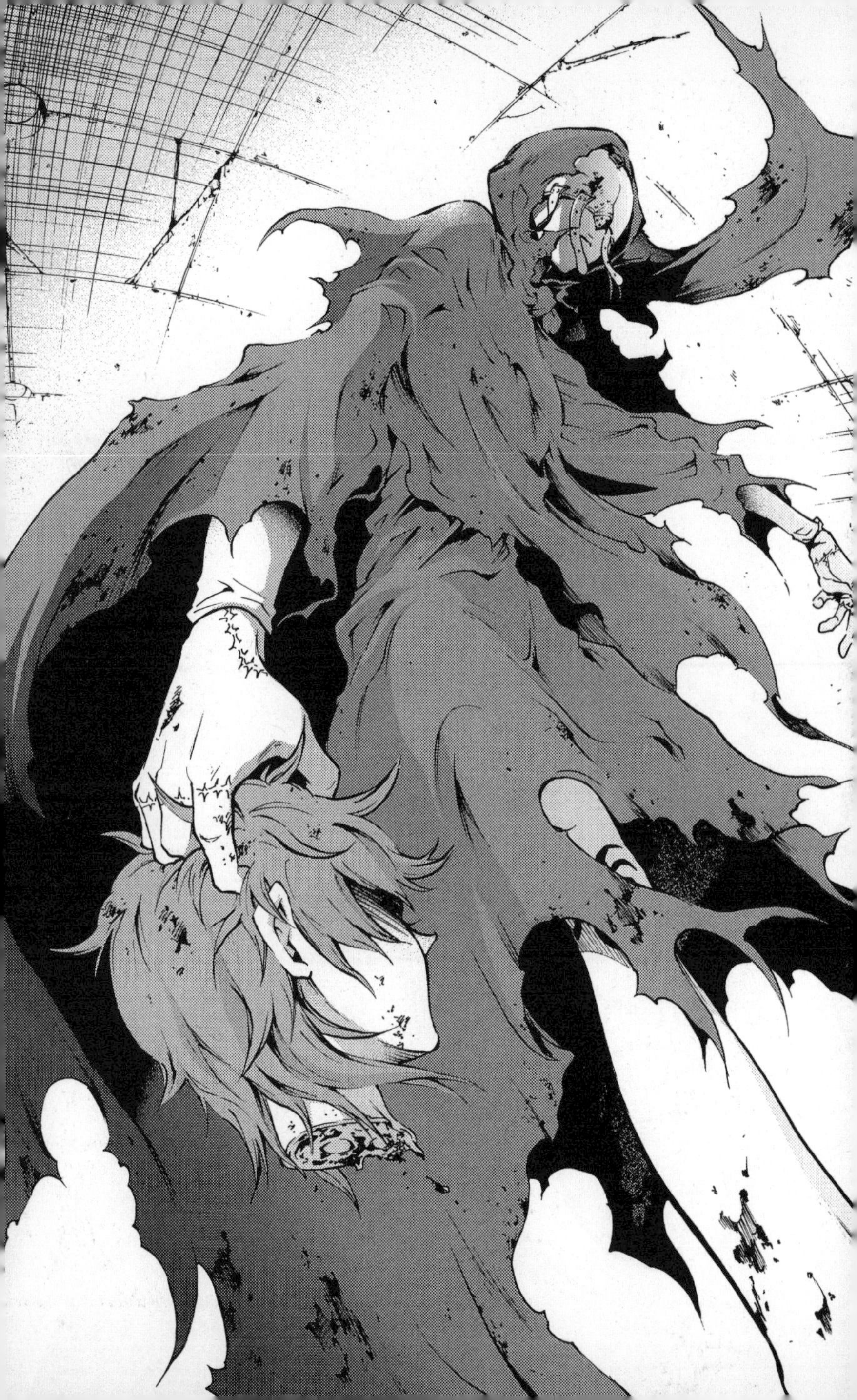

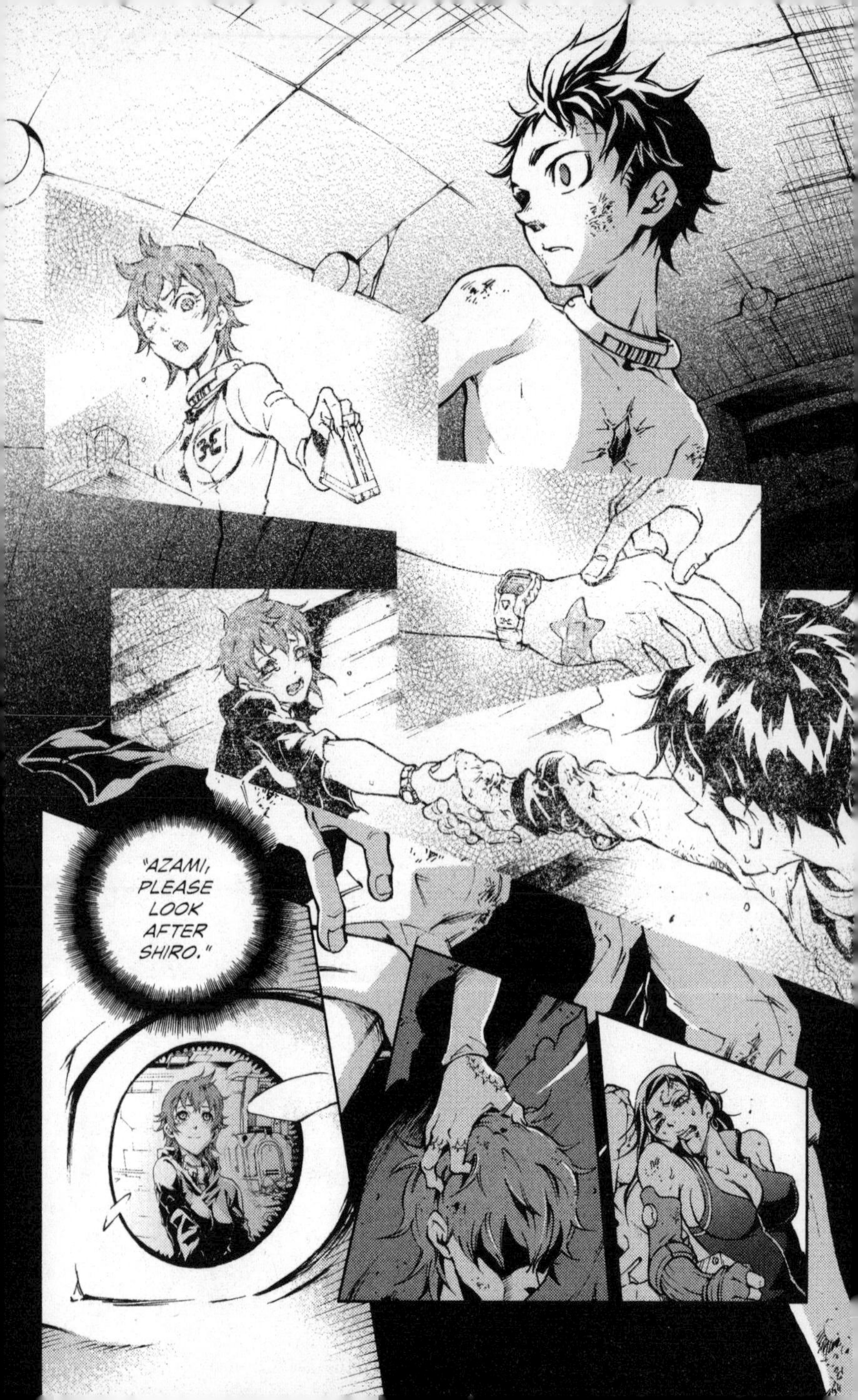
"AZAMI, PLEASE LOOK AFTER SHIRO."

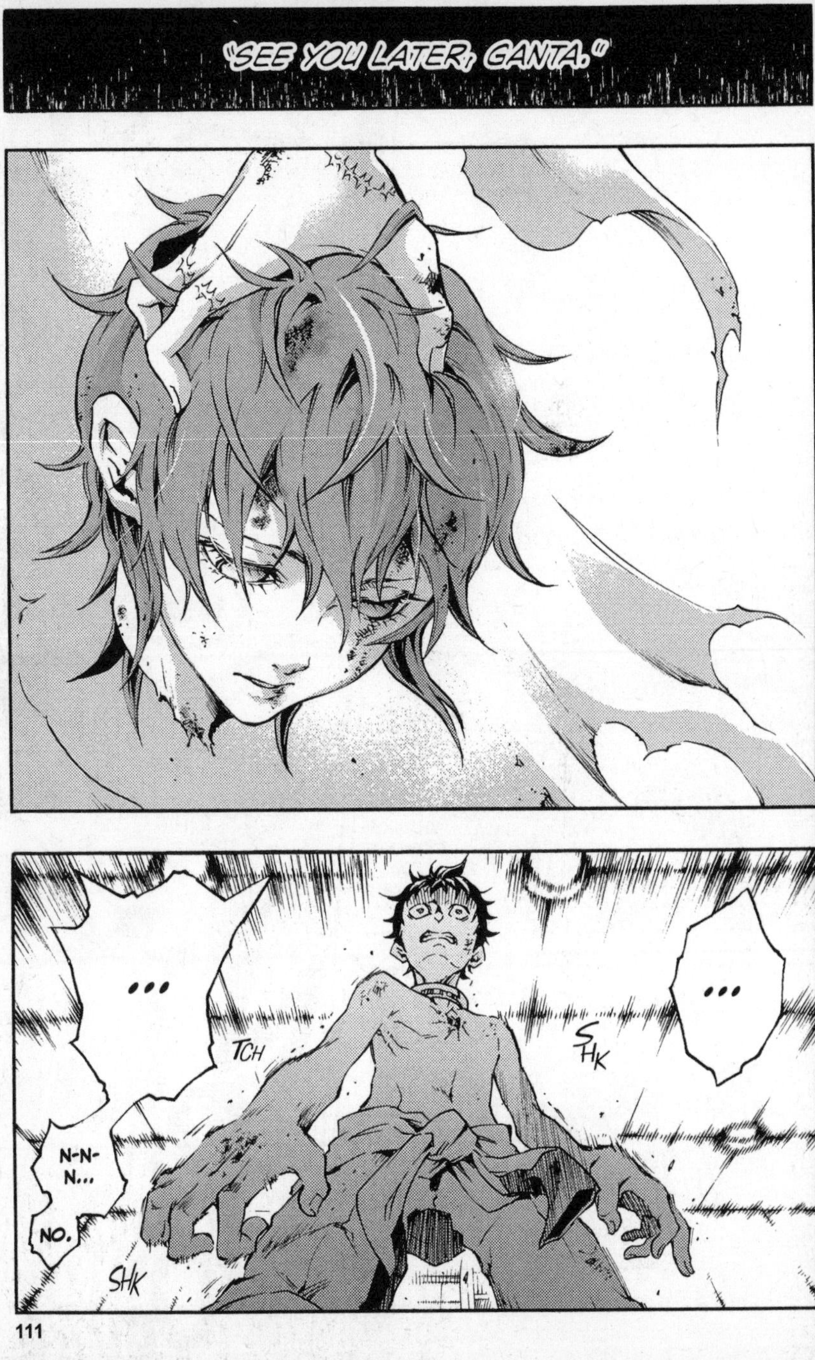
"SEE YOU LATER, GANTA."
...
SHK
...
TCH
N-N-N...
NO.
SHK

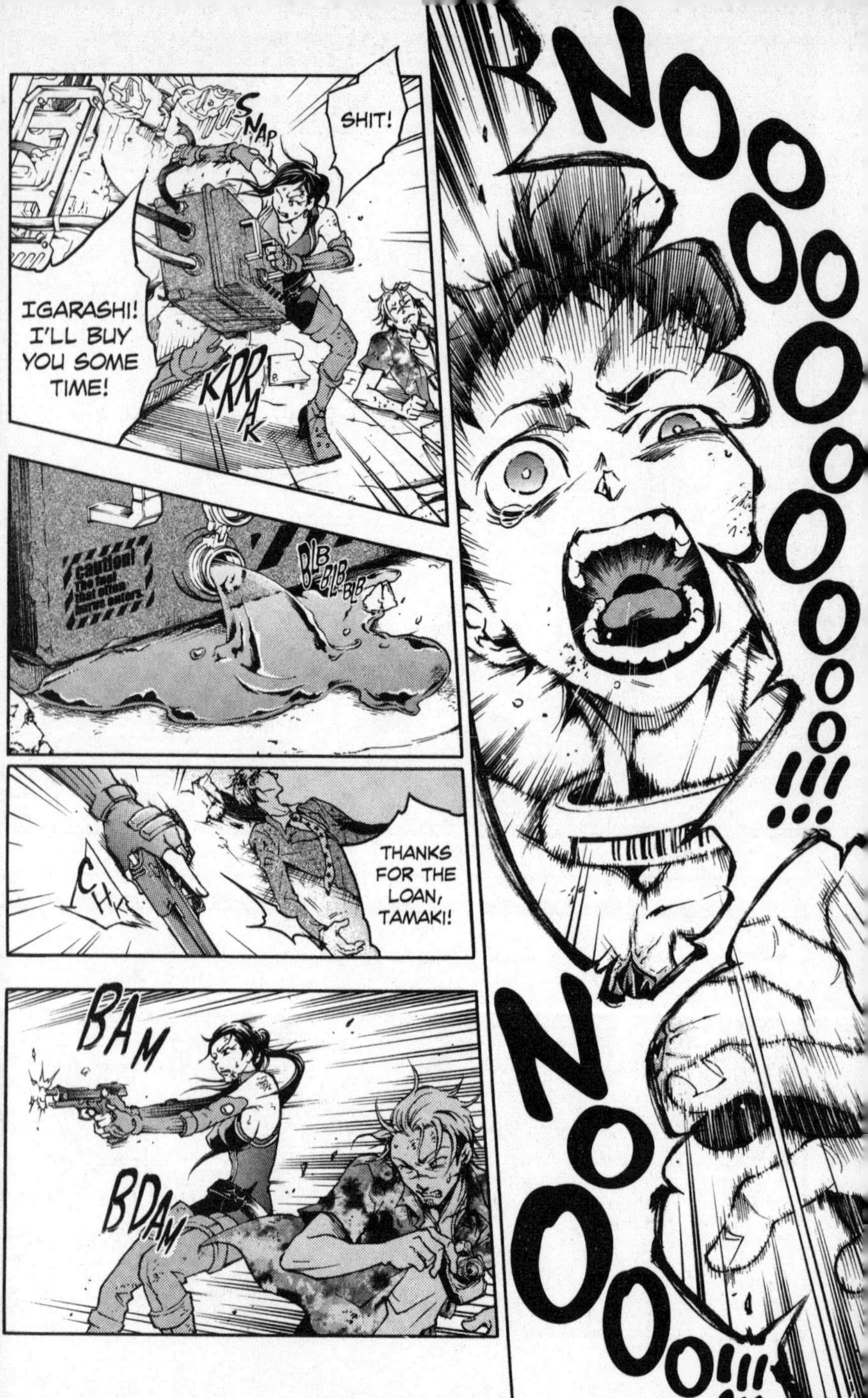
NOOOOOOOOOOO!!!
NOOOOOO!!!
SHIT!
SNAP
IGARASHI! I'LL BUY YOU SOME TIME!
KRRAK
Caution!
BLB BLB BLB
THANKS FOR THE LOAN, TAMAKI!
CHK
BAM
BDAM

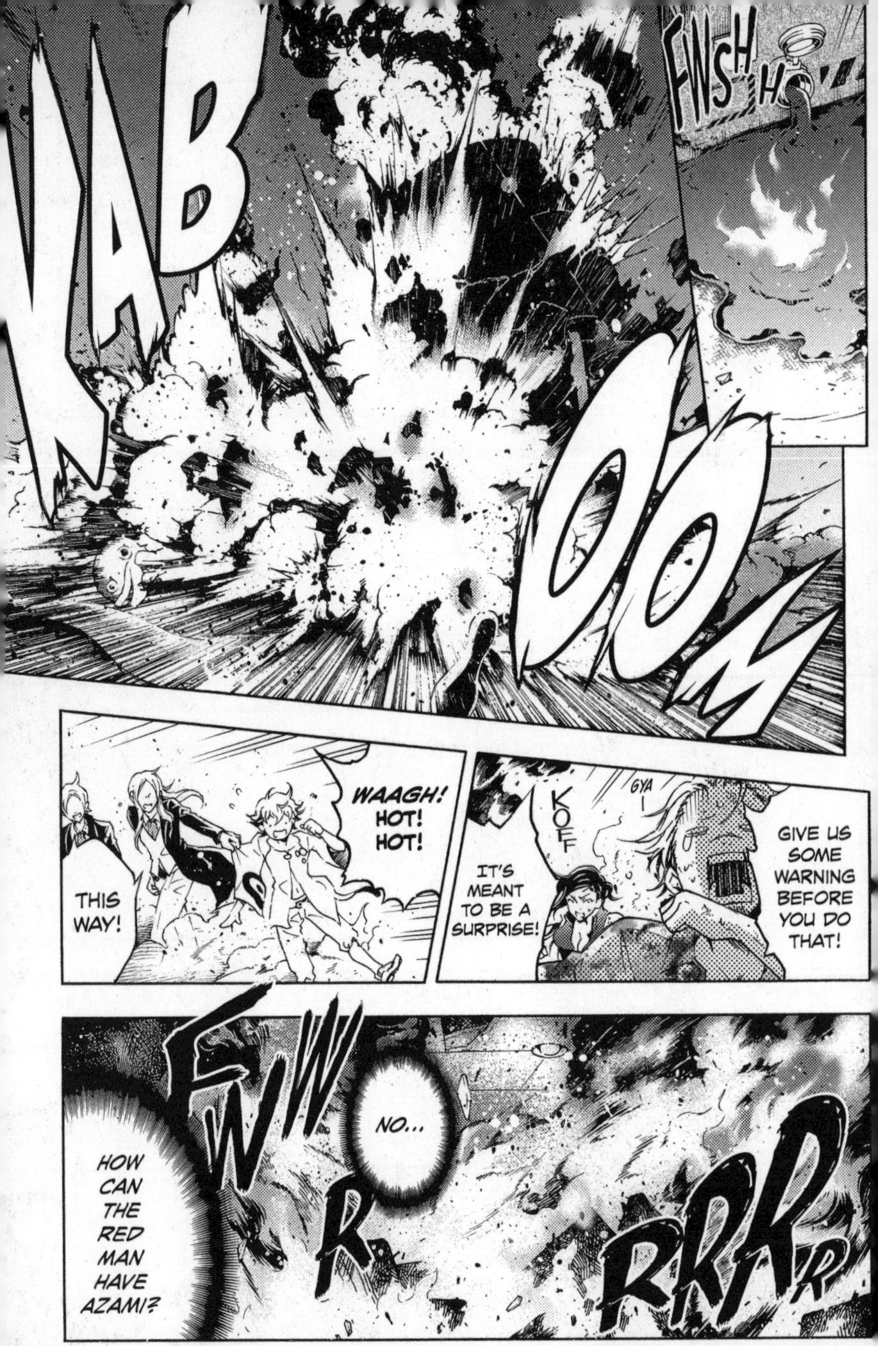
FWSH HO
KABOOM
GYA
GIVE US SOME WARNING BEFORE YOU DO THAT!
KOFF
IT'S MEANT TO BE A SURPRISE!
WAAGH! HOT! HOT!
THIS WAY!
FWWRRRRR
NO...
HOW CAN THE RED MAN HAVE AZAMI?

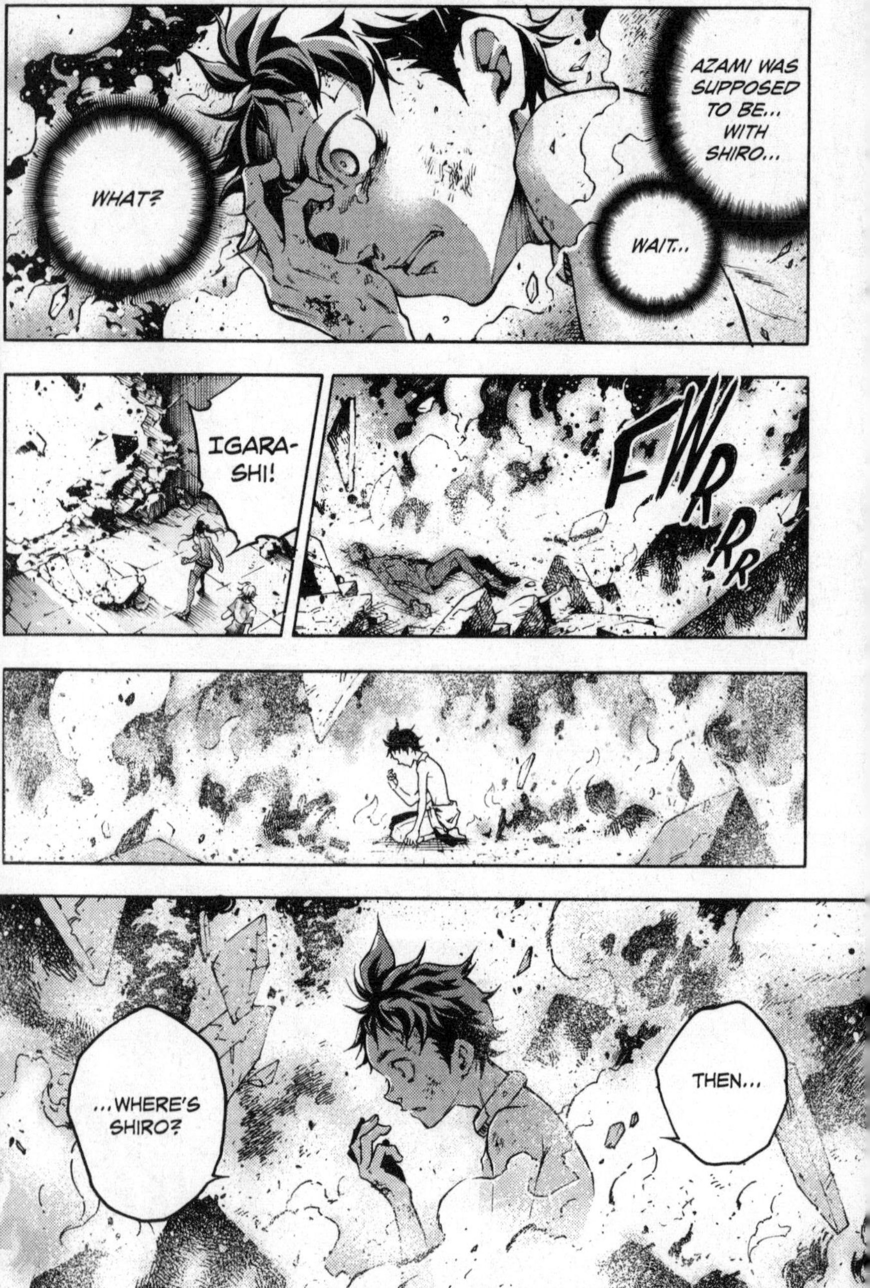
AZAMI WAS SUPPOSED TO BE... WITH SHIRO...
WAIT...
WHAT?
FWRRRR
IGARA-SHI!
THEN...
...WHERE'S SHIRO?

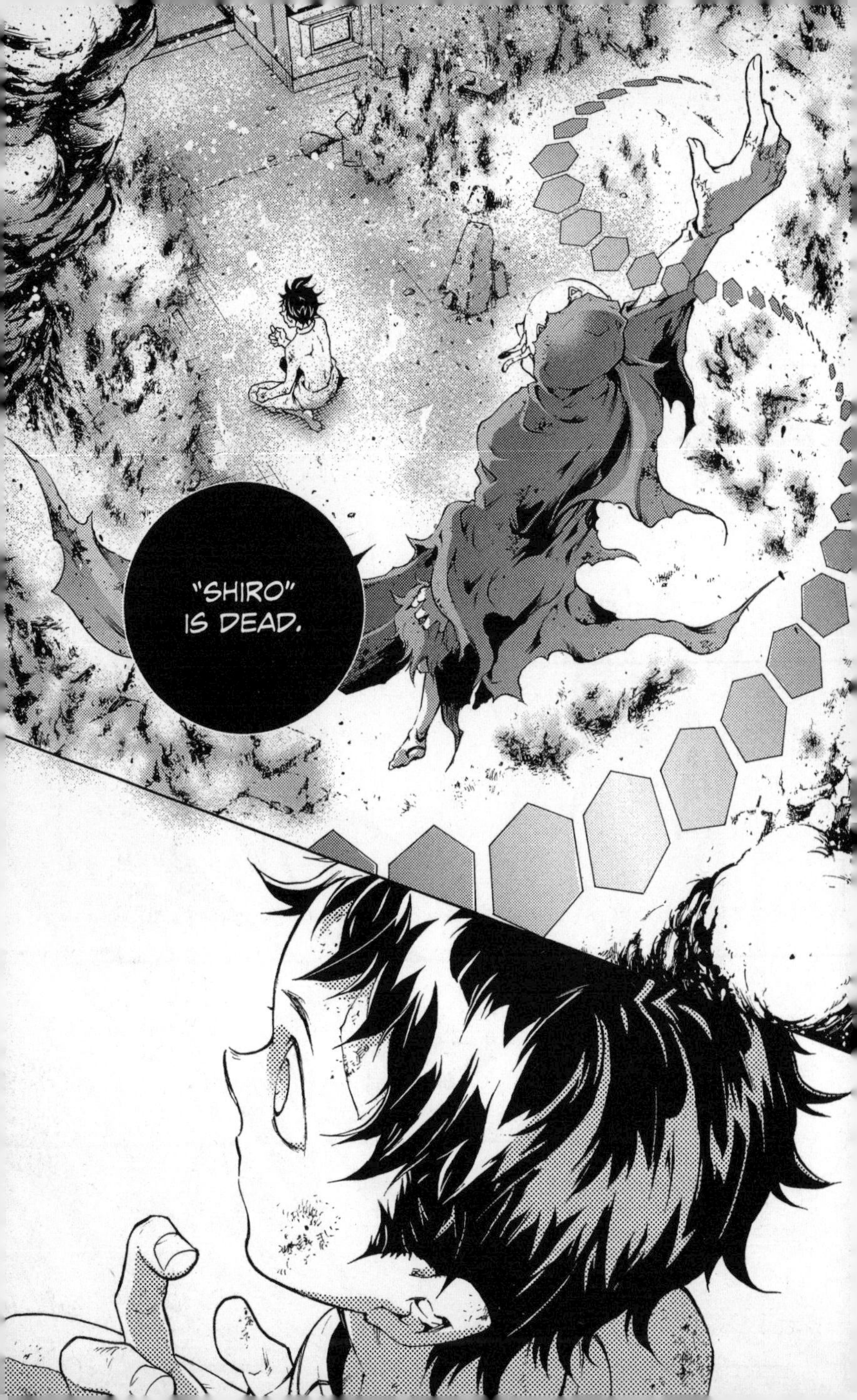
"SHIRO" IS DEAD.

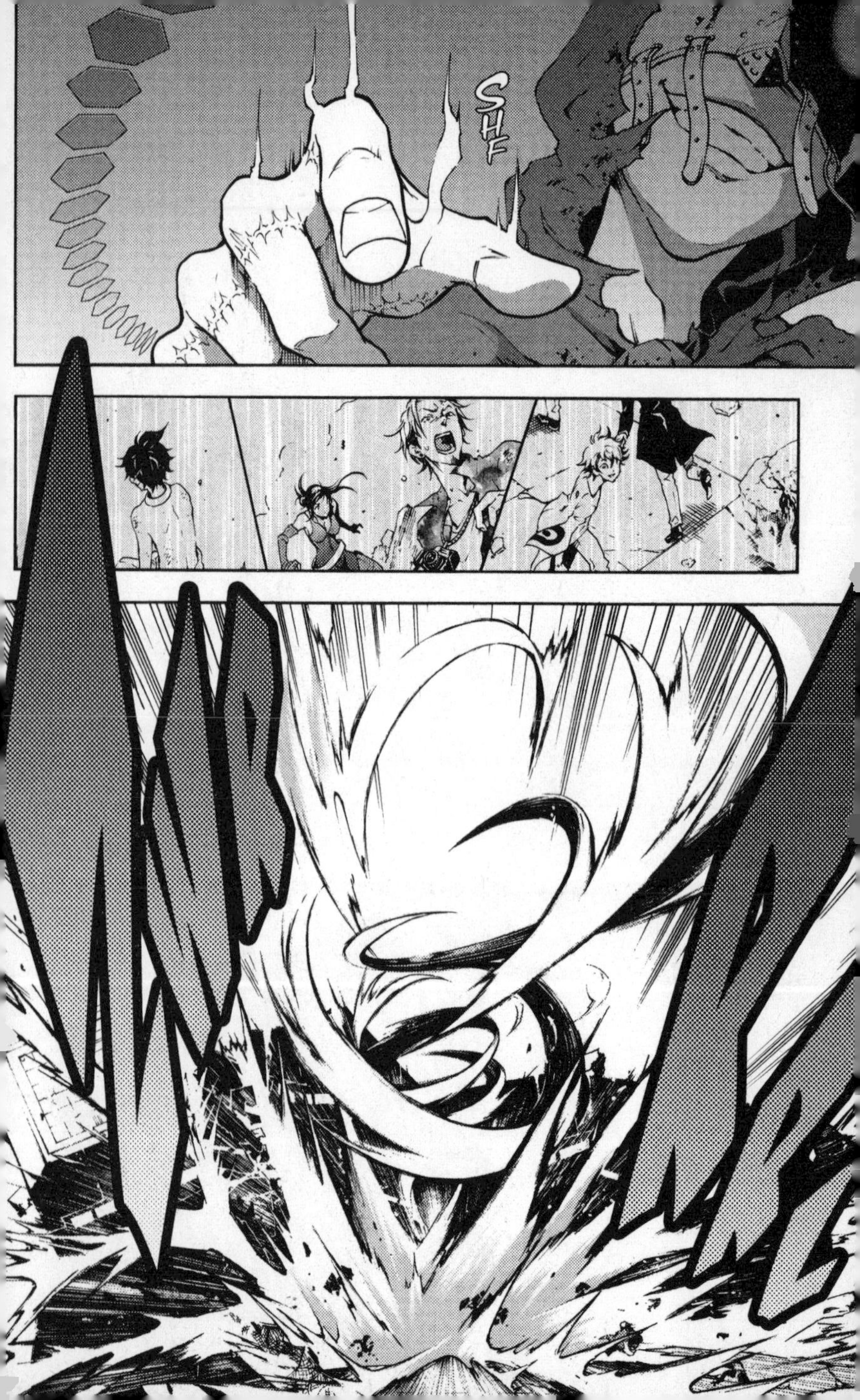
SHF

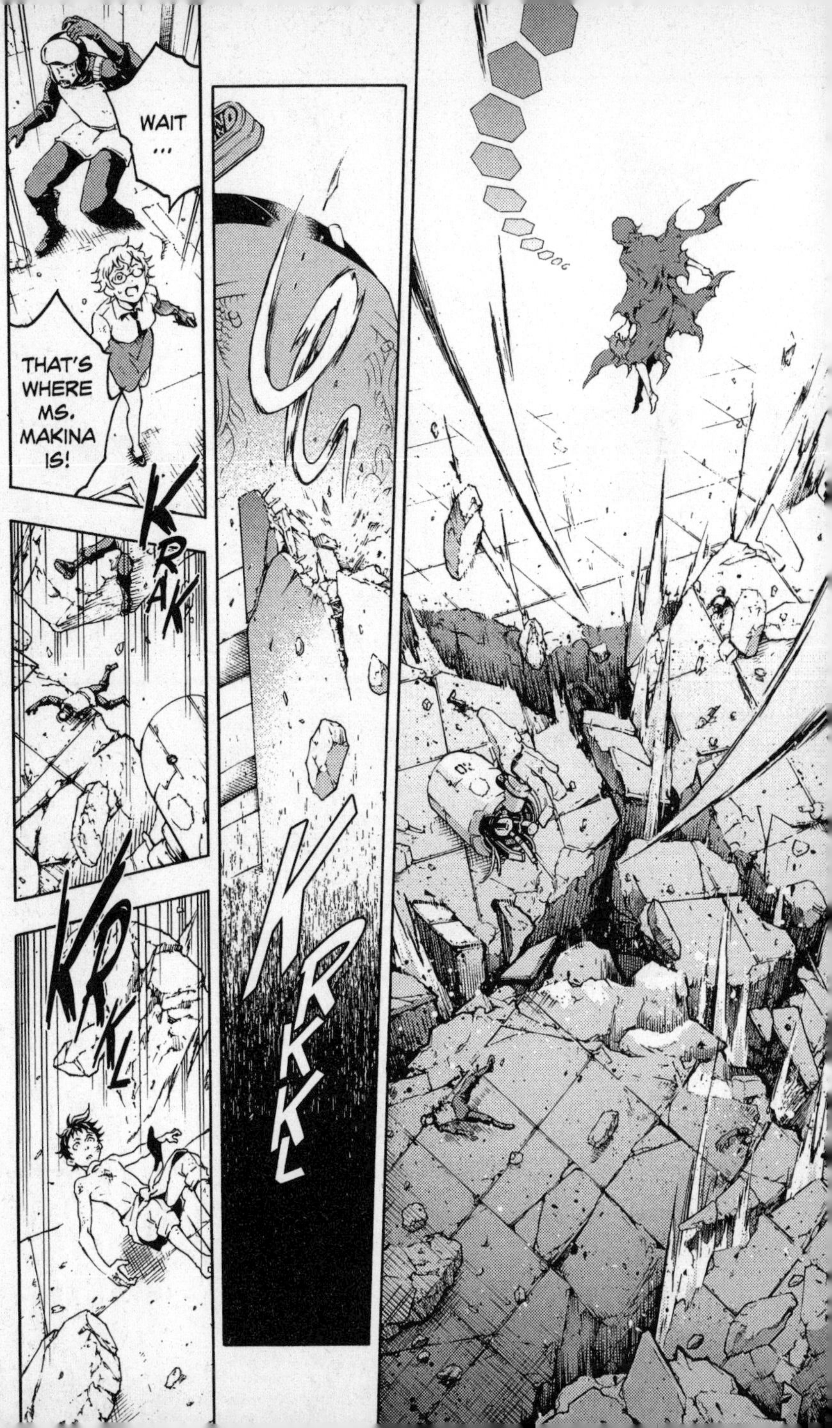
KRKKL
WAIT ...
THAT'S WHERE MS. MAKINA IS!
KRAK
KRKL

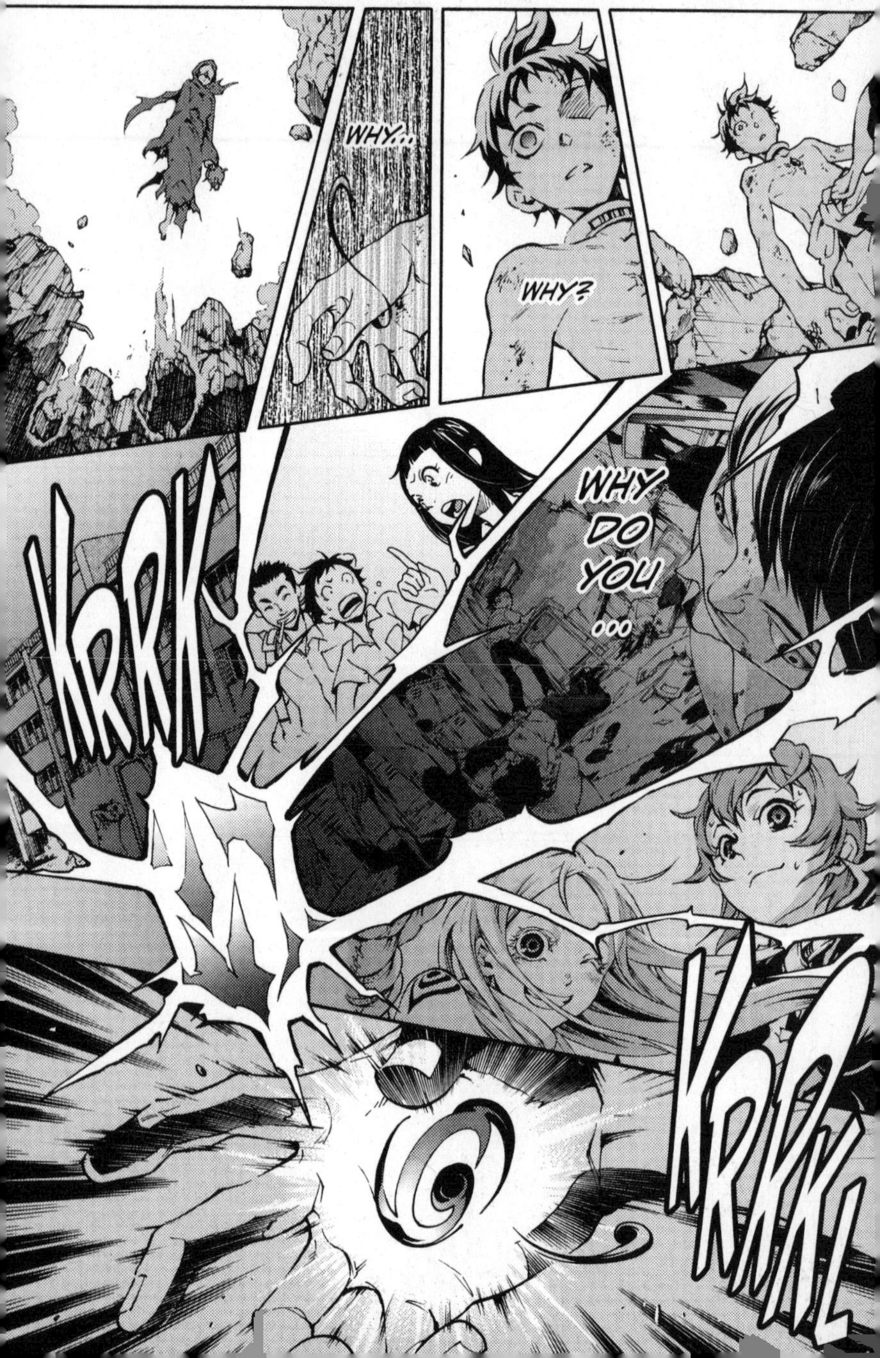
WHY?
WHY...
WHY DO YOU ...
KRRK

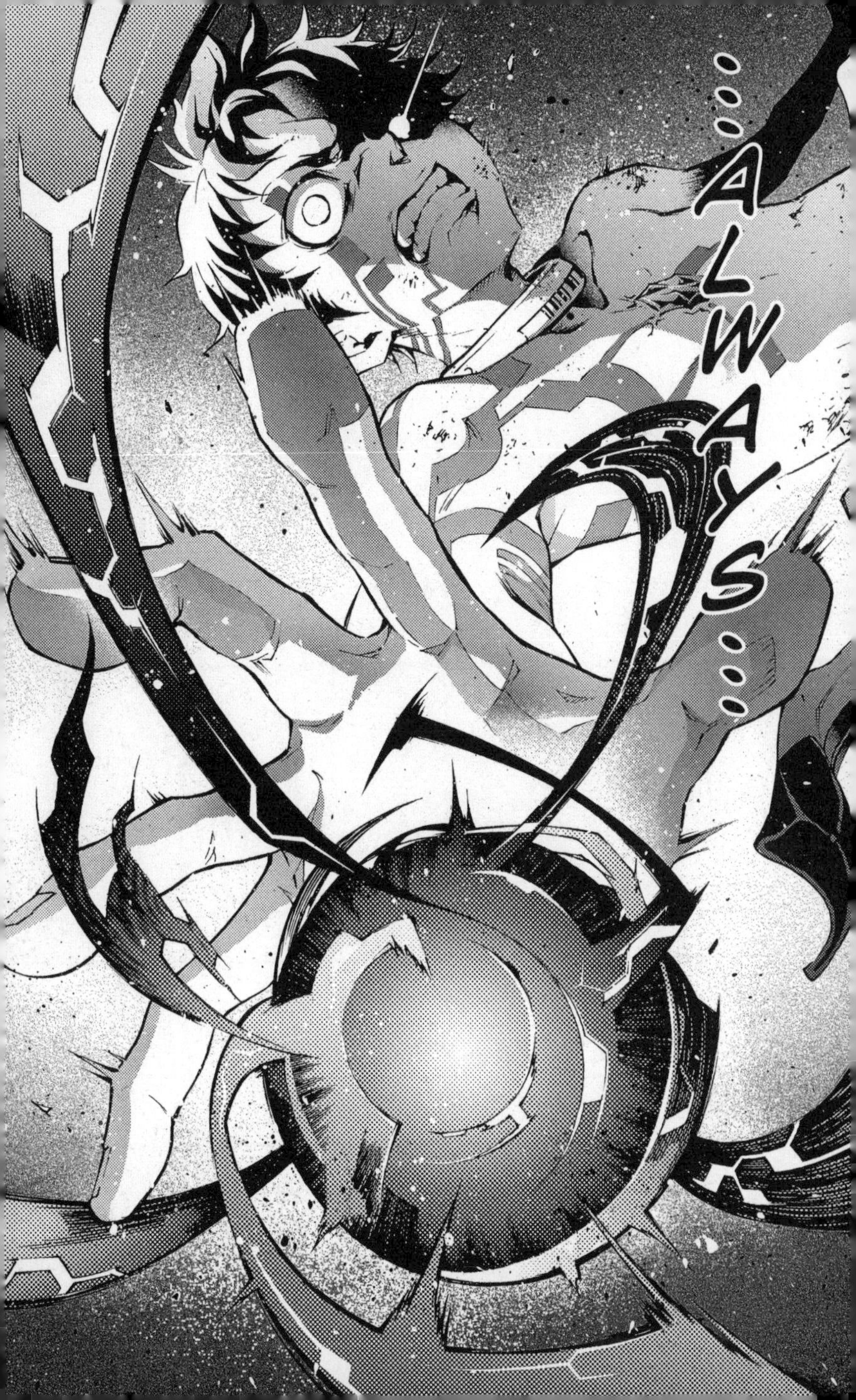
...ALWAYS...

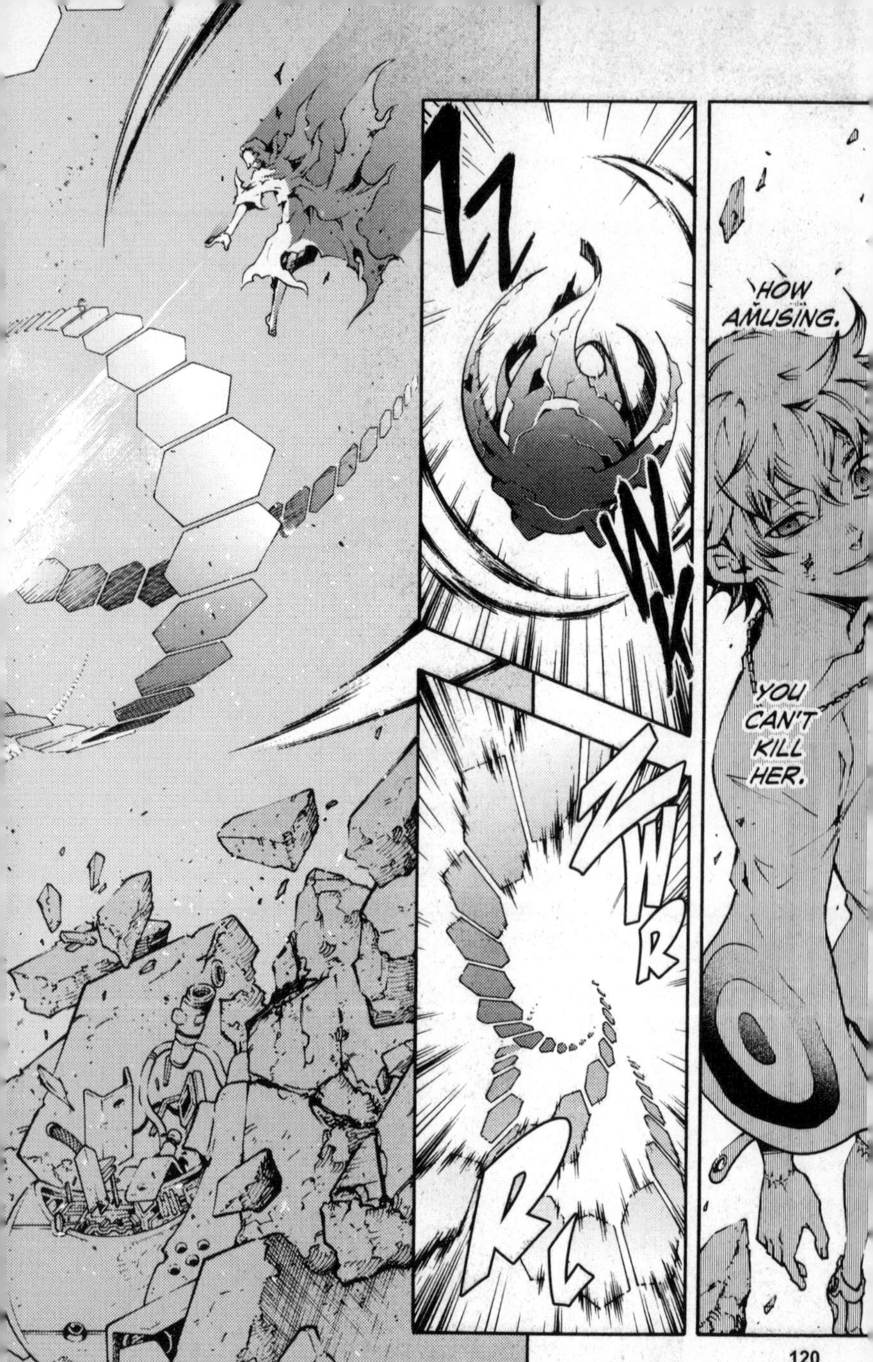
HOW AMUSING.
YOU CAN'T KILL HER.

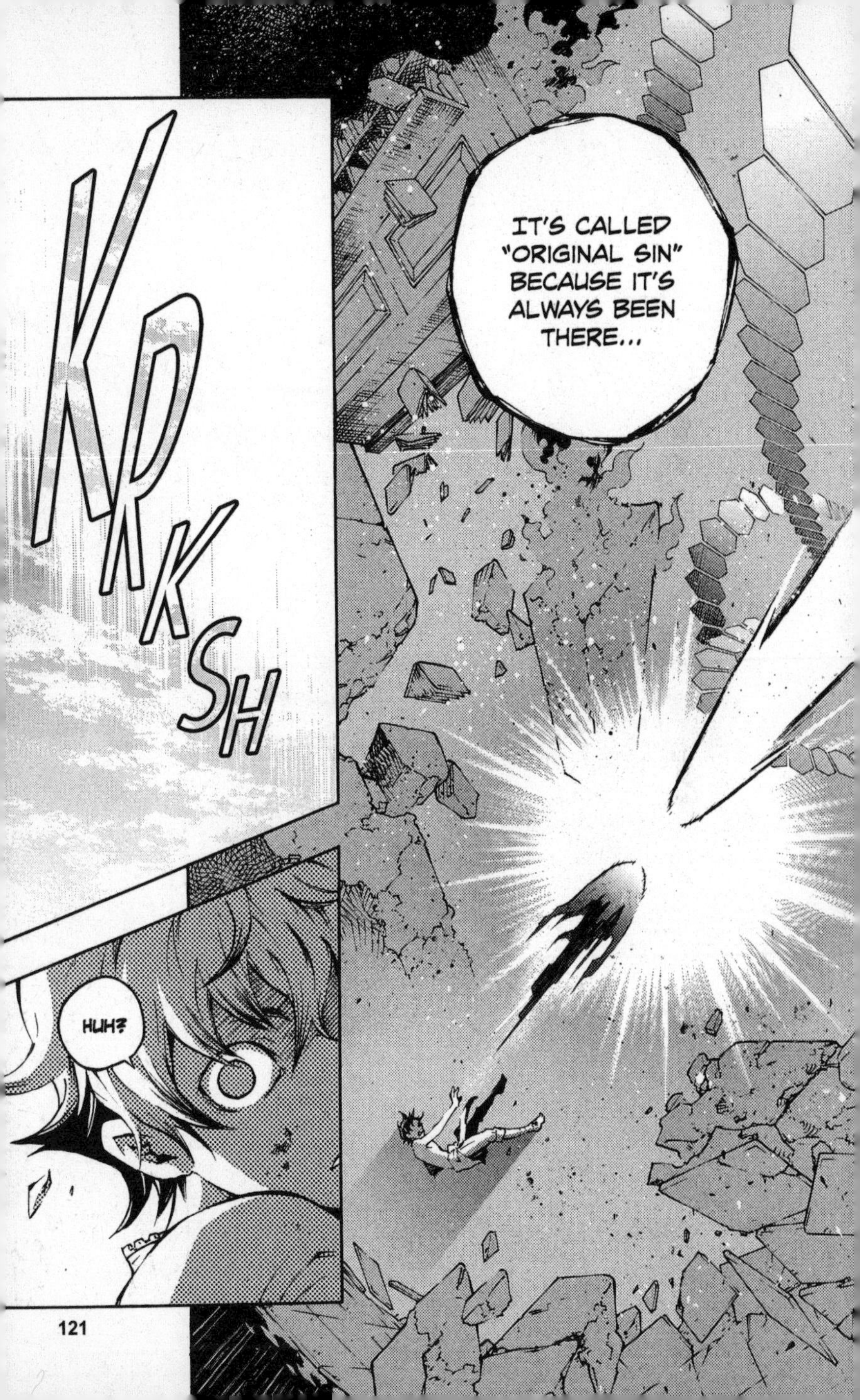
IT'S CALLED "ORIGINAL SIN" BECAUSE IT'S ALWAYS BEEN THERE...
KRKKSH
HUH?

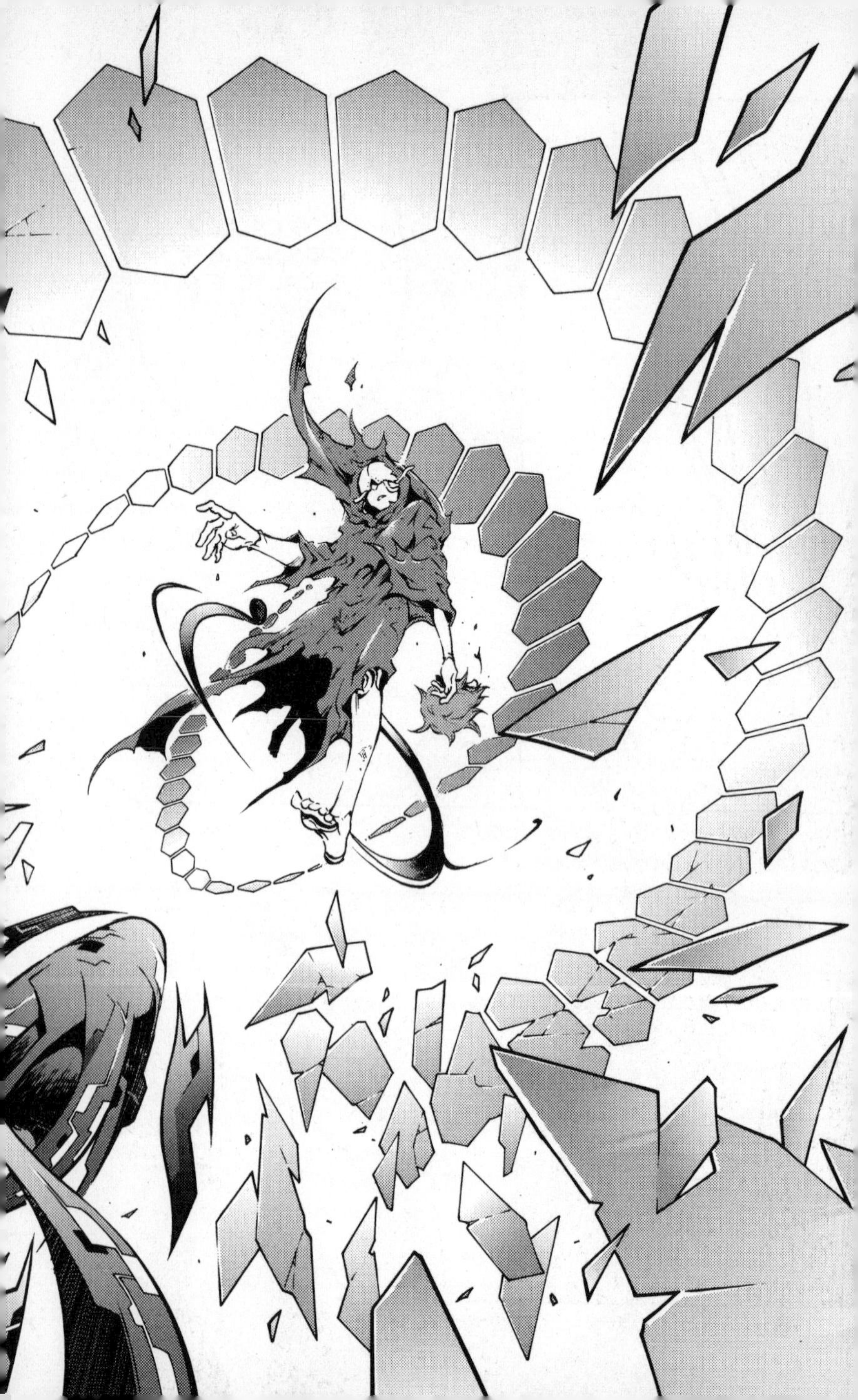

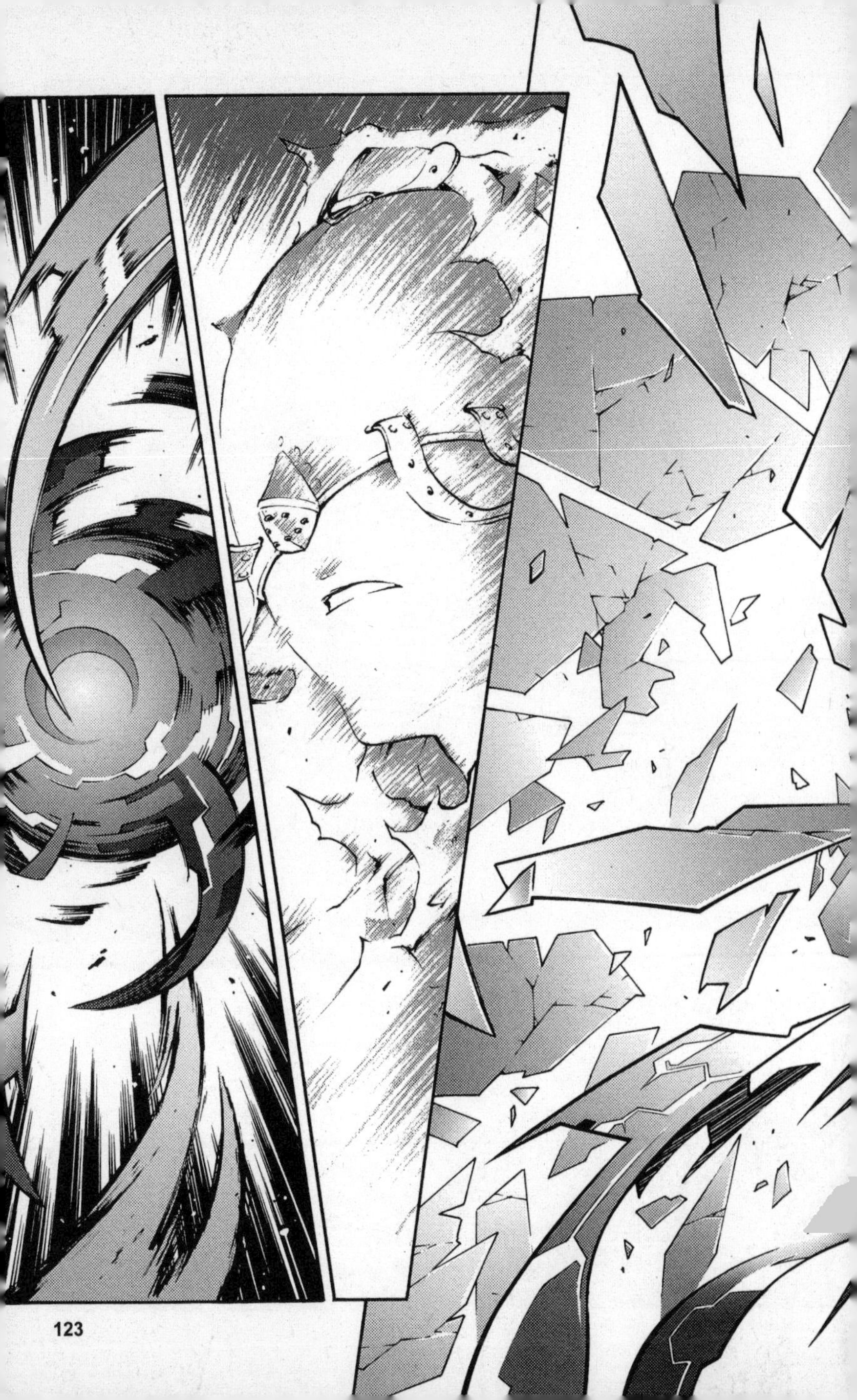

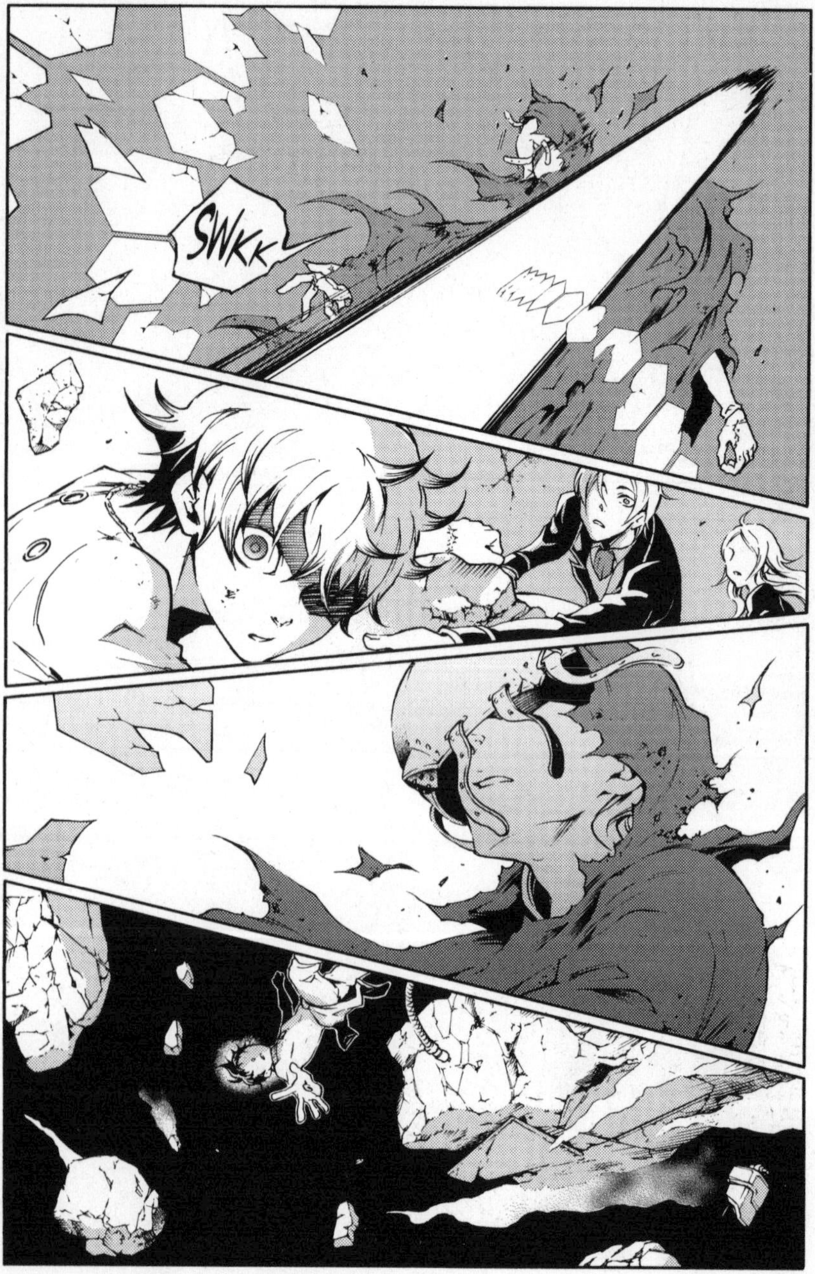
SWKK

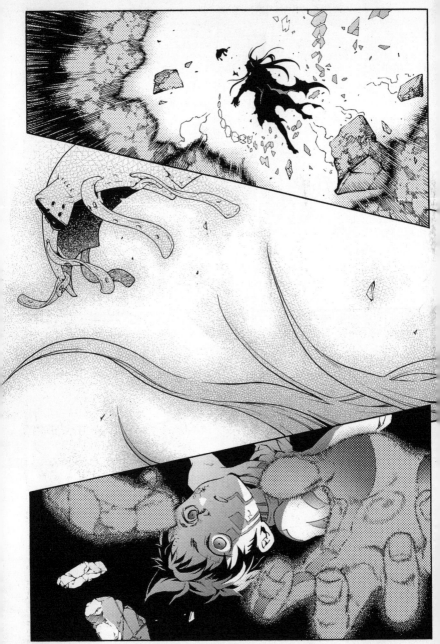

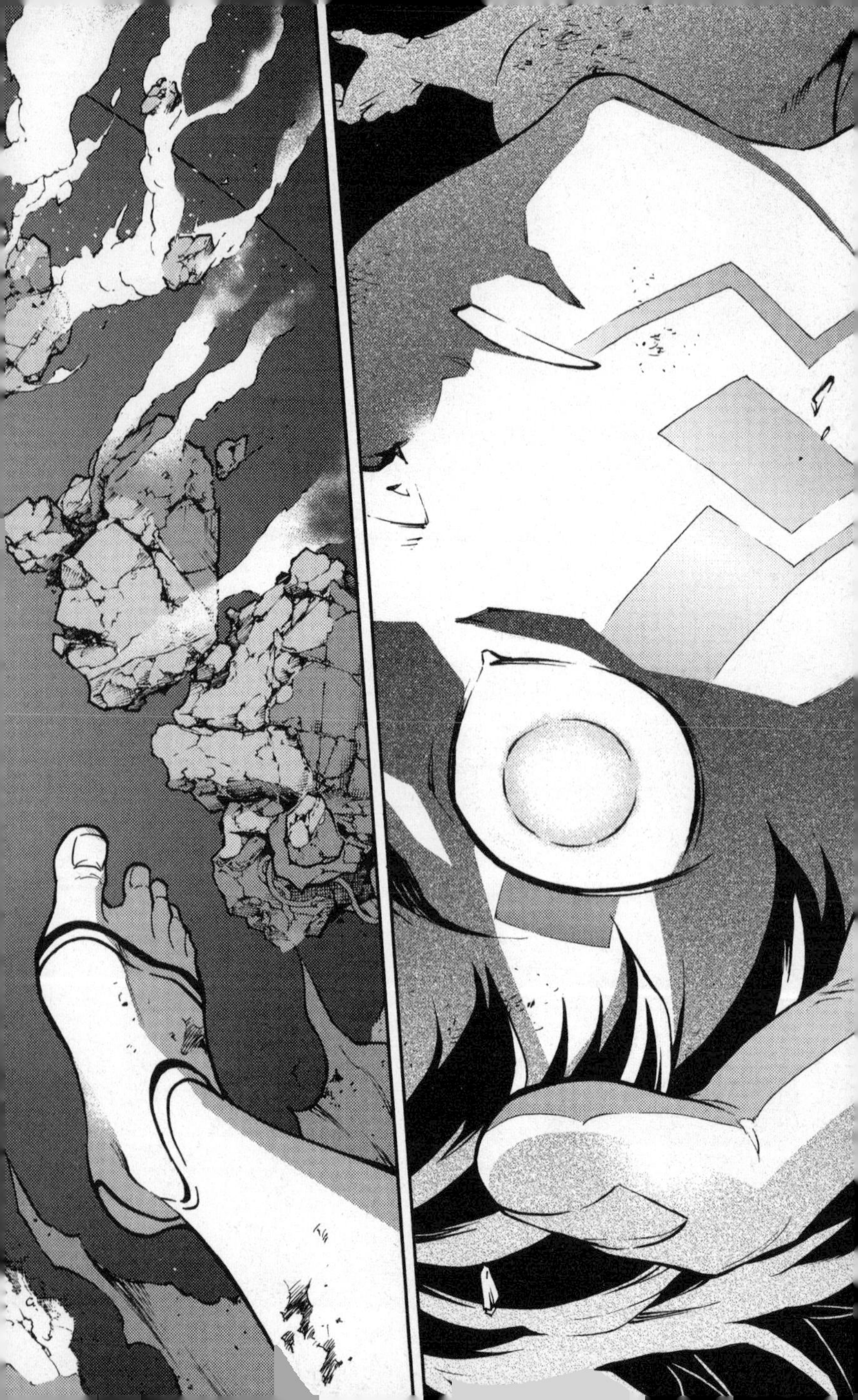

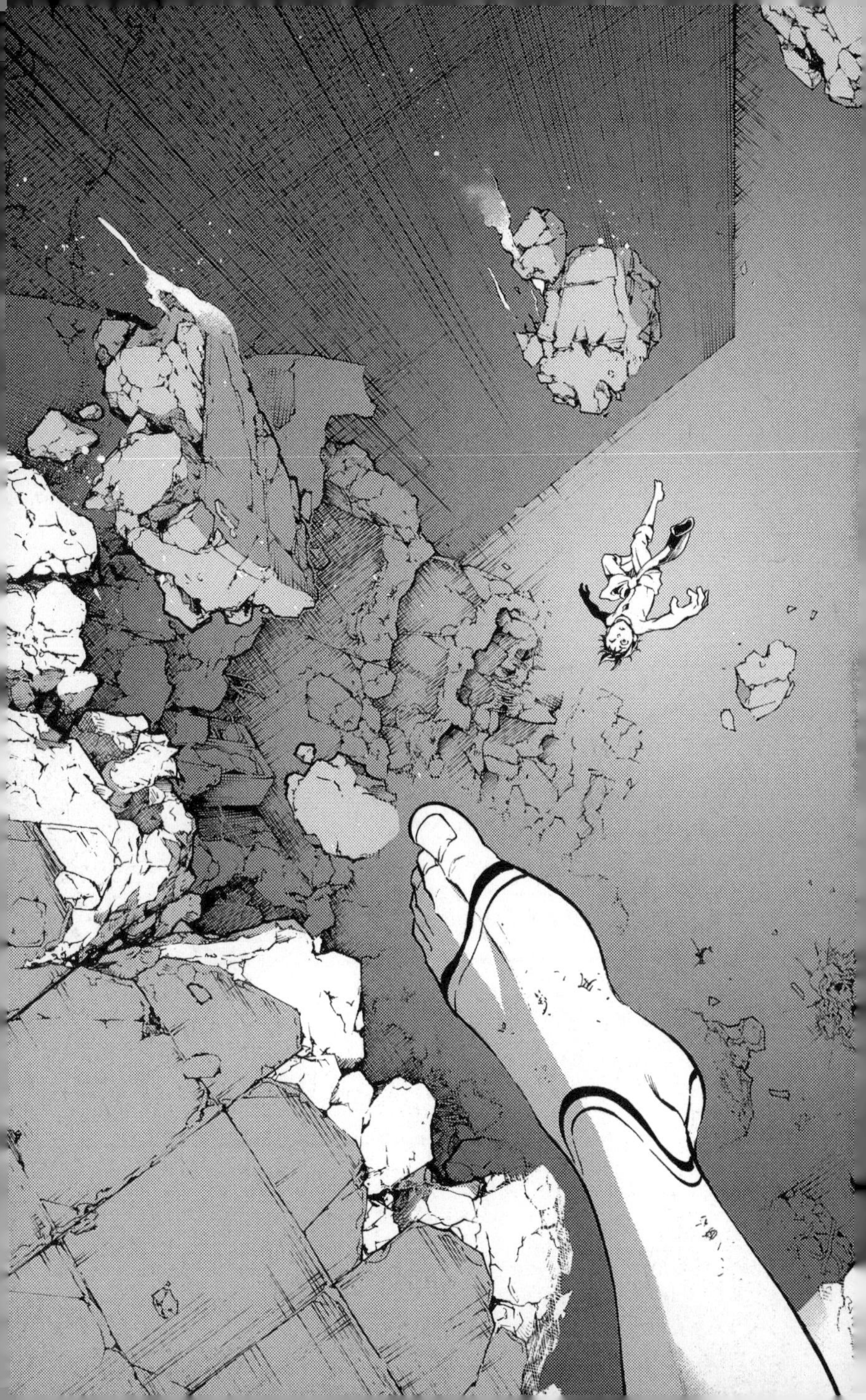

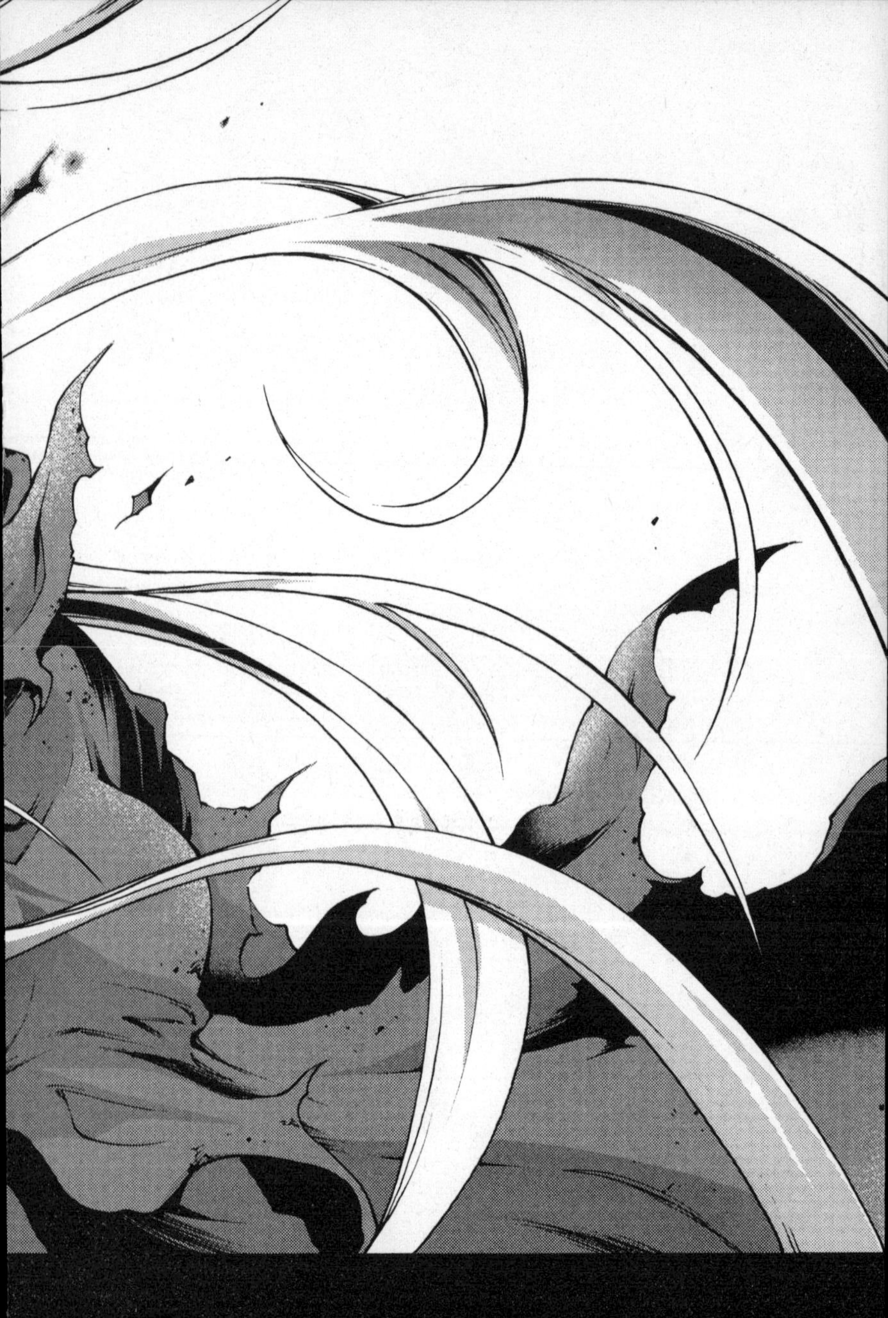

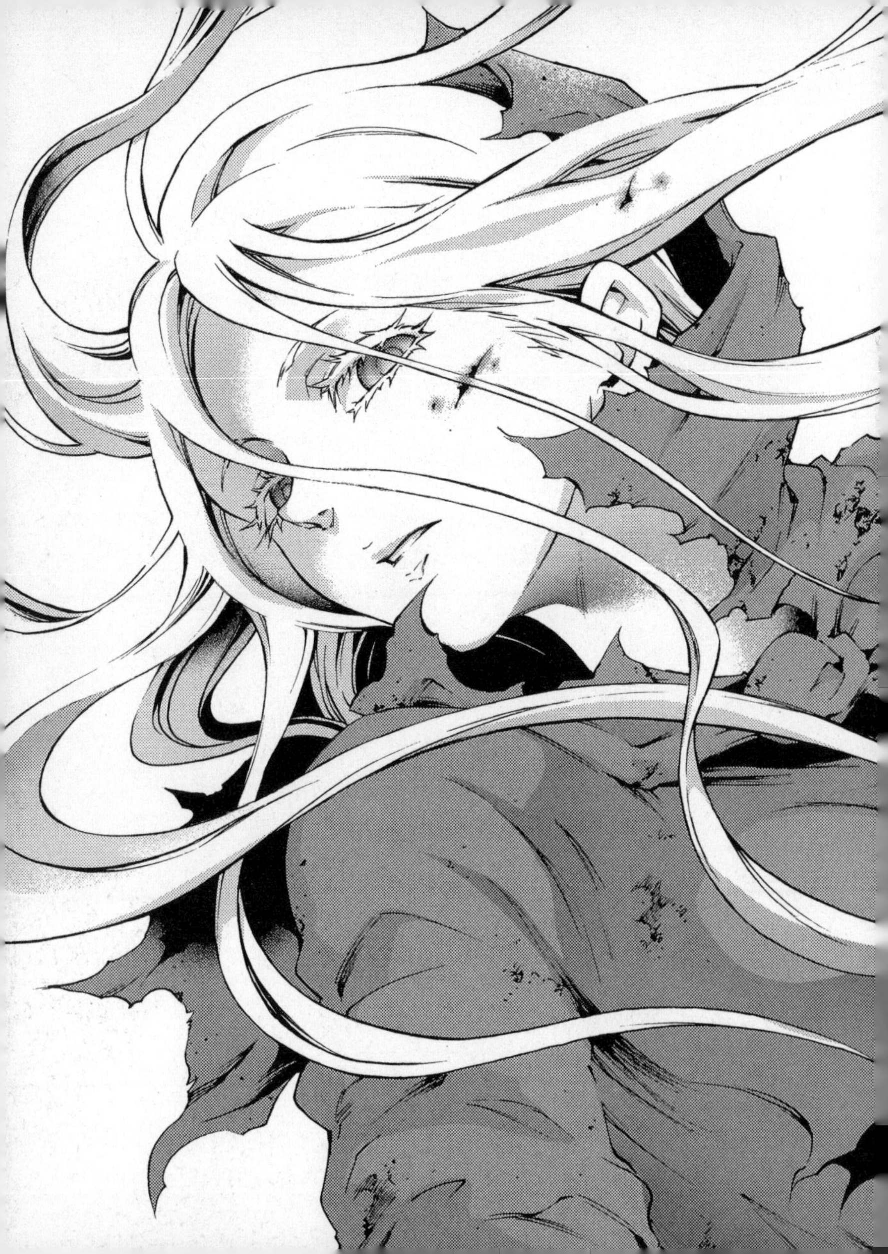

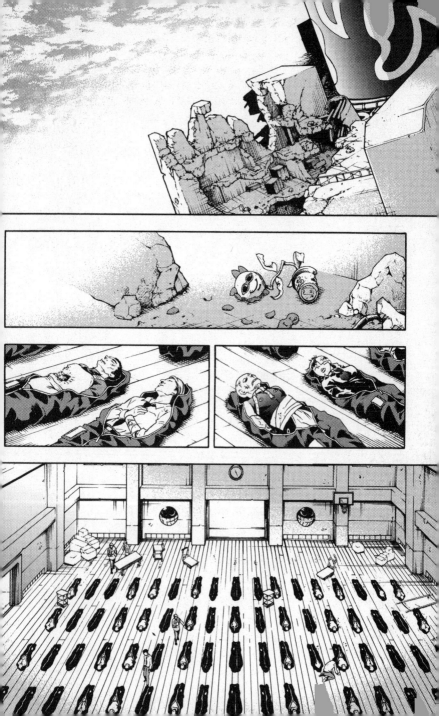

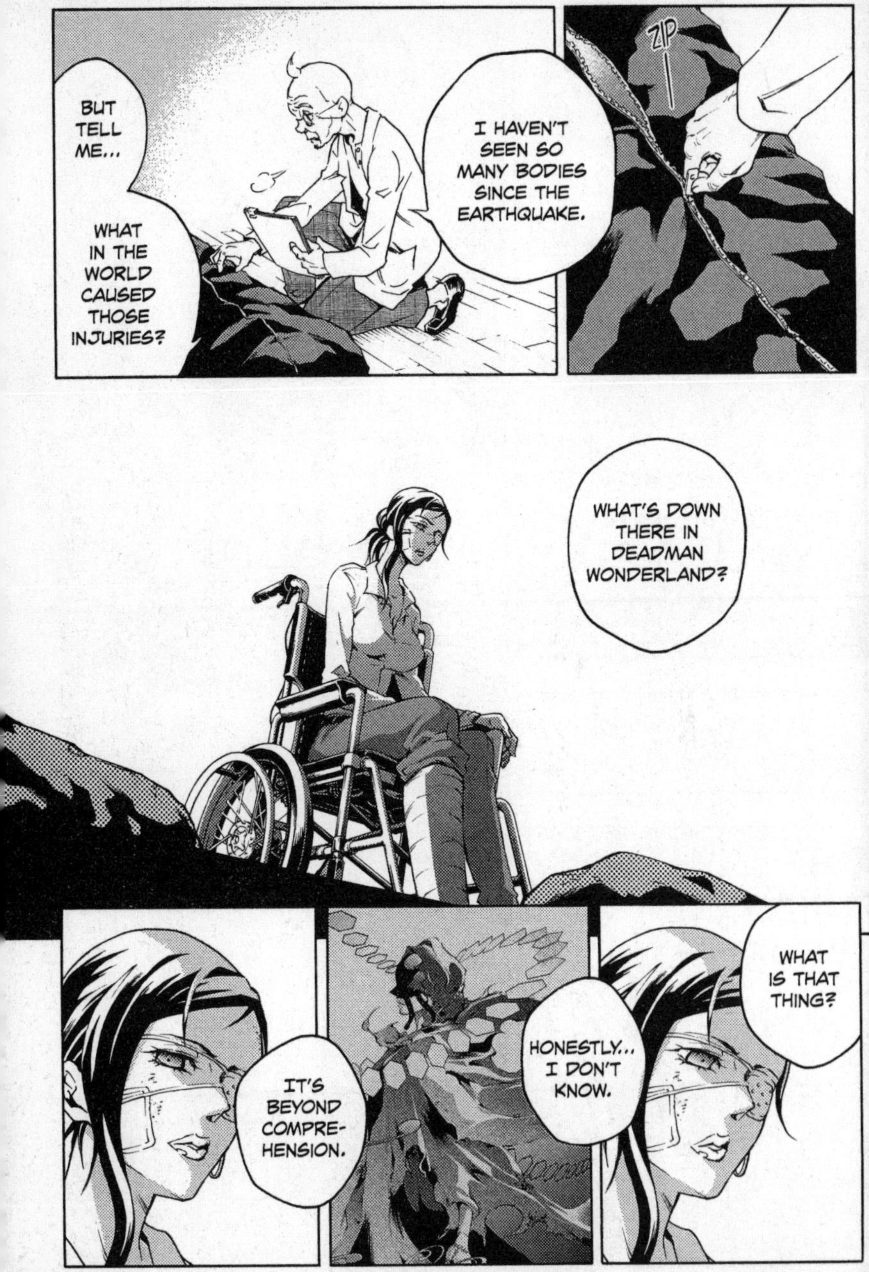
ZIP
I HAVEN'T SEEN SO MANY BODIES SINCE THE EARTHQUAKE.
BUT TELL ME...
WHAT IN THE WORLD CAUSED THOSE INJURIES?
WHAT'S DOWN THERE IN DEADMAN WONDERLAND?
WHAT IS THAT THING?
HONESTLY... I DON'T KNOW.
IT'S BEYOND COMPRE-HENSION.

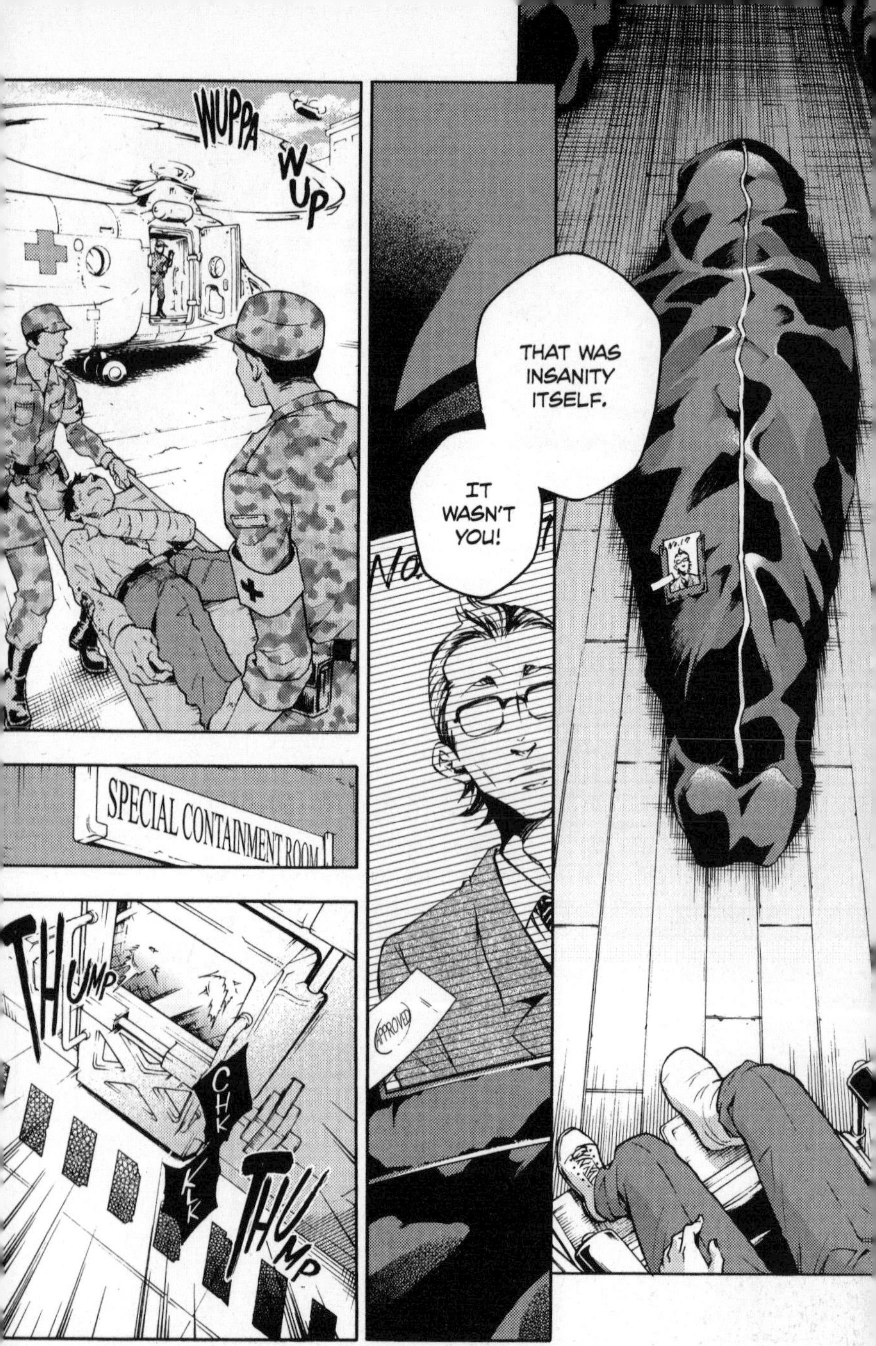
THAT WAS INSANITY ITSELF.
IT WASN'T YOU!
APPROVED
WUPPA
WUP
SPECIAL CONTAINMENT ROOM
THUMP
CHK
KLK
THUMP

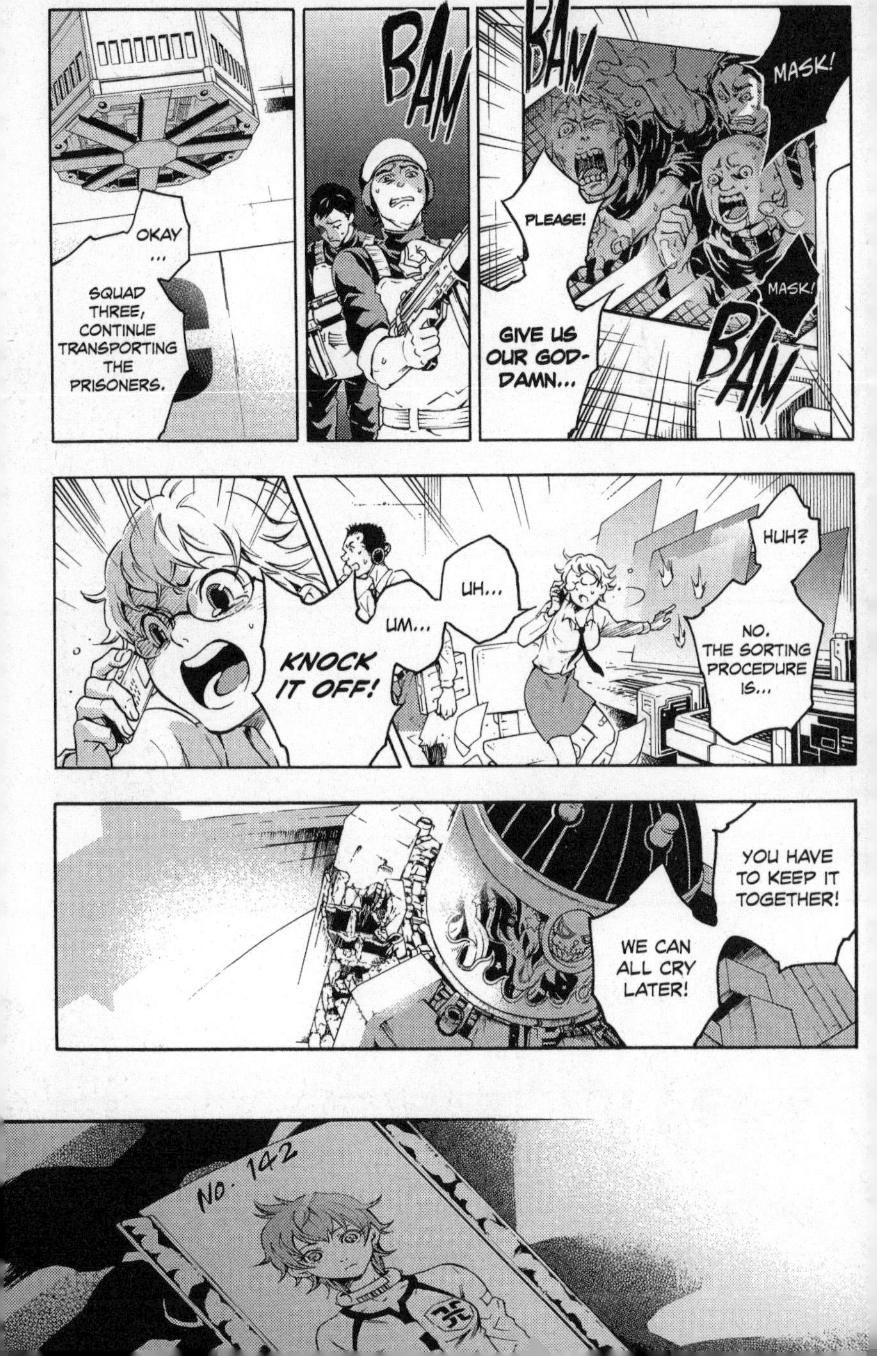
MASK!
BAM
PLEASE!
MASK!
BAM
GIVE US OUR GOD-DAMN...
BAM
OKAY ...
SQUAD THREE, CONTINUE TRANSPORTING THE PRISONERS.
HUH?
NO. THE SORTING PROCEDURE IS...
UH...
UM...
KNOCK IT OFF!
YOU HAVE TO KEEP IT TOGETHER!
WE CAN ALL CRY LATER!
NO. 142

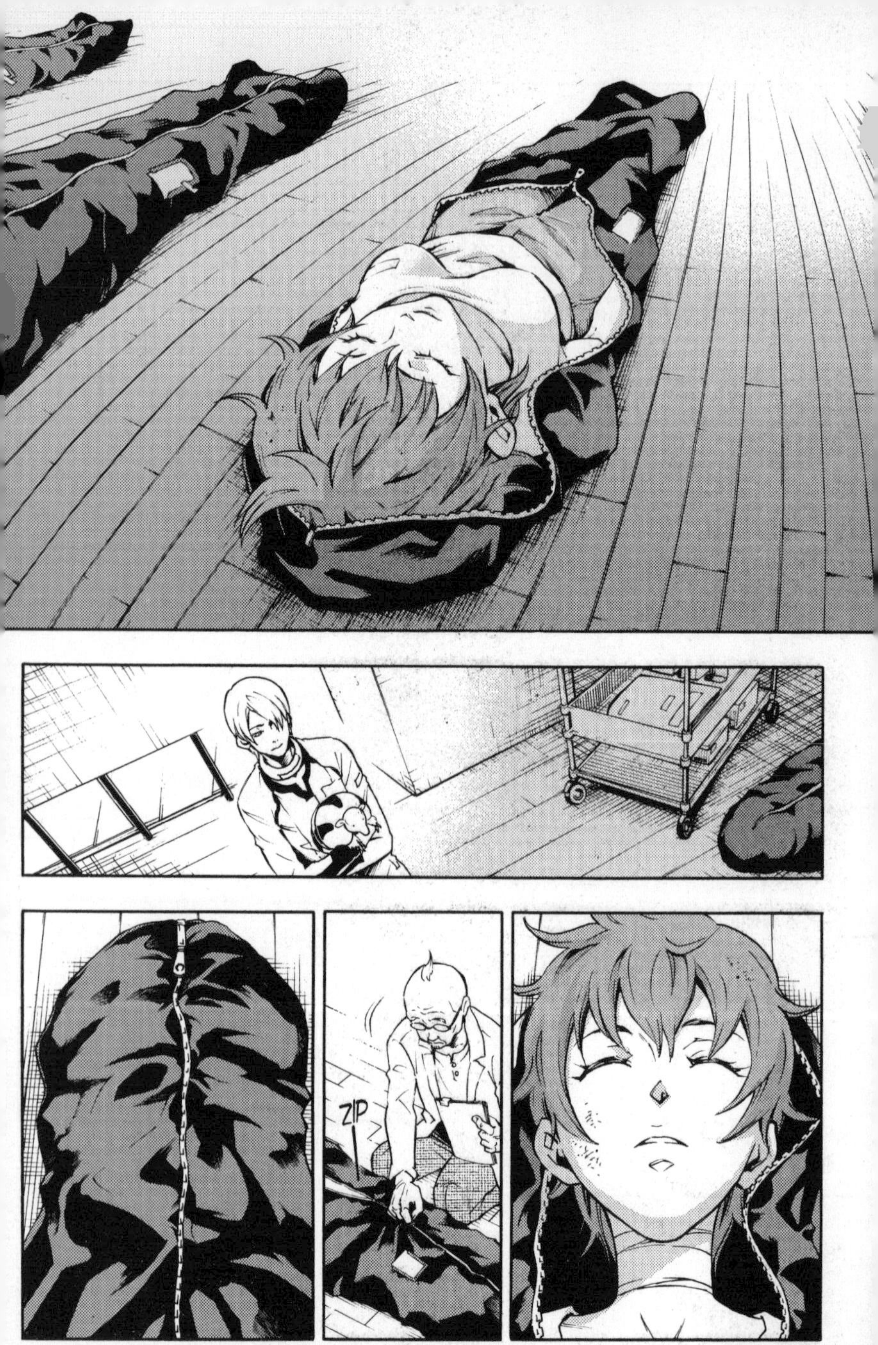
ZIP

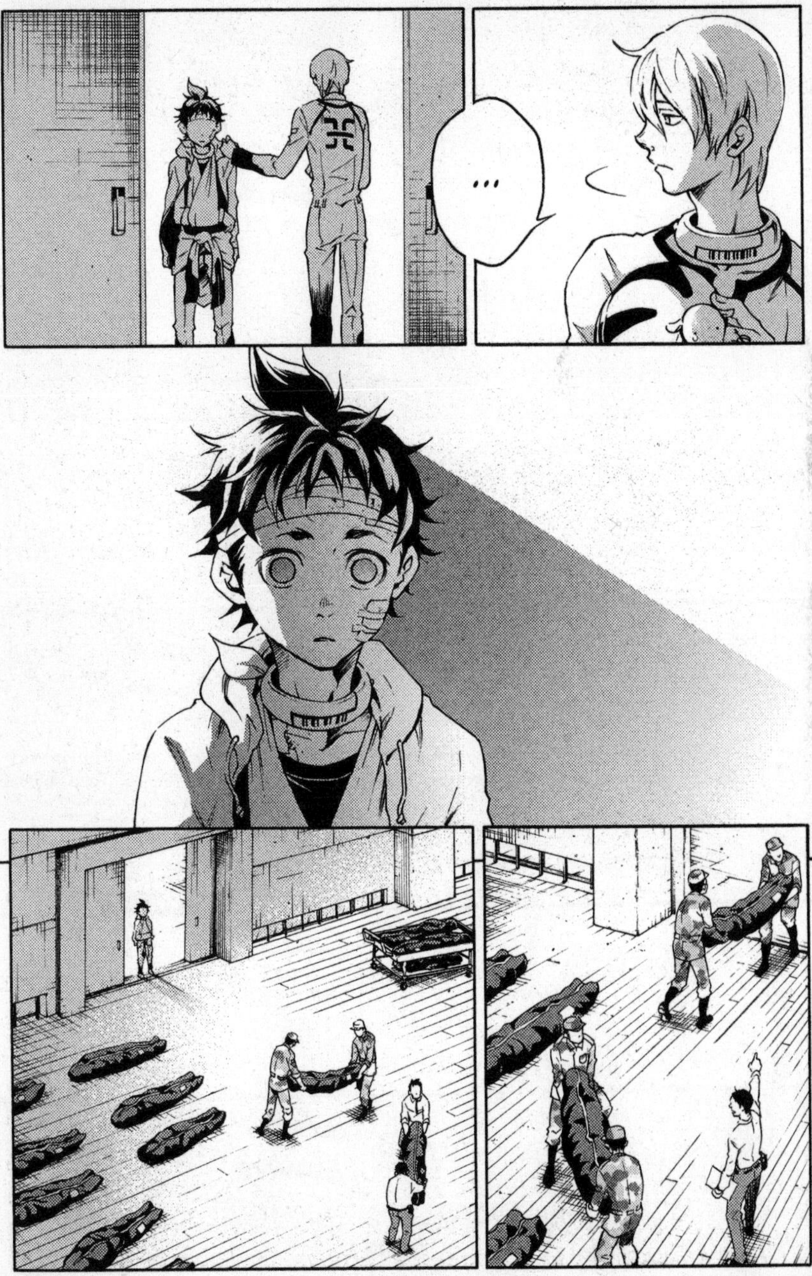
...

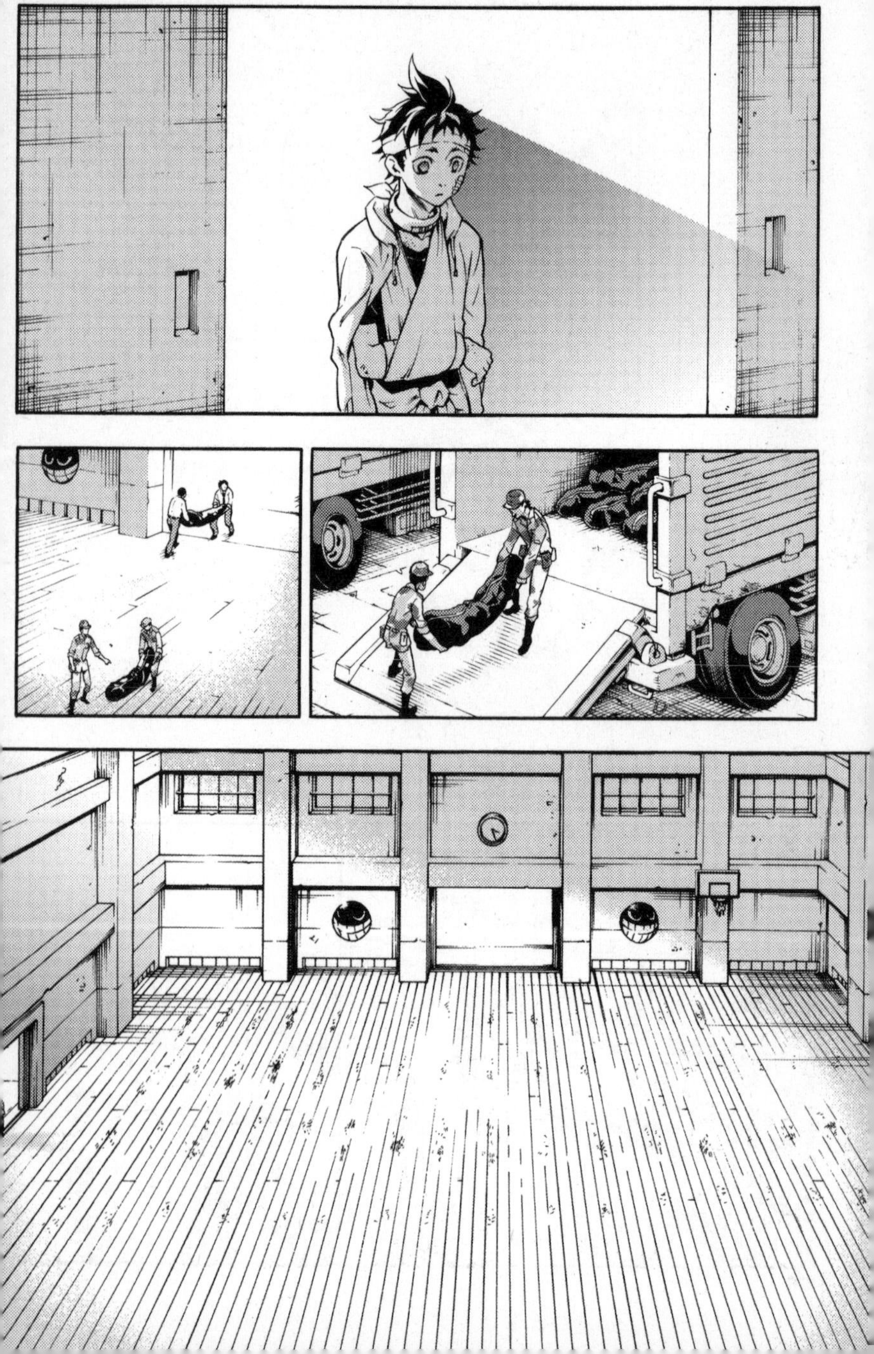

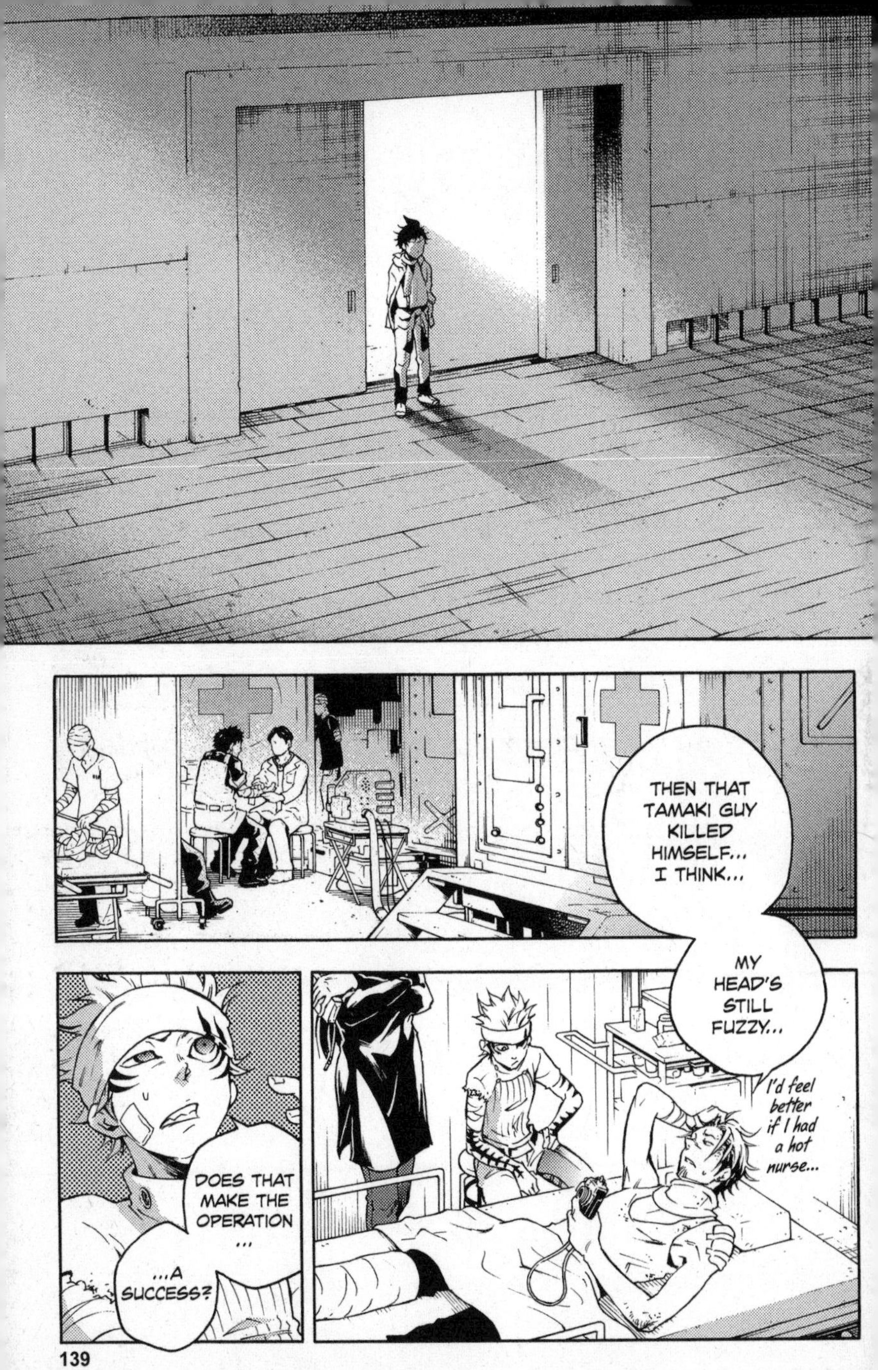
THEN THAT TAMAKI GUY KILLED HIMSELF... I THINK...
MY HEAD'S STILL FUZZY...
I'd feel better if I had a hot nurse...
DOES THAT MAKE THE OPERATION ...
...A SUCCESS?

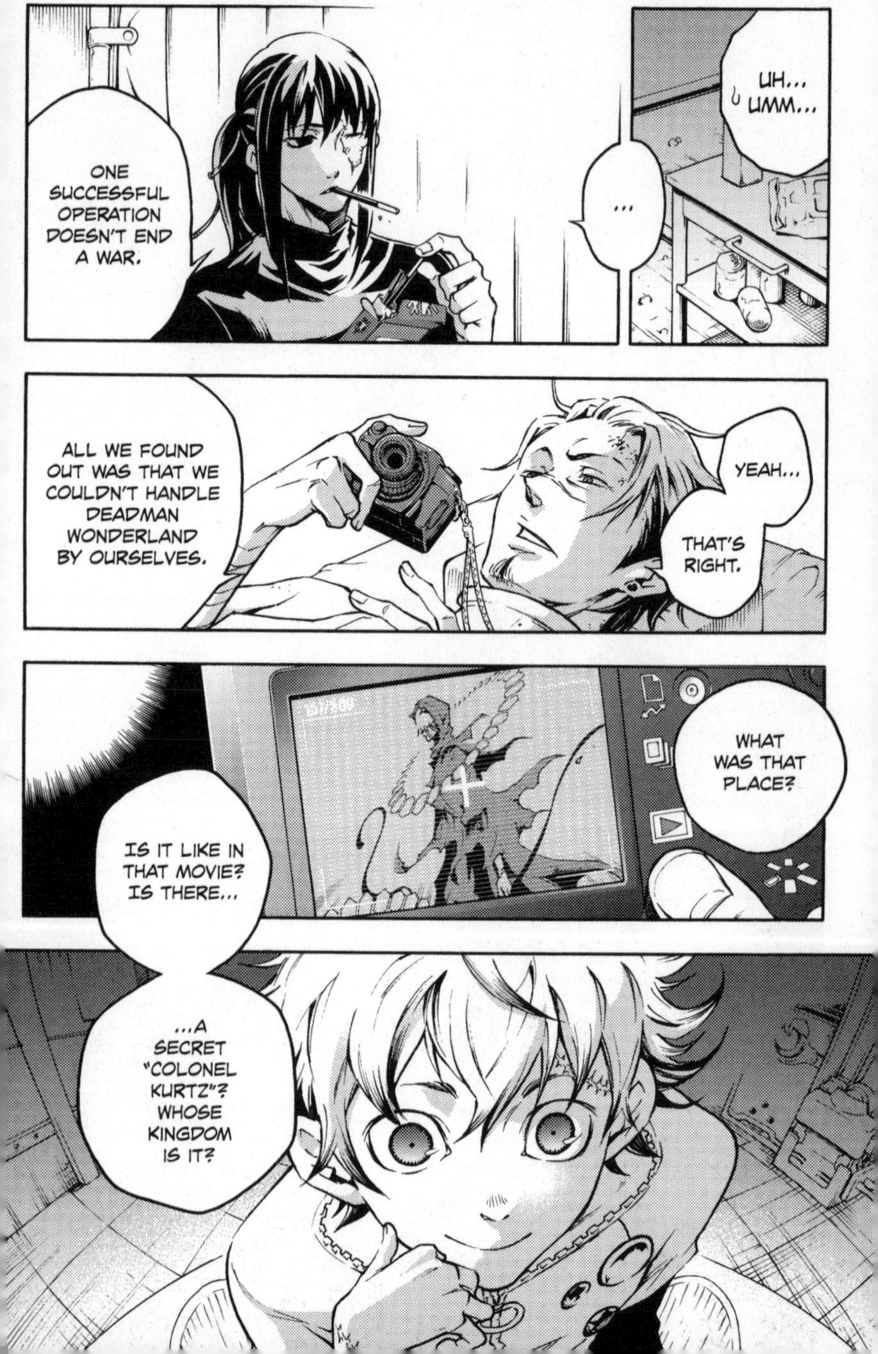
UH... UMM...
...
ONE SUCCESSFUL OPERATION DOESN'T END A WAR.
ALL WE FOUND OUT WAS THAT WE COULDN'T HANDLE DEADMAN WONDERLAND BY OURSELVES.
YEAH...
THAT'S RIGHT.
WHAT WAS THAT PLACE?
IS IT LIKE IN THAT MOVIE? IS THERE...
...A SECRET "COLONEL KURTZ"? WHOSE KINGDOM IS IT?

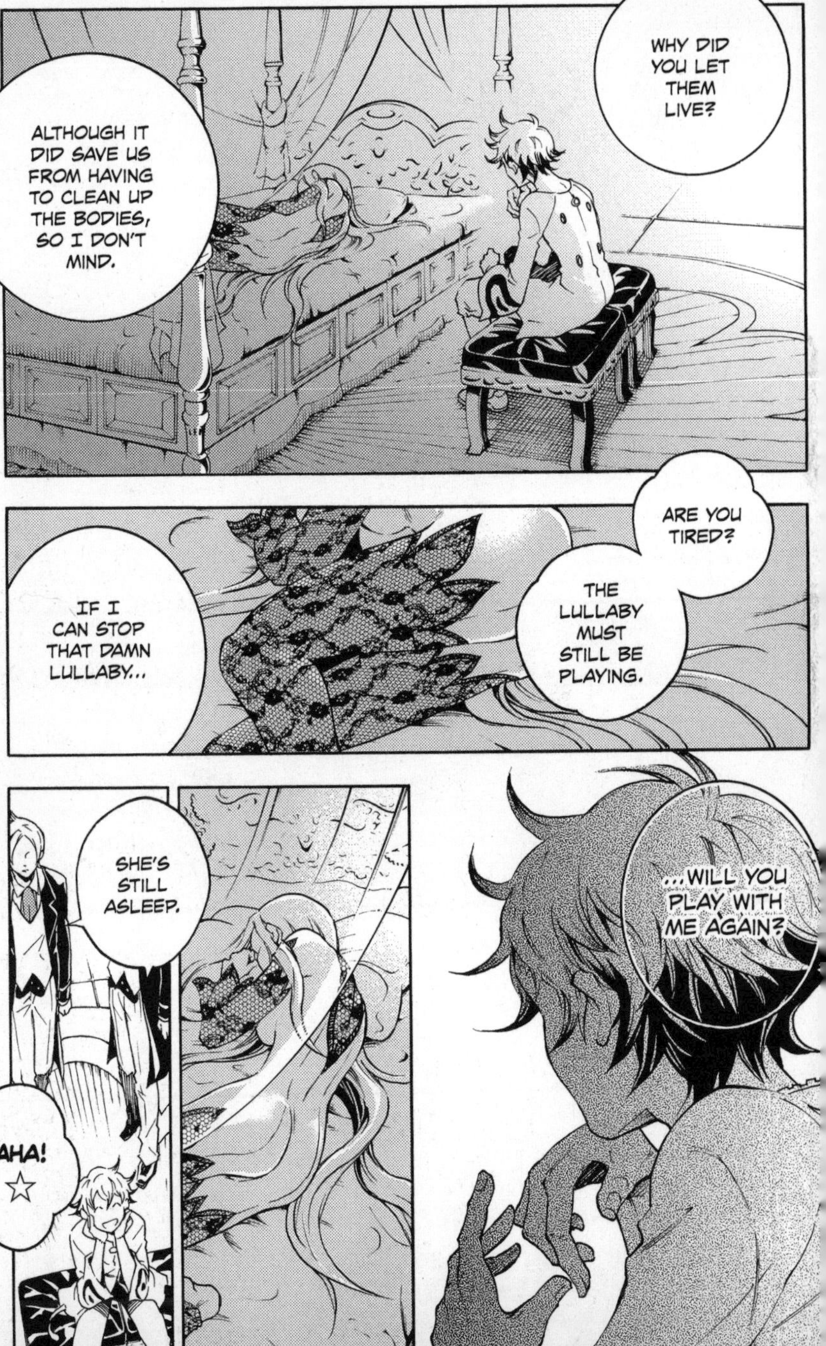
WHY DID YOU LET THEM LIVE?
ALTHOUGH IT DID SAVE US FROM HAVING TO CLEAN UP THE BODIES, SO I DON'T MIND.
ARE YOU TIRED?
THE LULLABY MUST STILL BE PLAYING.
IF I CAN STOP THAT DAMN LULLABY...
...WILL YOU PLAY WITH ME AGAIN?
SHE'S STILL ASLEEP.
AHA! ☆

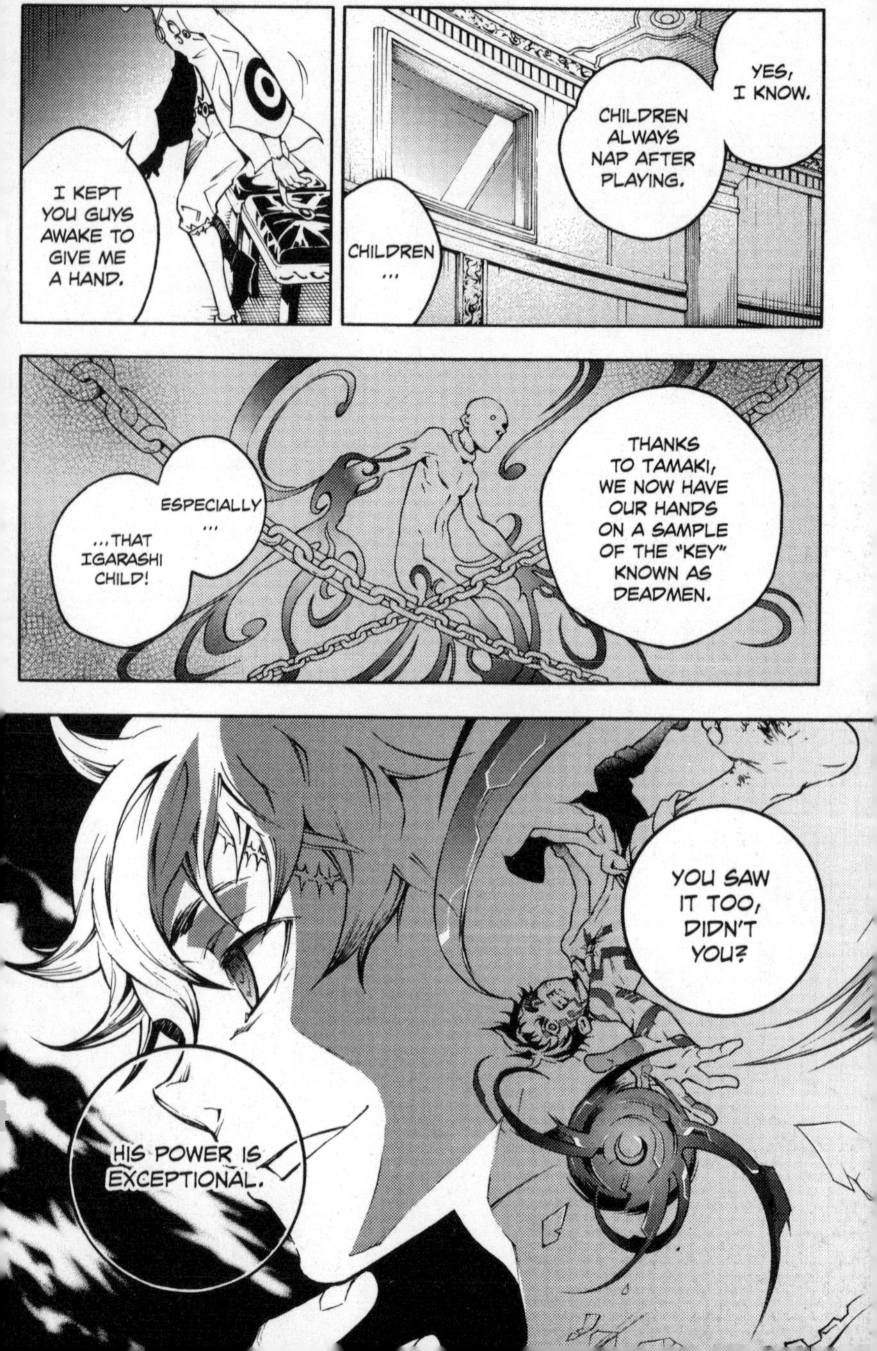
YES, I KNOW.
CHILDREN ALWAYS NAP AFTER PLAYING.
CHILDREN ...
I KEPT YOU GUYS AWAKE TO GIVE ME A HAND.
THANKS TO TAMAKI, WE NOW HAVE OUR HANDS ON A SAMPLE OF THE "KEY" KNOWN AS DEADMEN.
ESPECIALLY ...
...THAT IGARASHI CHILD!
YOU SAW IT TOO, DIDN'T YOU?
HIS POWER IS EXCEPTIONAL.

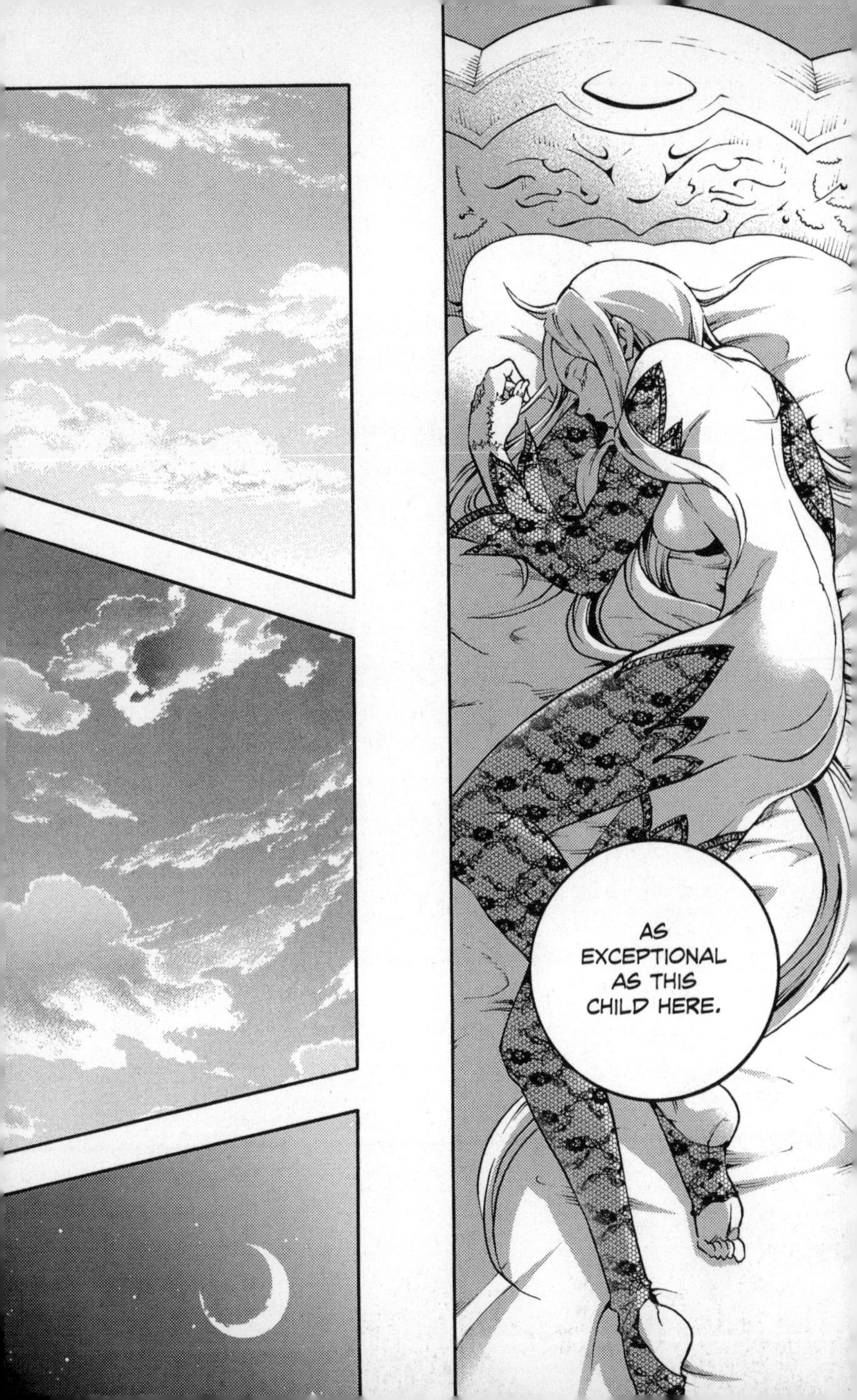
AS EXCEPTIONAL AS THIS CHILD HERE.

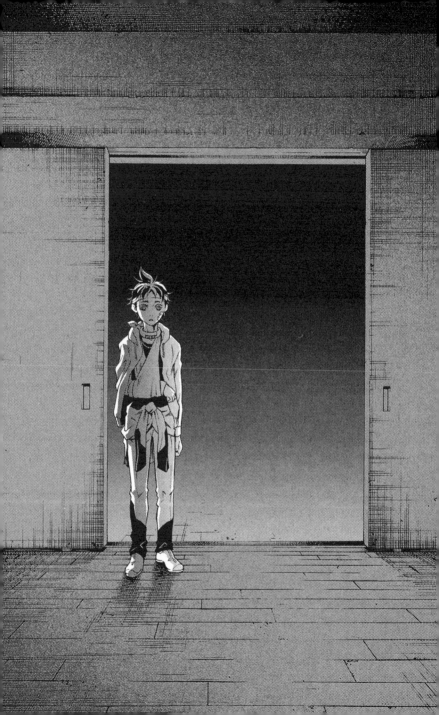

DEADMAN

WONDER LAND

DEADMAN

WONDER LAND

DEADMAN

WONDER LAND

DEADMAN

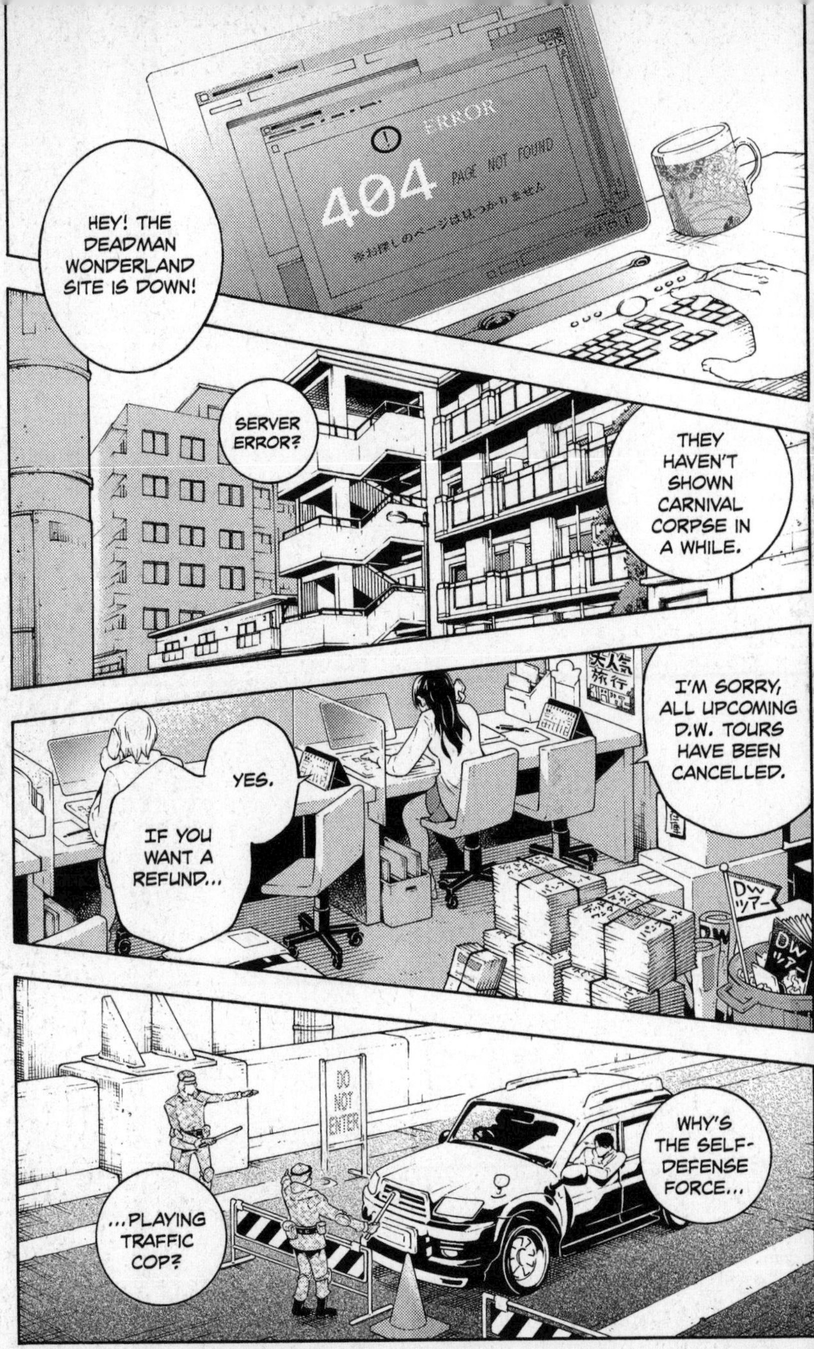
HEY! THE DEADMAN WONDERLAND SITE IS DOWN!
ERROR
404
PAGE NOT FOUND
THEY HAVEN'T SHOWN CARNIVAL CORPSE IN A WHILE.
SERVER ERROR?
I'M SORRY, ALL UPCOMING D.W. TOURS HAVE BEEN CANCELLED.
YES.
IF YOU WANT A REFUND...
DW ツアー
WHY'S THE SELF-DEFENSE FORCE...
DO NOT ENTER
...PLAYING TRAFFIC COP?

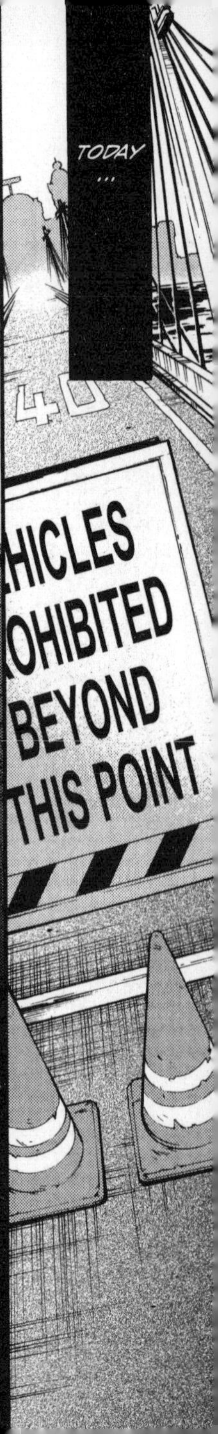
TODAY ...
40
HICLES
OHIBITED
BEYOND
THIS POINT

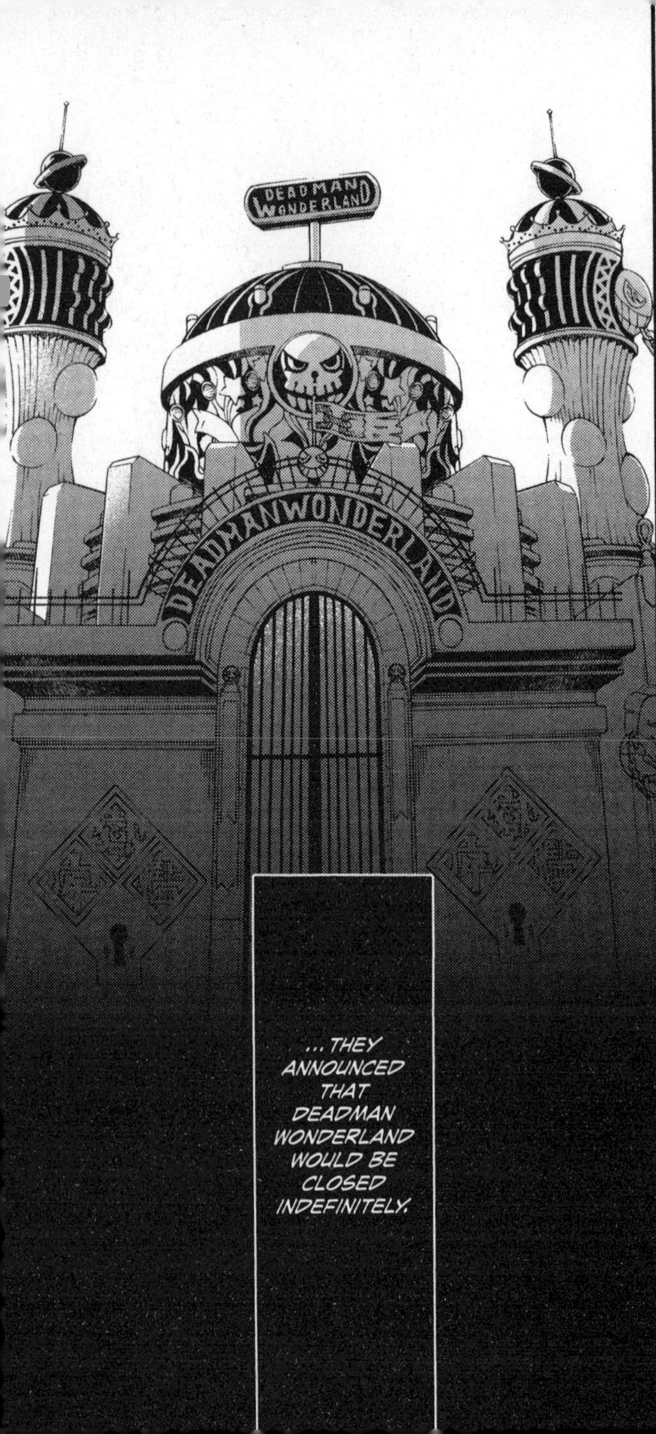
DEADMAN WONDERLAND
DEADMANWONDERLAND
...THEY ANNOUNCED THAT DEADMAN WONDERLAND WOULD BE CLOSED INDEFINITELY.

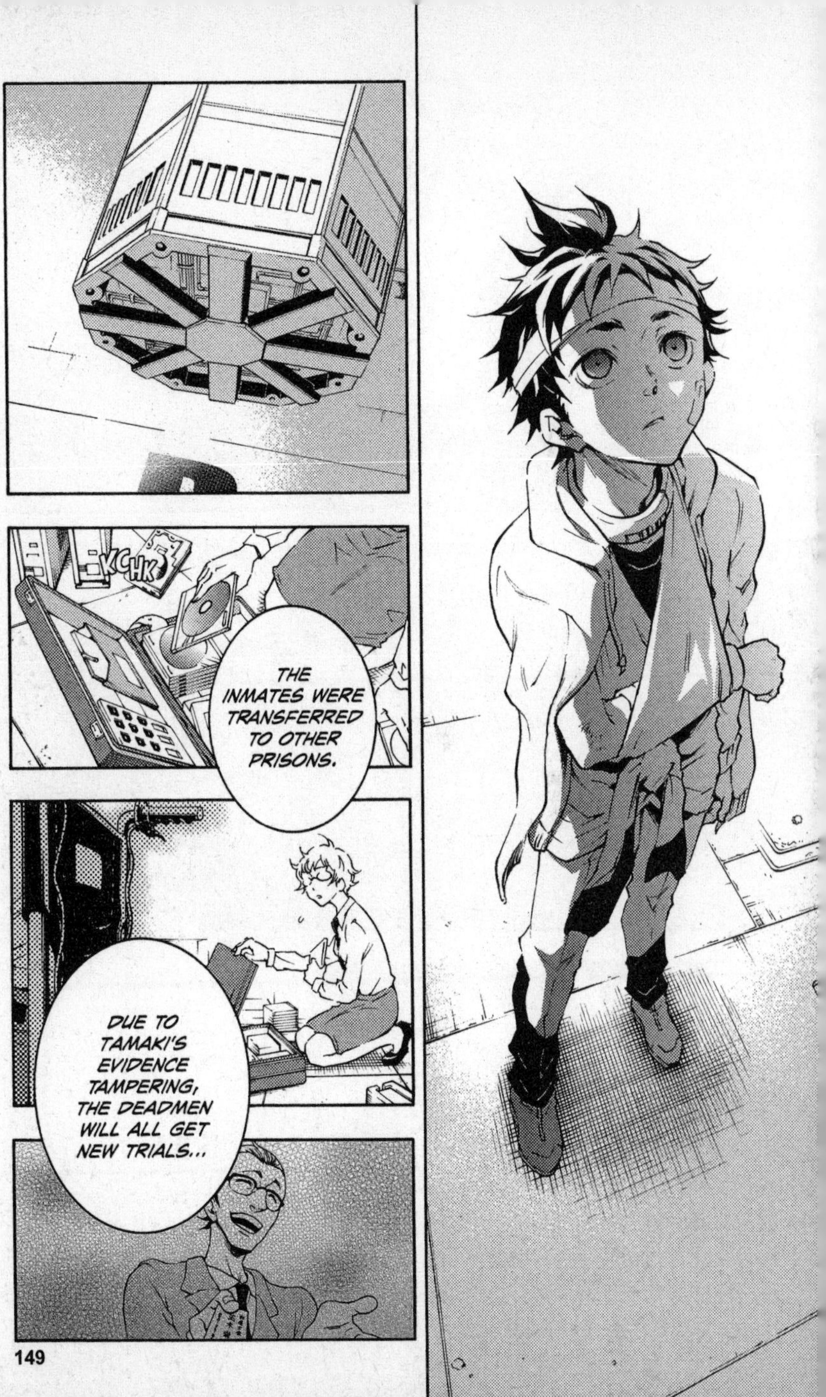
KCHK
THE INMATES WERE TRANSFERRED TO OTHER PRISONS.
DUE TO TAMAKI'S EVIDENCE TAMPERING, THE DEADMEN WILL ALL GET NEW TRIALS...

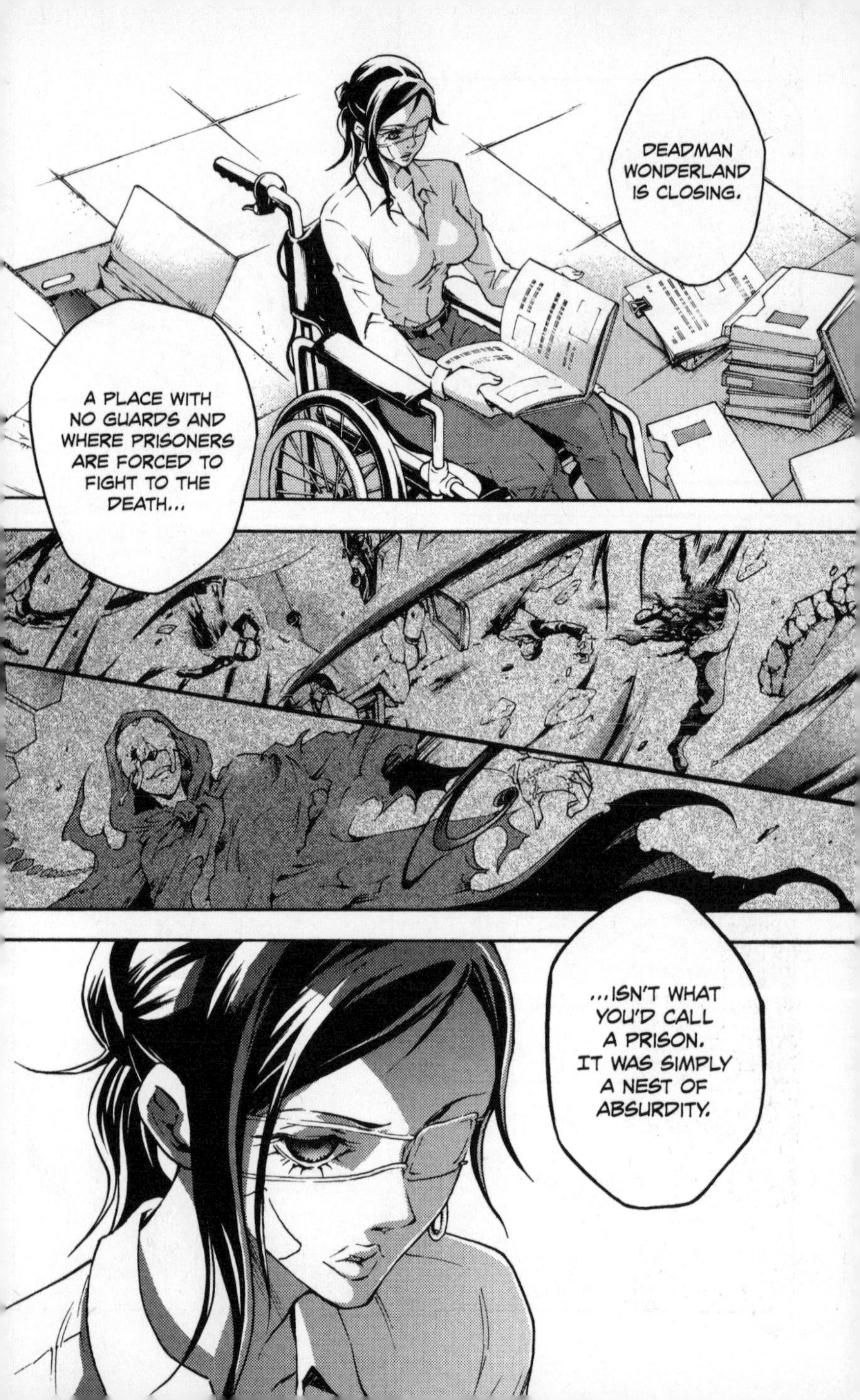
DEADMAN WONDERLAND IS CLOSING.
A PLACE WITH NO GUARDS AND WHERE PRISONERS ARE FORCED TO FIGHT TO THE DEATH...
...ISN'T WHAT YOU'D CALL A PRISON. IT WAS SIMPLY A NEST OF ABSURDITY.

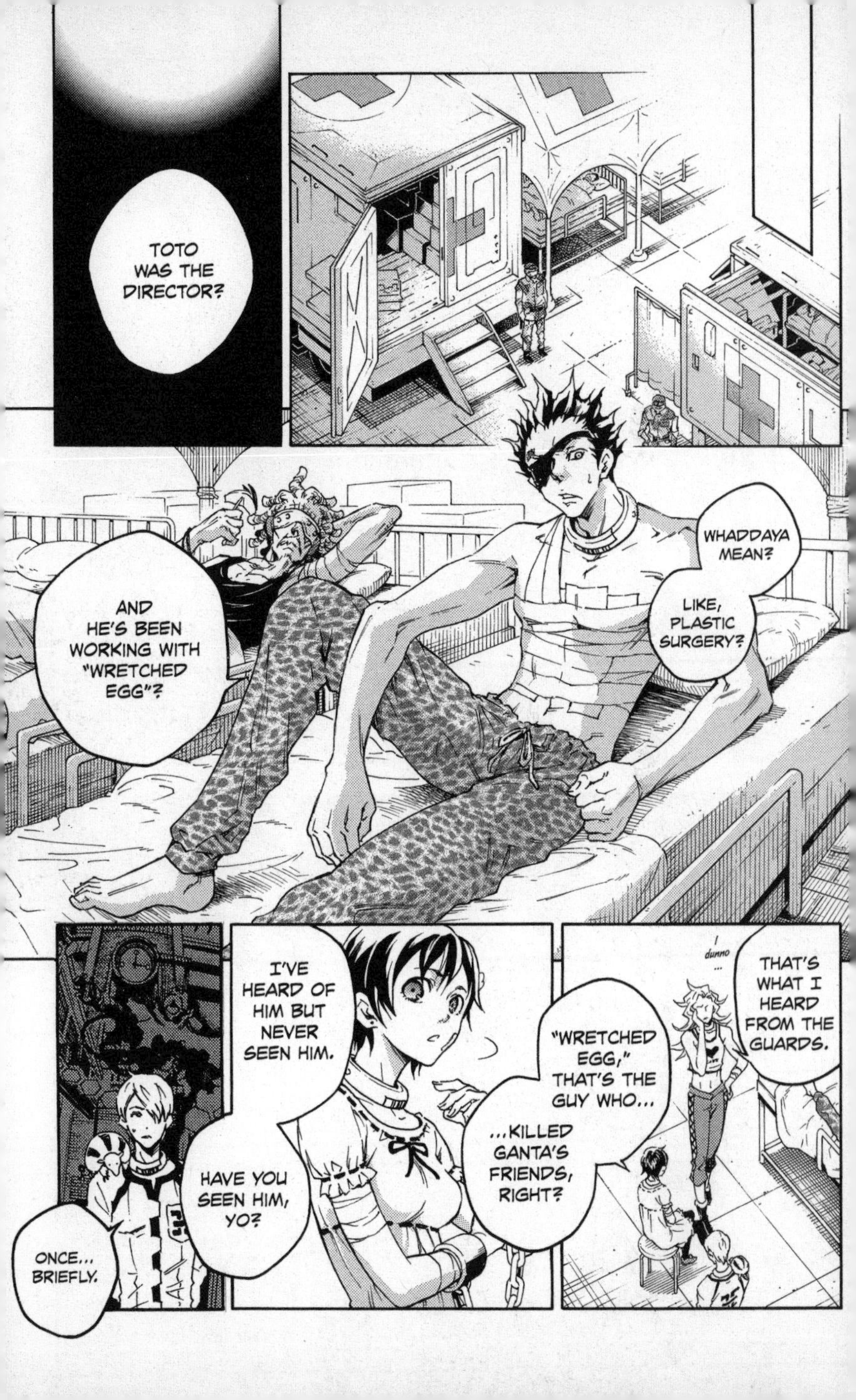
TOTO WAS THE DIRECTOR?
WHADDAYA MEAN?
LIKE, PLASTIC SURGERY?
AND HE'S BEEN WORKING WITH "WRETCHED EGG"?
I dunno...
THAT'S WHAT I HEARD FROM THE GUARDS.
"WRETCHED EGG," THAT'S THE GUY WHO...
...KILLED GANTA'S FRIENDS, RIGHT?
I'VE HEARD OF HIM BUT NEVER SEEN HIM.
HAVE YOU SEEN HIM, YO?
ONCE... BRIEFLY.

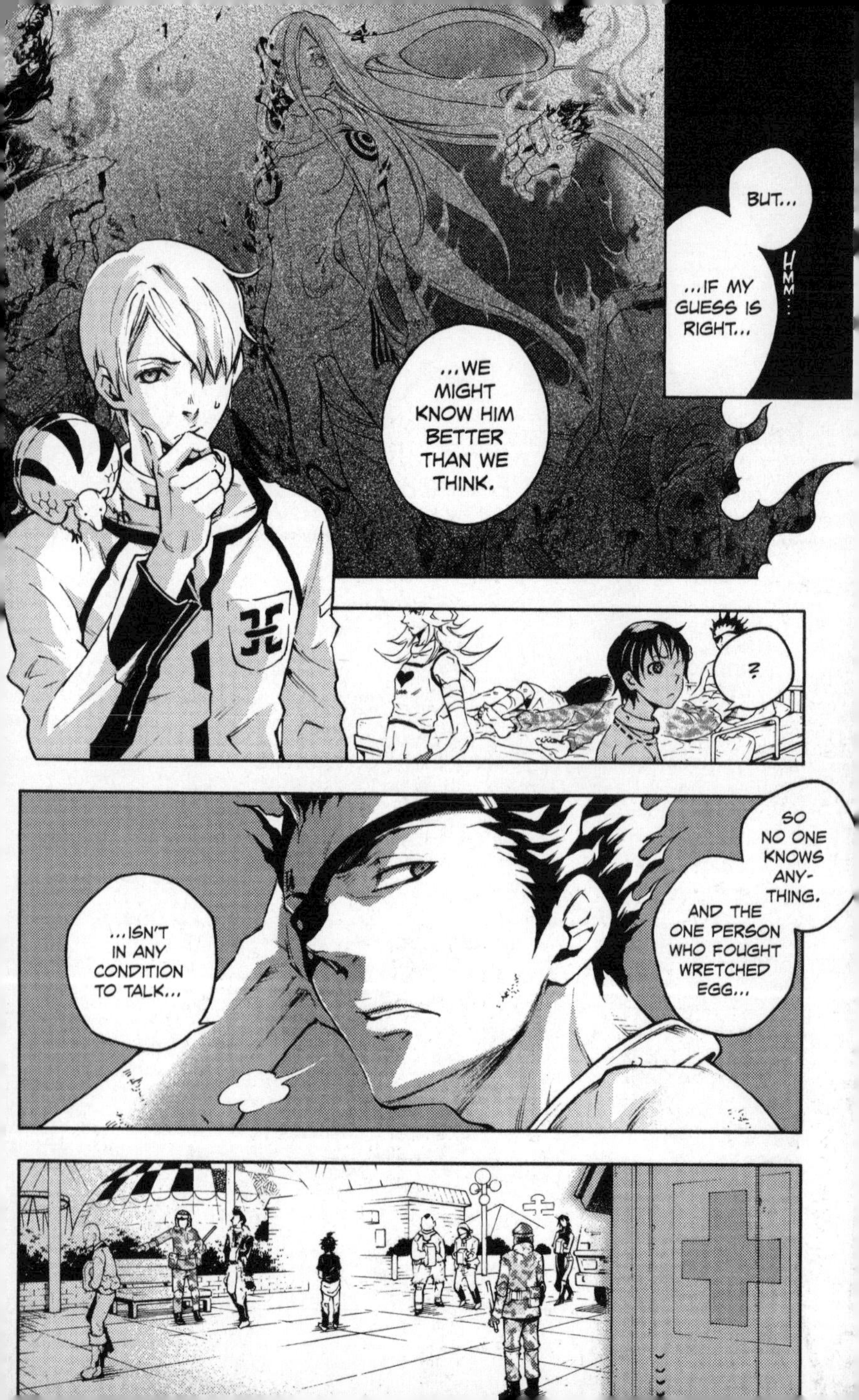
BUT...
HMM...
...IF MY GUESS IS RIGHT...
...WE MIGHT KNOW HIM BETTER THAN WE THINK.
?
SO NO ONE KNOWS ANYTHING.
AND THE ONE PERSON WHO FOUGHT WRETCHED EGG...
...ISN'T IN ANY CONDITION TO TALK...

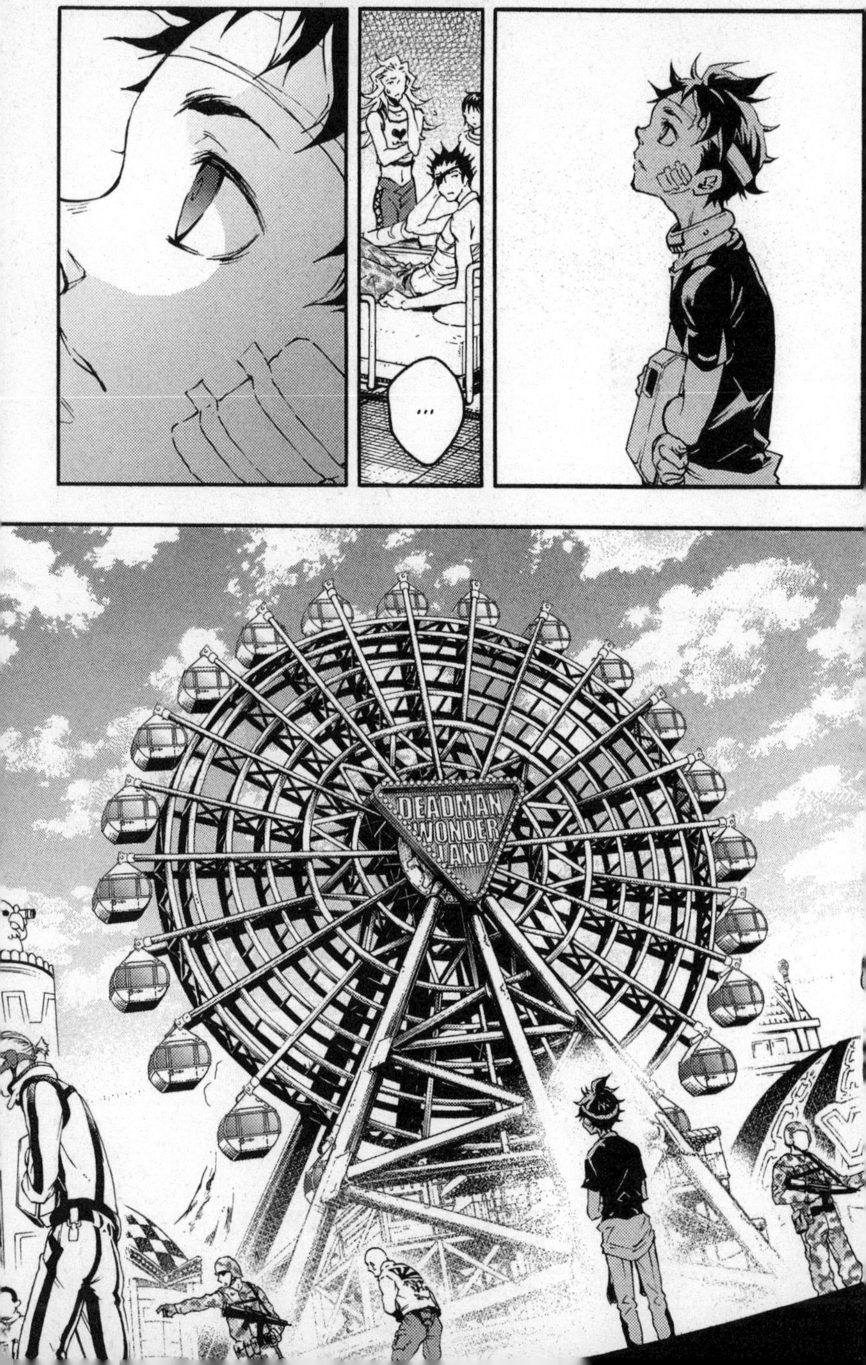
...
DEADMAN WONDER LAND

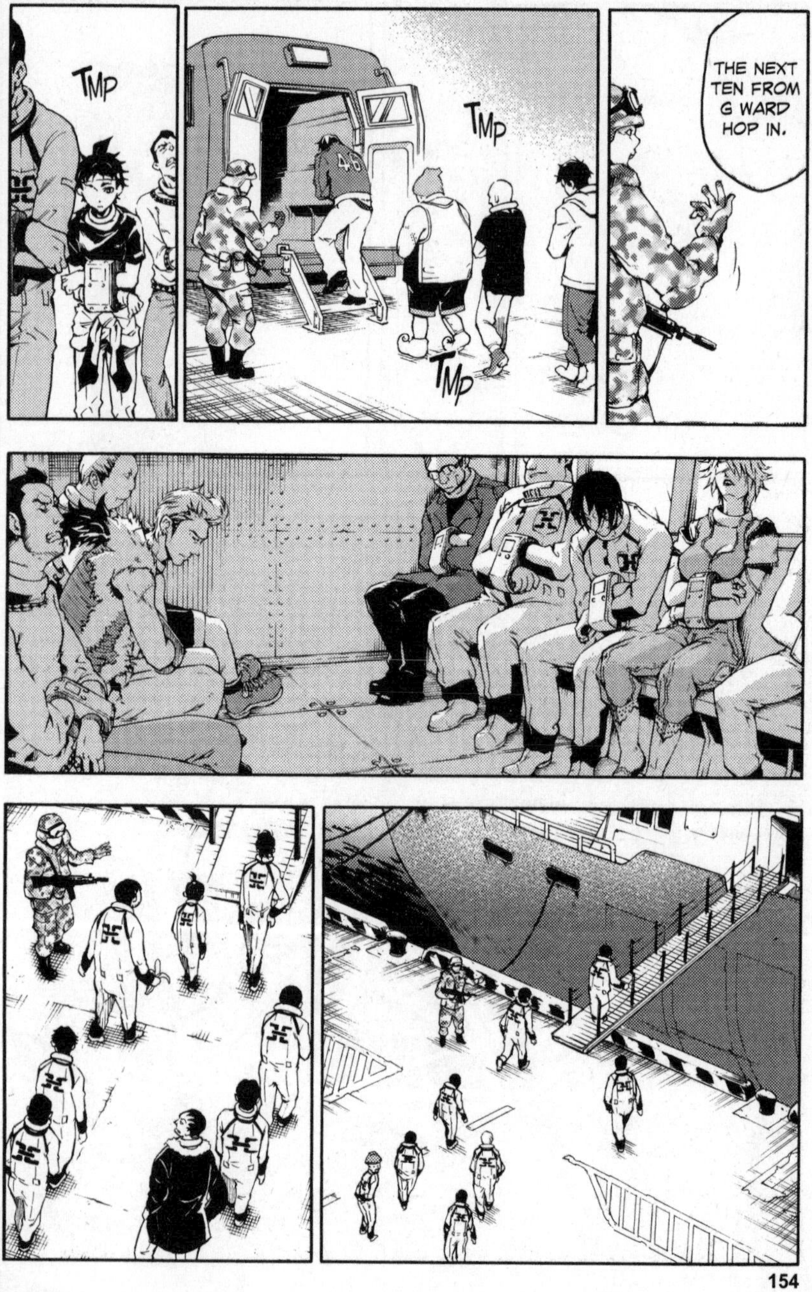
THE NEXT TEN FROM G WARD HOP IN.
TMP
TMP
TMP

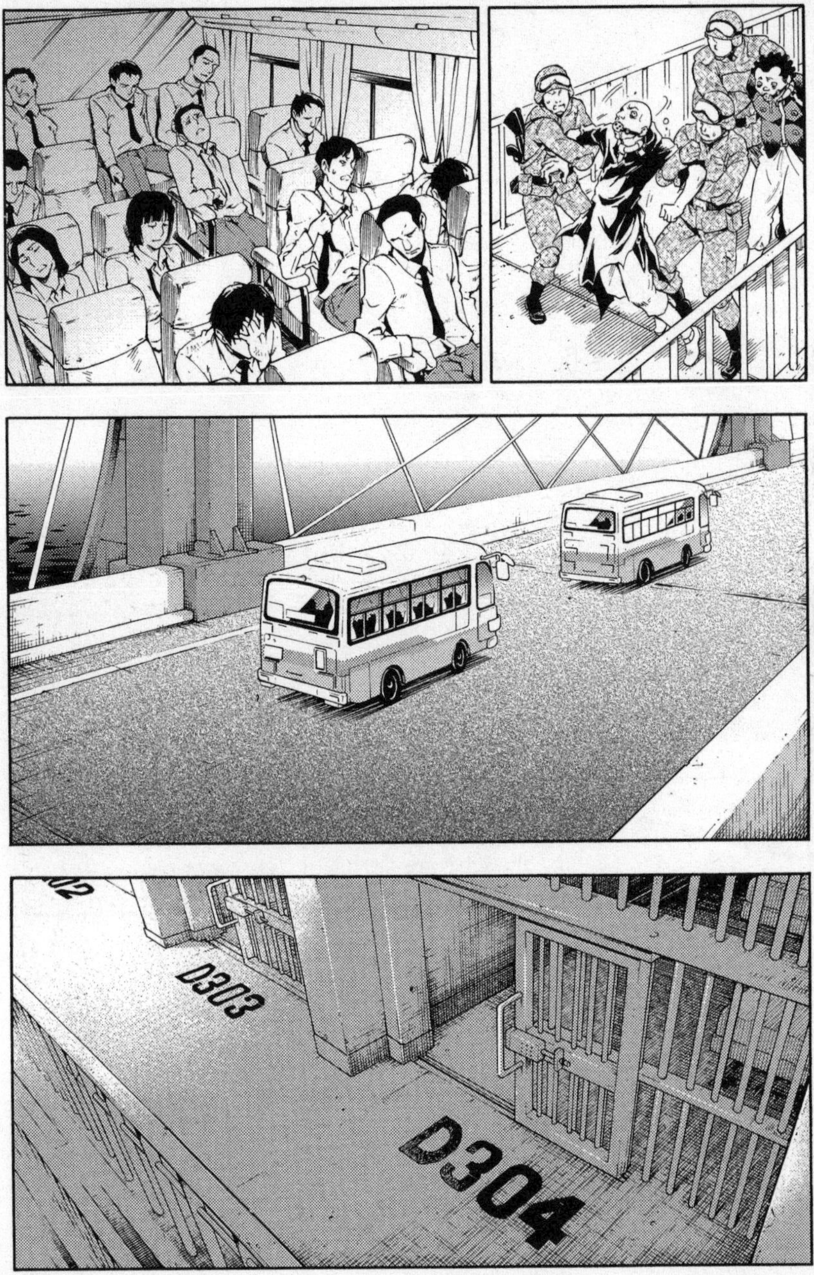
D303
D304

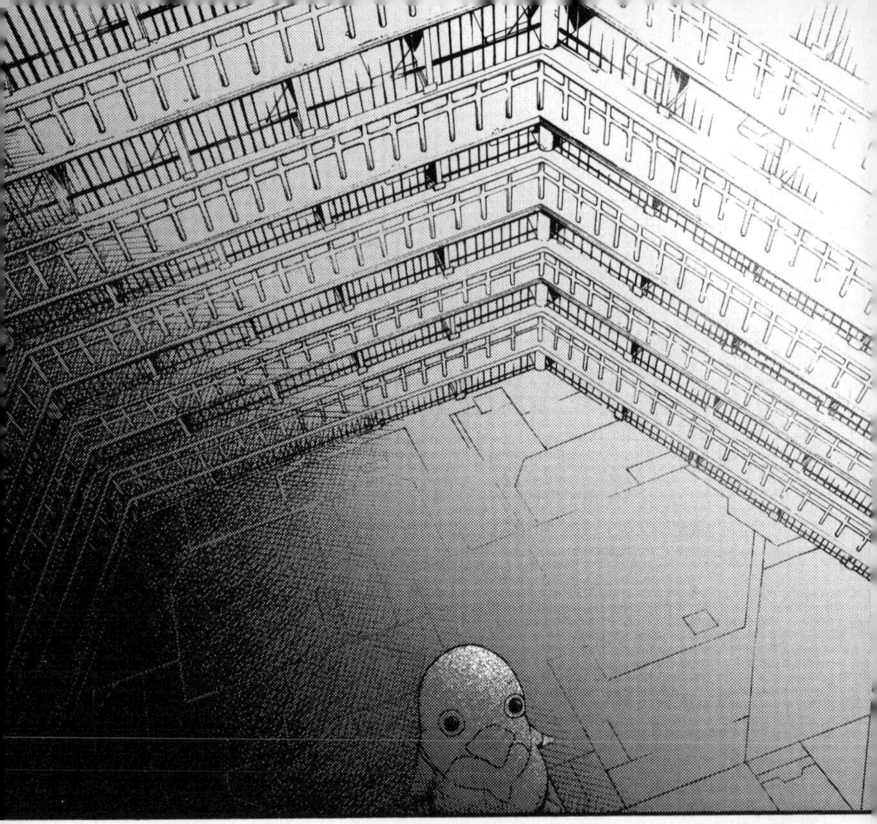

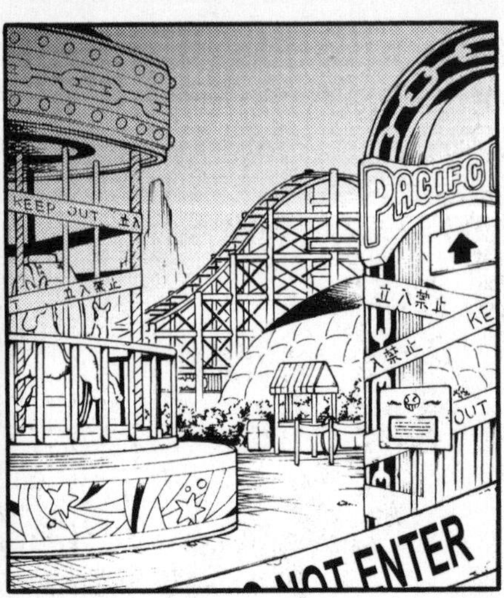
PACIFC
KEEP OUT 立入
立入禁止
立入禁止
入禁止
KE
OUT
NOT ENTER

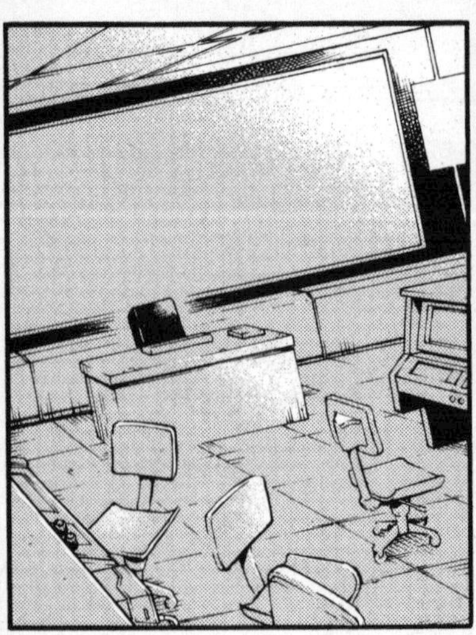

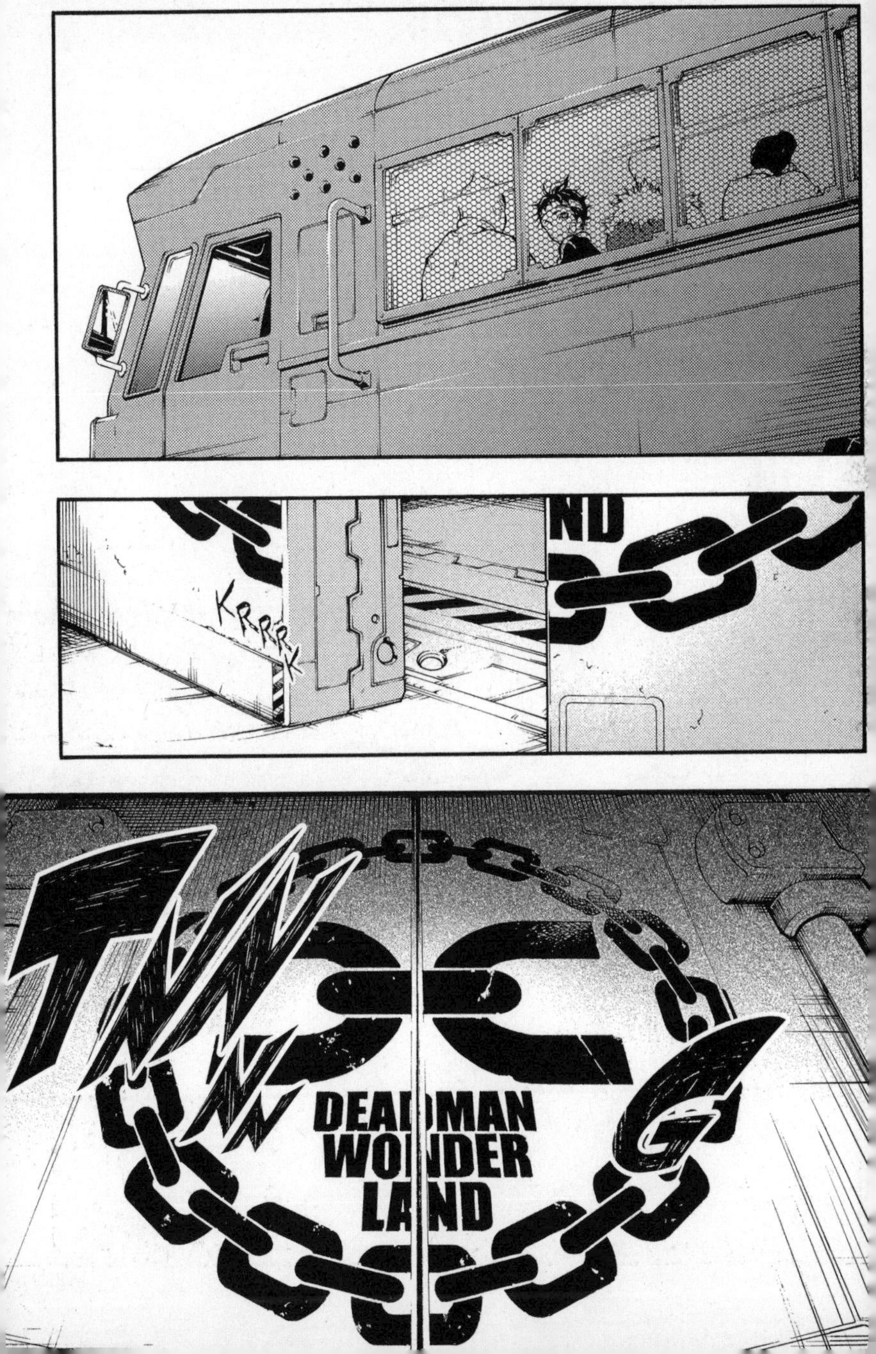
KRRRRK
TWANG
DEADMAN
WONDER
LAND

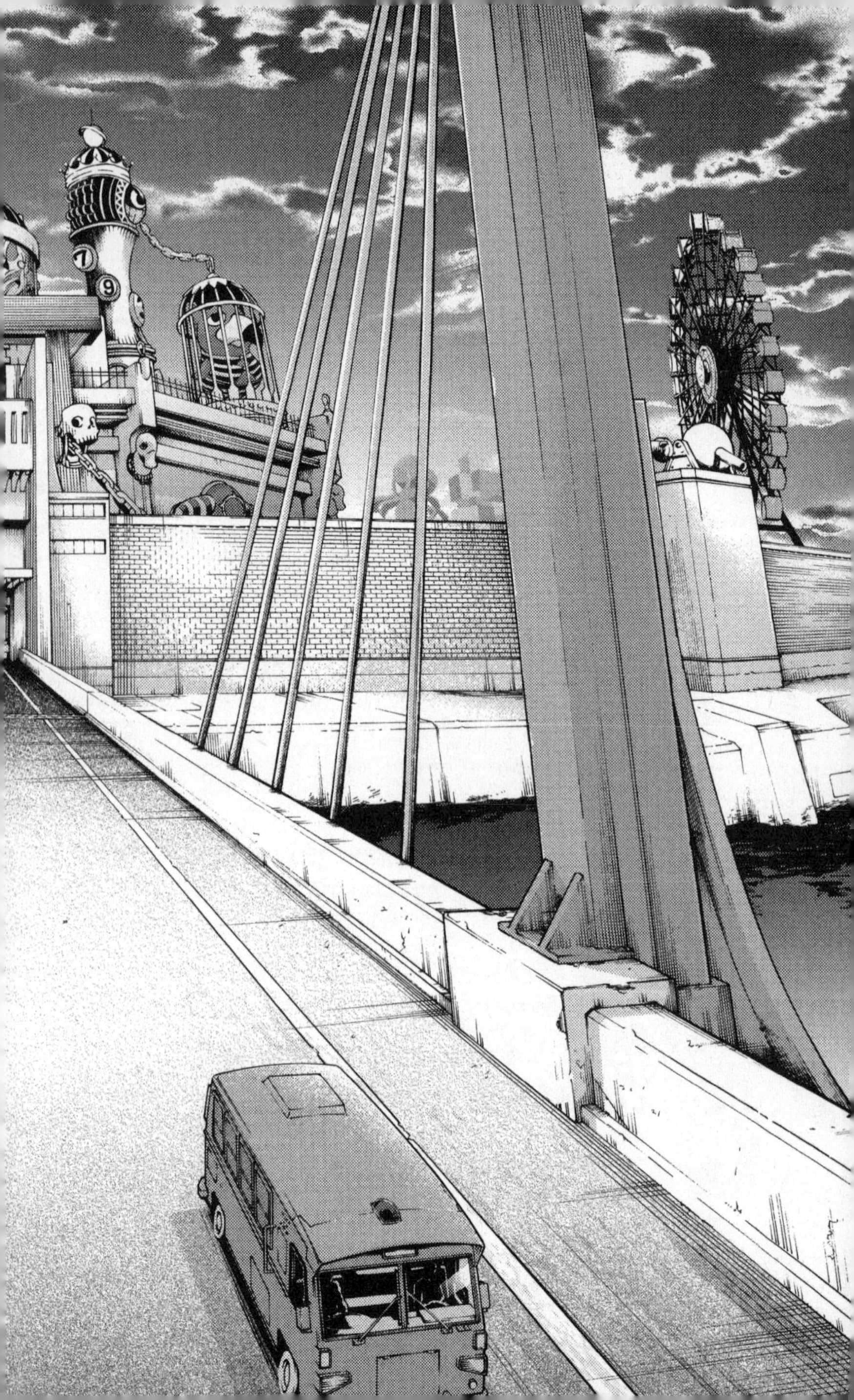

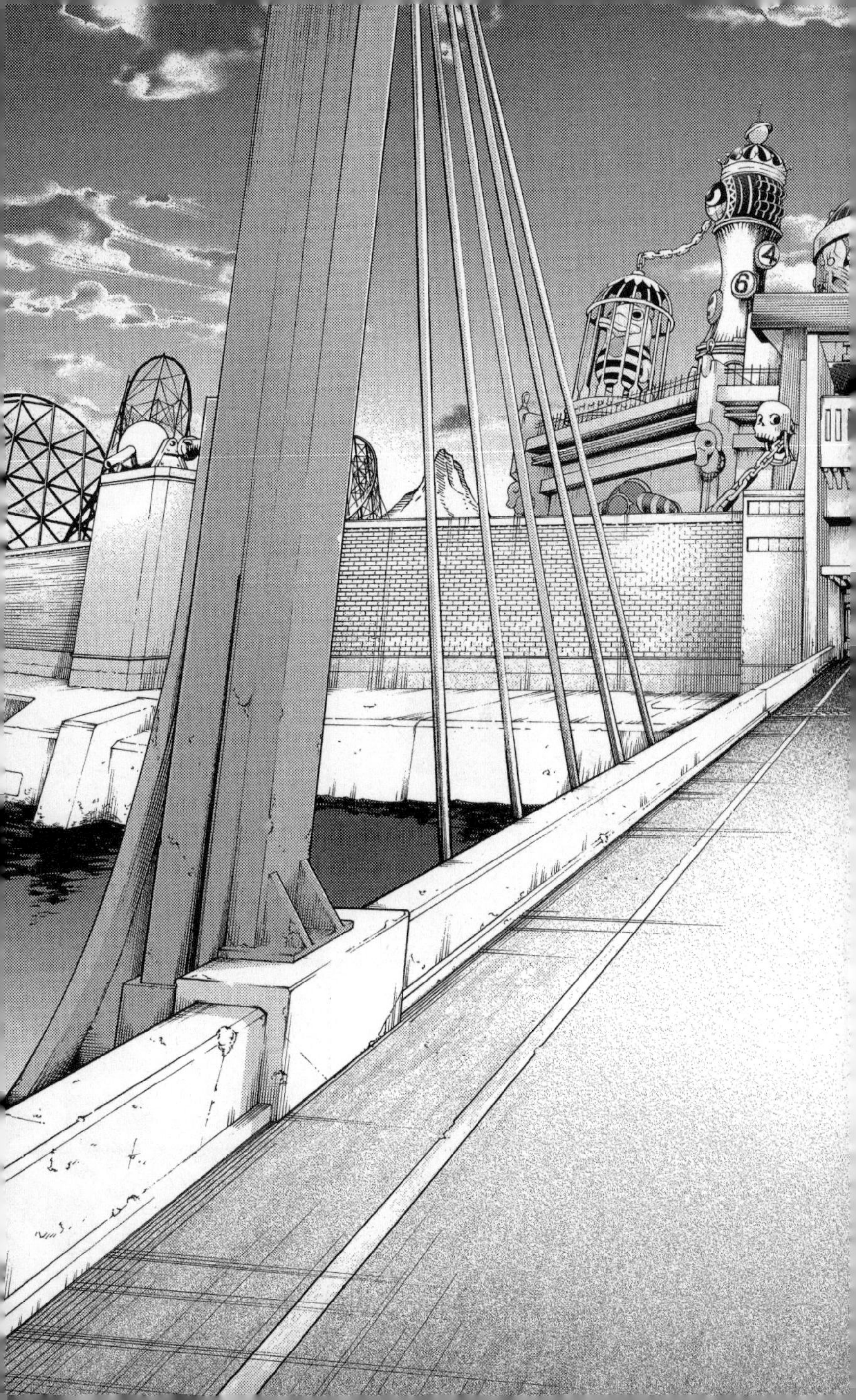
4
6

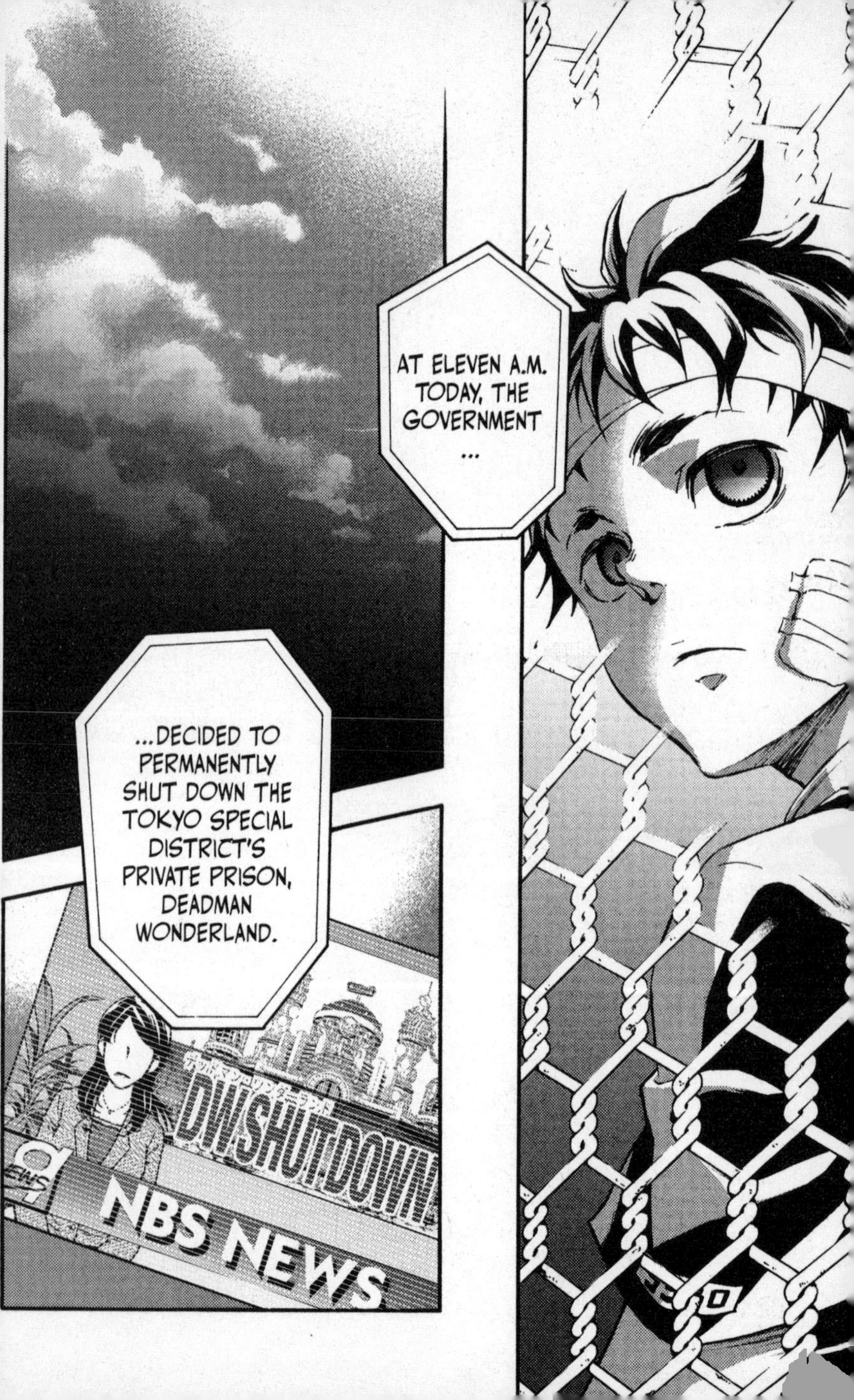
AT ELEVEN A.M. TODAY, THE GOVERNMENT ...
...DECIDED TO PERMANENTLY SHUT DOWN THE TOKYO SPECIAL DISTRICT'S PRIVATE PRISON, DEADMAN WONDERLAND.
DW SHUT DOWN
NBS NEWS

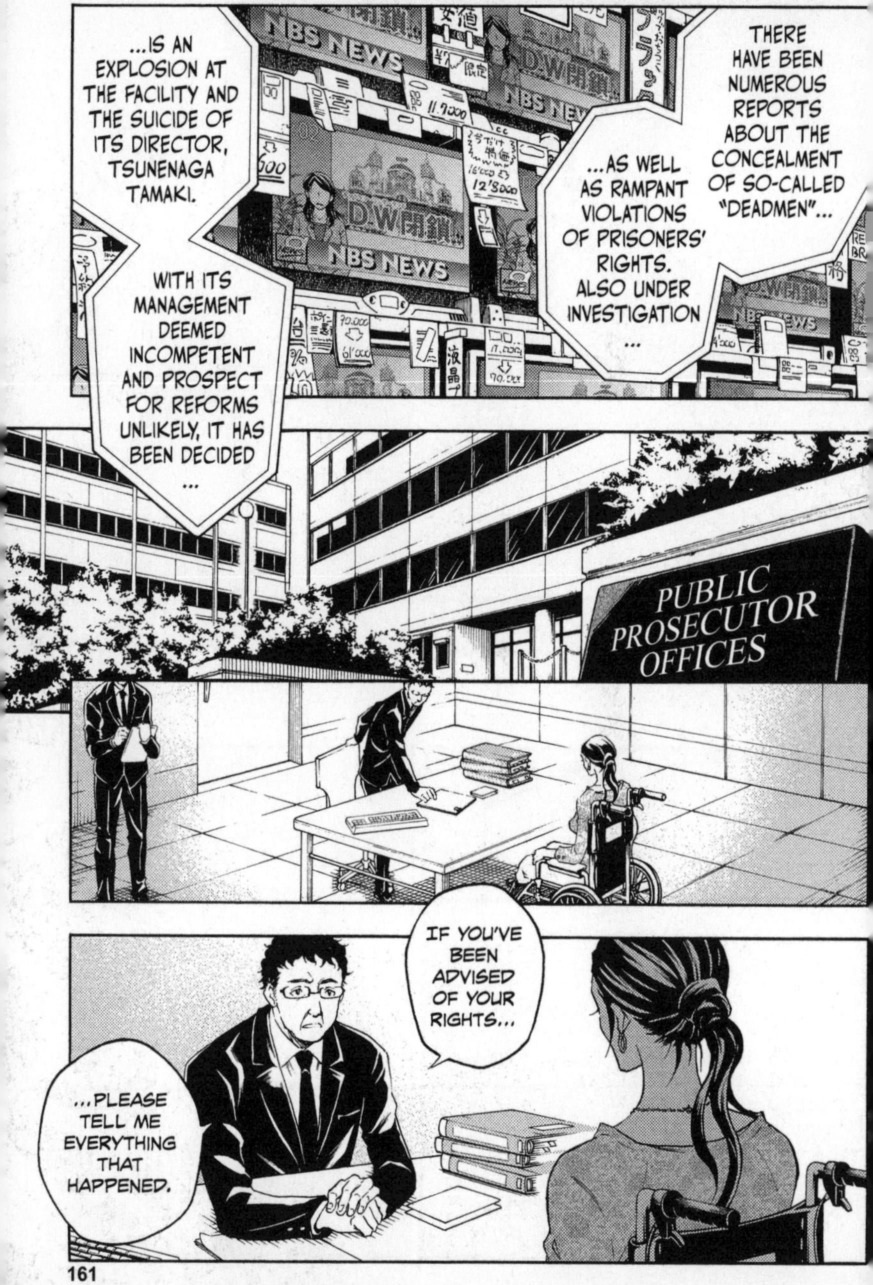
NBS NEWS
THERE HAVE BEEN NUMEROUS REPORTS ABOUT THE CONCEALMENT OF SO-CALLED "DEADMEN"...
...AS WELL AS RAMPANT VIOLATIONS OF PRISONERS' RIGHTS. ALSO UNDER INVESTIGATION ...
...IS AN EXPLOSION AT THE FACILITY AND THE SUICIDE OF ITS DIRECTOR, TSUNENAGA TAMAKI.
WITH ITS MANAGEMENT DEEMED INCOMPETENT AND PROSPECT FOR REFORMS UNLIKELY, IT HAS BEEN DECIDED ...
PUBLIC PROSECUTOR OFFICES
IF YOU'VE BEEN ADVISED OF YOUR RIGHTS...
...PLEASE TELL ME EVERYTHING THAT HAPPENED.

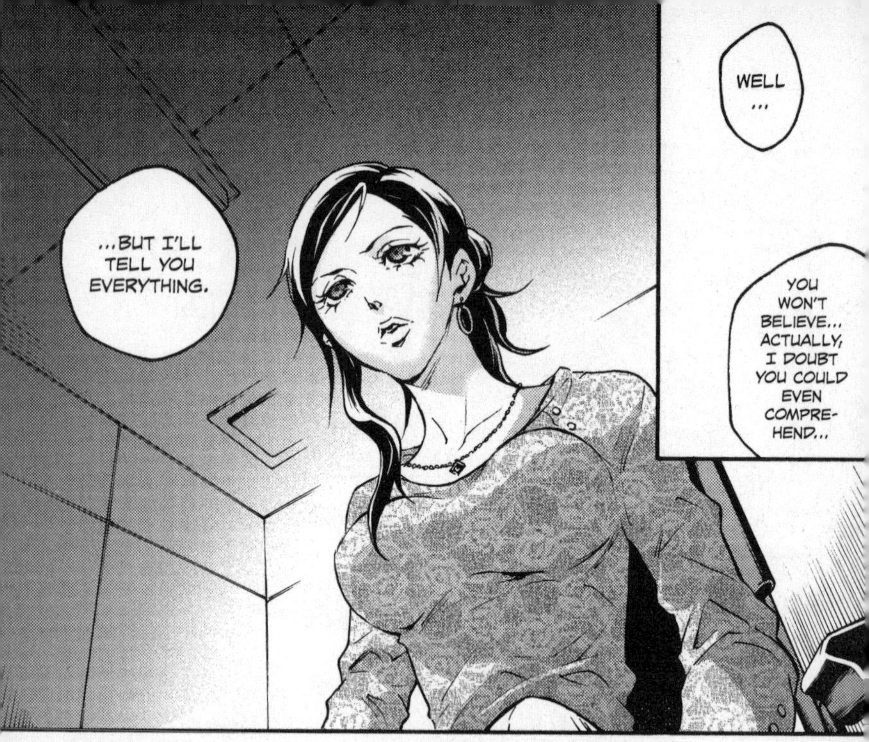
WELL ...
YOU WON'T BELIEVE... ACTUALLY, I DOUBT YOU COULD EVEN COMPRE-HEND...
...BUT I'LL TELL YOU EVERYTHING.

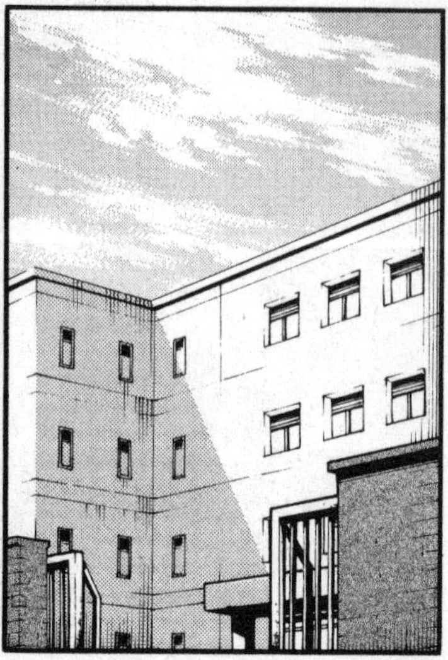

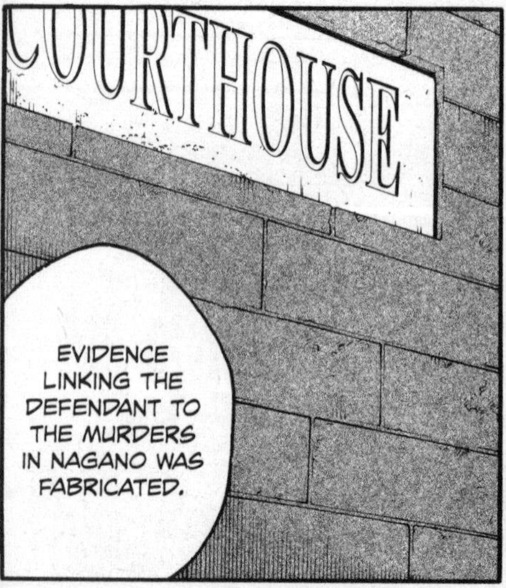
COURTHOUSE
EVIDENCE LINKING THE DEFENDANT TO THE MURDERS IN NAGANO WAS FABRICATED.

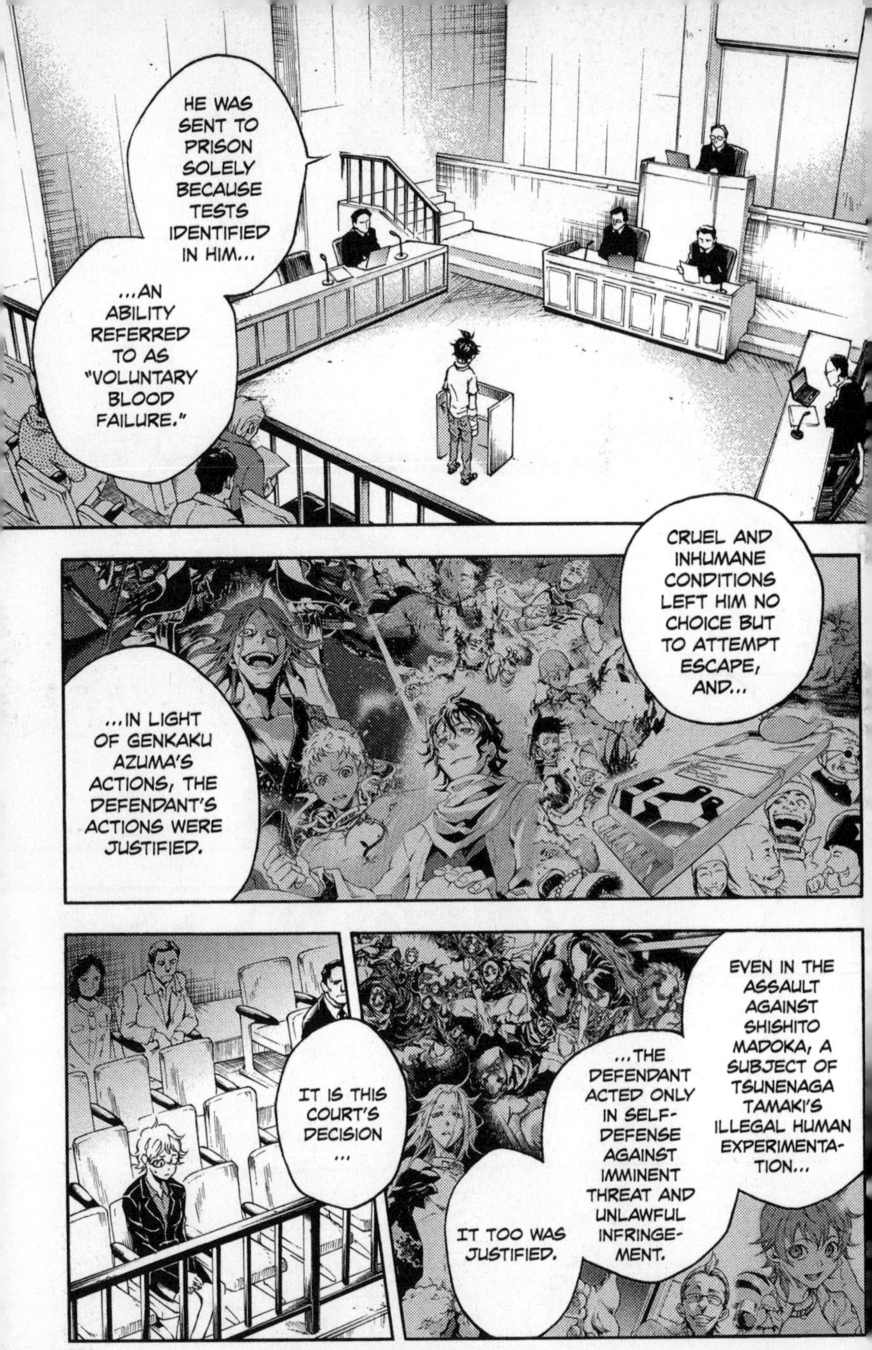
HE WAS SENT TO PRISON SOLELY BECAUSE TESTS IDENTIFIED IN HIM...
...AN ABILITY REFERRED TO AS "VOLUNTARY BLOOD FAILURE."
CRUEL AND INHUMANE CONDITIONS LEFT HIM NO CHOICE BUT TO ATTEMPT ESCAPE, AND...
...IN LIGHT OF GENKAKU AZUMA'S ACTIONS, THE DEFENDANT'S ACTIONS WERE JUSTIFIED.
EVEN IN THE ASSAULT AGAINST SHISHITO MADOKA, A SUBJECT OF TSUNENAGA TAMAKI'S ILLEGAL HUMAN EXPERIMENTATION...
...THE DEFENDANT ACTED ONLY IN SELF-DEFENSE AGAINST IMMINENT THREAT AND UNLAWFUL INFRINGEMENT.
IT TOO WAS JUSTIFIED.
IT IS THIS COURT'S DECISION ...

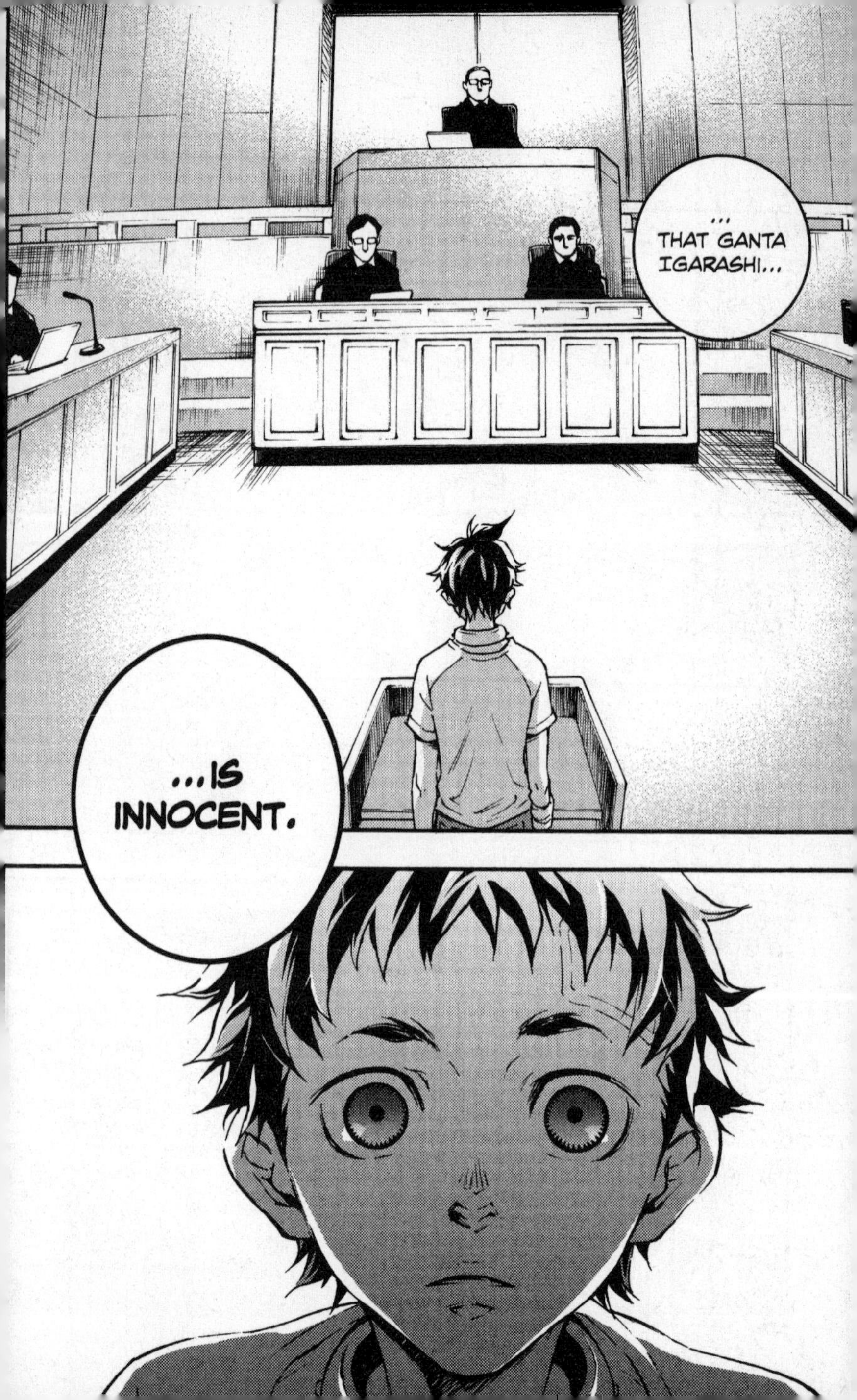
...THAT GANTA IGARASHI...
...IS INNOCENT.

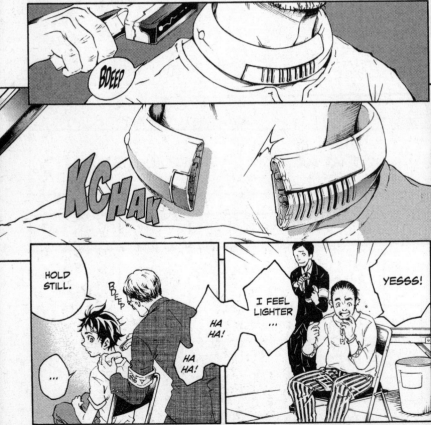

BDEEP

KCHAK

HOLD STILL.

BDEEP

...

HA HA!

HA HA!

I FEEL LIGHTER ...

YESSS!

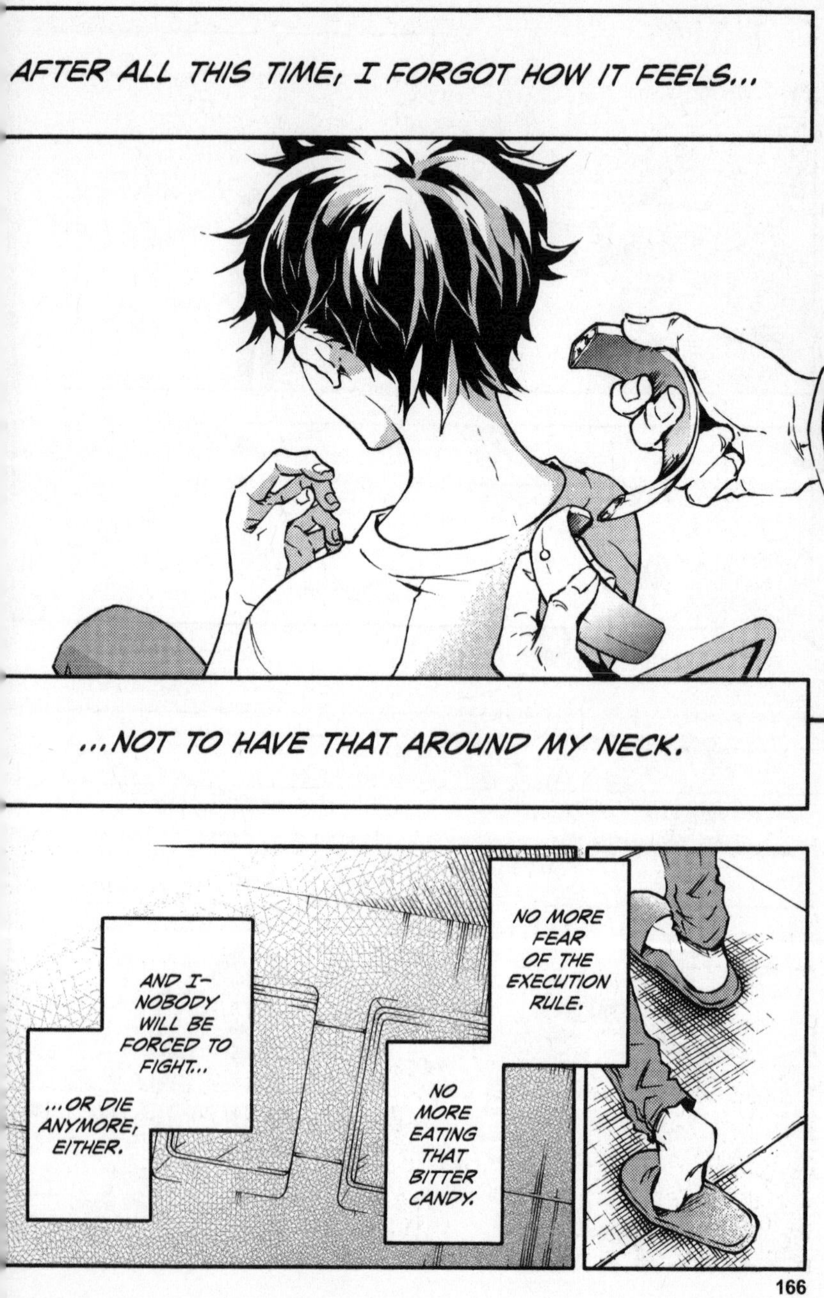
AFTER ALL THIS TIME, I FORGOT HOW IT FEELS...
...NOT TO HAVE THAT AROUND MY NECK.
NO MORE FEAR OF THE EXECUTION RULE.
NO MORE EATING THAT BITTER CANDY.
AND I— NOBODY WILL BE FORCED TO FIGHT...
...OR DIE ANYMORE, EITHER.

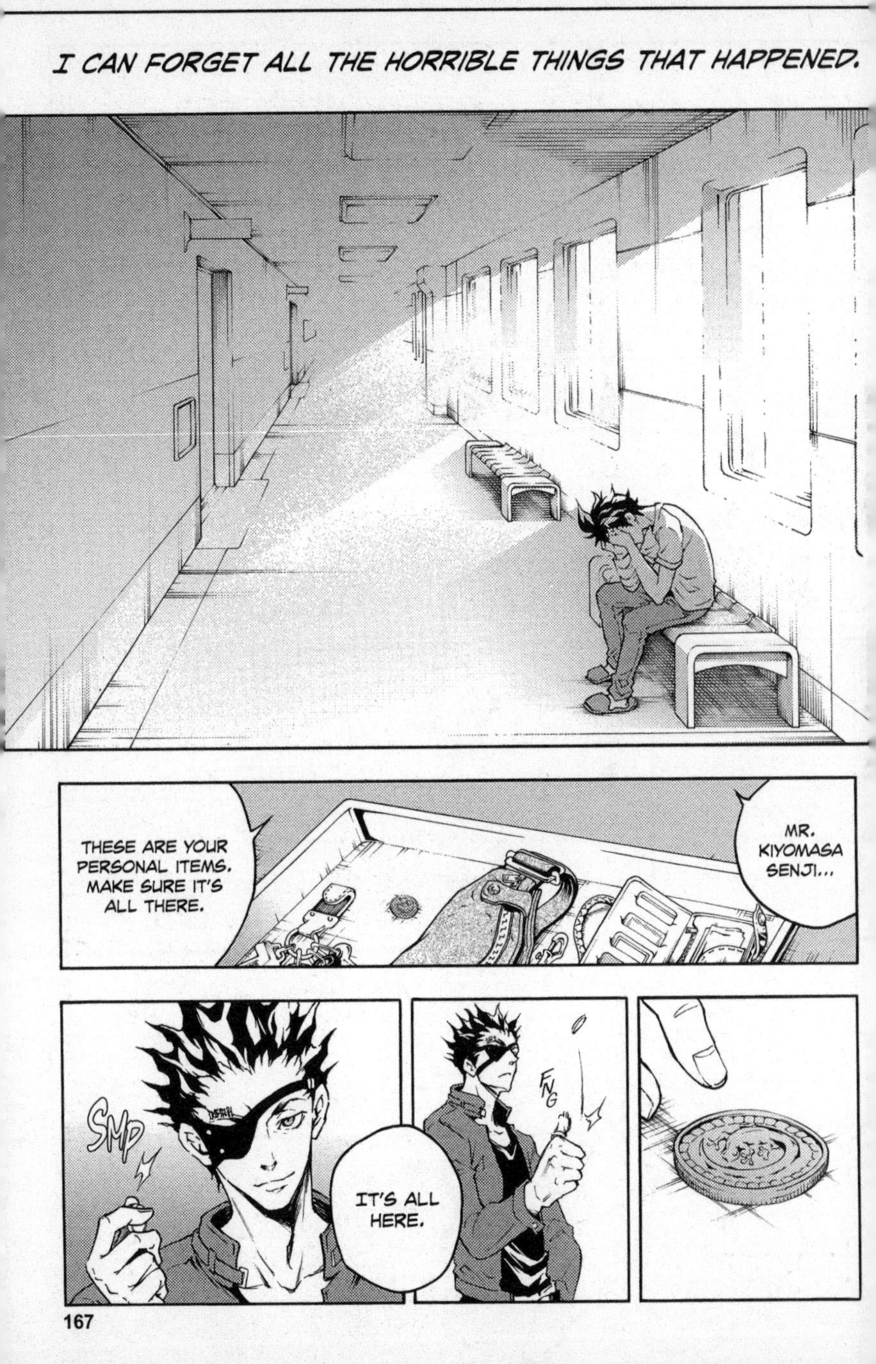
I CAN FORGET ALL THE HORRIBLE THINGS THAT HAPPENED.
MR. KIYOMASA SENJI...
THESE ARE YOUR PERSONAL ITEMS. MAKE SURE IT'S ALL THERE.
FNG
IT'S ALL HERE.
SMP

MY OLD CLOTHES ARE AWFULLY TIGHT NOW.

THERE'S NOBODY LEFT FOR ME TO CALL...

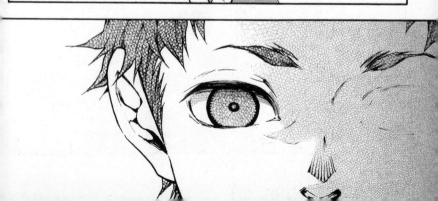

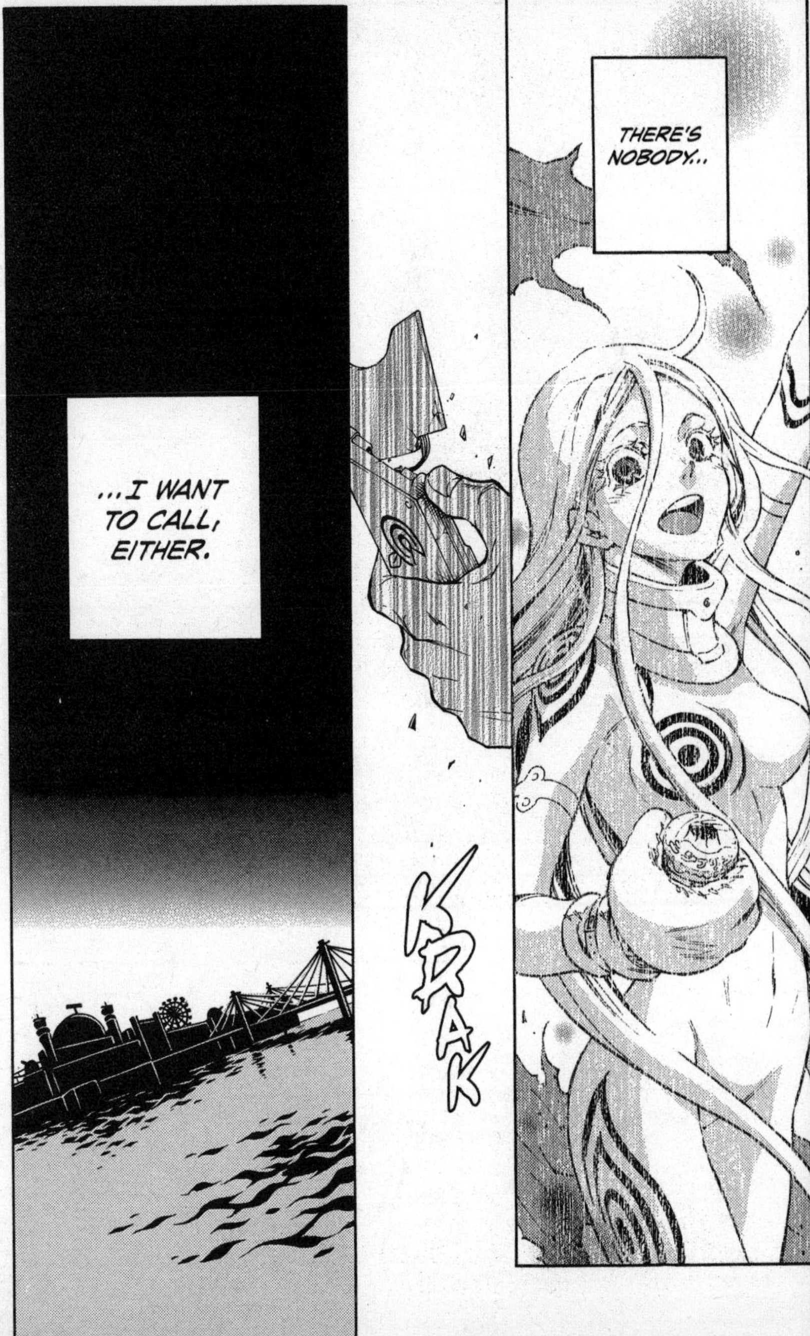
THERE'S NOBODY...
KRAK
...I WANT TO CALL, EITHER.

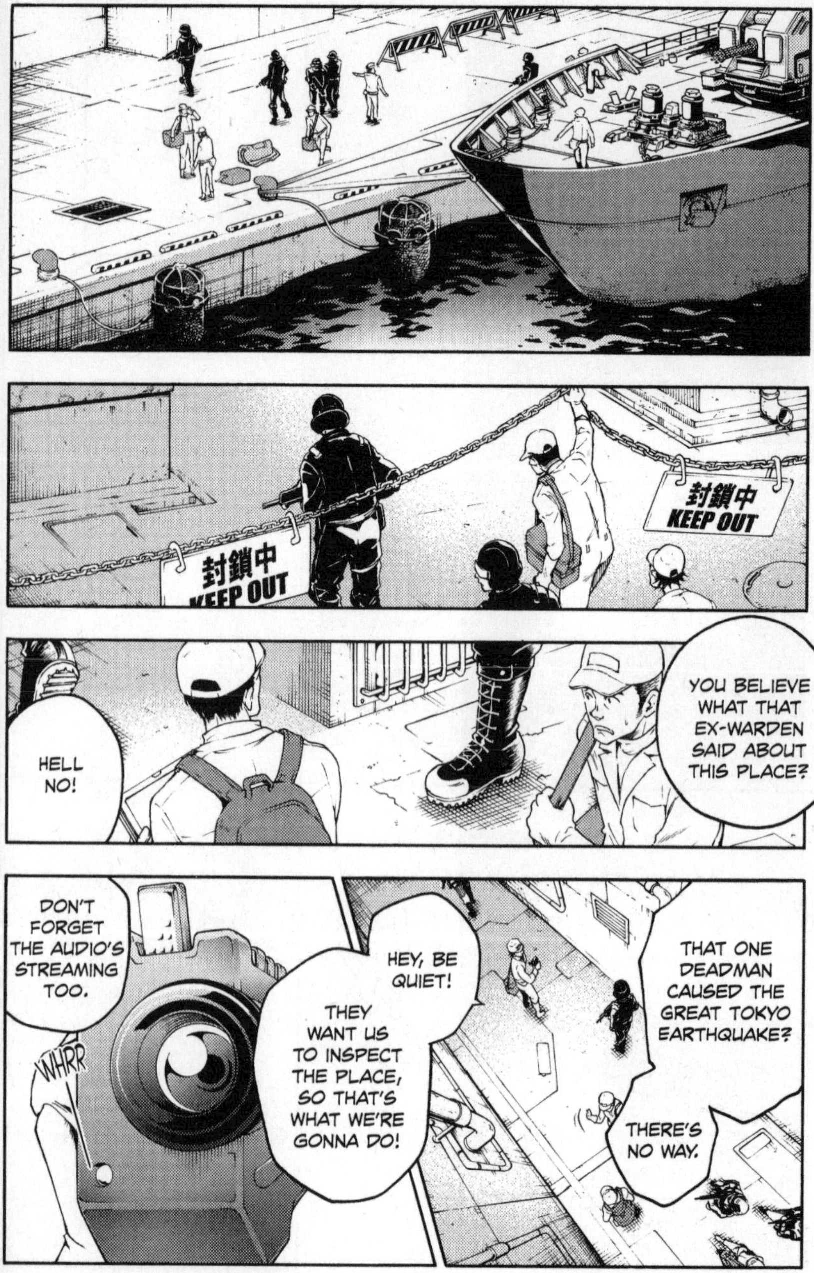
封鎖中
KEEP OUT
封鎖中
YOU BELIEVE WHAT THAT EX-WARDEN SAID ABOUT THIS PLACE?
HELL NO!
THAT ONE DEADMAN CAUSED THE GREAT TOKYO EARTHQUAKE?
THERE'S NO WAY.
HEY, BE QUIET!
THEY WANT US TO INSPECT THE PLACE, SO THAT'S WHAT WE'RE GONNA DO!
DON'T FORGET THE AUDIO'S STREAMING TOO.
WHRR

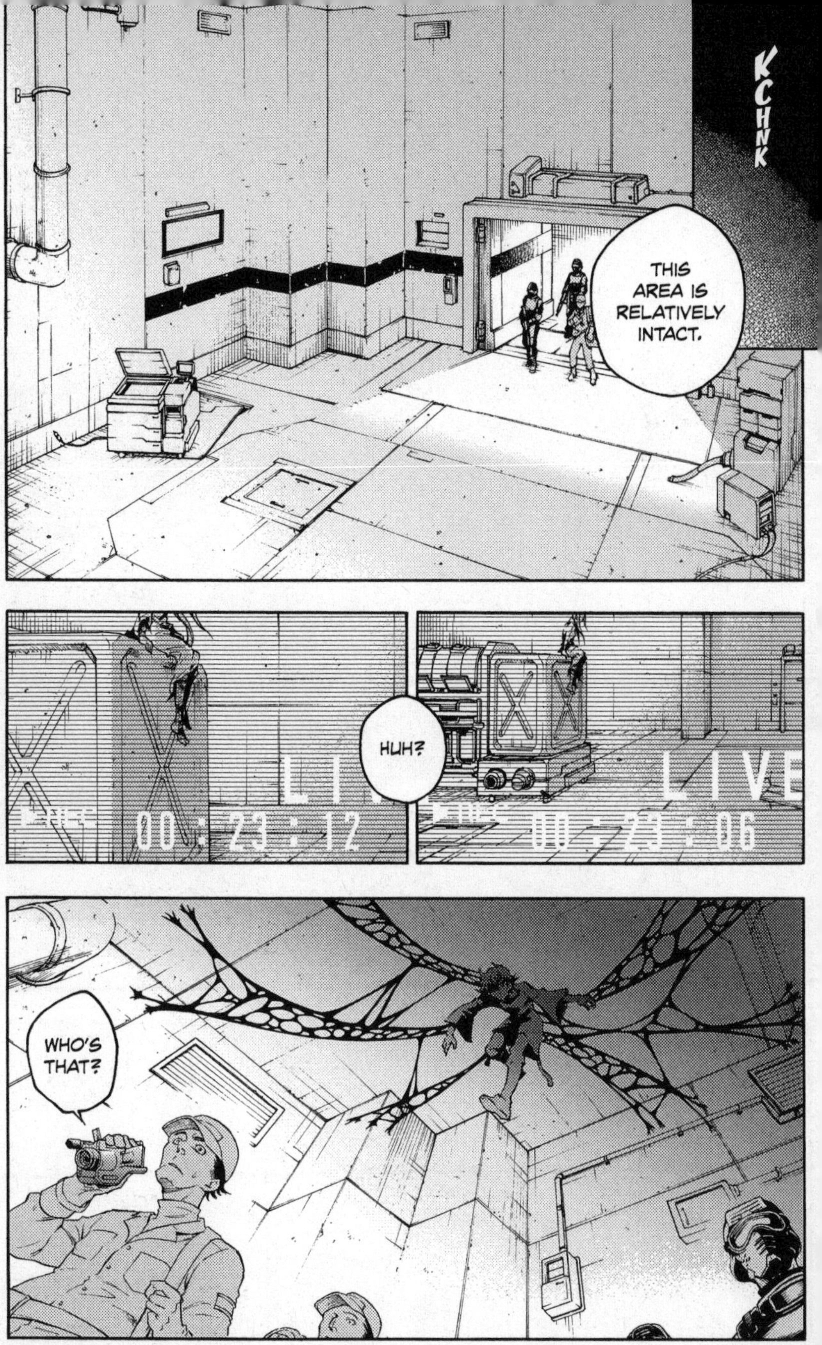
KCHNK
THIS AREA IS RELATIVELY INTACT.
LIVE
00 : 23 : 06
HUH?
00 : 23 : 12
WHO'S THAT?

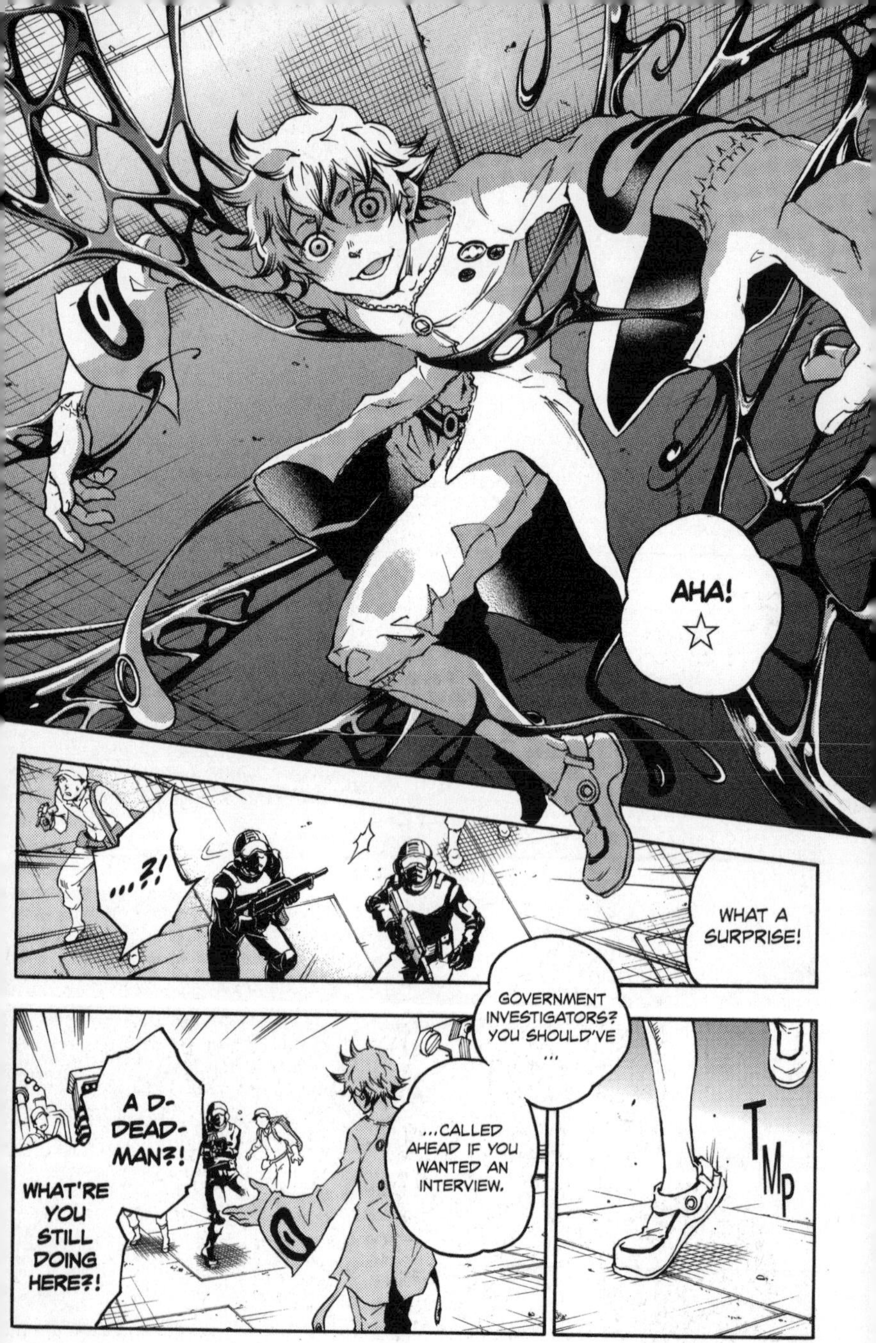
AHA! ☆
WHAT A SURPRISE!
...?!
GOVERNMENT INVESTIGATORS? YOU SHOULD'VE ...
TMP
...CALLED AHEAD IF YOU WANTED AN INTERVIEW.
A D-DEADMAN?!
WHAT'RE YOU STILL DOING HERE?!

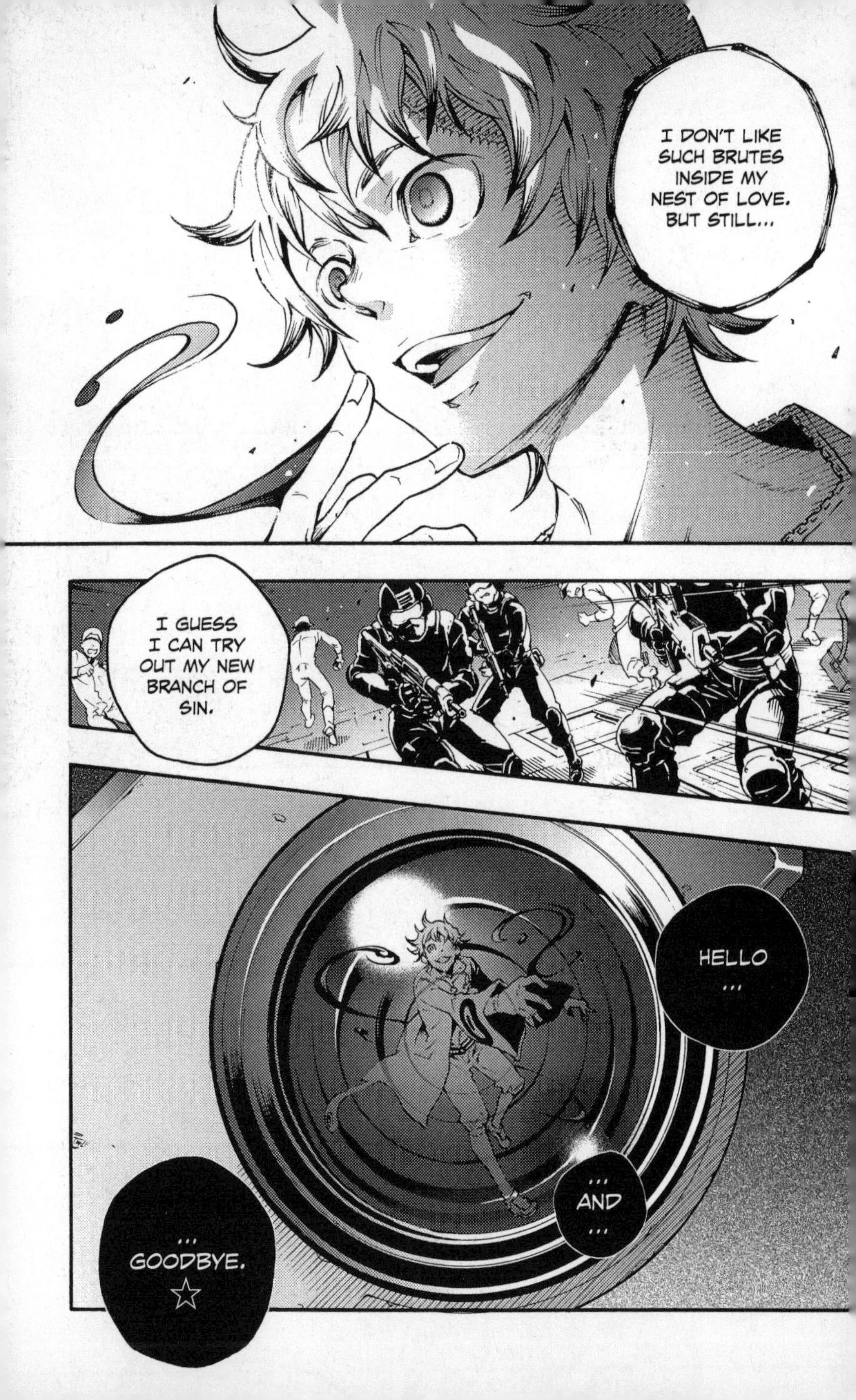
I DON'T LIKE SUCH BRUTES INSIDE MY NEST OF LOVE. BUT STILL...
I GUESS I CAN TRY OUT MY NEW BRANCH OF SIN.
HELLO ...
... AND ...
... GOODBYE. ☆

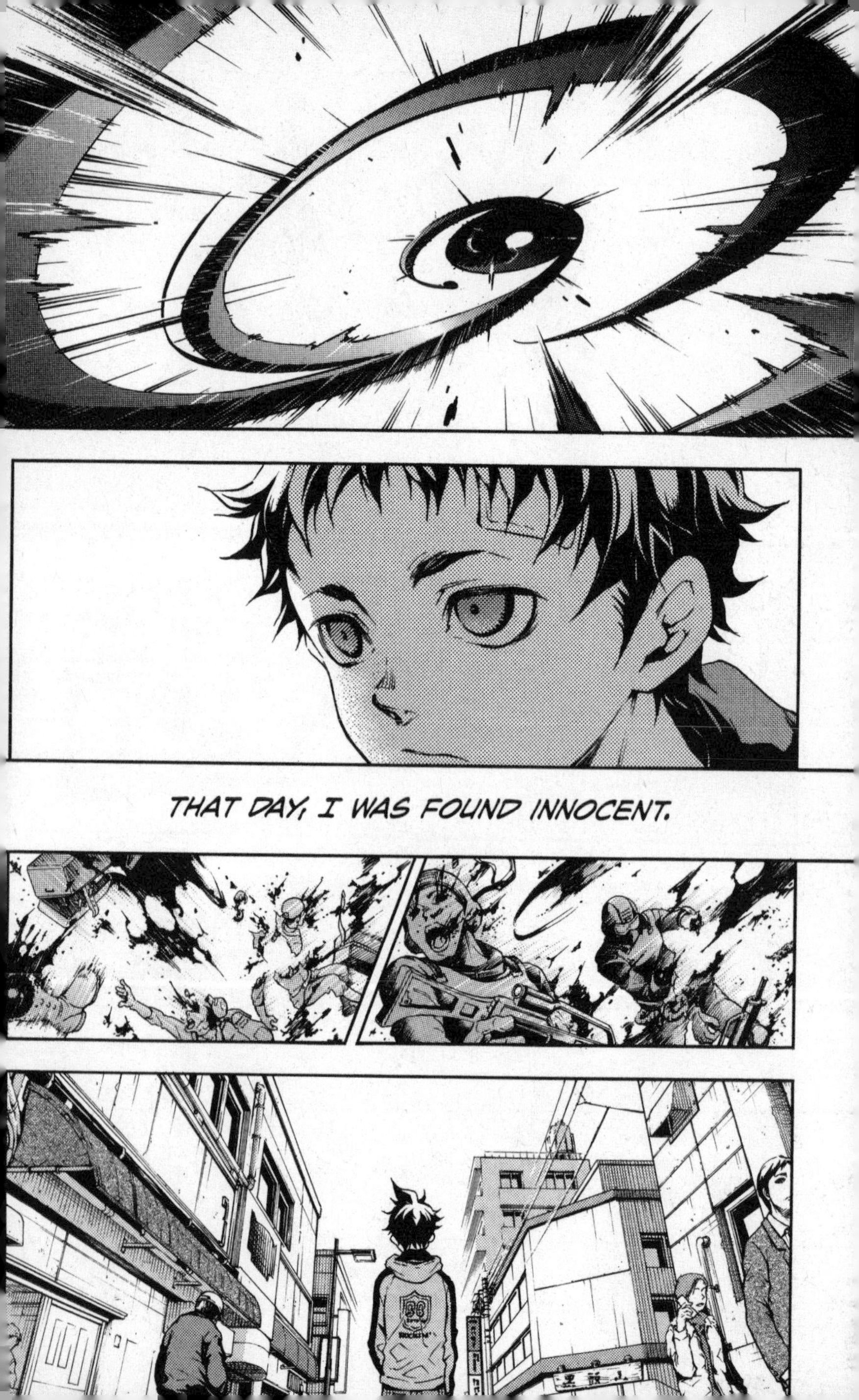
THAT DAY, I WAS FOUND INNOCENT.

BUT...

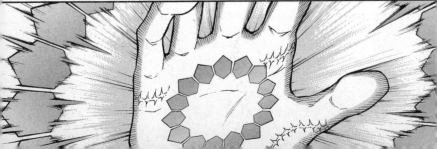

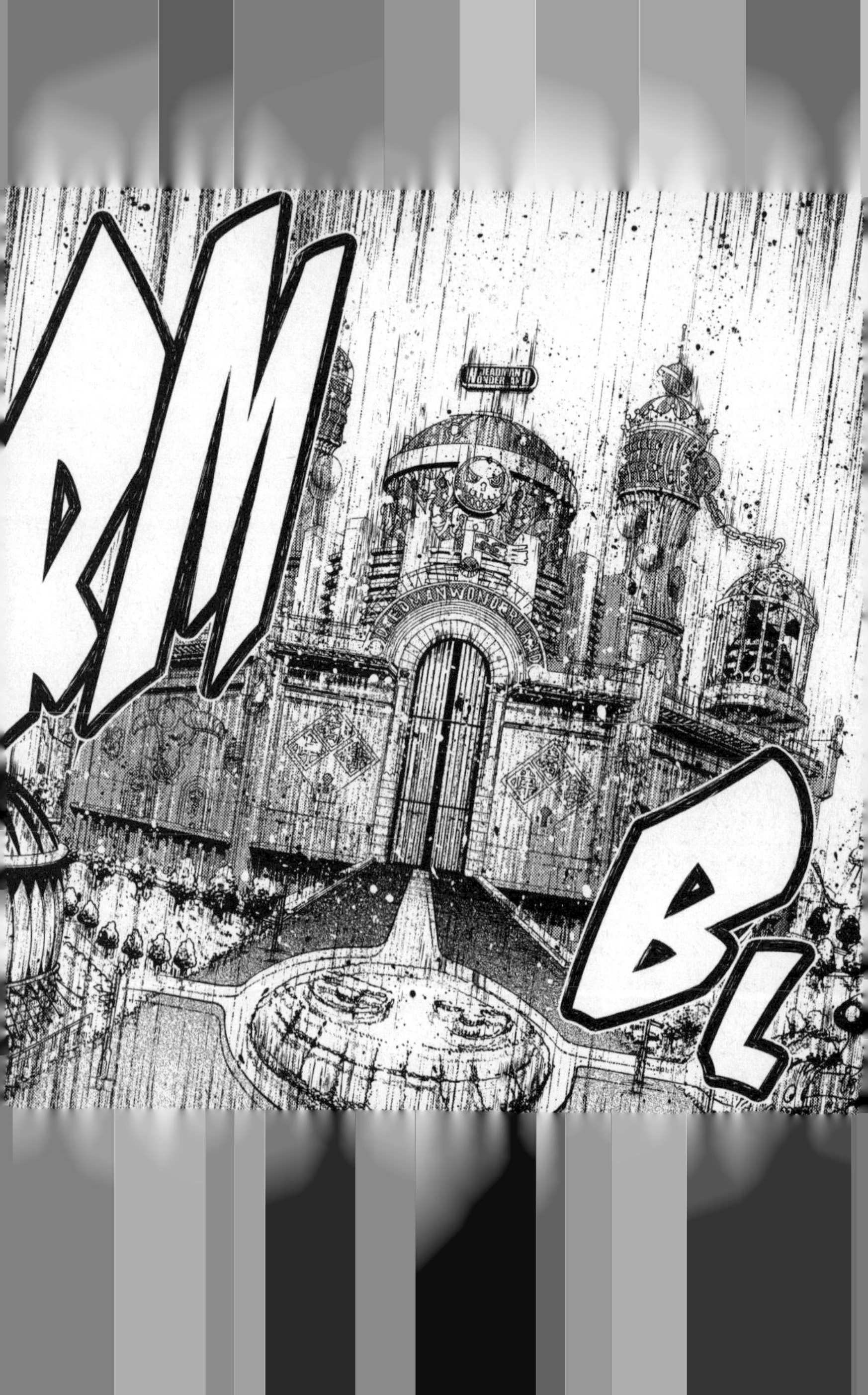
BL
DEADMAN WONDERLAND
AM

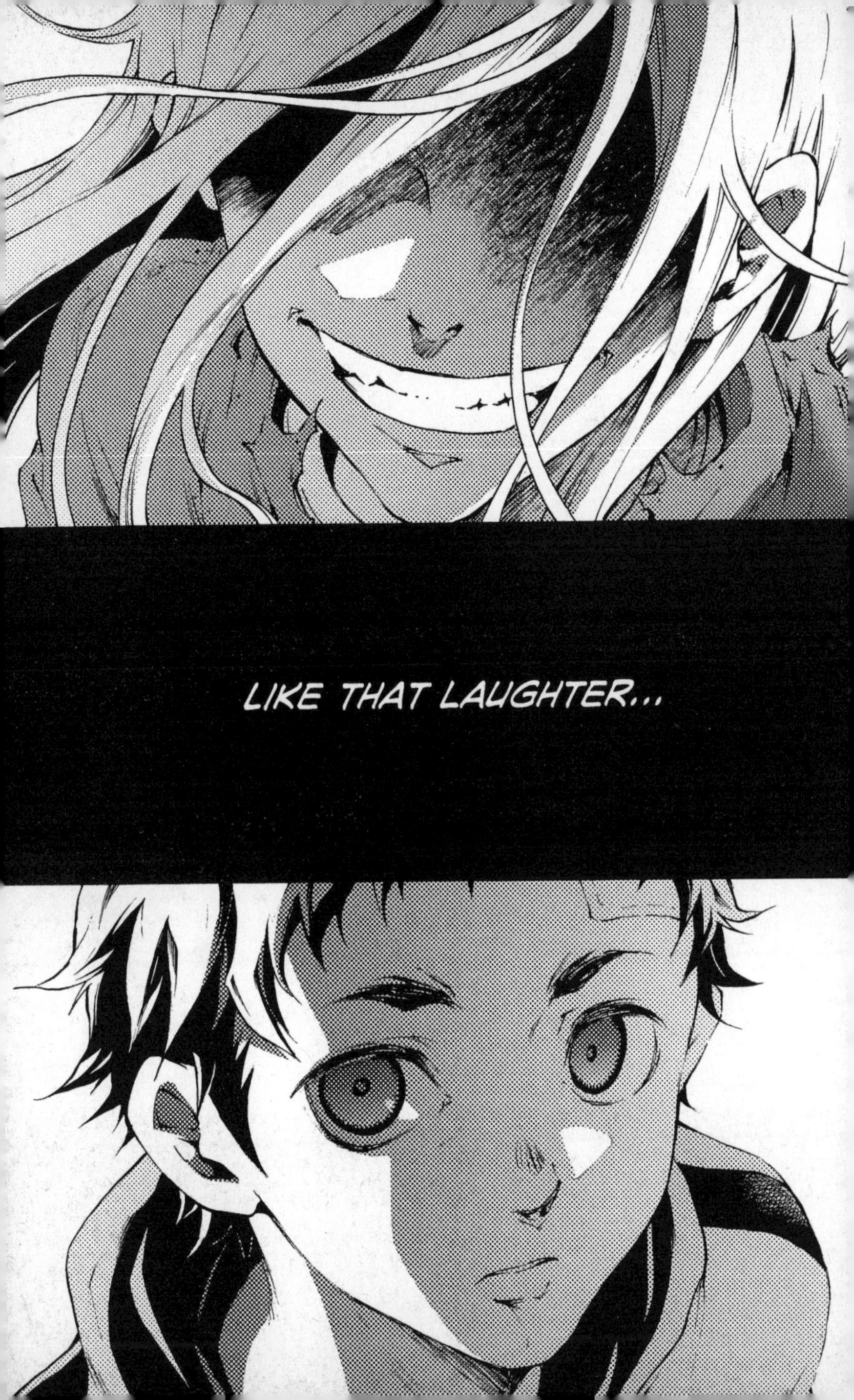
LIKE THAT LAUGHTER...

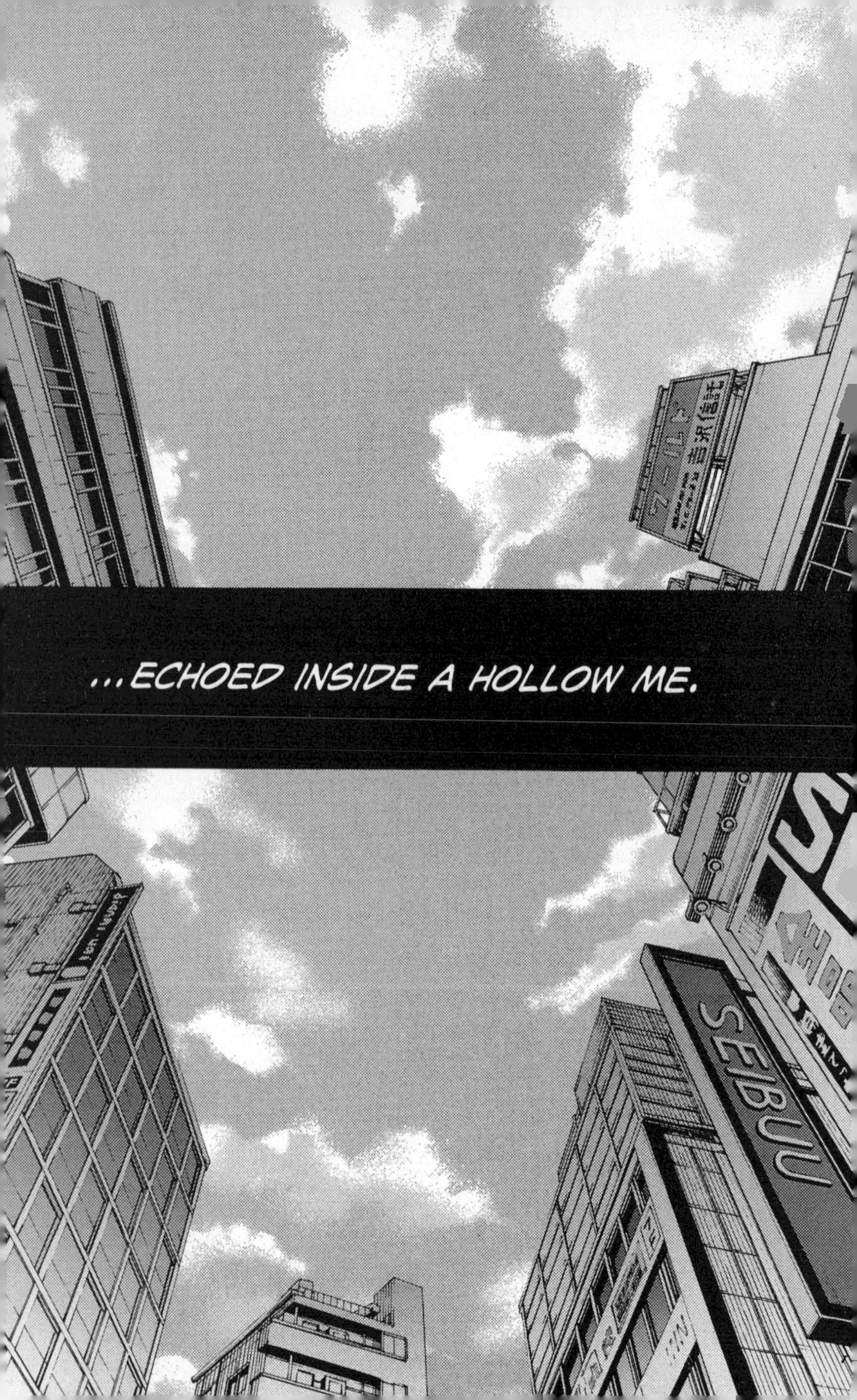
...ECHOED INSIDE A HOLLOW ME.
SEIBUU